Lord Macaulay

FROM A PHOTOGRAPH BY CLAUDET.   ENGRAVED BY C. COOK

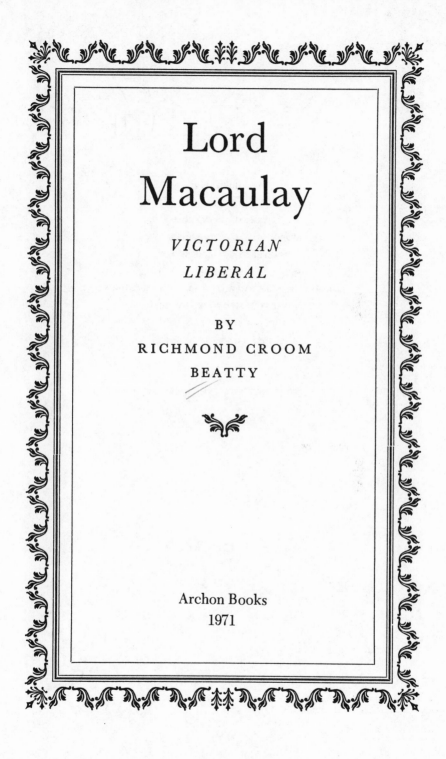

Lord Macaulay

VICTORIAN LIBERAL

BY
RICHMOND CROOM
BEATTY

Archon Books
1971

COPYRIGHT 1938

BY THE

UNIVERSITY OF OKLAHOMA

REPRINTED WITH PERMISSION IN AN

UNALTERED AND UNABRIDGED

EDITION

LIBRARY OF CONGRESS CATALOG CARD NUMBER: 72-116905

INTERNATIONAL STANDARD BOOK NUMBER: 0-208-01037-8

THE SHOE STRING PRESS, INC.

HAMDEN, CONNECTICUT 06514

PRINTED IN

THE UNITED STATES OF AMERICA

TO FLOY

Acknowledgments

MUCH of the material which appears for the first time in this book would have been inaccessible to me except through the kindness of Professor George Macaulay Trevelyan, by whose permission I was allowed to examine Macaulay's eleven volume *Journal* at the library of Trinity College, Cambridge. For the fact that the study does not contain a good many more flaws than at present, I can thank three friends of mine who read it over patiently in manuscript: Dr. Edwin Mims and Dr. Daniel M. Robison, of Vanderbilt, and Professor James B. McMillan of the University of Alabama. I am also indebted to the Social Science Research Council for a timely Grant-in-Aid, which expedited considerably the later stage of my work.

Contents

Introduction

THE TERM *liberal* has been handled so often that it seems today almost too slippery to take hold of. It has become vague and amorphous, and like many other once useful general labels has had its meaning stretched to flabbiness. For its users have for several generations, and in many lands, employed it to serve the particular purposes of their hour, often to cloak deeds that, if more accurately identified, would perhaps have been roundly condemned, if not forbidden. To put the matter differently would be to say that this formerly nice word has become suspect through long sorting with questionable company. To restore it, in some measure, to its lost state of innocence is an undertaking which assumes, then, the proportions of a distinct social service.

This book attempts, among other things, to clarify the concept as it was made manifest in England during the decade before and the two decades after the accession of Queen Victoria. What were the men who thought of themselves as liberals then attempting to do for their country and for the world? What were the legislative methods they followed and the nature of the opposition they were compelled to face? What compromises did this opposition force upon them? Where, if anywhere, did their liberalism stop; in what respects did they abandon their views for the sake of keeping untouched the privileges of their own particular class? And, finally, what has been the more nearly ultimate fruit of their philosophy, insofar as it can be stated today?

The issues, as drawn in Macaulay's age, were defined with comparative simplicity. In 1830, say, there were, at one extreme, the Tories, or the party of the Established Church and the wealthy landholders. These men, politically, were still ruling England, but they were aware that the necessary sanction of their rule, popular support, was fast crumbling beneath them. They were definitely alarmed, some of them terrified, lest the growing discontent of hungry millions prove finally unstayable until a revolution had made the mass will dominant. At the other extreme, to speak broadly, were the radical groups, the dispossessed lower social strata whose leaders felt that the time had come to seize the sources of power for their own purposes. These men wanted universal male suffrage. They wanted labor unions. They wanted a system of public education, a limit to working hours, and many other concessions which appeared as extravagant then as they appear commonplace now. And between these two was still another party. Its members were called Whigs by their own generation, but essentially they were the Liberals. They favored compromise. They endorsed such timely reforms as the abolition of the rotten boroughs. They would extend the franchise to the upper middle class. They would allow the new and growing industrial towns a fair representation in Parliament. But, above all, they were committed to protect "the sacred institution of property." And the class from which they would protect it was the highly populous group below them, the group that was without property. That class, lacking tangible wealth, lacked also, they contended, a sense of stability; it could not, therefore, be trusted to share in the highly cautious business of government.

Yet these multitudes, whom Macaulay termed conveniently "the lower orders," were not to look upon their prospects as hopeless. They were hewers of wood and drawers of water —true; but it should be perfectly plain to them that as the "middle orders" prospered, they, in turn, would also prosper. Wealth would come down to them in streams that, if little more than trickles at first, would grow in time to be floods. For they should be able to see, with little persuasion, that Science with its giant strides was working tirelessly to pile up in their interest material blessings of which their grandfathers had lacked, literally, the remotest conception. All good things would come their way at length, thanks to world trade and to the new instruments of production.

It was in many ways a serene assurance, one in which, I have little doubt, Macaulay sincerely believed. But that one should not question too closely the implications of those blessings was another thing he believed as well; for he treated with scorn and contempt those who did—such men as Ruskin and Carlyle. He did not feel, that is to say, that the problems which the industrial age was trailing in its wake— periodic unemployment, specialization, the loss of freedom and initiative on the part of the laborer—should even be generally discussed. Nor did he for a moment consider as valid the question of what would happen when the policy of world trade to which his country was dedicated came into conflict with the policy of a rival nation as strong as his own. The debacle of 1914-1918, one of the fairly early fruits of his philosophy (one already budding, too, in Macaulay's day, as his good friend Lord Palmerston could have told him)— that was another creeping nightmare with which honest men need not trouble their heads.

His liberalism, in brief, was an economy designed to minister to the materialistic ambitions of a single class, a class whose interests, he came to think, were identified inextricably with the welfare of the entire nation. It was a view also which—from his first speech in the house of Commons in 1830 to that bitter January day three decades later, when he was laid to rest with the immortals in Westminster Abbey— men appeared as if by instinct to associate with his name. The middle orders, as H. J. Laski has declared (I am not endorsing Mr. Laski's political philosophy), grew to be regarded as the material representatives of the human race.

As an organized society, the state which this class created had at bottom "no defined objective save the making of wealth, no measurable criterion of function and status save ability to acquire it. If in England, for example, it sent an occasional poet, a rare man of science, an infrequent doctor, to the House of Lords, after the middle of the nineteenth century it doubled the size of that chamber by its elevation of business men to the peerage. And just as it reduced the medieval craftsman to the status of a factory hand or a tender of machines, so it assumed that a successful man was simply and literally one who had made a fortune. So obsessed had it become by its material achievements that it was unable to think of success in any other terms."

The major tenet of this philosophy of government was, in Macaulay's phrase, "the sanctity of property." Property rights, in other words, he looked upon as eternal and inviolable. As far as we can learn, he never seems to have considered the fact that such rights have no meaning outside the realm of law, that, in Walter Lippman's words, no man can hold or enjoy property openly except by virtue of the readiness of the state to enforce his claims. He failed likewise to bother himself much with setting forth the responsibilities of the property class toward society. He never concerned himself, for instance, with the question of natural resources—the extent to which any single generation may justifiably squander them for selfish ends. Convinced that the England of his day was governed by a set of God-fearing gentlemen, he was content to ask few questions about the future.

Here, then, is one type of liberalism. It contained within its sharply defined limits no shadow of room for the outstanding liberals of history. It was clearly not the radical individualism of a man like Thomas Jefferson, of whom—as I have pointed out in detail in one chapter—Macaulay emphatically disapproved. Nor did it resemble, in the least, the liberalism of that sometime American Tom Paine, whom Macaulay pronounced to be "a worthless, drunken, dirty beast." How this philosophy of government revealed itself in action is one of the central problems of the book, a problem which, in the text itself, I have tried to present objectively.

2

Yet Macaulay was a great deal more than a political figure, and a volume that pretends to treat his career fully must concern itself with many questions which bear only slightly upon statecraft, if they touch it at all. Moreover, one might well be inclined to ask what excuse there is for tracing out his life again, in view of the fact that it was ably set forth more than half a century ago by his nephew, G. O. Trevelyan. It is certainly true that that eminent author's detailed study remains, to this day, one of the few really great biographies that were written during the nineteenth century. It is not a specimen of blind hero-worship; many frailties of its subject are described side by side with his virtues. And the style of the book is both entertaining and distinguished.

Yet that work suffers, none the less, because of inadequacies which the author of it could scarcely have foreseen. It assumes, for one thing, a rather thorough knowledge of English history between the years 1820 and 1850; and this assumption having been made, the life of Macaulay is presented with little factual adumbration as a background. The result, for most readers of the present day, is that the famous Whig appears to exist in a kind of vacuum. His actions are not revealed in terms of the complex age of which he was a part.

Again, no systematic attempt is made by Trevelyan to suggest the full scope of Macaulay's literary work in connection with his life itself. I do not believe that the two can be separated. A man's writings, that is to say, are a part of his life, often its most important part; and to take for granted a general knowledge of them, or to divorce them from the narrative of the events of his biography, involves an unfortunate exclusion which can result only in a distorted or unfinished

[xv]

picture. I might add, however, in this connection, that I have made little effort to indicate the strict literary sources of Macaulay's ideas. I have avoided this item mainly because it seems to me that he borrowed much more often from experience than from earlier writers. I have very little faith in the theory that authors, when competent, feed only upon other authors in their quest for expression. Literary influences there certainly are; but there are also non-literary influences —those which stem from the state of one's digestion, from one's political rivalries, or from one's age and the confused problems which that age must struggle with. To recreate, in little, that interval of history, always in terms of the personality of one's subject, is, it seems to me, the first duty of a biographer. It is a duty the imperfect fulfillment of which will lead him often seemingly far afield—into labor problems, into questions of etiquette, into the state of religion, and into countless other matters. It is a duty, moreover, which he can never feel himself to have accomplished with much satisfaction. For the past, it seems, is irrecoverable, really, except in fragments, or through glimpses, as by poets.

RICHMOND CROOM BEATTY

Vanderbilt University,
October, 1938.

Lord Macaulay

We are wiser than our ancestors. — MACAULAY, "ESSAY ON MACK-INTOSH."

Of lawgivers in whom the speculative element has prevailed to the exclusion of the practical, the world has during the last eighty years been singularly fruitful. To their wisdom Europe and America have owed scores of abortive constitutions, scores of constitutions which have lived just long enough to make a miserable noise, and have then gone off in convulsions. But in English legislation the practical element has always predominated, and not seldom unduly predominated, over the speculative. . . Never to innovate except when some grievance is felt; never to innovate except so far as to get rid of the grievance; never to lay down any proposition of wider extent than the particular case for which it is necessary to provide—these are the rules which have, from the age of John to the age of Victoria, generally guided the deliberations of our two hundred and fifty Parliaments. Our national distaste for whatever is abstract in political science amounts undoubtedly to a fault. Yet it is, perhaps, a fault on the right side. That we have been far too slow to improve our laws must be admitted. But, though in other countries there may have occasionally been more rapid progress, it would not be easy to name any other country in which there has been so little retrogression.—MACAULAY, HISTORY OF ENGLAND.

Much talk with Lord Grey. He told me that he thought of publishing his father's correspondence with Fox and asked me whether I would advise the suppressing of the very unfavorable judgments which they both, from a very early period, passed on the public and private conduct of Sheridan. I was quite against the suppression. In truth their fame requires that the truth should be known.—MACAULAY, JOURNAL.

I. Scion

THE NIGHT had come down, warmly. It was September 27, 1794, and a little group of officials of the Sierra Leone Company were just completing their prayer service. The Lord in His mercy had blessed them and their work. Planted precariously on the west coast of Africa and threatened alternately by slave-hunting Americans and rum-besotted native chiefs, the colony of freedmen had none the less prospered. Their trade with the interior tribesmen was growing. And growing, too, in a knowledge of the ways and manners of the civilized, and thus in favor with God, were the colonists themselves—twelve hundred of the liberated who had been brought there from the bleak shores of Nova Scotia[1] and the filthy mews and alleys of London. Here, for the world to see and marvel at, was to rise up the answer to those who had termed the ignorant African incapable of advancement. The settlement of Freetown would silence them. But as prayers were ended this particular evening, two cannon shots from the darkened harbor thundered ominously down the still air.

Governor Zachary Macaulay was agitated. With several of his secretaries he began a hurried search for the *Table of English Signals*. Finding it, he looked up "two shots": It meant that a squadron was coming to anchor. A rumor had already reached him that a fleet of seven or eight vessels was seen up the coast a few days before, beating its way south-

1. These negroes from Nova Scotia had been granted land there by the British in return for service during the American Revolution.

ward; but its colors could not be made out. In the harbor they were invisible now. The twenty-six year old Governor passed an anxious night. If they were French, as some feared, the results of his entire seven months leadership and work would probably be destroyed. But they couldn't be French! Since the Revolution, and with the Reign of Terror still going on, the French were unable to muster so large a fleet for the simple purposes of piracy! But he was up at dawn to make certain.

The first sight he met with was formidable, but somewhat reassuring. There they were, eight of them, riding smoothly, all flying English colors. What kept the Governor from being completely at ease was his knowledge of an old trick of French raiders; the trick of substituting an enemy flag for their own until they had obtained an advantage. Macaulay, at all events, would simply have to await developments; for Freetown was almost completely unarmed.

Many others thought differently about waiting. Since resistance was out of the question, they favored a precipitate flight to the woods with as much of their property as could be carried away. But the Governor was resolute; and resolution in this Governor, they had already learned, was a force before which most men were inclined to submit without murmur. They kept their glasses on the ships—and said their prayers.

Shortly after nine o'clock their uncertainties were ended. "Perceiving some men in one of the frigates with great care pointing a cannon into my piazza, we were relieved from all our doubts." Soon, Macaulay continued, writing in his *Journal*, shots were whistling over their heads. As Governor, he gave hurried orders to haul down their own colors and run up the flag of truce. The French fired for half an hour more, killing a negress and a child and giving one unlucky Englishman a fright that ultimately brought him to his grave.[2] "Several of the grape and musket shot fell into my piazza.

2. G. O. Trevelyan, *Macaulay's Life and Letters*, I, 30.

We then hailed them, and told them we had surrendered, and the firing stopped."[3]

The young Governor's conduct for the next seven days was a model of shrewdness and diplomacy, both futilely expended. At about ten o'clock he noticed a number of men from one of the ships, busy with preparations to land. He sent one of his clergymen to meet them, with a request that the commanding officer come to his house. But when the clergyman got to them they were already ashore, had entered the central warehouse of the Company, and several of the officers' houses, and were "pillaging and destroying in a shocking manner." Macaulay himself soon learned one of the causes of the raid: he had prevented the return of several slaves who had escaped from the vessel of a Yankee captain named Newell. Newell, in revenge, had told the French captain of the wealth and lack of belligerency at Freetown. This Yankee was soon at his door, in person, backed by a mob of ragged sansculottes. Macaulay's own words are best on what followed:

"Newell, almost foaming with rage, presented a pistol to me and demanded instant satisfaction for the slaves who had run away from him to my protection. I made very little reply but told him he must now *take* such satisfaction as he judged equivalent to his claims, as I was no longer master of my actions. He became so very outrageous that, after bearing with him a little while, I thought it most prudent to repair myself to the French officer, and request his safe conduct on board the Commodore's ship. As I passed along the wharf the scene was curious enough. The Frenchmen who had come ashore in filth and rags were now, many of them, dressed out with woman's shifts, gowns, and petticoats. Others had quantities of cloth wrapped about their bodies or perhaps six or seven suits of clothes upon them at a time.

"The scene which presented itself upon my getting on board the flagship was still more singular. The quarter deck was crowded by a set of ragamuffins whose appearance beggared

3. Viscountess Knutsford (Margaret Trevelyan), *Zachary Macaulay*, p. 65.

every previous description, and among whom I sought in vain for one who looked like a gentleman. The stench and filth exceeded anything I had ever witnessed in any ship, and the noise and confusion gave me some idea of their famous Mountain.

"I was ushered into the Commodore's cabin, who at least received me civilly. His name was Citizen Allemand. He did not appear to have the right of excluding any of his fellow citizens even from this place. Whatever might be their ranks they crowded into it, and conversed familiarly with him."

The Governor began immediately to set forth a hot but formally worded protest. "I told the Captain that I expected to find in Frenchmen a generous enemy, but that on the contrary we had been dealt with in a manner which I believed was unusual except in places taken by storm. I then represented to him the unrestrained pillage which had taken place and the manner in which private houses and private property were violated, and requested him to put a stop to it." The first question the Captain asked his guest was "Have you removed anything from the town?" Macaulay, warned to speak the truth, assured him that no goods had been hidden. The Captain then promised that nothing belonging to servants of the Company would be damaged or destroyed. "This promise, however, gave me little consolation, as he would make no written engagement, and as he told me, in the same breath, that if the seamen and sailors were disposed to pillage, he would not be able to prevent them."[4] The Governor was beginning to see, at first hand, what happened to law and discipline when men subscribed to the newfangled French madness of Liberty, Equality, and Fraternity.

The Captain had not finished, however, and what he went on to say was not pleasant. He firmly intended to burn every house in the place belonging to Englishmen. "I made use of every plea I could think of to dissuade him, representing the nature of the establishment to him in a way which I thought

4. *Ibid.*, 66.

[6]

might interest him, but to no purpose." The American, Newell, had poisoned his mind.

When Macaulay became convinced of the Captain's inveterate hatred of England, he changed his line of argument. "I then represented to him the case of the settlers, who at least were not Englishmen, but who were now sharing our fate in having their houses broken into and pillaged." The Captain promised, at length, to save their homes from fire, but added again that his men were beyond restraint.

Macaulay's next demand was for food for the colonists, and for "other things absolutely necessary to keep us alive—wine, small craft, tobacco, medicines, firearms. He promised, but I found in the end how little reliance there is now to be placed on the word of a sansculotte." The Commodore asked him to drink and to dine. But Macaulay excused himself, professing an indisposition that was probably by this time not at all feigned. He went back to Freetown.

The goings on there were villainous indeed! At the wharf he found a party of drunken sailors emptying a case of port they had stolen from the Company's warehouse. Farther along were others, an American among them, loaded with spoils and cursing the English. In his own office every desk, drawer, and shelf, together with the printing and copying presses—used in turning off religious tracts—"had been completely demolished in the search for money. The floors were strewn with type, papers, and leaves of books—the labor of several years entirely destroyed."

"At the other end of the house I found telescopes, hygrometers, barometers, thermometers, and electrical machines lying in fragments." The view of the town library, which was kept in his house, distressed him almost more than he could bear. "The volumes were tossed about and defaced with the utmost wantonness, and if they happened to bear any resemblance to Bibles they were torn in pieces and trampled on." He looked at his collection of natural curiosities of which he had been so proud. Plants, seeds, stuffed birds, specimens of

[7]

insects—they had been scattered madly in all directions, and "some of the sailors were busily killing a beautiful musk-cat, which they afterwards ate." Every house, an official informed him, was full of Frenchmen, furiously engaged in hacking and tearing up everything for which they could find no use. The slaughter of livestock had been sickening—14 dozen fowl in Macaulay's own yard, 1200 hogs in the town. And the drunken, reeling knaves were potshotting wildly at any other animal hapless enough to venture within sight.

So the time passed, Macaulay making the rounds of the town to see for himself the extent of the depredations. When he returned to his dwelling in the afternoon, he learned that it had been converted into a guardhouse, and that a number of the Company's officers had been herded there for safe-keeping.

What could they do at this dark interval—Christian men among howling savages—except to take council of one another and reflect on God's mysterious ways? This they did as the hours passed, "moralizing on our late and present situation." In large measure—larger than at first they had hoped—comfort came to them, the consolations of an ageless faith. "We found, in casting up the accounts, that we had lost very little by the change. We were free from pain; we felt neither cold, nor hunger, nor thirst; in short we found that our happiness does not consist in the number of things we possess, but in the mind being so indifferent to externals as neither to feel their weight when present, nor their want when absent. We had likewise come to feel the calamities attendant on war, of which we had so often read with indifference. We now found out, too, how much better the mind of man is fitted to bear adversity than prosperity, and surely it is in mercy that God has so ordered it, seeing our course is so strewed with thorns." Their minds grew reconciled to their losses, assumed their accustomed attitudes toward even the comedy in the situation about them. They could, at length, amuse themselves with the strange and ludicrous appearance of their captors—"their savage manners, their wanton rage against our aristocratical lamps, decanters, looking glasses and tumblers, their extravagant boastings of their nation, and their violent railings against Pitt and King George." There was not a boy among them, Macaulay declared, who had not learned to accompany the name of Pitt with an execration. All night long he was forced to listen to oath upon oath, as the sentinels who stood guard at his door broke in upon his sleep with stories of the revenge they were holding in store for Pitt, against the time when they would have him, a desperate captive, in Paris. [5]

The second day was as bad as the first. Macaulay went again to see the Commodore, finding him at mess with the officers and crew. The filth and confusion at the meals was terrible—a chorus of boys ushering in and finishing the dinner with a wild version of the Marseillaise, ceaseless ecstatic shouting for the revolutionary government and army, ceaseless praise of the guillotine, and ceaseless denunciations of the English. Seeing Macaulay, they asked him if the day before had not been Sunday. He replied that it had. "Oh," said they, "the National Convention have decreed that there is no Sunday and that the Bible is all a lie." Yet he obtained from Citizen Allemand permission to distribute among the settlers five tons of rice that had been overlooked in his warehouse. He returned to the town, gave directions about the food, sent several natives down to the cape to warn away any incoming vessel, and went about reassuring his people. Meanwhile news had come that the central church had been almost destroyed—the pulpit broken in pieces, the Bibles and prayer books torn and defaced. And every bottle of medicine in the apothecary's shop had been smashed. His spirit was being sorely tried.

For another full week this sort of villainy continued, during which that spirit faltered but once. Bit by bit, he extracted concessions from the Commodore. He persuaded him to have put in irons four of his sailors who had hauled off a sick man's bed. He persuaded him to warn his American enemy that if

5. *Ibid.*, 68.

he committed any violence on shore "his head would be in jeopardy." He got a supply of flour and a cask of pork. He got brandy, a doctor's services, and a little medicine. Later on he got several sacks of sugar.

One thing he did not get, despite his bitter desire for it. To others it was so contemptibly little! An English ship, entering the harbor at night, had been captured by the enemy squadron. Searched while Macaulay was on board, it was found to contain a number of dispatches and personal letters for him. He begged for them. But the Commodore refused, said it was too late, and then had them thrown into the harbor. Still Macaulay implored him to help—to lend him a boat to retrieve them. But the Commodore, though obliging in other particulars, this time proved thoroughly obstinate. Macaulay was forced to remain on deck and watch them sink. "Nothing had yet happened materially to disturb my mind, but this stroke affected me quite materially. My regret for the loss of the letters, and my indignation at such unworthy treatment, such wanton cruelty, unhinged me not a little."[6]

His language is restrained. This was the comparatively trivial act that was to bring all his smouldering resentment to a white fury and keep it white. In his heart there developed a relentless hatred of the French as a race, a hatred that was to lead him, years later, to follow as if rapt the rise and fall of Napoleon's fortunes. He would take that hatred to the grave with him. But it was not to rest even there. It would live on in his son, sublimated perhaps, differently motivated perhaps, but as tangible and as implacable as stone.

On the morning of October 13 the raiders departed. Macaulay began immediately the tedious job of reconstruction. He set out, first, to reclaim in the Company's name all goods that the natives had secretly conveyed off during the enemy occupation. The value of these goods was considerable, and their unwillingness to return them more considerable still. But return them they did—all except foodstuffs, which they

6. *Ibid.*, 75.

were permitted to keep—under the persuasive but stern insistence of the Governor. Meanwhile came reports of further French depredations upon other towns, and, nearer home, constantly agitated rumors that the settlers were planning, definitely, to revolt. Some of the officials were certain of it! That outrageous American captain had informed the blacks that no harm would have been visited upon Freetown had Zachary Macaulay and his psalm-singing Abolitionists not been tolerated there. Zachary went on with his work, unmoved. He was preparing an estimate of damages to send to his directors in London, and supervising the rebuilding of the Company's warehouse. Two million dollars worth of property, in all, had been destroyed by the French on the West Coast. The value of captured Liverpool vessels alone he set at $600,000.[7] He was ill with a fever, seriously ill, but he kept on working, and placating, and comforting.

Indeed, he did not leave the place until May of the following year, and the manner of his leaving was characteristic of his nature. All through the months that had intervened since the raid, his fever had lingered. The Directors, learning of it, had insisted that he come home for a rest. But he would not book passage on a ship direct for England. Instead, he boarded a slaver that was taking a cargo of unfortunate negroes to the West Indies. It meant a long voyage, under filthy conditions, but, ill though he was, he risked it "in order to judge for myself at close quarters of the situation and treatment of newly captured Africans." The vessel was the *Anna*, its destination the slave markets of Barbadoes.

He saw his fill of one aspect of slavery—slaves murdered on tables by ignorant surgeons; others, in irons, whipped and handcuffed for trying to drown themselves; still others beaten with a cat-o-nine-tails for being too exhausted to respond to the captain's command that they dance for him.[8] The quarter deck was packed with them. Macaulay's own condition was

7. *Ibid.*, 85.
8. *Ibid.*, 88.

difficult, he felt, though he had for consolation the thought of friends he would soon be joining; and, beyond that, and with him always, the blessings of religion, circling him with refulgent glory. But what had these miserable wretches to look to? There they lay on the stinking deck, "extended naked on the bare boards, unable when sick to reveal the cause of their complaints, ignorant of the fate which awaited them, filled with fear either of a horrid death or a cruel servitude, and without even the most distant prospect of ever beholding again the face of one of those friends or relatives from whom they had been forcibly taken. Their cup," he concluded, "is full of pure unmingled sorrow, the bitterness of which is unalloyed by a single ray of hope." They reached Barbadoes after a voyage of four weeks. The Captain had been very civil to him; he had not sworn once, on board, in his presence.

Macaulay did not see England until late summer. He visited the Directors and made his reports. One of these directors, a brother-in-law, Thomas Babington, took him to his country seat for a long rest. By February, 1796, the young man had recovered sufficiently to begin paying court to an attractive young lady.

Miss Selina Mills was the daughter of a kindly Quaker gentleman, a bookseller, of Bristol. Some years before, she had been sent for her education to the school kept by the remarkable More sisters, Hannah and Patty, at Blagdon, some 10 miles from the city. One of the sisters, Patty, had taken so strong a fancy to her as to wish her never to marry at all, but to domesticate herself in their household at Cowslip Green. But Miss Hannah was more reasonable. Intensely concerned with the cause of slavery herself, she saw in the very earnest young suitor all that eyes bent mostly heavenward could require. She espoused his cause to Miss Mills, against the counter and rather less glamorous proposal of her sister.

To have Hannah More's support was no mean honor in the life of any gentleman of the late eighteenth century. The fourth of five daughters of Jacob More, she had been brought up, like her sisters, with the firmly rooted idea that young women should make their own way in the world. Jacob More, however, gave her a fortunate start: her nurse had attended the gout-afflicted Dryden in his last illness. Two great uncles had been captains under Cromwell. From her own father she had learned Latin and mathematics, from an older sister French, from the masters of a school her other sisters had set up in Bristol, Italian and Spanish. A year before Zachary Macaulay was born, she had waited at the altar for a bride-groom who never came. When Zachary was a lad of seven, she was taking tea with Burke and Reynolds, and bandying compliments with Dr. Samuel Johnson. Before Zachary was ten, Garrick had played for twenty-one consecutive nights in her moving drama, *Percy*.

But Garrick's death in 1779 wrought a singular change in her life. She began to frequent less and less often the gay scenes of her early years. Playgoing, she decided, was definite-ly wrong. She turned to more edifying concerns—notably to the encouragement of the Bristol milkwoman-poet, Anne Yearsley, whose study of the Bible, she agreed with the blue-stocking, Mrs. Montagu, had enabled her to soar above Pindar and Aeschylus in her verse making. Already, too, she had met the churchman John Newton, and had made him her spiritual adviser. By 1788 she had published the first of her more serious works, *Thoughts on the Importance of the Manners of the Great*. Like those to come later, this book had been widely read. From the royalties of it the sisters retired from their school, well-to-do. Miss Hannah was now interested in the founding of Sunday schools, in raising the moral status of the clergy, in teaching the serving classes the blessedness of their condi-tion ("I allow no writing for the poor. I do not think the purpose of education is to make the poor scholars and philos-ophers."),[9] in decrying the excesses of the French Revolution, and in the abolition of slavery. Until her death she was to remain a friend of Zachary, and of all his family.

9. *Dictionary of National Biography*, XXXVIII, 415-20.

In Zachary's case, therefore, the sisters arrived at a compromise. The engagement he desired with Selina was sanctioned, and duly announced. But there could be no thought of his marrying her and taking her with him to his tropical Eden. He must go back there—for so the Company desired—without her, do the work which was designed for him in his new capacity as Minister of Public Worship, and, when he had finished it and returned, the marriage could take place, not before. Zachary agreed, and departed early in 1796, taking with him, instead of his Eve, a band of Methodist, Baptist, and Wesleyan Methodist missionaries.[10]

These disseminators of the faith tried his patience to the limit. No sooner were they on board than they began to talk about theology. Talk led to discussion, discussion to argument, and argument, as so often happens, to bitterness and vituperation. Perhaps it was the monotony of the long voyage and the crowded cabins, but at any rate they soon became through their vehemence the butt of even the common seamen's jests. Zachary as their superior was compelled seriously to exert his prerogative. But still they grumbled and were disorderly, while "rank antinomianism" spread among them apace. All this he must suffer for the salvation, and ultimate emancipation, of the negro.

Arriving at the colony, he found that his first job was far from clerical. He was compelled to sit in judgment on the ringleaders of an outbreak which had taken place during his absence. He dealt with them firmly, but kindly. He admonished the Baptists of the place to attend more scrupulously to family worship. He advised the Methodists to live more conventional lives. He worked to temper the emotional excesses of the Wesleyan group, newly swollen by a revival. He stayed on with them all, enduring their trying humors and their defections, until something resembling order had been restored, until something like discipline had grown respected again, and until something like a profit for the supporters of

10. Trevelyan, *op. cit.*, I, 36.

the enterprise had become reasonably certain. When he returned to England in May, 1799, he brought with him twenty-five negro children.

He had great hopes for these youngsters. One Mr. Haldane, a Scotch philanthropist, had agreed to pay for their education. Fully trained and civilized, they would go back to spread the Transcendent Illumination into the darkest reaches of Africa. Zachary had held classes with them regularly on board, teaching them their catechism. But almost within the hour of his arrival he received a summons from the Company's directors to hurry at once to London. They were attempting to put through Parliament a measure confining the slave trade within certain limits on the African coast. The House of Commons had already passed their measure, but the Lords, dominated by the planter aristocracy, were doubtful. Macaulay was wanted to testify before them. Duty won out. He left his charges on board, gave up his hopes of an early meeting with Selina, and complied.

For almost two months this measure was fought out before the Upper Chamber. Macaulay contracted a case of African fever, and was forced to advise with the directors from his bed. Ill, and irked by many unforeseen demands upon him, he would write Selina of his impatience to visit her, of the strange perversity of certain English law makers, and of his negroes, from whom he expected so much:

"On Wednesday my black children got to Clapham in good health, and excited no small admiration among our friends, who account them a favorable specimen of African youth. Miss More. . . . began to catechize one of them a little, and was much pleased with his ready answers, though I find on an examination which I instituted this morning that they have rather lost ground during our separation. . . . I have been to the smallpox hospital to arrange for their innoculation."[11]

He also told Miss Mills of the way their ship, the *Fairy*,

11. To Miss Mills, June 1, 1799. Knutsford, *op. cit.*, 221.

was chased by the French for 32 hours, the privateer for a great part of the time having been within three miles of them. "I expected to be taken, in which case there was cause to fear all my children would have been carried to South America and sold." He added a remark that was possibly construed not altogether generously by his waiting fiancée: "I had resolved to follow them, if taken, to the farthest corner of the earth."

Great interest in these black children was taken by the inhabitants of Clapham. Mr. Haldane sent a missionary from Edinburgh to inspect them. The missionary, Mr. John Campbell, was delighted with their aptitude; he took them for a walk across the Common. But when the walk was over, nearly half of the lot were found missing. Zachary explained the reason. People dining in nearby houses "astonished to see such a cloud of young Africans" sent out their servants to catch specimens for them. And the specimens, trained already in meekness, "willingly went along with anybody."

But now came news that disturbed him greatly. Zachary had begun to hear stories—much too insistent and circumstantial to be doubted—that Mr. Haldane's religious and political convictions were dangerous. He had become a dissenter, and some of his doctrines could only be termed both "heretical and socialistic." This would never do! Not to the end of making radicals of his little Africans had Zachary brought them this perilous two thousand mile journey. He wrote to the philanthropist a modest proposal. Its terms were that Haldane should be "allowed" to bear the expense of their education (since he was the "originator" of the scheme), but that they be kept at Clapham, in London, and that Zachary himself should select their instructor. Mr. Haldane was unwilling. His curt reply declared: "We will not so mix the work. Either you or I shall have the whole charge."[12] Help came though, finally and providentially, from the directors of the Company and certain of their friends.

12. *Ibid.*, 224.

Zachary was able at length to exclaim to his patient Selina: "At last my children are rescued from the grasp of Mr. Haldane."

At about the same time, in July, 1799, the House of Lords rejected the Slavery Bill. Recovered from the fever, Zachary turned over his negroes to an instructor and set out to visit his betrothed.

Their plans for the wedding were already completed. It was to take place the twenty-sixth of August. But before Zachary would venture upon so solemn a step he desired to know one thing truly, no matter how distressing it might be to have it told him. He desired to know the truth about himself—all his faults and shortcomings, to the end that, as far as mortal could, he might undertake to correct them. He turned to his brother-in-law Babington, of Rothley Temple. Babington had known him well from childhood; he had made his African experience possible; he understood Zachary, as few men or women were ever to understand him:

"Your chief faults, my dear Zachary, seem to me nearly connected with natural ardour of mind and firmness of character. These qualities are excellent when kept within due bounds, but their very excellence tends to relax the watch which should be set over them. The first is apt to encroach on that smiling serenity of soul which is so amiable in itself, and so duly connected with Christian love and meekness; and the latter tends to destroy, in some instances, and to deaden in others, the sensibilities which are the proper concomitants and the most pleasing expression of those dispositions." The remedy for these frailties, Babington continued, was the simple formula—Christian humility. He went on: "As to positive faults, I have not seen one of your old ones which does not seem to have been greatly weakened, if not apparently destroyed. . . . I allude particularly to impatience, self-confidence, and a love of praise. May you still be able to foil these fell adversaries! Shall I mention the instances in which, as far as I now recollect, they used most

[17]

to appear? In the style of your letters and your tones in reading being too oratorical, in something of this in your own conversation also at times; in a boldness in your looks, and a hardness and spirit of opposition in arguing, and in joining in conversation sometimes as a master, sometimes as an equal in knowledge, on subjects on which your degree of information would have made it more decorous and useful for you to have taken a lower station."

But this was not all. Babington, wise in the ways of the world, and of ladies, went on to remind him that for the past several years he had been a grave and active governor, away from female society. Selina, on the other hand, had been "entirely with females." He must try to adjust himself to her point of view, without departing, of course, from his "proper sphere" as master of the household. Only one thing, really, did this change involve in him—that he acquire the art of relaxing, "an art you have never yet studied." He must not expect his fellow traveler, during the thorn-ridden journey they were about to set out on together, to be pleased entirely with the adventure "if you drag her over deserts or through swamps, or bury her in the depths of a forest. Though she will not dislike a good deal of these occasionally, yet in general you should lead her through cheerful cornfields and pastures, and when opportunity offers go out of your way a little to show her a flowery meadow or a winding stream."[13]

It is difficult to say what all this probing of the young man's mind came to. Certainly, as month succeeded month, he was to grow more humble, was to lose his impatience wholly, and was to become, it appears, all but inarticulate in speech, trusting almost altogether to his thunderous printed revelations of the iniquity of the slave trade. But was the path of Selina, ever, between successive childbirths, to be made less thorny through occasional glimpses of the green serenities Babington had mentioned? Alas, this blessing was scarcely to be. She would have to content herself with blessings more

13. *Ibid.*, 232-34.

ancient and certain—the blessings, chiefly, of a family of children, growing methodically more numerous with the advancing years; while her husband was to withdraw more and more completely into himself and his work, to the end that there might be finally accomplished the overwhelming task of emancipation that God had meant him to direct.

But all this was in the untroubled future. Meanwhile, the directors of Sierra Leone had appointed him Secretary of the Company at a salary of four hundred pounds a year. His prospects were promising. Duly, as planned, therefore, the marriage took place in Bristol, and duly, also, as planned and as was proper, the couple set out for Rothley Temple for their honeymoon, "with the inevitable sister in the carriage between them." After some weeks they returned to London to visit friends until their rooms at the Sierra Leone office could be made ready.

In addition to his routine duties, Zachary soon became interested in the formation of the Religious Tract Society. This society was the natural outgrowth of an earlier enterprise whose objective had been the distribution of Cheap Repository Tracts. Here were, in embryo, the Bible societies that years later were to spread incalculable blessings throughout the world's darkest centers, that would inform George Borrow's ablest work, and would grow at length into organizations like the Gideon's, founded to deposit in each hotel room of America the Holy Word against the forgetfulness of desperate men. And when leisure presented itself from this duty, and his accustomed duties as secretary, he devoted himself to his duty as husband, and to his other duty as guardian of his little Africans. Already he had had them placed under a trusted Clapham rector, John Venn, who had selected as their schoolmaster an equally trusted gentleman, Mr. William Greaves. But the winter was proving too much for them. When the spring of the new century arrived, half a dozen had already died, despite prayers and the closest care.

But if Death was showing no mercy on his negroes, Life,

with its no less ancient ritual, was busy too—elsewhere, nearer home. Mrs. Macaulay was near her confinement. She must come for the event, Mrs. Babington insisted, back to Rothley Temple; for the advantages of country air far outweighed, to her thinking, the more dubious advantages of London doctors. Come she did, gladly; and there—"in a room paneled from ceiling to floor, like every corner of the ancient mansion, with oak almost black from age"[14]—her first child, Thomas Babington Macaulay, was born the twenty-fifth of October, 1800. It was a date he was to recall with fondness throughout his remarkable career. For on it, at various intervals down the revolving centuries, Chaucer and Hogarth had died, and the field of Agincourt had been won by the impetuous Henry. It was also, he liked to add, the day of St. Crispin, the patron of shoemakers. Zachary was more than pleased, though his pleasure was to be but short-lived. For the next day his horse, shying at the noise of a spinning jenny, threw him and broke both his arms. Strapped from shoulder to fingertips, he was led in to join his convalescing wife, and spent with her there, his grandson declares, the last holiday of his life.

14. Trevelyan, *op. cit.*, I, 38.

II. Prodigy

THE HEREDITY of Zachary's first born was Scotch, solid and respectable. Four generations back, in the first decade of the eighteenth century, Aulay Macaulay, Zachary's grandfather, is heard of as minister of Tiree and Coll. Losing his stipend there through the machinations of a powerful laird, he was forced to preach for a while in the open air, "exposed to the violence of the weather at all seasons." This condition, obviously, could not last. Dissatisfied with it, he removed to Harris, "to the great regret" of the parisioners he left behind him, and for the next half century discharged his duties there in peace.

Aulay begat a sizeable family—fourteen in all. One of them, Kenneth, lives briefly for us in the crowded pages of Boswell. A minister like his father, he had done a *History of St. Kilda;* and though eager, according to Dr. Johnson, to be known as "a most modern thinker," he nevertheless had proved himself willing to set down without cynicism a few superstitions about the island. Later, in 1773, Johnson paid him a visit. The evening, as often happened where the great lexicographer was involved, began with compliments, but ended with insults. Johnson finally pronounced Kenneth Macaulay incapable of having written the book that went by his name, a decision which, in Trevelyan's words, gives those curious enough to have read the volume "a very poor notion of my ancestor's abilities." [1]

1. Trevelyan, *op. cit.*, I, 21. Trevelyan is, of course, best on Macaulay's ancestry. See pp. 20-24.

The eldest son of Aulay, Zachary's father, was born in the year 1720 and christened John. He, too, was a minister, living chiefly in his earlier days at Invary, under the patronage of the influential Argyll family. John had also enjoyed the honor of a rebuke from Dr. Johnson, a rebuke earned, it appears, for defending the perfectly respectable point that people were not in earnest in good professions if their practices belied them. But the two men spent the following morning together as friends, the doctor declaiming in Macaulay's presence "some of the finest lines ever written." As the century advanced, John's reputation advanced with it. In 1774 he moved to Cardross, and there on the banks of the estuary of the Clyde he passed the last fifteen years of his life. His first wife had died at the birth of their first child. Seven years later, in 1757, he had married a second, Margaret Campbell, of Inverseger, who followed the now well established Macaulay tradition by bearing him a round dozen children.

At least three of these children became fairly eminent in the world. Aulay the younger was ordained a clergyman in the Church of England. He was known as a scholar and antiquary; he published pamphlets and treatises; he was for a time a tutor to royalty. Mr. Babington married his daughter Jean, in 1787. Then there was Colin. Colin entered the Indian army when quite young, and in 1836 died a scholarly General sufficiently well off to leave his nephew, Thomas Babington Macaulay, a £10,000 inheritance. Throughout his later years he remained an intimate friend of the Duke of Wellington. The third son of importance was Zachary.

And Zachary, if a son of importance, was already, in 1800, in close association with other gentlemen more important still. Some of these gentlemen deserve attention; for in one way or another they were to shape not only his own destiny but that of his illustrious son, were to fashion that destiny in ways that became fixed as adamant before that son knew what had happened to him. There was William Wilberforce, for example:

Wilberforce had entered St. John's College, Cambridge, in 1776, a frail wealthy youth with pleasant manners and an excellent voice. As a student he had entertained lavishly, had drunk and gambled like a typical blade of fashion, and in 1780, at the age of twenty-one had, "bought" a seat in Parliament from Hull at a cost of £9,000. In London his career of gaiety continued. He joined five exclusive clubs and kept up at once his drinking, his entertaining, and his gambling. And then one night he won £600 from men who could not afford the loss. He stopped this diversion and, worried in spirit, set out from France with a friend, William Pitt, whom he was growing increasingly to admire.

The year 1785 is significant because of his conversion. He traveled in Italy, France, and Switzerland with his mother and the Cambridge Churchman, Isaac Milner. Nightly they discussed the subject of religion. Wilberforce, at length, saw the evil of his ways, and resolved to lead from that time forth a life of piety and good works. It was a resolution from which he was never once to waver. Pitt was sympathetic. The chastened young man returned to London, and almost immediately set out to carry through the House of Commons a bill amending the Criminal Law. In 1787 the Anti-Slavery forces won him over, and from that date, until his death nearly half a century later, this delicate Christian, whose health had been totally despaired of in early manhood, was to work at their cause in the rôle of its Patron Saint. Among the many new obligations he assumed was that of a director of the Sierra Leone Company.[2]

Another director and wealthy member of Parliament was Henry Thornton. This capitalist statesman, eight years Zachary's senior, was the son of the philanthropist John Thornton, who had given away his fortune to charity at the rate of £6000 a year, who had befriended the poet Cowper, and had backed the budding Evangelical or Low Church group in its efforts to circulate the Bible in all parts of the world. He sent his son

2. *Dictionary of National Biography*, XXI, 208-15.

Henry, the youngest of four, first to Cambridge for a classical education, and then into the banking business. Henry's fortunes were soon prospering. In 1782 he was elected M.P. from Southwark, despite his refusal—then not common—to buy votes at a guinea apiece. Thornton at once identified himself with the liberal party in the government. He favored the French Revolution and those two apparently then lost causes, Lord Grey's first reform bill and Catholic emancipation. And almost from the start of his career he was looked upon as an authority on national finances. His personal generosity was the talk of the country. Until his marriage, in 1797, he devoted to charity six-sevenths of his yearly income. Afterwards, he continued to give away one-third of it to good works, feeling, as had his own father, that the best legacy he could leave to his children was the example of his liberality.

One of the first interests Thornton developed in Parliament was the slave trade. Wilberforce was already an old friend: they would labor together in the cause of righteousness. Thornton bought a home at Battersea Rise, in Clapham, and Wilberforce, then unmarried, came to live with him. It was the real beginning of the Clapham Sect, of that body of earnest, devout men who were to affect in so fundamental a manner the fortunes and attitudes of Zachary Macaulay, of his illustrious son, and of the world. Thornton was soon made another director of the Sierra Leone Company.[3]

But if Wilberforce and Thornton formed the center of this "brotherhood of saints," others scarcely less esteemed made up its shining periphery. One of those others was Dr. Thomas Bowdler, from whose name there was to stem before long a new and valuable English verb, thanks to his edition of Shakespeare in which "all expressions are omitted that cannot with propriety be read aloud" in the family circle.[4] Then there was John Venn, the Evangelical Clapham rector, busy, in 1800, with supervising the activities of the Church Missionary

3. *Ibid.*, XIX, 781-83.
4. *Ibid.*, VI, 44-46.

Society and the waning fortunes of Zachary's little Africans. John Shore, Baron Teignmouth, was another. Already, when Zachary first met him during the earliest years of the new century, he had been honored with a paraphrase of one of the odes of Horace, addressed to him by Warren Hastings, had served on the Supreme Council of India, and later as Governor General. Finally, one should mention Charles Grant. For more than a quarter of a century Grant had been active in the Missionary Movement. When the Sierra Leone Company was chartered, in 1791, he was named to its board of directors.[5] Later he had moved to Clapham, to be near his enterprising associates, who would listen to the stories of how he founded the first Sunday schools in Scotland, or of how, as a living testament to Godliness, he had built the inspiring Church of St. John amid Calcutta's heathen temples and mosques.

It was, in short, an impressive group, this band of unselfish and tireless men that had settled now within the suburbs of London, a band whose significance it would be difficult to overstress. Intellectually they were part of a movement of sweeping importance, one that had as its objective nothing less than a reshaping of the social and moral structure of English society. Looking about themselves upon the late eighteenth century aristocrats who were their friends, they found them, and most of the ideals they stood for, shot through with corruption and spiritual indifference. Cynicism was abroad in the land and a chilly Deism that was freezing up the ancient warm fountains of apostolic faith. Nowadays, wrote the Reverend Isaac Milner, "only the lower orders regard such things as the gospel. The great and the high have, all over Europe, forgotten that they have souls."[6] It was time for an awakening to come, yet an awakening that would be, somehow, free from the violence and soon exhausted emotionalism of the more vulgar sects. The intelligence, not the passions of

5. *Ibid.*, XVIII, 148-49.
6. Elie Halévy, *History of the English People in 1815* (E. A. Watkins and D. A. Barker, trans.) I, 393.

[25]

men, must be appealed to. And that could be done best by showing them, plainly, the many good works that ought to be wrought in the world, the multitudinous abuses that fairly cried out for correction. A practical religion was needed, one that would appeal to gentlemen schooled during the incomparable Age of Reason. And behind the plea for the reforms in question, a grim threat against their postponement, loomed the solemn red shadow of the French Revolution. The lesson to be learned from that shadow was that a people cannot be expected to endure oppression forever in silence.

What was it, to be exact, that most grievously clamored for remedy? To begin with, there was the vice of duelling. Addison and Steele had protested against the practice without avail; in the army and navy it was still far more widespread than it should be. Next there were cockfights, bear baitings and bull baitings, to say nothing of boxing matches, at which otherwise rational Englishmen were too prone to lose their heads altogether. Still more serious was the habit of employing as chimney sweeps thin, underfed children of six or seven years of age. Then there was wholesale Sabbath breaking, blasphemy, drunkenness, obscene literature and immoral amusements—all alike in their need for suppression. And there was the Established Church itself. The "Saints," or Evangelicals as they in fairness should be called, felt that basic reform should begin with it. Parson Doolittle and Parson Merryman ought, they insisted, to be expelled from the pulpit, ought to be replaced by Parson Lovegood, [7] who would remain in the village to which he had been assigned instead of rushing away to London to spend months at a time in that citadel of sin and abandon. Finally, of course, there was the lingering curse of the slave trade. God's creatures stolen, beaten, and sold in shrieking violation of all human instincts and divine injunctions.

Two influential groups were behind this effort to awaken the drowsy conscience of England. One was centered at Cam-

7. *Ibid.*, I, 394-401.

bridge, where the Evangelical party possessed two men of unquestioned ability—Isaac Milner and Charles Simeon. Milner, as we have seen, had effected the conversion of Wilberforce. Awe inspiring he was, an overwhelming personality; indeed, according to one admirer, the impression he wrought upon erring souls was like that of a sledge hammer used against pliant iron. He was wealthy and lived like a thoroughgoing gentleman, but his tastes did not prevent him, as vicar of Christ Church, from preaching to the poor farmers of the shire, or from freezing with a fixed look of his eyes the wealthy and cynical undergraduates in his audience.[8] The settled fury that lurked in those eyes became the terror of the noise maker and skeptic. They heard him out in silence; and many —including one of Macaulay's early teachers—went away from his services indelibly impressed.

Simeon was less sensational than his inspired friend, but his influence was equally important. Methodically, and with infinite perseverance, he was going about his business of training and recruiting a body of Low Church ministers, ministers alike at least to the extent of sharing the conviction that a new pietism should be brought to inform the pulpit utterances of the Establishment. These men, who owed their awakened spirituality to Simeon, were scattered throughout the country by the year 1800. The Rev. John Venn of Clapham was one of their number, a vigorous link between the "Saints" and that center of saintliness beside the never troubled Cam.

The Clapham group was variously busy. To it had been recruited a nucleus of kindred spirits, men who were either members of Parliament or of considerable indirect influence there. Throughout the first third of the nineteenth century they constituted a bloc which no one politically ambitious could ignore. At the time of their greatest authority they controlled sixty votes in the House of Commons; politically, therefore,

8. *Ibid.*, I, 379-80. See also James Stephen, *Essays in Ecclesiastical Biography*, II, 309.

they could ruin a ministry. In general, they seem to have been concerned with reforms of a humanitarian nature.

For the ambitious Sierra Leone company, for example, they were to raise in all a total of £240,000, before that noble but finally bankrupt venture passed to the Crown in 1808. In 1795 they had founded the London Missionary Society, basing it on "the principle of united action by all denominations of orthodox Christians." The next year they pushed through Parliament a bill that raised by fifty per cent the stipends of Episcopal curates. In 1804, in keeping with the Englishman's chronic enthusiasm for "societies," they were to form another—the Bible Society—whose sweeping influence we have already mentioned.[9] And already, in 1800, they were planning a magazine to be called the *Christian Observer*, which would trace the course of world events from the point of view of a vigilant orthodoxy. Zachary Macaulay was seriously being talked of for the position of editor.

These leaders were meeting regularly, at times as often as thrice a week for lunch, frequently during the evenings, and always, literally always, on Sundays. They would attend church together, repair home for a simple meal, and then set out for Mr. Henry Thornton's salon, where "Anglican clergymen, non-conformist ministers, gentlemen of means, lawyers, business men, and representatives of all the oppressed races on earth—Spaniards and Portuguese from both Europe and America, negroes, hindus, and chinese"—talked with passionate intensity of the future of mankind. William Pitt, relaxing once from his budgets and subsidies, had designed that inspiring oval drawing room. Books lined its walls on every side, except one, which opened "on a far extended lawn reposing beneath the giant arms of elms and massive tulip trees."[10] Young Tom Macaulay, with the children of his father's friends, played there many mornings and afternoons. And there or in his own scarcely less noisy home—or alone

9. *Ibid.*, I, 391.
10. Stephen, *op. cit.*, II, 388.

in his study, long after these childhood idols were sunk in dust
—the shadow of Clapham and the moral earnestness it represented remained with him, directing his judgments in practically all that he wrote.

2

The Macaulays lived on at the Sierra Leone office for two
more years after the birth of their eldest son, before the lure
of more intimate companionship led them to move to the
High Street of Clapham. Zachary, as soon as his family was
settled there, immersed himself in his new and added undertaking, that of editor of the *Christian Observer*. The magazine
began with an impressive program, a program, one might
add, which was never once lost sight of until the publication
sank at length, forever, under the weight of its own too
ponderous godliness. Its first number appeared with the new
year, 1802, its contents arranged in the following divisions:
1. Religious Communications—which contained an article
on the history of the Church, in the form of a biography of
St. Ignatius. 2. Miscellaneous, comprising essays on the
"Proprieties of Female Character," "Cruelty to Animals,"
and "Field Sports." 3. Reviews of New Publications—chiefly
devoted to comments on religious books. 4. Reviews of Reviews—a discussion of rival magazines. 5. Literary and
Philosophical Intelligence—wherein a list of important new
books was published. 6. Religious Intelligence—which gave
news of missionary work. 7. A View of Public Affairs—
devoted mainly to Napoleon. 8. An Obituary Column—
which listed important churchmen recently deceased and
9. Answers to Correspondents.
A solemn intellectual supper, in short, awaited the limited
but hardy subscribers who undertook to digest this diet. To
make its future career even more difficult, the Devil was
already at work, raising up an adversary to appear in the
fall under the caption *The Edinburgh Review*. But the *Chris-*

tian Observer held hard on its course, despite Hannah More's complaint, in 1804, that it needed "a little salt, a little sprinkling of manners as well as principle"; and despite Wilberforce's even more frank avowal that it was "heavy, and if not enlivened will sink."[11] Yet sink it did not! Instead, it went on and on, growing in righteousness and influence every hour, and growing also, and more importantly, in the practical item of circulation. And this growth continued, it should be added, despite the indignant protests of many readers that the editor was treating religious matters with excessive frivolity, and that many of his papers were entirely out of place "in well regulated Christian families."[12]

Zachary was unperturbed. The discipline to which he had committed himself, in fact, left scant interval for either perturbation or leisure. At four in the morning, summer and winter, he arose, and set about his already fixed routine. There was early breakfast, and afterwards, family prayers. Then, with the day little more than begun, he went to his office and started work on the Company's business, a business which seemed to have, quite literally, neither beginning nor intimation of end. And all day long, during pauses in that business, he wrote letters on the slavery question to interested gentlemen scattered over at least three continents; he supervised the packing of pamphlets; he composed the arguments for other pamphlets yet unwritten. When Parliament was in session, moreover, he attended its meetings regularly, supplying Wilberforce and Thornton with facts which he alone had at ready command. And always there was the magazine to be looked after. Even his rare holidays were spent at the watering places to which more prosperous members of the sect had repaired. Plans were discussed then, bills were drafted, and the sacred cause to which he was now solely devoted received new impetus against the rival forces that threatened it.

11. Knutsford, *op. cit.*, 257.
12. *Ibid.*

Meanwhile Zachary's eldest son was showing the first of his many symptoms of precocity. "From the time that he was three years old, he read incessantly, for the most part lying on a rug before the fire, with a book on the floor, and a piece of bread and butter in his hand."[13] He never cared for toys. It was much better to entertain the parlor maid with elaborately amplified summaries of stories he had recently read, or to tell, during walks with his mother or nurse, other stories, far more fanciful, that had been freshly minted by his astonishing imagination. Always he would be talking, moreover, in "quite printed words," words which he had retained without effort from the latest volume to come within the range of his ravenous curiosity. Once, when about four years of age, he answered a knock at the door. The visitor, none other than the almost sanctified Miss Hannah More, heard with no little interest from a slight, fair, curly headed child the announcement that though his parents were out, they would soon return, and would she be so good as to wait for them? Miss Hannah decided she would, and was shown into the parlor. The young man then inquired if he could bring her "some fine old spirits." Now to a lady whose furthest dissipation since Dr. Johnson's death had been a rare glass of cowslip wine, this offer was little short of startling. What did he know about old spirits? The child replied with entire naturalness that Robinson Crusoe had often enjoyed them. A little later in the year he was taken to visit Lady Waldegrave, at Strawberry Hill. He went through the art collection, manifesting great interest, until he was summoned to tea. But while the tea was being served, a maid spilled a cup of the hot liquid flush on his legs. It proved intensely painful. Yet Tom complained very little. And after a while, when his solicitous hostess inquired how he felt, he answered her with the simple remark: "Thank you, madam, the agony is abated."[14] He was already proving himself no ordinary youngster.

13. Trevelyan, *op. cit.*, I, 39.
14. *Ibid.*, I, 40.

Thus he passed his earliest years, inventing or retelling stories, or startling people ten times his age with remarks almost incredible to hear. Clapham Common was the general playground of the neighborhood. In Macaulay's childhood it was "a delightful wilderness of gore bushes, poplar groves, gravel pits and ponds, great and small."[15] On each recess and green secrecy of the place he bestowed a nomenclature of his own devising. A slight ridge intersected by ditches toward the west of the Common was christened the Alps. An elevated island in the pond was called Sinai. So it went. In the family's own garden he had marked out with oyster shells a plot of ground which he claimed as his own. Sally, the maid, one afternoon threw away those shells as rubbish. The child was irate. He walked into the drawing room, where his mother was entertaining a number of visitors, and reaching the center of the circle pronounced his judgment: "Cursed be Sally; for it is written, Cursed is he that removeth his neighbor's landmark."

While still very young, his parents sent him to a day school run by Mr. Greaves, who had been brought to Clapham to teach Zachary's little Africans. The arrangement made with Mr. Greaves had been that, when one of the negro children died, he would be permitted to take in a white scholar in his place. And as we have seen, these unfortunate lads were fast finding the English climate beyond their endurance.

Tom was not happy to leave home even for the day, for home was already beginning to prove a place of fairly endless excitement. Three sisters and two brothers had "joined" the family circle by June of 1808. There was Selina, born in 1802; Jane, born in 1804; John, born the year after Jane; William, born the year after John; and then Frances, born a year and a half after William.[16] Young Tom had thus, at the age of eight, become the major influence in a hierarchy of no mean pretensions. It was much nicer, he felt, to remain in his own

15. *Ibid.*, I, 40.
16. Charles Booth, *Zachary Macaulay*, 212.

house, to direct the ranging energies of these dependents, and to continue his now quite serious literary activity.

Indeed, although he wrote a great deal in his later years, this interval of pre-adolescence was likely the most productive of his life. It went on, moreover, without any special encouragement; in fact, his parents were sorely tried, at times, to satisfy his insistent demands for foolscap. They had already agreed to take all that he did, howsoever unusual, as a matter of course, convinced that, if brought up to consider himself a perfectly normal person, his chances of getting along agreeably in the world would prove far greater than would be the case were he reminded too often of the fact of his genius. And so it happened that they received without astonishment a copy of his Compendium of Universal History, a manuscript which set forth with fair continuity the leading events from the creation to the year 1808,[17] and which proclaimed the rather remarkable judgment that Cromwell was both "an unjust and a wicked man."

Other sweeping documents were being turned out, in hurrying sequence. He wrote a paper which a friend was to translate into Malabar. It was a treatise enjoining the people of that country to embrace the Christian religion "with some strong arguments" appended. Shortly afterwards, he fell under Scott's witchery, memorizing in its entirety the *Lay of the Last Minstrel*, and, almost in its entirety, the moving romance of *Marmion*. He was stirred by this reading to begin a glamorous saga of his own, to be entitled *The Battle of Cheviot;* and in two days' time he completed three cantos of 120 lines each. Then he tired of Cheviot, tempted by subjects nearer home. Why not do a poem in the heroic manner, a poem that would also celebrate, somehow, the past and future fortunes of his family! He began this work at once. It sketched the careers of General Macaulay in India, and of his own father Zachary, "deliverer of the wretched Africans." And of course, he wrote religious hymns, hymns that seemed with

17. Trevelyan, *op. cit.*, I, 42.

[33]

entire propriety to emerge from an environment so steeped in the sanctities. In spirit, at least one of these hymns is remarkably like work he produced years later. It is addressed to God the Father:

Almighty God of all below,
Thou canst protect from every foe;
The heavens are made by Thy great hands,
One word of Thine the Earth commands.

Some men make gods of red and blue
And rob their Sovereign of his due:
The good shall go to heaven. The fell
Blasts of Thy wrath can bear to hell.

As one critic has recently pointed out, it is hardly fanciful to list as characteristic of Macaulay both the ease with which he divides mankind into two antithetical classes, and the sureness with which he forecasts the respective destiny of each.[18]

The education which young Tom was receiving under Mr. Greaves' tutelage was being supplemented, during holidays and the summers, at the home of the More sisters. Barley Wood indeed, with the exception of Rothley Temple, was perhaps to him at this date the finest place in England. Educators both, the Mores knew how to encourage a child without spoiling him. Miss Hannah was his particular favorite: she would listen to him while he read prose almost endlessly, or while he declaimed poetry, or while he discussed, "under all points of view," his heroes, literary, historical, and legendary. As early as his seventh year she had begun to correspond with him, expressing the hope that he would become a good scholar long before he became a grown man, and sending him, by way of encouragement, a small sum of money with which to lay "a little tiny cornerstone for your future library." She

18. S. C. Roberts, *Lord Macaulay; the Preëminent Victorian* (English Assn. Pamphlet, No. 67), 6.

even discussed the authors he might start with—Isaak Walton, Cowper, and Milton in English, or in French, Racine, "the only dramatic poet I know in any modern language who is perfectly pure and good."[19] She added, in this note to the young author, a hope which the Lord never saw fit to grant: "I want you to become a complete Frenchman." But Tom was grateful for her advice and for her more tangible patronage. He dedicated to her one of his most ambitious odes.

But Miss Hannah went considerably beyond the rather simple business of writing to Tom. She consciously set about helping Zachary to plan his future. They exchanged long letters about the problem, both of them now fully aware of his genius and therefore of the importance of directing it rightly. One thing it was necessary to make plain to him immediately—the fact that not all youngsters could be expected to equal him in mental endowments. In May, 1810, Miss More wrote his father:

"I will tell you honestly. . . . that his superiority of talents make competitors necessary for him, for he is a little inclined to undervalue those who are not considerable or distinguished in some way or other. I have talked with him gently on the subject, telling him how valuable and worthy people may be who are neither brilliant in talent nor high in situation. He listened to me meekly."[20]

The following year she was sending along still more advice. "Tell him," she wrote Zachary, "that he must apply hard to business, and that of a sober, severe cast. He must be very neat and improve his handwriting, as qualifications for repeating his visits to Barley Wood. You need not add a part of my message, though it is very true; that he is a jewel of a boy."[21]

Yet now, at the age of twelve, it was fairly evident that Tom was outgrowing the limited educational facilities of Clapham. He had already begun the study of Greek and

19. Trevelyan, *op. cit.*, I, 47.
20. Knutsford, *op. cit.*, 336.
21. *Letters of Hannah More to Zachary Macaulay* (Arthur Roberts, ed.) (London, 1860), xi.

Latin, and Miss Hannah, at the end of one of his visits, reported happily to Zachary that his son's "classicality had not extinguished his piety."[22] But another school must be found for him—a boarding school. This implied that he must leave home, a compulsion that was to prove one of the most difficult of his life.

At first, though, the school itself had to be selected. Zachary had thought of enrolling him at Westminster, and wrote his friend for her opinion. That opinion, which soon came, was quite positive: Zachary should place his son under some clergyman who kept students; nothing less edifying would do. She went on to say that she compared "the sending a boy to a public school or college to the act of the Scythian mothers, who threw their new born children into the sea. The greater part, of course, were drowned; but the few who escaped with life were uncommonly strong and vigorous."[23]

Miss Hannah's judgment prevailed. In the fall of 1813 Tom was sent away to a private school kept by the Rev. Mr. Preston at Little Shelford, a village near Cambridge. It meant that, in a day before railroads, he would have to live, during most of the year, some sixty miles from home, and from the family of children, now eight in number, of which he was logically and by right of priority the head. He left that family in overwhelming sadness, and with joy equally overwhelming, as we shall see, he returned to it as often as an increasingly serious minded father would permit. For his family to Tom had already become what, essentially, it was destined to remain throughout his life—the center of his interest and affection, a center so closely and guardedly kept that little room would ever be left in it for affections of a different nature.

22. *Ibid.*, xii.
23. *Ibid.*, 109.

III. Student

INDUSTRY AND PIETY were the twin gods that received academic homage at the Rev. Mr. Preston's school. He was a follower of the saintly Mr. Simeon, and a close friend of the esteemed Dean Milner, both of whom dined often at his table. The educator, it should be added, had scant respect for those churchmen who insisted that holy matters should be presented only in attractive form. He felt himself justified at any time in introducing into talks with his students searching queries on the state of their souls, or lengthy sermons on the thirty-nine articles which, as punishment for lack of diligence, any one of them might be requested to summarize in writing. The result of this menacing obligation was that young Tom Macaulay took particular pains to see that his assignments were scrupulously worked up. Of sermons, and the epitomizing of sermons, he had already, he felt, had more than his share.

Aside from Mr. Preston's system of penalties, therefore, the young scholar found life at his school fairly pleasant, except, of course, for the fact that he was away from home. He wrote to his father in February, 1813, with an almost contagious enthusiasm. In the first place, he noted, he was working hard at his Greek—Xenophon every day and the *Odyssey* twice a week. Twice a week, also, he was writing Latin verses, so successfully that "I have not yet been laughed at." In addition, there was Greek grammar to be memorized every evening, and regular intervals set aside for tests in composition, both English and Latin. And he had already begun to take considerable interest in the school debating society, a gathering at which subjects like "Whether Ld. Wellington or Marlborough was the greatest general" were certain to elicit the most savage discussions. In another letter home, he described his room. It was "a delightful snug little chamber, which nobody can enter as there is a trick about opening the door. I sit like a king with my writing desk before me; for (would you believe it?) there is a writing desk in my chest of drawers; my books on one side, my box of papers on the other, with my armchair and my candle; for every boy has a candlestick, snuffers and extinguisher of his own." [1]

A note to his mother the following April told of more significant matters. Dean Milner, who had met the boy at Dr. Preston's and who had been much taken with him, had had him as a guest at Queen's College, showing him all around the university and generally amusing him "with the greatest kindness." Also, he was doing some fairly remarkable reading for a lad of his years: Plutarch's *Lives* and Milner's *Ecclesiastical History*, in English; and, in French, Fénelon's *Dialogues of the Dead* and the *Petits Romans* of Madame de Genlis. All this, of course, was in addition to his regular methodical study of the classics. [2] But perhaps, he was inquiring a week later, his father should like to have word of his son's activities on Sunday:

"It is quite a day of rest here, and I really look to it with pleasure through the whole of the week. After breakfast we learn a chapter in the Greek Testament. . . We then go to church. We dine almost as soon as we come back, and we are left to ourselves till afternoon church. During this time I employ myself in reading, and Mr. Preston lends me any books for which I ask him, except for one thing, which, though I believe it is useful, is not very pleasant. I can only ask for one book at a time, and can not touch another 'till I have

1. Trevelyan, *op. cit.*, I, 50-51.
2. *Ibid.*, I, 52.

read it through. We then go to church, and after we come back I read as before till tea time. After tea we write out the sermon. I can not help thinking that Mr. Preston uses all imaginable means to make us forget it, for he gives us a glass of wine each on Sunday, and on Sunday only, the very day when we want to have all our faculties awake; and some do literally go to sleep during the sermon and look rather silly when they wake. I, however, have not fallen into this disaster."[3]

He went on, in later letters, to discuss politics with his father, whose interest in the struggle with France was still profound, although the old tragedy at Sierra Leone was now almost two decades past. The East India Company was seeking in Parliament a renewal of its charter, and the Clapham Sect was insisting that this renewal should be granted only on condition that missionaries be allowed to enter the country with their gospel. Petitions endorsing this view were being circulated throughout the island, all of them drawn up by the restless pen of Zachary.

"I am very pleased," his son wrote home in May, "that the nation seems to take such interest in the introduction of Christianity into India. My Scotch blood begins to boil at the mention of the seventeen hundred and fifty names that went up from a single country parish. Ask Mama and Selina if they do not now admit my argument with regard to the superior advantages of the Scotch over the English peasantry."[4]

Meanwhile, Tom was continuing his literary effusions at a pace rather too rapid to please his family: there was danger that he would become too facile and careless. His mother finally decided to warn him: "I know you write with great ease to yourself and would rather write ten poems than prune one; but remember that excellence is not attained at first. All your pieces are much mended after a little reflection, and

3. *Ibid.*, I, 52-53.
4. *Ibid.*, I, 53-54.

therefore take some solitary walks, and think over each separate thing." She went on to tell him that he should seek always to render each work as nearly perfect as possible, to remind him that every faculty of his mind should be disciplined and improved, now, to the utmost, in order that, in the future, he might "be better enabled to glorify God. . . . You see how ambitious your mother is. She must have the wisdom of her son acknowledged before angels and an assembled world." [5]

The summer holidays came, and Tom was able to return home. The family of children had now reached eight in number; and already he had developed an affection for the two youngest—Hannah More, age three, and Margaret, not yet two—which was to grow with each year, until the prospect of even a temporary separation from them came to appear almost unendurable. More than ever, during this vacation, did that family and his place in it absorb the limitless affections of his nature. When the time came for him to return to Shelford, it seemed as if his heart would break. Once there, he was still unconsoled. "Everything," he wrote his mother, "brings home to my recollection. . . . Not an hour passes in which I do not shed tears thinking of it." His mother had tentatively promised that he might return for a visit during the fall holidays. He began to count the hours until that wished-for time should come. Might he be allowed to select the date himself? He should like best for it to be October 25, his birthday. "I think I see you sitting by Papa just after this dinner, reading my letter, and turning to him, with an inquisitive glance, at the end of the paragraph. I think too that I see his expressive shake of the head at it. Oh, may I be mistaken! You cannot conceive what an alteration a favorable answer would produce in me." [6]

But this apprehension about his father proved true. Instead of permission to return to Clapham, he received a letter "of

5. *Ibid.*, I, 55.
6. *Ibid.*, I, 56.

strong religious complexion." Already, in fact, Zachary was beginning to hear stories about his son's conduct at school, stories which began soon to evoke rather solemn lectures, instead of the innocent indulgence he longed for. Tom had apparently been too lustily critical of some of the townsmen of Shelford. One of them he had actually contradicted at Mr. Preston's table. The news of his arrogance soon reached his parent, who had already warned him against the evil of "vociferous debate." "I have been in hopes," Zachary wrote, "that this half-year would witness a great change in you in this respect. My hopes, however, have been a little shattered by something which I heard last week through a friend, who seemed to have received an impression that you had gained a high distinction among the young gentlemen of Shelford by the loudness and vehemence of your tones." His father proceeded to confess that this report gave him great pain. "I do long and pray most earnestly that the ornament of a meek and quiet spirit may be substituted for vehemence and self confidence."

Let his son and his school mates remember that, if no better, the people of Shelford were certainly no worse than men and women elsewhere in the world. If ungrateful for his lectures to them, for his kindness and solicitude, it still did not become one of his immaturity to denounce them openly at the dinner table! There was a more effective way than that, and he and his friends should take it. Instead of railing at the citizens of the town, "you and your school fellows should try to reform them. You can buy and distribute useful and striking tracts, as well as Testaments, among such as can read. The Cheap Repository and Religious Tract Society will furnish tracts suited to all descriptions of persons; and for those who cannot read—why should you not institute a Sunday school, to be taught by yourselves, and in which, appropriate rewards being given for good behaviour, not only in school but through the week, great effects of a moral kind might soon be produced." [7]

7. *Ibid.*, I, 57-58.

The picture of a set of none-too-modest youngsters lecturing the respectable natives of Shelford and giving them prizes for good behavior was one which seemingly did not appeal to Tom. But he did promise to mind the tone of his voice, to keep it subdued on all occasions except three: "*Imprimis*, when I am speaking at the same time with three others. Secondly, when I am praising the *Christian Observer*. Thirdly, when I am praising Mr. Preston or his sisters." Yet these fine promises, so engagingly made, were alas! scarcely to be kept. Tom Macaulay's endless torrent of words was soon to be known about wherever he went, until some no doubt envious contemporary finally christened him anew Thomas Babble-tongue. And even this fairly devastating pun was to prove ineffectual against the surging energies it sought to restrain.

During the year 1814 Mr. Preston moved his school to Aspenden Hall, near Buntingford, Herfordshire. Young Macaulay began here a period of almost four years of wide and industrious reading, reading which, as the months progressed, took him further and further beyond his not ungenerous classroom preparations. His room and that of a brilliant rival scholar, Malden, were sacrosanct; no classmate could enter them without invitation, upon penalty of a shilling fine. A gift that was to remain with him throughout his life began first to make itself prominent here: the ability to take in the contents of a printed page almost at a glance and to retain those contents, letter perfect, in his memory. Few men in the history of English or American literature have had that gift to such an amazing extent. Later in his career he was to make the now well known observation that "if by some miracle of vandalism all copies of *Paradise Lost* and *Pilgrims Progress* were destroyed off the face of the earth, I would undertake to reproduce them both from recollection."[8] But like most gifts of nature, this one, as we shall see, was to exact its price and impose its penalties. For as he matured, he came increasingly to rely on it; recollection and endless citation came increasing-

8. *Ibid.*, I, 60.

ly to replace the more exacting labor of thinking until he found himself, at length, in conversation after conversation, pursuing allusion after allusion around those pointless verbal circumferences that lead nowhere, except to flatulence and monotony.

Tom Macaulay cared nothing for games: he was clumsy and awkward to the day of his death. Even in 1856, he thought of shooting a pistol as of something the art of which one had laboriously to be taught.[9] The months at Aspenden Hall were spent, therefore, mainly in stretches of varied reading. He was indifferent of the opinion of those classmates who were beginning to think of him as abnormal. Already, too, regarding the direction of that reading, he was beginning to show a marked disregard for books by contemporaries. Southey, Scott and Byron he noticed, if at all, almost apologetically. It seemed much more valuable, he felt, to "hold high converse with the mighty dead."[10] It was the time of the great romantic revival; everywhere was talk of the beauties of nature, rural innocence, and the joys of country life, but this sort of rapture was meaningless to him. He infinitely preferred, so he confessed to a friend, the smoky atmosphere and the muddy river of the capital, the splendid variety of life there, "the fine flow of London talk and the dazzling brilliance of London spectacles." And this same urbanity was traceable in other ways:

What books he was devouring, for example—books mellow with age and reputation! He was excited over the *Decameron* of Boccaccio and—rather oddly—recommended the volume to his mother. "I prefer him infinitely to Chaucer." He had gone through *Gil Blas* with boundless enthusiasm. Then he had read Mrs. Montagu's essay on Shakespeare, "a great deal of Gibbon," and much of Dryden. So month succeeded month, Tom as they passed growing taller, stouter, and more healthy, and making of himself, beyond doubt, a truly very fine

9. See *Journal*, XI, 41 (September 28, 1856).
10. Letter to Hudson, August 22, 1815. *Ibid.*, I, 64.

"classic."[11] He was also—which was more important to his father—giving evidence of great "moral improvement." His love for truth had "acquired very considerable strength" as had his "disrelish for what is low and sensual." Hearing this, Miss Hannah More was fully as pleased as she should have been. Already, in her will, she had made over her large library to Tom.

During holidays he continued, as eldest son, to reign as lord of the children at home. The family's growth had finally stopped with the birth, in the fall of 1813, of the Macaulay's ninth child, Charles Zachary. Tom's eight brothers and sisters fairly idolized him; long before he became a lion in London society he had mastered his rôle by being lionized in the household at Clapham. Always even-tempered he was, always talking, always in fine spirits, and never tired of improvising games for the wholesome amusement of everybody. Frequently he read to the entire household. "He hated strangers," his sister Hannah once wrote, "and his notion of perfect happiness was to see us all working around him while he read aloud from a novel." In the summer of 1816 they all went to Brighton. Tom read to the other children every page of Richardson's *Sir Charles Grandison*. His mother would frequently join in the entertainment, reading from Shakespeare or Miss Edgeworth. Tom's presence in the home, in fact, was a sign that one of its sterner disciplines might be relaxed: except when he was there, poetry and novels could not be perused in the daytime. Such laxity, Zachary had decreed, was on a par with "drinking drams in the morning."[12]

This question of fiction reading had already involved Zachary in something of a distasteful controversy. Back in 1814 he had received an anonymous letter, addressed to him as editor of the *Christian Observer*. The letter sought, quite elaborately, to justify the existence of works of fiction, and concluded with a defense of the prose writings of Henry

11. Letter of Zachary Macaulay to Hannah More, January 30, 1816. Knutsford, *op. cit.*, 337.
12. Trevelyan, *op. cit.*, I, 67.

Fielding and Smollett. Zachary, in an incautious moment, had published this letter in the magazine.

Its effect was sudden, and shocking! He was abused in vile language by subscriber after subscriber. He was ordered to cancel subscription after subscription. One reader committed his copy to the flames. It was some time before the editor learned that the writer of the mischievous defense was his own eldest and equally mischievous son.

2

But the year 1818 had arrived; it was time for Tom Macaulay to go to the University. Cambridge was chosen almost without question, for the original inspiration of the Clapham Sect had stemmed from there. As for Trinity College, which Macaulay finally selected, it was an institution of long and honorable reputation: Bacon had studied in its halls. Newton was a graduate, and the spacious library, backed by the Cam, had been designed by the distinguished Christopher Wren.

Zachary accompanied him to the school. Once there, he wrote his wife to say that, as prearranged, Tom was settled in lodgings with the son and namesake of his late friend, Henry Thornton. From the start, the boys seemed to take to each other. Their tutor, Mr. Browne, promised "to select from among the thirty laundresses of Trinity College one of exemplary virtue for our youths." Zachary also pointed out that he had taken measures "to prevent any association beyond the merest civility with certain cousins who had asked Tom to take a walk with them, but whose characters had not met with the parental approval." [13]

Soon after he entered Trinity, a Parliamentary election took place in the town. There was great excitement in the lane adjoining Macaulay's lodgings, and with young Thornton he rushed out to discover its cause. He found it soon enough. A mob was breaking in the windows of the successful candi-

13. Knutsford, *op. cit.*, 339.

date; stones, oaths and various perishables were being hurled in profusion. One of these objects, a dead cat, struck Tom Macaulay flush in the face, But an apology soon followed. The man who had flung the animal rushed up to explain at great length that it was not a question of town against gown, that the cat, in truth, had been meant for a Mr. Adeane. "I wish," replied Macaulay, wiping his cheeks, "that you had meant it for me and hit Mr. Adeane."[14]

He took his new duties most seriously; it was testing time. What one did at the university, he felt, was, largely, a promise of what one would do later in the world. He attended Chapel and all lectures unfailingly. No college law did he ever think of violating. But these laws, it should be remembered, were relaxed during the summer vacations—vacations which Macaulay spent occasionally at the school. Often, at such times, after a lengthy argument over a literary problem, he would walk out in the moonlight with several intimate friends, their discussions continuing noisily down the winding lanes that led from the village. On into the night they would walk, and talk, about the merits of this or that writer, or about abstruser matters unrecorded and now unfortunately long forgotten. Once the subject was Wordsworth's merit as a poet, a question that was still requiring fresh examination since the appearance, in 1814, of the lengthy *Excursion*. Macaulay would acknowledge no merit whatsoever. Finally, certain relatives of Coleridge who were present took such pointed issue with him that he was driven to prove his point by suggesting a test. Who, in all the company, had managed to control his boredom sufficiently to get through the damnable poem? His friends were abashed. Not a one had succeeded. Macaulay himself, it developed later, had alone been able to endure those verses to the end.

Macaulay's reputation as a talker was spreading. In truth, when he and one friend, Charles Austin of Jesus College, crossed one another on a particular question, the audience

14. Trevelyan, *op. cit.*, I, 79.

as a rule squared off and gave them gladly the coveted center of the stage. Once, when they were visiting Lord Landsdowne at Bowood, an argument—the subject has never been mentioned—developed over the breakfast table. The two young men went on without interruption until the table was cleared. Then immediately drawing up their chairs at opposite sides of the hearth, they continued their discourse until suppertime, allowing their wide-eyed listeners only a short intermission for lunch.

This craving for an audience led Macaulay to take a keen interest in the debates of the Cambridge Union. Fearing too much undergraduate freedom in the expression of political points of view, the university authorities had decreed that no question should be debated there unless it antedated the nineteenth century. But the students were not dismayed. They argued motions censuring the cabinet then sitting in London under guise of a discussion of a cabinet of George II. The issue of Catholic Emancipation—then violently being discussed—was brought up in terms of a motion that the Catholics should have been relieved of their disabilities in the year 1795. The very live issue of Free Trade was contested from a motion that Free Trade would have been a sound English economic policy before 1800. Even the cause of Greek Independence, in the interest of which Byron was to give his life in 1824, managed to obtrude and was hotly argued when one member proposed, in Greek, that "the Hellenic Trumpet do lie upon the table." The ultimate effect of this Union experience was far reaching. Macaulay joined it a mild Tory, like his father and the Clapham Fellowship. But he left it a ramping, arrogant Whig; and Whig he remained, in body and in soul, to the end of his days and to the dismay of many a friend.

Tom Macaulay competed for a good many of the honors which the University bestowed. Twice, in 1819 and 1821, he won the Chancellor's medal for English verse—an honor which during the next decade was to come, among others, to

W. M. Praed, to E. G. L. Bulwer, and to Alfred Tennyson. The titles of the poems submitted by these men are interesting. Macaulay versified upon "Pompeii," and "Evening"; Praed upon "Australasia" and "Athens"; Bulwer upon "Sculpture";[15] Tennyson upon "Timbuctoo": they were all objective and impersonal in nature. Macaulay later roundly agreed with Sir Roger Newdigate—who had established the poetry prize at Oxford—that such poetry ought, above all, to be short. Sir Roger had decreed that fifty lines should be the limit, a law, said Macaulay, which had a solid basis in reason, since the world "is pretty well agreed in thinking that the shorter a prize poem is, the better."[16]

Macaulay twice failed in his efforts to gain a Trinity Fellowship, an honor highly sought after since there went with it an annual stipend of £300, together with certain perquisites. The reason for his failure is fairly evident. For one thing, he took little interest in the detested labor of manufacturing Greek and Latin hexameters in cold blood, a practice regularly demanded by the authorities. More important still was his contempt for mathematics. How he groaned over the exactions of that cursed subject! "Oh for words," he had exclaimed to his mother in 1818, "to express my abomination of that science, if a name sacred to the useful and embellishing arts may be applied to the perception and recollection of certain properties of numbers and figures. Oh, that I had to learn astrology, or demonology, or school divinity; or that I were compelled to pore over Thomas Aquinas, and to adjust the relation of Entity with the two Predicaments, so that I were exempted from this miserable study! 'Discipline' of the mind! Say rather starvation, confinement, torture, annihilation! But it must be. I feel myself becoming a personification of Algebra, a living trigonometrical canon, a walking table of logarithms. . . . Farewell, and tell Selina and Jane to be thankful that it is not a necessary part of female education to

15. See "Lord Macaulay and his Friends," *Harpers*, XLIII (1873), 93-94.
16. Trevelyan, *op. cit.*, I, 85.

get a headache daily without acquiring one practical truth or beautiful image in return."[17]

During his stay at the University he had a series of annoying differences with his father. The first of them dealt with the question of what emphasis one should devote to the matter of morals. There was his poem "Pompeii," for example. Sent home for parental approval, it was returned with the parental complaint that it was faulty because it did not pointedly admonish the erring to virtue. The young man was firm in his demurrer: As to your "more momentous charge, the want of a moral, I think it might be a sufficient defense that, if a subject is given which admits of none, the man who writes without a moral is scarcely censurable." His reply went on, seriously and respectfully, but bravely: "Is it the real fact that no literary employment is estimable or laudable which does not lead to the spread of moral truth or the excitement of virtuous feeling? Books of amusement tend to polish the mind, to improve the style, to give variety to conversation and to lend a grace to more important accomplishments. . . . Is no useful end served by that writer whose works have soothed weeks of langour and sickness, have relieved the mind exhausted from the pressure of employment by an amusement which delights without enervating, which relaxes the tension of the powers without rendering them unfit for future exercise?"

This sharp but transitory difference had developed in February, 1819. The following August one of the most disgraceful episodes in the history of English official government took place at St. Peters Fields, Manchester. "An orderly and unarmed crowd" of 60,000 men, women, and children—members largely of the underprivileged classes—had met to listen to the radical "Orator Hunt," who was demanding universal suffrage in their interest. They were permitted to gather unmolested, but when the magistrates noticed the size of the crowd, they became alarmed. A number of yeomanry, on

17. Trevelyan, *op. cit.*, I, 91-92.

horseback, were ordered to charge them and to arrest the speaker. "Their impact drove the dense mass of human beings, cursing and shrieking, off the field, while the yeomanry, who were Tory partisans, used their sabres with gusto. In the disturbances of that day some eleven persons, including two women, were killed or died of their injuries; over a hundred were wounded by sabres and several hundred more injured by horse hoofs or crushed by the stampede. The women injured were over a hundred." [18] The radical press took advantage of this ill advised act and, recalling another somewhat more glorious day of three and a half years before, christened it the Charge of Peterloo. A Peterloo medal was struck.

Tom Macaulay and his friends at Cambridge sided vigorously with this dispossessed rabble. Here was a shrieking example of the incompetence of that Tory leadership which had dominated England for almost two full decades. Zachary was alarmed. He had decided, with the saintly Wilberforce, that the authorities ought to be supported; that, after all, the real trouble with society was not who spoke or who was not allowed to speak, but rather that men were so wrapped up in the world's affairs as "to leave only a few scanty and lukewarm thoughts" for the vaster treasures awaiting them in heaven. Having thus agreed with his leader and friend, Zachary wrote Tom to know if certain information that had reached him from Cambridge was true.

It was true, and Zachary's son gave him a lecture he seems to have sadly needed. "I am not," he began by reminding both his parents, one of those advocates "of anarchy and confusion with whom you class me. My opinions, good or bad, were learned not from Hunt and Waithman, but from Cicero, from Tacitus, and from Milton. . . . I may be wrong as to the facts of what occurred at Manchester; but if they be what I have seen them stated, I can never repent speaking of them with indignation. When I cease to feel the injuries

18. G. M. Trevelyan, *British History in the Nineteenth Century*, 189.

of others warmly, to detest wanton cruelty, and to feel my soul rise against oppression, I shall think myself unworthy to be your son."

Why, he went on, striking much nearer home, "should a few democratical sentences in a letter, a private letter, of a collegian of eighteen he thought so alarming an indication of character," when a statesman like Brougham—one of Zachary's friends—has been known to express himself much more freely without the slightest rebuke from Clapham? But let the family's anxiety be stilled. "There are not so many people in the world who love me that I can afford to pain them for any object of ambition which it contains."[19] It was a generous reply throughout, forbearing and dutiful, and one thinks that the father should have been quieted upon receiving it, if not actually ashamed of having called it forth.

Yet the fact is that Zachary was neither of these things, or if he was he did not remain so for long. The following January, he heard something else about his son, something which awakened in his spirit another interval of sore distress. This time, so the rumor alleged, his son was fast acquiring a disgraceful reputation—the reputation of a novel reader. Some busybody had declared to Zachary that, having dined at the same table with Tom, the young man had showed a minute acquaintance with every bit of fiction that was named during the meal. It was a most disturbing report.

Tom was forced, simply, to tell his father that the nameless John-a-nokes against whom he was being asked to plead was an arrant liar, if he had declared that his reputation at Cambridge was that of a man interested exclusively in modern fiction. But after all, what would his parent have? There were too many "mere mathematical blocks" at Cambridge, too many men who, after plodding through the required work of the university, "leave the groves which witnessed the musings of Milton, of Bacon, and of Gray without one liberal idea or

19. G. O. Trevelyan, *op. cit.*, I, 97.

elegant image." Did Mr. Zachary Macaulay desire his son to approximate that pattern? It is within these circles, he proceeded to explain, "that a knowledge of modern literature is called novel reading. . . . To me the attacks of such men are valuable as compliments.

"As to the question whether or not I am wasting time, I shall leave that for time to answer. I cannot afford to sacrifice a day every week in defense and explanation of my habits of reading."

This specie of annoying warfare with his parent went on throughout young Macaulay's career. He expressed himself once rather freely in a letter about the conduct of the new king, George IV. His father took him to task for so doing, almost as if he had published a signed statement in the *Times*. Again, he wrote some burlesque verses for the *Morning Post*, some harmless doggerel entitled "Tears of Sensibility." Even his mother was greatly upset, and missing the point of the burlesque altogether, addressed him a solemn rebuke. In sober fact Macaulay was never free of this trying parental solicitude until he announced to his family, in October 1824, that the authorities had elected him a fellow of Cambridge and that £300, two pats of butter for breakfast, and a yearly grant of the school's best audit ale were to be his for the coming five years. Suddenly then, it seems to have struck both mother and father, their first born child had grown up.

Yet although he had grown up, and although he had, with his growing, suffered many now ended trials from both of his parents, it would be wholly misleading to conclude that the influence of Clapham ended with his maturity. That influence was never to end. It was to endure, rather, as long as life in his body endured, steady but powerful to the last. Tom Macaulay never shared his father's religion. It is doubtful, indeed, whether he had any formal religion at all: he rarely went to church, nor did he support a church regularly at any time during his career. But these distillations of a religious environment remained: an "impeccable demeanour," the never quite relaxed sense of self righteousness, and a censoriousness that descended, like iron weights, upon those who, for causes mostly trivial or forgotten, fell short of his exacting ideas of the way gentlemen should think and live.

IV. Barrister

THE CONTROLLING PASSION in Zachary Macaulay's life was settling upon him more fixedly than ever, when news of his son's fellowship reached the family home at Clapham. He was editing now a more specialized organ, the *Anti Slavery Reporter*, a magazine founded with the single purpose of exposing the multiplying villainies of the slave interest. Every violation of existing law that was committed, every flouting of the human rights of the negro that took place, seemed, somehow, to reach the ubiquitous and relentless intelligence of this editor. To expose the inhumanity of slavery had grown to be the burden of all his waking thoughts, in spite of the fact that his own business was becoming more and more involved, his family more and more worried about its condition, and less and less certain about what future awaited its members, now withered to such a plainly subordinate place in his regard. Those anti-slavery societies that were formed during this period were formed under his direction. Those particular facts about the iniquities of the slave system that reached the attention of Parliament in the 1820's were facts which he had personally gathered. He wrote speeches for members of both houses of that body. He drew up petitions demanding removal of the West Indian sugar bounty; he framed others, more radical, demanding the boycott in the mother country of all sugar grown by planters who owned slaves.

But this holy crusade was not waged without its exactions.

Zachary was compelled to neglect more and more his private affairs. This sacrifice, moreover, was not insignificant; for as a collateral interest during the decade before and following Napoleon's downfall he had managed to develop a certain mercantile interest of his own to a highly profitable degree. This enterprise went under the name of the house of Macaulay and Babington. It was an interest, or business, concerned with nothing less than the supplying of newly liberated areas in Africa with clothing and other manufactured articles which would naturally be demanded in a civilized society. The firm had grown up quite normally after the Sierra Leone venture was taken over as a Crown colony, in 1808. Zachary, in short, was managing a thriving wholesale business, a business that promised to prosper so well that his eldest son became justified in thinking of himself as the ultimate heir to a fortune of no mean proportions. And then, after building upon this prospect for nearly ten years, a sad and shocking revelation broke. It developed that the house of Macaulay and Babington was bankrupt.

Zachary's business ability, however, was not impugned by the revelation. His associate was his own nephew, the son of Mr. Babington, of Rothley Temple. At first Zachary had himself been active manager. He had been a very conservative manager, too. He had maintained only one trading post on the continent—the one at Sierra Leone. He had shipped down only necessities for the consumption of the liberated negroes, and he had employed only industrious clerks, at moderate wages.

But the slavery cause—grandly interminable in its limits and exactions—began as the century progressed to engross him more and more determinedly. Soon after Tom reached maturity, that cause, as we have seen, had come to render wholly insignificant all other causes that flesh is heir to. He hit upon a plan: he would turn over to young Mr. Thomas Gisborne Babington the controlling interest in their prospering venture; he would give him, in future, the major share of its income.

Only one stipulation would he make: The business must be run in accordance with its present policies. No basic changes might be attempted without Zachary's consent. Babington agreed. The Macaulays began to adapt themselves at once to their more straitened income by moving into a less attractive house in Great Ormond Street, near the British Museum, and by giving up their carriage. This was in 1823.

It required young Babington exactly three years to ruin the enterprise. He started out by keeping open house at the Sierra Leone office. Any trader who touched there, whether of high or low reputation, could be certain of a bibulous and continuing welcome. Had this trader looked about the Company warehouse, moreover, he would have found it stocked to the limit with luxuries that were practically unsaleable. The whole spirit of the place had altered since the pious Zachary had served as his own chief clerk. The salaries of those now in charge had been raised from three hundred to five hundred per cent. Branch houses had been set up in neighboring settlements, and at heavy cost, and a fleet of boats was maintained to convey the resident officials of the firm, or their clients, from one office to the other. Babington had already run heavily into debt when Zachary, after hearing a report from a friend who had witnessed the drunken revelry at the Sierra Leone center, rose up in indignation and demanded a sight of the books.

That sight, once it came, was a sad one, past any doubt. Babington had been borrowing systematically from several more wealthy members of the Clapham group, men who had advanced the money with the certainty that Zachary knew of his partner's acts. Further study of the records disclosed that, in a fit of generosity, Babington had underwritten the credit of another African trading firm that had since become insolvent. Macaulay estimated conservatively that his obligations were something more than £100,000. Babington, meanwhile, was indisposed and surly. He would fly into a temper if the subject of the firm's business were mentioned. The truth seems to be that he had envisioned for himself the position of director of a nebulous Royal West African Company, dispensing, with a royal hand, the favors and privileges that such a position implied.[1]

2

Meanwhile, T. B. Macaulay, Esq., the promising fellow of Trinity College, had not been wasting his time. He had, for one thing, turned rather ambitiously to literature, writing for *Knight's Quarterly Magazine* articles of more than normal promise. This publication had been founded by a printer who recognized that at the University at this period were gathered a group of very bright young men. Derwent Coleridge, a relative of the aging poet, was one of them. W. M. Praed was another; John Moultrie was a third. Under pseudonyms they all, with Macaulay's help, turned enthusiastically to the new venture in belles lettres. Macaulay was signing himself, euphemistically, Tristram Merton, and in the first number he sighed languidly, in lush verses, for the fair and incomparable Rosamond.

His father's concern was at once aroused. What did this flippant laxity mean? Did this son know that *Knights* was being sold, in London, alongside other works of a definitely improper cast? Did he realize that his good name was in jeopardy? Was he aware of the general lack of moral earnestness in the publication? So the complaints ran, solemnly and insistently, each one requiring a long and patient answer.

As a matter of fact, Macaulay's part in the venture was entirely harmless. Between the months of June, 1823, and November, 1824, he contributed to it nine prose essays and sketches, as well as several poems. The more important of these works, as we shall see, dealt with lengthy criticisms of two Italian writers, Dante and Petrarch, with a very successful "Conversation between Mr. Abraham Cowley and Mr. John

1. Knutsford, *op. cit.*, 395-406.

Milton touching the Great Civil War," and with a stimulating review of Mitford's *History of Greece*. There was also another surprisingly sane article disparaging the idea of an English Royal Society of Literature.[2] The article revealed, among other things, that Macaulay had already come to be aware of one of the major curses of authors—jealousy, a curse which was later to beset his own mind to an extent now almost incredible. Yet his father, after the first issue appeared, practically demanded that his son cease his connection with Mr. Knight. He was placated, at length, only when, through the influence of Tom, a lengthy diatribe against the slave trade was run. And it was a diatribe that proved so ponderously righteous as almost to submerge the entire publication. Zachary's criticisms stopped. He never guessed, apparently, that but for his son's work for this quarterly, Francis Jeffrey, of the *Edinburgh Review*, would possibly never have encouraged him as a writer.

What was the young man like at this period? Two lively pen portraits are available, one in verse, the other in prose, both the work of fellow authors and students. "Tristram Merton," cried Praed in a sketch, "come into court. Then came up a short manly figure, marvellously upright, with a bad neckcloth, and one hand in his waistcoat pocket. Of regular beauty he had little to boast, but in faces where there is an expression of great power or of great good humor, or both, you do not regret its absence."[3] Moultrie's sketch, written some sixteen years later, is more detailed.

> "*Little graced*
> *With aught of manly beauty—short, obese,*
> *Rough featured, coarse complexion, with lank hair,*
> *And small grey eyes. . . . his voice abrupt,*
> *Unmusical.*

2. See *The Works of Lord Macaulay* (Edinburgh edition, 8 vols. London, 1900, Edited by Lady Trevelyan. Referred to henceforth as *Works*), VIII, 561-703.
3. Frederick Arnold, *The Public Life of Lord Macaulay* (London, 1862), 38.

> "*To him*
> *There was no pain like silence—no constraint*
> *So dull as unanimity: he breathed*
> *An atmosphere of argument.*
>
> "*Meanwhile*
> *His heart was pure and simple as a child's,*
> *Unbreathed on by the world—in friendship warm,*
> *Confiding, generous, constant.*"[4]

That he was talkative, upright, untidy, heavy, and ugly seems, in short, to have been the verdict of his contemporaries from the period of young manhood to the year of his death.

It was during the summer of 1824 that Tom Macaulay first distinguished himself before a public gathering as an orator. He spoke, appropriately, to a meeting called to protest the unforgivable iniquities of slavery. The occasion was that of the annual meeting of the Anti-Slavery Society, held in Freemasons Hall, London, and attended by such leaders of English public opinion as Henry Brougham, the Whig Reformer; O'Connell, the fiery advocate of Irish and Catholic rights; Orator Hunt, of Peterloo fame, and the Duke of Gloucester, who was in the chair. Of course, the entire Clapham brotherhood was present in a body.

Present too, and unsuppressed, was a spirit of almost incandescent bitterness. It was the outgrowth of a series of attacks that had been running for months now in the columns of *John Bull*, a widely read Tory publication founded to oppose all manner of reform, especially reform that touched the wealthy planter interest. Its editor was the brilliant, but volatile and somewhat more than faintly disreputable Theodore Hook,[5] who had concentrated his savage literary fire upon Zachary. Such comment as the following was typical of the quality of his notices: "Far are we from wishing to ask any question

4. *Ibid.*, 37. See also Moultrie's sonnet to Macaulay in his *Poems* (3 ed. London, 1852), 341-42.
5. See J. G. Lockhart, *Theodore Hook* (London, 1853).

of Mr. Zachary Macaulay, the once needy overseer, now elevated into an opulent merchant, touching the sum of £129,951. 11s. 11d. paid to him on account of Sierra Leone; nor do we mean to inquire how much philanthropy was blended in the exertion to capture negroes for which upwards of £275,000 has been paid by government."[6]

Worse insinuations followed: Zachary Macaulay, one of the most saintly of the "Saints," was renting out personal property at Sierra Leone at ten times its real worth. Also it was widely known that blacks could be found there, in abundance, who bore his name. By implication, they were his bastards. So these scurrilities went, contemptible entirely, but none-the-less maddening. It seemed to Zachary and to his family and friends that the forces of the Adversary, in one grand and unholy union, were joined together to nullify his good works.

But the soaring eloquence on this particular evening did much to drown the odium of these charges and apprehensions. Wilberforce spoke with a piety that was irresistible. Then followed Charles Denman, who not many months before had distinguished himself, as Solicitor General, by defending in an ecstatic peroration the innocence of Queen Caroline and imputing to her husband George IV "the vilest vices of the court of Nero."[7] After Denman came Orator Hunt. Now Hunt almost always produced alarms when he rose to speak among gentlemen, and on this occasion he behaved according to custom. He stood up, he declared, to request one thing only, a simple answer to a simple question: Why, with thousands of their countrymen starving almost at their very doorsteps, did this body of citizens insist upon concerning itself with the condition of ignorant black men in Africa and the West Indies? Why, in other words, were gentlemen so manifestly unwilling to do anything toward ameliorating the deplorable status of their own neighbors? Charity, he thought, should begin at home.

6. Arnold, *op. cit.*, 40.
7. Lloyd Sanders, *The Holland House Circle* (London, 1908), 278.

Orator Hunt was shouted down. He was ruled out of order. He was hissed and even cursed. Then Brougham proceeded to answer him. Later the impassioned Henry Drummond shouted the sentiment, widely acclaimed, that "moderation is out of place—is thrown away. Slavery will never be got rid of until some black O'Connell, some swarthy Bolivar, shall rise to strike off the chains."[8]

Tom Macaulay, in other words, was facing no mean oratorical gathering when he set forth to make his initial contribution to the cause of the oppressed. Yet the critics were unanimous in praise of his remarks, though far from unanimous in the item of his given name. He was referred to consistently in one account as Mr. J. Macaulay. But "loud cheering" greeted his words; and he sat down, the report continues, "amid the repeated plaudits of the meeting." "This very eloquent address," declared another commentator," produced a strange impression on the Assembly."[9] Even the distinguished *Edinburgh Review* went so far as to say that Tom Macaulay had "made a speech that was greeted with a whirlwind of cheers," adding that his performance was distinguished by an eloquence so rare and matured that "the most practiced orator might well admire how it should have come from one who then for the first time addressed a public assembly."[10]

The text of Macaulay's speech has unfortunately not been preserved. We know from excerpts from it, however, that in one place he brought the crowd to its feet by declaring that the hour was at hand when the oppressed African and West Indian Negro "will no longer crawl in listless and trembling dejection round a plantation from whose fruits he must derive no advantage, and a hut whose door yields him no protection; but, when his cheerful and voluntary labor is performed, he will return with the firm step and erect brow of a British citizen from the field which is his freehold to the cottage which

8. Knutsford, *op. cit.*, 420-21.
9. Arnold, *op. cit.*, 40-41.
10. Quoted in "Lord Macaulay and his Friends," *Harpers* LIII (1873), 95.

is his castle.""[11] The passage has already the balanced, sweeping, metallic ring of the essential Macaulay. And yet, though that ring is unmistakable, and although, swayed by the distinction of it, Wilberforce and many others rushed to the platform to grasp Tom's hand, the taciturn Zachary was taciturn still. We are told—and it is credible—that his heart was overflowing with devotion, and with gratitude to the Lord for having given him such a son. But as they walked homeward, his only remark to that son about his speech was a rebuke for having, while delivering it, folded his arms in the presence of royalty.[12]

3

Thomas Babington Macaulay was called to the bar in 1826 and joined the northern division of the Circuit Court at Leeds. This statement, when met with by anyone seriously interested in Macaulay, provokes no little surprise. One is not prepared for it. Trevelyan, his nephew and most detailed biographer, tells us nothing about his preparation for the law. Did he read for it at Cambridge, or in a law office in London, or did he attend one of the Inns of Court, where for centuries the most illustrious barristers of England had received their legal training?

This last conjecture appears unlikely: more than a year and a half would have been required there—even of Macaulay, and he would almost certainly have mentioned so distinguished a training later. Moreover, he would have known more law than he apparently knew at the beginning of his career. As for his reading in a law office, there is no evidence to indicate that this was ever done. Henry Brougham, a great admirer of Zachary, had advised such a procedure for Tom in the spring of 1823, along with a good many other things, such as having him memorize the best speeches of Burke, Fox,

11. Quoted in G. O. Trevelyan, *op. cit.*, I, 111.
12. *Ibid.*, I, 113.

[62]

Demosthenes, and Cicero.[13] Yet it is difficult to imagine Tom spending a year in a London law office, when he might have remained at Cambridge, enjoying the privileges of a fellowship, a fine library, and the atmosphere of a place now mellow and familiar to him. The probability is that—in between stretches of much more agreeable reading—he got through enough law at the University to pass the rather perfunctory examinations then required.

At all events, he kept up this more agreeable reading after his work on the circuit had begun. Having ended his first dinner with his colleagues, he was observed by one of the veteran jurists of the company to be carefully picking out the longest candle in the room. Observing, also, that he had a volume under his arm, the veteran admonished him concerning the danger of reading in bed; one might set the place on fire. The young man, whose rapidity of utterance was soon to become proverbial, answered this gentleman in short order: "I always read in bed at home, and if I am not afraid of committing patricide and matricide and fratricide, I can hardly be expected to pay any special regard to the lives of the bagmen of Leeds."[14] So saying, his nephew remarks, "he left his hearers staring at one another and marched off to his room, little knowing that before many years were out he would have occasion to speak much more respectfully of the Leeds bagmen."

The year before, he had begun also—in a high jubilation that was to vanish completely within the next two decades—another practice that brought him at first an all but infinite satisfaction. He was invited to contribute to the *Edinburgh Review*, the outstanding Whig publication of the age. Francis Jeffrey, who had edited the quarterly since its founding in 1802, was looking around for new and rising talent. He had already met Tom Macaulay. Back in 1817, Tom had toured Scotland briefly with his father, and the two had called on

13. H. G. J. Clements, *Lord Macaulay, his Life and Writings*, London, 1860 (2 lectures), 24-27.
14. G. O. Trevelyan, *op. cit.*, I, 109.

the sprightly little editor at his home in Edinburgh. The visit was hardly a success. Jeffrey "was so terrified by the religious reputation" of his elder guest that he seemed afraid to utter a joke. Zachary the while proceeded to tell his host how he had been progressing from manse to manse, and how everywhere devout prayer services had been held for him. Yet no one could have spent an evening in Tom's presence, even when laboring in the throes of a transcendent awe, without realizing pretty clearly that here was a young man of more than average promise. Jeffrey kept up with his progress at the University, and was no doubt more than normally pleased to learn that, by the time he began his career as a barrister, Macaulay was as whole-hearted a Whig as could be found anywhere in England.

It would be difficult to overstate the influence which Mr. Jeffrey's publication exercised, during the first third of the nineteenth century, upon English life and thought. Even to suggest that influence involves some mention of the intellectual tradition behind it, and that mention involves, in turn, some notice of Dugald Stewart. Stewart is scarcely remembered now. A professor of moral philosophy at the University of Edinburgh, he proved to be more an eclectic than the originator of a system, and more the hard-headed rationalist than the mystic. The metaphysical theorizing of the great German thinker, Immanuel Kant, for example, remained, from first to last, beyond his comprehending—just as from first to last it remained beyond the grasp or the interests of Macaulay. But even so, Stewart came into authority at Edinburgh at a peculiarly fortunate time. By the year 1789, the year of the French Revolution, he had won a place of eminence in Scotland, and with war throwing its desperate shadow across the continent, many promising young men of the British Isles who might otherwise have gone abroad for study came to him, and absorbed his doctrines.

These doctrines, looked at in perspective, were simple enough, and faithfully in line with the rational tradition of

English thinkers from Bacon and Locke to Hartley. Condensed, they implied merely that men should trust their common sense, should work faithfully to leave this earth better off than they had found it. Stewart applied these ideas in his class lectures to all phases of the world's wide interests. He had taught mathematics, he had studied political economy under Adam Smith's influence, and he knew a good deal about literature. And, above all, how eloquent he was! Victimized by asthma, he was forced often, in the midst of his lectures, to pause for the purpose of clearing his throat; but, explained one rapt admirer, "there was eloquence in his very spitting."[15]

Among this scholar's more distinguished students six stand out with unusual brilliance. They are Jeffrey, Brougham, Francis Horner, Sydney Smith, Palmerston, and Lord John Russell. The first four gentlemen in this list formed the nucleus which, during the third year of the century, launched the review upon a public that needed its message sorely, and that had unconsciously long awaited it.

It was a public already laboring too heavily under those Tory doctrines which were soon to be epitomized by Lord Chancellor, later the Earl of Eldon (John Scott) and his followers of the school of Burke and Pitt. They were conservatives—men who had learned but one lesson from all the savagery and bloodshed across the channel. That lesson taught them that, to avoid a similar tragedy in England, the government should practice one routine only, the routine of a savage repression. Writs of habeas corpus should be suspended, the press should be effectively throttled and fractious editors sent to prison, public gatherings should be suppressed or forbidden, the organized drilling of armed men should be stopped. These measures were not formally enacted until 1819, but the spirit which dictated them had been active and in control in Parliament since the French sacked

15. *Dictionary of National Biography*, XVIII, 1169-83.

Zachary's innocent African village a quarter of a century before.

What, then, was the point of view of these restless intellectuals from Edinburgh? What did the term Whig mean, when applied to them? Walter Bagehot, writing specifically of the group just named, had this to say: "In truth Whiggism is not a creed; it is a character. Perhaps as long as there has been a political history in this country there have been certain men of cool moderate resolute firmness, not gifted with high imagination, little prone to enthusiastic sentiment, heedless of large theories and speculations, careless of dreamy skepticism; with a clear view of the next step, and a wise intention to take it; a strong conviction that the elements of knowledge are true, and a steady belief that the present world can, and should be quietly improved."[16]

These men, Bagehot does not fail to add, were enslaved by sharp imaginative limitations. They were blind to the significance of that renascence of wonder which we call the romantic revival; Wordsworth and Keats were foolish and moonstruck, to their way of thinking; the "nature" movement was mainly affected and absurd to them. But with their vigorous insistence upon the improvement of political and social conditions, they brought into English life one of the first and most concerted attacks against the conservative order that were to develop during the century; and it was an attack the impetus of which spread finally into every recess of the awakened consciousness of England.

It was also an attack that was to find reenforcement from elements that never proved entirely to the taste of those who led it. The Utilitarians represented, to the Whigs—and to Macaulay, as we shall see—a fringe of liberalism that was considerably too radical for acceptance. But radical or not, they had to be reckoned with in any reform program that statesman of the first half of the century proposed. They had power, and they had an organizing ability that kept that

16. *Literary Studies* (London, 1879), I, 13.

power from being aimlessly dispersed. For this ability, and for the common sense that developed it, Jeremy Bentham was mainly responsible.

Bentham was, in every sense of the phrase, a highly remarkable person. Born in 1748, fully as precocious as Macaulay, he had already by the time of the French Revolution distinguished himself as a thinker and as a reformer. Entering Oxford at the age of twelve, he had been irritated from the start by being required, against his will, to subscribe to the Thirty-Nine Articles. "I learnt nothing while there," was his final verdict. He had not even made friends at college with anyone of later distinction. The students there, he declared, were all given over either to stupidity or to dissipation. Graduated at 16, he turned to the law, only to be disgusted, as Carlyle was later, with its "shapeless mass of absurdity and chicane." To his father he seemed, in his middle twenties, a young man of astonishing promise who had turned out, unaccountably, a failure. And then, in 1776, he published his *Fragment on Government.*

The slender volume opened for him a good many doors which had before stood shut. A prominent Whig of the day, Lord Shelburne, read it and admired its sentiments. He sent for Bentham and, soon afterwards, introduced him into the society of a number of important public men. Yet the young and earnest critic of political institutions proved scarcely a conversational ornament. He was slow in speech, he was incapable of insincerity or flattery, and, above all, he was diffident—the torture of bashfulness, it has been said, "clung to him like a cold garment all through life." But the brief experience with Lord Shelburne's friends proved valuable to him in at least one sense. He learned how the leaders of society thought; he came to understand their prejudices.

Many worthy gentlemen of the age set Bentham down as hopelessly one-sided. Many called him a misanthrope, even. He lived the life of a recluse; he seemed always busy; and he despised the graces, and such cultural studies as literature and history. Fundamentally, it was reverence that he lacked. Yet irreverence is the price the world has often been compelled to pay for emancipation. This quality, active and ceaselessly vigilant, he owned to an unholy degree—the irreverence of Erasmus satirizing the monks, of Bacon scoffing at the schoolmen, of Pascal denouncing the Jesuits, or of Voltaire riddling the superstitions of the Church.[17] With a similar zest for the preeminence of rationality in human affairs, Bentham was devoting his energies toward making over the legal system of England. Sir Henry Maine, writing a century later, confessed that he did "not know a single law reform effected since Bentham's day which cannot be traced to his influence."

What had happened by the time he began his work was, simply stated, this: the growth of English law in complexity had far exceeded any efforts to systematize it. Antiquated and obsolete statutes still commanded respect. Legal terminology was prolix and technical. The curse of legal fictions was general. And above the doors that harbored this confusion hung an old maxim contending, smugly, that "Ignorance of the Law Excuses No One."

What, exactly, is a legal fiction? Bentham wanted to know. He asked his own question and answered it, bluntly. "It is a falsehood." By whom invented? "By judges." On what occasions? "On the occasion of their pronouncing a judicial decision." For what purpose? "One may conceive two—*either* that of doing in a roundabout way what they might do in a direct way, *or* that of doing in a roundabout way what they had no right to do in any way at all."

Take, he went on—if one needs proof of the absurdity of existing law—the legal fiction called "corruption of blood." The statutes decreed that the innocent son of a father who has been executed for high treason shall not only be deprived of his father's goods but that he shall not be allowed to inherit

17. See, on this discussion of Bentham, the excellent work by John MacCunn, *Six Radical Thinkers* (London, 1910).

[68]

even from his grandfather.[18] The assumption was that the family strain had been corrupted. It was a ridiculous assumption. *What is the good of it?* So ran his question—sullen, insistent and never relenting, while his intellect swept, like a burning light, into corner after corner of musty English jurisprudence.

He was making no defense of any ridiculous "rights of man" theory; Bentham was too tough-minded a philosopher to be led astray by the talk of poets and idealists. Man, he insisted, has no natural rights whatever. All that he inherits at birth is a set of inclinations, of desires and appetites. Those other rights, so invaluable, so difficult to preserve—the rights of life, of liberty, and of property—are not his at all until he has received them at the hands of law. The law is the only source of them, since law alone defines those natural inclinations which are compatible with the public good, and those which should be suppressed.

Considered from this luminous perspective, that particular system of law, the unwritten English constitution, needed a vast deal of looking into! Bentham proceeded to look, long and sharply; and he found it hedged about with fallacy upon fallacy; all of them reared up to guard the privileged and wealthy orders against the encroachments of the dispossessed.

Take the arguments set forth against reform (Macaulay was forced to do battle against them), arguments that assailed any reformer who was interested in breaking down the Tory domination. There was, to begin with, "the wisdom of our ancestors, or the Chinese argument." It read as follows: "Why must the constitution be looked into? It was the work of our holy forebears. It was good enough for them; it should be good enough for us." Then came "the hobgoblin argument, or, no innovation!" No reading, no writing, no education of the masses, cried the authors of this kind of reasoning. Change means anarchy!

And there were a great many others: the arguments of those official malefactors who shouted that "When I am attacked,

18. *Ibid.*, 10.

government is attacked"; arguments of the quietists with their "no complaint is best" contention; and those advocates of the snail's-pace doctrine who cried, "One thing at a time. Be slow and sure." And so forth. These views and demurrers, Bentham felt, represented the fixed bias of a class that had long controlled England but that was now set, with a perverse blindness, upon ruining it. As a reformer he was doing no very remarkable thing. He merely wanted to see to it that the legal precedents of the country be brought into reasonable conformity with the demands of his time. He was a child of the eighteenth century, in England one of "the best representatives of the humanitarianism and enlightenment of that age."[19] But so desperate was the plight into which that age had fallen as regards its canons of government that what he proposed was looked upon by many as a kind of unprecedented desperation. Worthy gentlemen cursed him, as they cursed his elder Tom Paine. His voice was the voice of revolution and chaos.

What were worthy gentlemen excited about, specifically? Mr. Bentham had contended that the principle which should inform every English law was the simple principle of utility. To use his own now memorable language—language he borrowed from Priestley—"the proper end of every law is the promotion of the greatest happiness of the greatest number." He did not mean to teach the absurdity that a law will really, and of itself, make men happy. What he did mean to say, and what he did say—with an insistence that half a century failed to diminish—was that enacting certain laws usually tended to favor the emergence of conditions under which persons subject to them may prosper.[20] And, mainly, he implied, these laws should be passed with the idea of leaving to the individual as much personal freedom as possible. The principle of *laissez faire* received his whole-souled endorsement.

Consider the dialogue advanced in a pamphlet he wrote under the title *Truth* vs. *Amhurst*, Amhurst representing the

19. A. V. Dicey, *Lectures on the Relation between Law and Public Opinion in England During the Nineteenth Century* (London, 1905), 136-37.
20. *Ibid.*, 137.

spirit of early nineteenth century Toryism, the Toryism of men like Lord Eldon. Truth, of course, is Bentham, or the Utilitarian point of view:

"Amhurst: *The law of this country only lays such restraints on the actions of individuals as are necessary for the safety and good order of the community at large.*

"Truth: I sow corn; partridges eat it, and if I attempt to defend it against the partridges, I am fined or sent to gaol; all this for fear that some great man, who is above sowing corn, should be in want of partridges.

"The trade I was born to is overstocked; hands are wanting in another. It I offer to work at that other, I may be sent to gaol for it. Why? Because I have not been working at it as an apprentice for seven years. What is the consequence? That, as there is no work for me in my original trade, I must either come upon the parish or starve.

"There is no employment for me in my own parish: there is abundance in the next. Yet if I offer to go there, I am driven away. Why? Because I *might* become unable to work one of these days, and so I must not work while I am able. I am thrown upon one parish now, for fear I should fall upon another, forty or fifty years hence."

What is the use of it? What is the use of it? The cry rang continuously down the bewildering corridors of English legislation. And it was a cry that proved generally unanswerable. Henry Brougham heard it and was convinced that, insofar as reform *could* be effected against the entrenched opposition it faced, he would work to effect it. Francis Horner, another product of Stewart's liberal doctrines, heard it also, and was awakened anew to the necessity of a liberal and generous reestimate of his government. Samuel Romilly heard it, and dedicated his life to the destruction, one by one, of legislative acts that had become obsolete and unjust in their effect upon the rising middle and lower classes.[21] Bentham, meanwhile, remained in his study, advising with friends, talking freely

21. Sanders, *op. cit.*, 269.

about the current of public affairs, drawing up particular proposals in the correct manner, but taking no public share in that movement which he had, in large measure, set moving. To the end, his spirit remained contemplative, not active.

His was, rather, the intelligence which bound together the scattered elements of political and social discontent in England into a single, determined, and finally irresistible force,[22] a force which encompassed in its ranging circuit the ideals of the Macaulays, both father and son.

The two last named gentlemen, as has been suggested, would hardly have confessed as much. Identified with the same age as Bentham, each saw him from a different plane, a plane which let in, unfortunately, a good deal of refracted and distorted light. Tom Macaulay felt that the whole Utilitarian school was made up of "codifying animals," though he did not coin the famous phrase that still clings to its leader. He even attacked the school in print. To Zachary the Utilitarians were simply too radical, and too prone to violence to be safe. Yet the friends of the Macaulays were friends of Bentham, and of his chief disciple and exegete, James Mill. And informing all their divisions, and levelling all their distinctions into a single stubborn and relentless protest, was the conviction that the government of England owed something to the eighty per cent of its inhabitants whom it had ignored in past ages. That government must broaden its sympathies. Those who in centuries gone had kept its vision narrow must give way. Another class—the middle class of property and respectability—was rising about them, with the rise of the new and impressive industrial order. And as prophet of that class, as its spokesman—and as, perhaps, an epitome of its ineradicable limitations—the Lord, in his wisdom, had reared up Tom Macaulay, who was already, in 1827, thinking seriously of a career in politics.

22. J. S. Mill, *Autobiography*, 69-70.

V. Whig

FEW MEN have been heroes to a large family of brothers and sisters, but Tom Macaulay proved an exception here, as in other ways. During the middle eighteen-twenties, between trips on the circuit as barrister, he spent many an afternoon and evening in the family's company.

No society ever pleased him more. He has been pictured to us as savage and unrelenting in his attacks upon literary or political opponents. Indeed, he has so pictured himself through his published works. But it was a savagery which he reserved exclusively for public figures or for relative strangers: his devotion to his immediate kin almost touched the abnormal. At a period in the life of most men during which the affections are rather more inclined to stray than to concentrate—and if to concentrate, to do so in fairly foreign areas—Macaulay preferred to stay at home, or to go endlessly walking and talking and laughing through the streets of London, in the company of his two favorite sisters.

The sisters especially favored were Margaret and Hannah, still youthful enough to idolize him, though old enough now to prove attractive young ladies and lively conversationalists. They both loved books and read them constantly—the best poetry, and novels of every sort, good and execrable, from Fielding, Richardson, and Jane Austen to the sugared inanities of Mrs. Kitty Cuthbertson or Mrs. Meeke. Reading was, in fact, their passion, as it had been for years the passion of their brother. Together, talking or shouting to one another

—in the language of Mrs. Bennett or Mr. Collins, or of some other Jane Austen character—what bewildering youngsters they appeared to the tired Zachary! He would lift his aging eyes from a slavery tract, wonder a moment, sigh, and go back to that never waning private passion of his own. He let the children have their way.

And what ways they had! They would not only carry on— the three of them—interminable conversations in the styles of their favorite eighteenth century characters; they would fall into quoting matches, reeling off, at great length, such gems as those containing the impeccable sentiments of Sir Charles Grandison. Macaulay once thought it probable that he could rewrite that book from memory: "Certainly," remarks his nephew, "he might have done so with his sisters' help."[1] Or they would read at night, in the family circle, just as they had read years before, from every level of literary endeavor. There was Mrs. Kitty's *Santo Sebastiano*, for instance. One of the girls would read it aloud—Macaulay pacing the floor in a circle— while everybody paused in unison to count the fainting fits that occur periodically in those five fat volumes. Macaulay once made a list of them, which is preserved. Julia de Clifford, one character, swooned in an ecstasy of fright a total of eleven times; Lady Delamore and Lady Theodosia followed, discreetly, with four fits apiece. So the list went, through the six other noble personages of the novel. And how beautifully they fainted away. A specimen will serve: "One of the sweetest smiles that ever animated the face of mortal now diffused itself over the countenance of Lord St. Orville, as he fell at the feet of Julia in a death-like swoon."[2]

If not enjoying novels, they were playing games, Tom serving as master of revels. He never tired of children, it seems, and on holidays, when fairly grown up children and cousins were visiting the Macaulays, he never tired of devising sport for their enjoyment: Hide-and-seek contests went on

1. Trevelyan, *op. cit.*, I, 129. The sister referred to is Hannah, the biographer's mother.
2. *Ibid.*, I, 130.

"for hours, with shouting, and the blowing of horns up and down the stairs, and through every room." And after that would come ballads. Tom would recite one—improvising it while he spoke—and the company would strike in at the chorus. These poems he attributed to the "Judicious Poet," a pseudonym covering a seemingly endless variety of works which he reserved exclusively for domestic consumption. There was at this period, among other dullards of his acquaintance, a country squire whom the entire family found more than normally boring. What chiefly bored them was this worthy squire's habit, while talking to people, of seizing them by a button of the coat or waistcoat. The "Judicious Poet" once characterized him thus:

> *His Grace Archbishop Manners Sutton*
> *Could not keep on a single button.*
> *As for right Reverend John of Chester,*
> *His waistcoats open at the vest are.*
> *Our friend[3] has filled a mighty trunk*
> *With trophies torn from Doctor Monk,*
> *And he has really tattered foully*
> *The vestments of Archbishop Hawley,*
> *No button could I late discern on*
> *The garments of Archbishop Vernon,*
> *And never had his fingers mercy*
> *Upon the garb of Bishop Percy.*
> *The buttons fly from Bishop Rider*
> *Like corks that spring from bottled cider.*

Meanwhile, during the period court was in session, he was traveling throughout northern England and on into Scotland, meeting, occasionally, men whom he had long wanted to know with some intimacy. Back in 1826, he had written his father about a call from one of these men: "The other day as I was changing my neckcloth which my wig had disfigured,

3. *Ibid.*, I, 131. Trevelyan declines to identify the squire.

my good landlady knocked at the door of my bedroom and told me that Mr. Smith wished to see me, and was in my room below. Of all names by which men are called, there is none which conveys a less determinate idea to the mind than that of Smith." Was he a special messenger from London, a beggar coming to prey upon a victim, a barber to solicit the dressing of his wig? "Down I went, and to my utter amazement beheld the Smith of Smiths, alias Sydney Smith, alias Peter Plymley. I had forgotten his very existence till I discerned the queer contrast between his black coat and his snow-white head, and the equally curious contrast between the clerical amplitude of his person and the most unclerical wit, whim, and petulance of his eye." [4]

His guest was, truly, a remarkable personage. A quarter of a century before, as we have noticed, he had helped to found the *Edinburgh Review*. Then, a year later, he had come down to London, attracted by stories that brilliant young Whigs there were being unusually well received. Once on the scene, he soon distinguished himself with an amazing series of lectures on moral philosophy, lectures so priced—£50 for the first set of twenty; £150 for the next—and so spiritedly talked up that "society" turned out almost in a herd to listen. Really, Mr. Smith's discourses brought on a serious traffic problem! Albemarle Street was blocked with "the concourse of carriages," and the Royal Institution, where he spoke, was packed and quite overflowing. The lobbies, the stairway, the steps of the arena, and of course the lecture room itself—they were all taxed to the limit with lords and ladies, wits, fellow philosophers, and with a few querulous parsons who had come to meditate upon the strange intellectual plumage of this new bird from the north. [5]

Smith had gone on, since those early triumphs, to distinguish himself in other ways, notably, by writing a series of letters on the Irish question under the signature of Peter

4. See letter of July 21, 1826. *Ibid.*, I, 137-38.
5. See "Lord Macaulay and his Friends," *Harpers*, LIII (1873), 239.

Plymley—letters that proved stirring enough to start a search for their author by the Tory government. Then he had retired to a modest parish in Yorkshire—Foston *le clay* he called it—a place of stubborn soil and stiff-necked farmers. And there he worked, long and faithfully, in a manner that one would be tempted to call heroic, except for the fact that heroism and wit find it usually so difficult to agree. He turned school-master to educate his sons, and farmer because he could not afford to lease his land. He served as village doctor, village parson, village comforter, and village magistrate. Unable to maintain a butler, he had made an excellent one of a young girl servant, Bunch. Unable to own a new carriage, he had bought an old one, only to find it grow newer and newer each year, as his neighbors supplied it periodically with new lining, new wheels, new paint, and a fresh assortment of straw.[6] And all this while, he was talking almost incessantly and writing for the *Review* articles which, among other topics, inquired, "who, in all the four quarters of the globe, *ever* reads an American book, or looks at an American picture, or goes to see an American play?"

Tom Macaulay, the new discovery of the *Review*, spent the weekend with this aging lion, and when he left he wrote his father a decidedly sane appraisal: "I have really," he said, "taken a great liking to him. He is full of wit, humor, and shrewdness. He is not one of those show-talkers who reserve all their good things for special occasions. It seems to be his greatest luxury to keep his wife and daughters laughing for two or three hours every day. His notions of law, government, and trade are surprisingly clear and just. His misfortune is to have chosen a profession at once above him and below him. Zeal would have made him a prodigy; formality and bigotry would have made him a bishop; but he could never rise to the duties of his order nor stoop to its degradations."[7] Socially, the two men had got along admirably, as they were to get

6. Bagehot, *op. cit.*, 323.
7. See letter of July 26, 1826. Trevelyan, *op. cit.*, I, 138.

along later, in London, when Smith settled there as canon of St. Paul's. As writers, of course, they would inevitably have admired each other. Both possessed styles of great vigor, styles which allowed of no nuances. The question with both was the polemic one, Will it tell? In a sense, they were both disciples of that master of polemic writing, their editor, Francis Jeffrey.

The long desired week-end with Jeffrey did not materialize until the spring of 1828, but when it did come it proved much more pleasant and satisfying than had the brief call Macaulay made with his father a decade before. He wrote his mother about it immediately afterwards lest, having so much to say when he reached home, he talk the entire family into exhaustion. It was Jeffrey's face that impressed him at first, or, rather, his faces, for he had twenty of them, each almost as unlike the other as his father's was unlike Mr. Wilberforce's. It was not, oddly enough, at all times an intellectual countenance. When quiescent, reading a paper, or hearing a conversation in which he took no interest, Jeffrey's features appeared as dull to Macaulay as Macaulay's appeared somewhat later to Carlyle—those of an honest fellow, made out of oatmeal.[8] But what changes could sweep over him, once a subject struck a response—what flash in his eyes, what violent contortion in his frown, what exquisite humor in his sneer, what brilliance in his smile! Garrick must have been like him. And his voice was equally variable and charming. "His familiar tone, his declamatory tone, and his pathetic tone are quite different things."[9] His power of mimicry seemed almost miraculous.

And yet how astonishingly domestic a person Mr. Jeffrey was—fond of his wife and daughter to downright absurdity. Not five minutes could pass without some affectionate word or gesture to them. He remained in Mrs. Jeffrey's presence almost constantly when at home, refusing, even when busy with

8. *Ibid.*, I, 22-23.
9. *Ibid.*, I, 142. See the entire letter (dated April 15, 1828), 141-44.

articles for the *Edinburgh*, to forsake his wife's boudoir or the drawing room for his ample study. Under such romantic circumstances would he sit, composing or editing article after article that damned the leaders of the Romantic Movement! Macaulay did not fail to notice this disparity between the critical opinions and the private conduct of his host. "I was surprised," he wrote, "to see a man so keen and sarcastic, so much of a scoffer, pouring himself out with such simplicity and tenderness in all sorts of affectionate nonsense."

The secret of Jeffrey lay, Macaulay felt, in a certain fastidiousness and vanity. He despised cheap literature, he despised blue-stocking ladies and the mutual flattery of authorial coteries. Indeed, did not the truth rest here: that while Jeffrey loathed affectation in other people, he was not wholly free from it himself? Was he not, like Congreve, when met by the great Voltaire, "a little too desirous to appear rather a man of the world, an active lawyer, or an easy careless gentleman, than a distinguished writer?" This, too, despite the fact that he had himself turned out seventy-nine articles during the first six years the *Review* appeared, had written forty more during a like period afterwards,[10] distinguished works almost every one of them, works that had counted largely in winning for his quarterly the reputation it enjoyed as the most important magazine of the age.

Macaulay's letter flowed on at length. It referred to Jeffrey's literary theories, to his well known contempt for the mystical and the rustic and to his cynical distrust of Wordsworth's "religion of nature." Bohemianism in conduct Jeffrey despised too; yet Macaulay complained that "we were never up till ten, and never retired till two hours at least after midnight." And he was definitely a hypochondriac, burdening his letters to friends with heavy accounts of imaginary maladies. The portrait Macaulay drew, in fact, is one of the richest and most complex in his long and uneven gallery, one of the few that really convince us still. With the exception of

10. Bagehot, *op. cit.*, 240.

that of William of Orange, he failed to equal it in his lengthy *History of England*, despite the exhaustive care that went into that work.

A welcome bit of luck came Macaulay's way in 1828. He was already having regularly to contribute to his family's support, and his income, though decent, was modest. The Trinity Fellowship amounted to £300, and he was realizing— as will shortly appear—about £200 more for his contributions to the *Edinburgh Review*. But the university grant was only for five years, four of which had already passed. In this year, however, just before the arch conservative Duke of Wellington accepted the office of Prime Minister of England, Lord Lyndhurst named Macaulay a Commissioner of Bankruptcy. It would probably not have happened had Wellington been in office, for the young man was already fairly well known as a Whig. The place added approximately £500 more to his income. It was only through such appointments as this that the legal profession ever proved profitable to him. There is no record, in other words, that any client, freely questing for a barrister, ever brought his woes to T. B. Macaulay.

He did not allow his new duties to interfere with his literary labors; they went on regularly, as payments of the amount named would imply. Since the essay on "Milton," which had made him famous, others had followed that kept that fame glowing. There had been a brilliant discussion of Machiavelli in the spring of 1827. It had been followed the next winter by a lengthy essay on John Dryden. Then, in the next issue, the great tribute to "History" had reminded his readers that to write history with excellence "is perhaps the rarest of intellectual distinctions."[11] A review of Hallam's *Constitutional History of England* came out the next fall. Readers were beginning to expect Mr. Macaulay's work regularly for, though unsigned, the brilliance and vigor of his style labelled at once whatever he wrote.

With the number that reached the newsstands in March,

11. *Works*, V, 122.

1829, Macaulay's ever widening audience found him engaged in a discussion that was to spread his name still more prominently through the country. The review of that date contained the treatise "Mill on Government." At last, it appeared to many liberal—but not too liberal—gentlemen, the menace of Utilitarianism had met with a mind capable of exposing its absurdities and extravagances.

In truth, liberal gentlemen were not far wrong. That the Utilitarians had enjoyed the ablest sort of leadership, Macaulay himself was the first to admit: Bentham did not teach people to pursue their "greatest happiness," for they have always done that; but he did something, Macaulay thought, which was a good deal more valuable. He taught them how to pursue it through law. "The whole science of jurisprudence is his."[12] Of James Mill, Bentham's chief evangelist, he spoke with almost equal courtesy and favor. With the single exception of its founder, "he is the most distinguished" of their growing school.

But with that, compliments trailed off abruptly. Like many other coteries of reformers, the Utilitarians had been unfortunate in their recruits. These recruits, arrogant and doctrinaire in their opinions and manners, were really, Macaulay declared, "in general, ordinary men, with narrow understandings and little information." The critic went on, roasting them royally in the best manner of the University bred statesman who is skeptical of all short cuts to learning. "The contempt which they express for elegant literature is evidently the contempt of ignorance. We apprehend that many of them are persons who, having read little or nothing, are delighted to be rescued from the sense of their own inferiority by some teacher who assures them that the studies which they have neglected are of no value, puts five or six phrases into their mouths, lends them an odd number of the *Westminster Review*, and in a month transforms them into philosophers."[13] Mr. Bent-

12. See "Westminster Reviewer's Defense of Mill," *Works*, V, 299.
13. *Works*, V, 240. See also, on Macaulay's attack, Elie Halévy, *The Growth of Philosophical Radicalism*, p. 485.

ham had founded that quarterly, and Mr. Mill was its chief contributor, but its gospel was leading to queer innovations: too many well meaning dunces, Macaulay thought, were being transformed by its pages to the dignity of sententious bores.

He went on to contend that the major fault of this group of men lay in one of their basic assumptions: that politics is a science and that, being so, "the principles which govern it may be synthetically deduced." They reminded one of medieval schoolmen; they had remained far too long in the cloister. Every *practical* statesman ought to realize at once that no profession—such as politics—which depends so completely upon the will of the voting classes can be comprised within the limits of a science. Human nature simply won't behave predictably! Men change their minds, they are subject to tempers, to fits of disgust and, alas, to a thousand things that leave dangling and helpless the frail threads of pure reason. Such is the dismaying truth, as every sensible statesman knows.

The subject matter of Macaulay's prose works will be considered more fully in another place, but one phase of this controversy must be noted now. It went on through the two succeeding issues of the *Edinburgh*. The *Westminster Review* replied to Macaulay, and Macaulay rejoined, in the summer number of the *Edinburgh*. Again the *Westminster* answered, and again, in the fall, Macaulay wrote further in elaboration of his views, the retort courteous giving way by degrees to words that came perilously close to the lie direct. In general, the series of discussions proved valuable to him in a number of ways. It forced him, in the first place, to acquire a much better understanding of this rival philosophy, an understanding that apparently led him in years to come to a gradual acquiescence to many reforms which the Utilitarians effected, if not actually to draw upon Utilitarian doctrine in his early speeches in Parliament.[14] It led him, again—in fact compelled

14. Halévy, *op. cit.*, 426-27.

him—to clarify his own ideas regarding the most pressing political changes then needed in England. Or perhaps one should say merely that it drove him to endorse publicly the set of ideas which nearly all good Whigs then held.

What forced this endorsement, incidentally, was an argument which the radical reviewers had over and over brought home—a point which struck at the root of Whig policy. The most elaborate statement of that point had appeared in the first number of the *Westminster*, in 1824. James Mill had established it in an article on the great Whig quarterly, an article more probing, if far less brilliant, than any Macaulay was ever to write.

Mill had begun by analyzing the characteristics of periodical literature in general. He pointed out that such literature cannot, like books, wait for success; it must succeed immediately or not at all. The misfortune in this fact is obvious: such writing must profess and inculcate the opinions already held by the public to which it is addressed; it can rarely afford the dangerous risk of attempting to rectify or to improve those opinions. With that preamble, Mill turned to an analysis, from the Utilitarian point of view, of the British Constitution. He emphasized its thoroughly aristocratic character —pointing out, among other items, the fact that a few hundred families had the privilege of nominating a majority of the House of Commons, and the further fact that country members of that body were almost exclusively identified with the great landholder interest. He went on to add, with a convincing array of evidence, that this narrow controlling oligarchy enjoyed the all but slavish support of both the Church and the Bar. Such a party, he continued, would naturally be divided into two factions—one in possession of the executive authority, the other seeking to displace its rival by a series of cursory overtures to that fraction of public opinion which voted or was otherwise influential. But this principle of deference to public opinion was confined within evident and sharply defined limits. Invariably it was opposed to any essential sacrifice of aristocratic control.

With that statement, he turned to the *Edinburgh Review*. He showed how, from its inception, it had coquetted with semi-popular principles for the patent reason that it desired popular support. It had opposed the excesses of Toryism—true; but what had it offered as a substitute for those excesses? Only, simmered down, the old exclusive brew—in new bottles, perhaps, but the old brew still. That brew was sour and needed changing. Essentially, in other words, the *Edinburgh Review* was a "see sawing" journal, a journal without morals, an opportunist publication.[15]

Perhaps James Mill overstated the case. Perhaps, from the start, the magazine he did so much to discredit had been dedicated to remedying the disenfranchisement of at least one order—the rising middle class. The question is debatable. But it is not debatable that the editor of the *Edinburgh*—Macvey Napier, who had succeeded Jeffrey—had been looking rather desperately for someone who could silence the enemy, and that he believed that, at long length, he had found such a person in Macaulay.

But Macaulay was forced to state his own political views, as we have mentioned. He did little more than state them, to be sure; arguing weakly, as excuse, that he "did not think it desirable to mix up political questions, about which the public mind is violently agitated, with a great problem in moral philosophy."[16]

Then he proceeded to commit himself in a pronouncement from the essentials of which he never afterwards departed. "Our fervent wish," he wrote, in the paragraph that closed the controversy, "and indeed our sanguine hope, is that we may see such a reform in the House of Commons as may render its votes the express image of the opinion of the middle orders of Britain. A pecuniary qualification we think absolutely

15. See, for an excellent summary of this article, J. S. Mill, *Autobiography* (N. Y. 1924, ed.), 65-66.
16. *Works*, V, 328.

necessary; and, in settling its amount, our object would be to draw the line in such a manner that every decent farmer and shopkeeper might possess the elective franchise. We should wish to see an end put to all the advantages which particular forms of property possess over other forms, and particular portions of property over other particular portions. And this would content us."[17]

It was a shrewd statement—the statement of a young man who in spite of his youth had already learned to write and to speak in the vague but reassuring terms of the politicians. He was declaring nothing radical. He was merely remarking, with a disingenuous clarity, what liberal statesman had been saying since Waterloo—that the middle classes were growing too wealthy, and therefore too powerful, to be longer ignored. It was the utterance of the traditional empiricist in politics, of one who looks daily upon a new scene and adjusts himself to it, but who adjusts himself, always, within the limits of his accustomed views. The middle classes, Macaulay reasoned, already controlled the wealth of Britain. Why not give them the power? The lower classes, he might have continued, are still dispossessed and helpless. To favor them would be radical and absurd. They must first teach us to fear them.

Macaulay's statements of his point of view, and his known brilliance and moral rectitude, were soon rewarded in the one way he chiefly desired. He had for months now been longing for a career in Parliament, but longing, he felt, rather hopelessly, since to run for office independently required a greater fortune than he could command. Then it was that his writing bore fruit. "In February, 1830," said his sister Hannah years afterwards, "I was staying at Mr. Wilberforce's when I got a letter." It was from Tom, and it enclosed another from Lord Landsdowne, a wealthy Whig who controlled several seats in the Lower House. His Lordship set forth that, impressed with the young man's articles on Mill, and with his high reputation, he desired him to stand for the vacant seat at Calne.

17. *Ibid.*

That seat he could bestow upon whomever he pleased. He went on to declare that he had no wish to influence Macaulay's votes; he would leave him entirely free to act "according to his conscience." Miss Hannah rushed into the sanctuary of the aging philanthropist and, speechless, put the letter into his hands. Wilberforce "read it with much emotion, and returned it to me saying, 'Your father has had great trials, obloquy, bad health, many anxieties. One must feel as if Tom were given him for a recompense.' "[18]

Macaulay, of course, lost no time in accepting an offer so entirely to his liking. He visited the Landsdowne home at Bowood, rejoicing in the pleasant society he found there, drinking "oceans of beer" and eating "mountains of potatoes" with the family, and revelling in the fine library at the estate. One critic has declared that Macaulay owed his elevation to Parliament to the feeling of his noble patron that he "had vanquished obnoxious radicalism"—or Benthamism.[19] Another has pointed out that Landsdowne was intimate with Charles Austin, Macaulay's Cambridge contemporary, implying that Austin probably urged his friend's case to advantage.[20] It does not matter. Whatever external influences were present, the fact persists that Macaulay reached his political goal almost entirely as a result of his own abilities.

One might add that he reached it in spite of at least one public and fairly insistent detractor. John Wilson, "Christopher North," was a professor of moral philosophy at Edinburgh University and a frequent contributor to *Blackwoods Magazine*. This publication was both Tory and cynical. Its editor had concluded that what was needed to combat the influence of the *Edinburgh* was a light and lively treatment of the shibboleths venerated by the Whigs. Professor Wilson had undertaken this task, collaborating with the critic James Hogg, who signed himself "the Ettrick Shepherd."

Macaulay meanwhile was continuing his articles for Napier.

18. Trevelyan, *op. cit.*, I, 136.
19. Alexander Bain, *James Mill* (London, 1882), 331-32.
20. See Lord Houghton, *Academy* (April 29, 1876).

His lengthy and disparaging review of the Tory Southey's *Colloquies* had appeared in January, 1830, to be followed by another disparaging review of the poems of Robert Montgomery in April, and by still another essay on Lord Byron in June. By that date Macaulay had already spoken in Parliament. "Christopher North," in other words, had had ample opportunity, by fall, to amass evidence that the young statesman was bitterly Whig in his politics and in his prose. He took his advantage:

"NORTH.—He's a clever lad, James.

"SHEPHERD.—Evidently; and a clever lad he'll remain, depend ye on that, a' the days of his life. A clever lad thirty years auld and some odds is to ma mind the moist melancholy sight in nature. Only think of a clever lad o' three score and ten, on his deathbed, wha can look back on nae greater achievement than haeing aince, or aiblins ten times, abused Mr. Southey, in the *Embro Review*."

These attacks, and others, went on. Indeed, the Macaulays grew at length accustomed to them; for since 1828, when Zachary had been assailed for championing the colony of Sierra Leone—where, according to the *Blackwood's* author, nothing flourished except "praying and concubinage"[21]—they had appeared insistently, one of the many trials of the just. But at least one of them contains enough of a kind of jaundiced truth, especially in its personal description, to sound fairly convincing still. It deals with Tom, and is in form another conversation, this time between North and Tickler.

"TICKLER.—. . . .It is the fashion, among a certain coterie at least, to talk of him [Macaulay] as 'the Burke of our age.' However, he is certainly a very clever fellow; the cleverest declaimer by far on that side of the House; and had he happened to be a somebody, we should no doubt have seen Tom in high places ere now.

"NORTH.—A son of old Zachary, I believe. Is he like the papa?

21. *Blackwoods Edinburgh Magazine*, XXIII (1828), 63-89.

"TICKLER.—So I have heard. But I never saw the senior, of whom some poetical planter has so unjustifiably sung:

How smooth, persuasive, plausible, and glib,
From holy lips has dropped the precious fib.

The son is an ugly, cross-made, splay footed, shapeless little dumpling of a fellow, with a featureless face, too—except, indeed a good expansive forehead—sleek puritanical sandy hair, large glimmering eyes, and a mouth from ear to ear. He has a lisp and a burr, moreover, and speaks thickly and huskily for several minutes before he gets into the swing of his discourse; but, after that, nothing can be more dazzling than his execution. What he says is substantially, of course, mere stuff and nonsense; but it is so well worded, and so volubly and forcibly delivered—there is such an endless string of epigrams and antitheses—such a flashing of epithets, such an accumulation of images, and the voice is so trumpet like, and he action is so grotesquely emphatic, that you might hear a pin drop in the House. . . . It is obvious that he has got the main parts at least by heart; but for this I give him the more praise and glory. Altogether, the impression on my mind was very much beyond what I had been prepared for; so much so, that I can honestly and sincerely say I felt for his situation most deeply when Peel was skinning him alive the next evening, and the sweat of agony kept pouring down his well-bronzed cheeks under the merciless infliction.

"NORTH.—The feeling does credit to your heart. Have you read his article on Byron in the *Edinburgh?*

"TICKLER.—Not I. I wonder how many articles on Byron we are expected to read. . . .

"NORTH.—Macaulay's paper is, however, an exceedingly clever thing, and you ought to glance your eye over it. The *Edinburgh* has had nothing so good these many years past. In fact, it reads very like a paper in one of their early numbers; much the same sort of excellencies; the smart, rapid, popgun impertinence; the brisk, airy, new-set truisms, mingled with cold, shallow, heartless sophistries; the conceited phlegm, the affected abruptness, the unconscious audacity of impudence; the whole lively and amusing, and much commended among the dowagers." [22]

But why go on? Let North sneer, let worthy gentlemen on the other side of the House or on the plush benches of the Lord's shudder in their sanctuaries or snort over their teacups at his speeches. Macaulay had joined with the forces of reform; he had taken his stand with the reasonable liberals. And the price of taking any stand at all, the price of speaking out boldly against any vested and jealous interest, was invariably the one he was paying now—unmerited abuse, cynical disparagement, and that broad distrust which at bottom was no more than the wailings of men whose instincts whispered to them that their day of authority was being swept away forever. He left them alone to ride the winds of their futile wrath.

22. From *Noctes Ambrosianna.* See Frederick Arnold, *Public Life of Lord Macaulay,* 84.

VI. Lion

IN THE summer of 1847, Macaulay, who had long represented Edinburgh in Parliament, ran for reelection. The campaign was desperate and long; he made many speeches—speeches that wore away his strength, for there were enemies in every audience who hissed and catcalled almost every statement he uttered. When the votes were counted, it was found that he had lost his place. It was the first political defeat of his career. An aging politician who had fought hard to no purpose, he went to his room and wrote a poem. It was the most personal poem he ever composed, one of the very few utterances in which his usually guarded emotions found release in the rhythms of a simple and convincing work.

The spirit of the piece is autobiographical—a vision poem in which in imagination he recalls the night of his birth and the visit of those faery queens who, rulers of the earth, passed his bed to decree his future. The Queen of Gain swept by without noticing him, and the disdainful Queen of Fashion followed. Then others came and departed, silently, taking no notice at all of the infant—the Queens of Power and of Pleasure, fay after fay in long procession. Finally one bent over him with sympathy; one whom he termed "the last, the mightiest, and the best."

So she proved indeed. She was the Queen of Knowledge and Imagination, and she declared that:

Mine is the world of thought, the world of dream
Mine all the past, and all the future mine.

He was destined, the Fay went on, "to love her with exceeding love," through all the changes and misfortunes the world might bring. It was true that the other queens had scorned him, but "let them go"; their gifts are transient and valueless. [1]

The poem, though in one sense his best, is sadly inaccurate. There were many goddesses, or queens, who smiled on Macaulay, and their favors began almost at the start of his public career. The Queens of Pleasure and Fashion smiled, the Queen of Power followed them, and the Queen of Gain was as generous as any reasonable man could wish.

To consider these imperious ladies in the order of their coming would be to treat first the Queen of Fashion. She appeared in the form of an invitation to visit Holland House. "His first great speech in the House of Commons," says his nephew, "at once opened to him all the doors in London that were best worth entering." "Whig doors," perhaps, would have been a more accurate statement, but at any rate there were few portals in London that, once crossed, revealed to a young historian and statesman a more intimate picture of England's past.

The House had been finished in 1607, and was first called Cape Castle after its original owner, Sir Walter Cape. King James I, the son of Mary of Scots, had visited there in 1612. Soon afterwards, Sir Walter died, £27,000 in debt, the house passing then into the hands of Henry Rich, Earl of Holland, who had married Cape's daughter and who had already established himself as, next to the Duke of Buckingham, the most celebrated courtier of the age. Alterations followed almost at once: the name of the place was changed to the one it bears today, Inigo Jones was commissioned to design a gateway in the courtyard, and Van Dyck was called in to

1. *Works*, VIII, 600-3.

do the portrait of the master of the estate. But ill fortune struck again before many years. The elegant Earl, who had sided with King Charles in his war with the Puritans, lost his head the same year that a like fate overtook his sovereign. "Arrayed in white satin waistcoat and white satin cap with silver lace," he faced his executioners proudly, an exquisite and cavalier to the last.

Afterwards, Cromwell held conferences there, though at times, even during the Protectorate, plays were given surreptitiously by the Earl's widow. Several decades later the house served briefly to accommodate the Court of William and Mary. And fairly early in the eighteenth century, in 1716, Joseph Addison married the widowed Countess of Warwick and Holland and went there to live, and three years later, to die "like a Christian" under its roof. Inauspicious days followed then; the estate was several times leased. Yet in 1767 its glory revived, when Henry Fox, the wealthy follower of Prime Minister Walpole, bought it and began to adorn it lavishly with fashionable paintings and with thousands of books.

Henry Fox had three sons—reckless bloods who managed to cost him a round £200,000 before they reached their majorities. He bought seats in Parliament for them all, while they were still in their 'teens and traveling on the continent. The eldest of them, Stephen, the second Lord Holland, died six months after his father. His title passed to his son Henry Richard who, born in 1773, had been sensibly reared by an uncle friendly with David Hume.[2] When young, this gentleman had visited the courts of Denmark and Prussia, a serious student of government. He had spent considerable time in the immoral Spanish household at Madrid, conversing with the simple-minded Charles III and his Queen, the mistress of Godoy, the Prince of Peace. From there he traveled to Italy, met Lady Webster, who bore him a son—known afterwards

2. Sanders, *op. cit.*, 1-37.

as General Fox—and, after her divorce from her first husband, married her and brought her to Holland House.

In 1806 Lord Holland had retired from politics. He was an excellent classical scholar and a great lover and collector of manuscripts. By the bedside of his uncle, Charles James Fox, the opponent of Pitt, he had sat during the statesman's last hours, reading aloud to him from Virgil, Dryden, and Crabbe.[3] Before that, in 1802, he had been a guest at the Court of Napoleon, after the Treaty of Amiens and, though an ardent supporter of republican principles, had come away feeling that the Corsican was little more than a badly spoiled child. His wife, however, disagreed, and to the end of Napoleon's life she corresponded with the fallen emperor, sending him delicacies or books when his name was anathema to almost the whole of Europe.

Before Macaulay met him, Lord Holland had done many other things of distinction. He had written a biography of Lope de Vega, confessing, however, with his usual candor, that he had read only fifty of that prolific Spaniard's four hundred odd plays. He had also translated some of the works of Calderon and Ariosto. And he had, without doubt, collected one of the finest private libraries in England. Books lined the shelves of the room set apart for them, stack after stack, reaching to the ceiling. And in one corner, to fascinate still more a student of the past century's life and manners, was the writing desk which Addison himself had used when a student in the Temple.

Macaulay seems to have admired this gracious gentleman as much, perhaps, as he admired any man he ever knew. His Lordship's fingers had been withered for life by a task imposed upon him by his fag master at Eton—the task of holding bread in his bare hands while he toasted it over an open fire. Also, like most of the Fox family, he was fat, and in later years an invalid from the gout. But his wit and joviality never seemed to desert him. A statesman just beginning his career could

3. *Ibid.*, 33.

nowhere have found a better adviser or a more valuable and stimulating friend.

Nor could he, if a scholar, have found a more exciting mansion within which that friendship might grow. Consider the first floor, for instance, a floor almost regal in its luxuriance! There was the entrance hall and the inner hall. Then, branching off, in several directions, came the smoking room, the breakfast room, the dining room, the china room, the map room, the picture room, the journal room, the print room, the library, the Sir Joshua Reynolds room, and the spacious white parlor. Chaste piers by Inigo Jones led off to pleasure grounds, flanked by the Dutch garden, with its ballroom set inspiringly in the center. There was also a conservatory, lined with busts of Europe's most distinguished figures, and, beyond, a dense green lane where, rumor contended, the mistress of the historic house met herself, in apparition, the day before she was fated to die. And what portraits might one find, in the picture gallery and elsewhere in the spacious mansion! There were, in sculpture, busts of Fox, of Henry IV of France, of Napoleon, and of the third Lord Holland, done in his youth, before the turn of the century. Then there were paintings, dozens of them, of Brougham and other contemporaries, of Addison, of Sir Philip Francis, of Robert Walpole, and of Francis Horner, the faithful Whig. Elsewhere Macaulay could find Rembrandt prints, Reubens engravings, sketches by Hogarth, and hundreds of other prints by German, Italian, Spanish, and noted English artists. [4]

Other curios, scattered about, made this mansion almost a museum. There were enamelled candlesticks which Mary Queen of Scots once owned, Addison's autograph, Napoleon's snuff box, and further reminders of the much maligned Emperor, sent there from desolate St. Helena—his arms, and a medallion, done in the height of his glory. Mementos of Byron all but cluttered up the place—letters written from

4. See Princess Marie Liechtenstein, *Holland House* (London, 1924), I, 134-75; II, 75, 156-57.

Italy by that passionate pilgrim, manuscripts of many of his poems, gifts he had sent to Lady Holland, and twelve water color illustrations of his works.

And yet, though freighted with all sorts of dispersed attractions, the house had a central emphasis that gave it unity and that made it, perhaps, unique among the many rival mansions of London. It was dominated by one of the most vigorous and astonishing personalities of the century, by a woman who, in an age growing increasingly conventional and formal, had preserved her individuality intact, a woman bent upon bringing the world around to a conformity with her own tastes and vagaries. One might call her, in a sense, a feminine Thoreau immersed in wealth, or a somewhat more cultured and intellectually curious Wife of Bath. She was a most invigorating but most trying person to know. For almost thirty years she was the social autocrat of London.

One never dined at her home, for example, without a formal invitation. He may have been detained, upon business, or by furious weather, until the butler was ready at the portals to announce dinner. Indeed, the butler might actually make his announcement, but one, lacking that invitation, was never asked to stay. When most of the members of the strictly professional classes called—members of the Bar or of Parliament, or medical men—they consistently left their wives at home: Lady Holland, having been once divorced, was not acceptable to their discreet mates.

Her table was small, as was the dining room itself, and most of her guests who have given us accounts of dinners there refer to that table as notoriously overcrowded. She could accommodate nine people comfortably, but usually there were fifteen or sixteen to be provided for. "Make room, Lord Grey," she would shout out abruptly, if a guest came late and she desired to seat him next the Prime Minister. So they would huddle together, more and more closely, higgledy-piggledy, profoundly uncomfortable. Once her commands nettled Lord Melbourne a bit too much. He had been shifted and crowded aside three times already when Lady Holland's "Make room, Lord Melbourne" rang out imperiously, once more. His Lordship arose and flung his napkin on the table. "I'll be damned if I dine with you at all," he shouted, and left the room. [5]

Away from the table she was equally dictatorial. She required always a large entourage of servants; on a visit to Woburn she had taken sixteen, all of them, naturally, to be looked after by her surprised host. When she traveled by stage coach, she insisted that her nerves could stand no speed greater than five miles an hour. Rather late in life she made a trip by railroad, and the furious wheels of the iron monster had to be subdued to a figure that suited her. She demanded of the director of the line that the train be run at less than twenty miles an hour, and her wishes were respected, despite the mass indignation of her fellow passengers.

So typically woman she was, in short: dreadfully afraid of the cholera, and likewise, dreadfully afraid of thunder, ordering, when a storm threatened, that all shutters be closed, all draperies drawn, and all candles lighted, though high noon might be reigning outside! And yet her kindness, upon occasion, could exceed the kindness of many others who were far less disturbing. When, in 1816, ill health beset that earnest young statesman Francis Horner ("that Marcellus of the Whig Party") she placed three rooms at Holland House at his disposal for the entire winter. "Pray spare me," she wrote, when extending the invitation, "all the commonplace compliments of giving trouble and taking up too many rooms. What you know I feel toward you ought to exempt me from any such trash." [6]

Yet there were reasons for coming to this home that were more important, even, than the privilege of being ordered about by its mistress. Holland House, by the time Macaulay entered Parliament, had enjoyed for more than a quarter of a

5. Sanders, *op. cit.*, 65-69.
6. *Ibid.*, 72.

century a reputation for liberalism which it had faithfully maintained, despite the overwhelming influence which the Tories, shuddering with fear of a resurgent Napoleon, had been able to exert upon the law makers of the country. Macaulay knew, for instance, that during the last twenty-five years, Lord Holland had staunchly opposed the law which permitted imprisonment for debt. He knew that his Lordship had actively supported Romilly's ill-fated bill providing that the sentence of death be removed for the theft of goods from warehouses and shops. He knew, also, that Holland had made a written protest against the exile of Napoleon, contending that such arbitrary and tyrannous treatment of a crushed enemy was beneath the dignity of a great nation. Finally, he knew that the aging liberal had consistently supported the opponents of slavery, despite the fact that he personally owned and received incomes from large holdings in the British West Indies.

This dwelling, in other words, was the most likely place for the new belligerent Whigs in Parliament to meet. Its master was, in a sense, the Nestor of the party—genial always, and always wise, with the wisdom of well spent intelligent years. For a young man just beginning his legislative career, like Macaulay, the experience to be gained at Holland House was incalculably useful. He could at once meet, on terms of intimacy and social equality, the leaders of his party, the men who, perhaps in his very presence, were discussing and formulating the policies that would soon be dominant in the state. The experience of dining and of visiting there precluded, in other words, the necessity of a tedious or uncertain climb to recognition; he was taken up the moment he was discovered to be a good speaker and a brilliant exponent of Whig doctrine, was put to use in the way that suited him best.

Yet men of letters also came to Holland House. Indeed they were there as often as statesmen, and found as cordial a welcome. Macaulay soon came to know them, almost as well as he knew the legislators. There were, among others, Sidney Smith, Tom Moore, the friend of Byron, Henry Luttrell, Samuel Rogers, and "Conversation" Sharp, the wealthy wit and critic. Greville the diarist of course visited frequently, and always present was the doctor and historical authority, John Allen, who resided there permanently as Lord Holland's medical adviser and librarian.

Macaulay first met Tom Moore in 1831, and he astonished the poet by quoting at length some stray doggerel that had appeared in the *Times* two decades ago. Moore was at this time a "dapper little man of fifty-two, who had already published, and fought a bloodless duel over, a volume of love verses which one of his critics had termed: a public nuisance." He had also dined with the Prince of Wales, later George IV, had traveled in America and pronounced the society of the country "low."[7] His volume *Lalla Rookh*, published in 1817, had followed the oriental tradition of Byron; to it mainly he owed his popularity. A gay, volatile, exuberant Irishman, Macaulay endured him because of Lady Holland.

Samuel Rogers, along with Luttrell and Sydney Smith, belonged to the "inner triad" of visitors. He was indeed a fortunate man, a bachelor with an income of £5000 a year and a discriminating taste in books, prints, and cuisine. He had to a marked degree the sharpness and cynicism of which bachelors are frequently the victims. "It matters little whom a man marries," he had once chirped in his weak voice, "for he is sure to find the next morning that he has married someone else." Women, and many men, feared his sharp tongue even in the early 1830's, when he was past seventy. Macaulay seems to have irritated him a good deal—the young man was too blustering and loud, too blind to the deferential niceties which an aging connoisseur had a right to expect.

Two of these other literary gentlemen must be at least hurriedly noticed. Henry Luttrell was still enjoying the reputation as the "premier wit of the Regency," thanks to

7. See "Lord Macaulay and his Friends," *Harpers*, LIII (1873).

that pleasant and mellow satire, *Letters to Julia*. They were all very lively verses, about things with which everyone in the city was familiar—the shoulder rubbing of high and low in Hyde Park, the Serpentine during skating season, and much talk of the horsemanship along Rotten Row. The London of George IV had discovered in him a faithful literary historian, and if, today, finding copies of his work has become an almost superhuman task, the fault cannot be laid to any neglect on the part of Holland House. There he was cherished at his true worth.

But John Allen really belonged to the family. Another Scotsman and Whig, a follower of Dugald Stewart, he had come down to the turn of the century already fortified with a medical degree—earned at the age of twenty—and with what seemed to the Hollands an immense amount of literary and historical learning. The stout, strong man with broad face, large round silver spectacles, a pronounced Scotch accent, "and the thickest legs one ever saw" soon won the favor of both Lord and Lady Holland and was offered the position we have already noticed. Macaulay—who considered Allen something of a rival historian and who, rival or not, could never understand a man taking orders from an arrogant woman—called that position one of a "Numidian slave." At times, too, it must have appeared so to many a visitor besides Macaulay, for Allen led what seemed to guests a decidedly cluttered and dependent life. Consider for a moment the nature of his duties: He attended Lord Holland as personal physician—though it is only fair to say that this office as the years passed was entrusted more and more completely to others. Then, before Holland's retirement, he helped his Lordship with his speeches, especially with the historical allusions in them.[8] But it was Lady Holland who seemed most exasperatingly to engross his energies. Allen must accompany her when she drove. Allen must chaperon her to the theater. Allen must make out the guest lists for dinners, and

8. Sanders, *op. cit.*, 82-84.

he must sit at the foot of the table and do the carving. When visitors came for a considerable time, it was Allen who assigned them to one or more of the twenty odd bedrooms in the house; and it was Allen who met them when they arrived. Yet, in spite of all these servile offices, he retained in a remote way something resembling independence. Sir Henry Holland —the distinguished physician of Queen Victoria's day— declares that the imperious lady of the house seems to have regarded him "with a certain dim awe." Byron, years before, had classified him as "one of the most learned men of his time." And he had, at least, written one notable book, the *Rise and Growth of the Royal Prerogative in England*, a book still esteemed by historians.[9]

Meanwhile, one may be curious to know how young Tom Macaulay impressed the distinguished guests whom Allen arranged for. One of the most reliable observers of the period was often present at Holland House. He was Charles Fulke Greville, the diarist, a man who should be reckoned among the most honest and therefore most reliable personal historians of the century. He met Macaulay early in his parliamentary career, at one of Lady Holland's crowded dinners. He had come in late and, oddly enough, had found a vacant place "between Sir George Robinson and a common looking person in black." Greville sat down without much formality; and soon afterwards began to speculate, as was natural, as to who his unknown neighbor might be. "As he did not open his lips except to eat, I settled that he was some obscure man of letters or of medicine, perhaps [remembering one of Lady Holland's chief phobias] a cholera doctor. In a short time the conversation turned upon early and late education, and Lord Holland said he had always remarked that self educated men were peculiarly conceited and arrogant and apt to look down upon the generality of mankind, from their being ignorant of how much other people knew; not having been at public schools, were uninformed of the course of general education.

9. See G. P. Gooch, *History and Historians of the Nineteenth Century* (London, 1913).

My neighbor [the hungry gentleman in black!] observed that he thought the most remarkable example of self education was that of Alfieri, who had reached the age of thirty without having acquired any accomplishment save that of driving, and who was so ignorant of his own language that he had to learn it like a child, beginning with elementary books. Lord Holland quoted Julius Caesar and Scaliger as examples of late education, said that the latter had been wounded and that he had been married and commenced learning Greek the same day, when my neighbor remarked that 'he supposed his learning Greek was not an instantaneous act like his marriage.' " Here was a queer visitor indeed. Was that last remark meant as humor, or was it a symptom of rather grotesque stupidity? Greville went on to note that the comment, and the manner in which it was uttered, gave him the notion that the guest was "a dull fellow." But surprises soon followed. With rather more astonishment than contempt the diarist listened while his neighbor continued the discussion of Scaliger's wound, heard him talk of Loyola having been wounded at Pampeluna. "I wondered how he happened to know anything of Loyola's wound. Having thus settled my opinion, I went on eating my dinner, when Auckland, who was sitting opposite me, addressed my neighbor 'Mr. Macaulay, will you drink a glass of wine?'"

Greville, as he admits, almost dropped in his chair. "It was Macaulay, the man I had been so long most curious to see and to hear, whose genius, eloquence, astonishing knowledge, and diversified talents have excited my wonder and admiration for such a length of time, and here I had been sitting next to him, hearing him talk, and setting him down for a dull fellow. I felt as if he could have read my thoughts, and the perspiration burst from every pore of my face, and yet it was impossible not to be amused at the idea. It was not till Macaulay stood up that I was aware of all the ugliness and ungainliness of his appearance; not a ray of intellect beams from his countenance; a lump of more ordinary clay never enclosed a powerful mind and lively imagination. He had a cold and sore throat the latter of which occasioned a constant contraction of the muscles of his thorax, making him appear as if in momentary danger of a fit."

The refined if informal Mr. Greville was not favorably impressed, as one may easily gather; and yet he was willing to record at least a few complimentary observations. Though Macaulay's manner struck him as "not pleasing," he acknowledged that it was not assuming, that it was unembarrassed, "unpolished, yet not coarse; there was no kind of usurpation in the conversation, no tenacity of opinions or facts, no assumptions of superiority." He acknowledged also, with equal candor, that the astonishing extent of Mr. Macaulay's information was soon apparent, for "whatever subject we touched on, he evinced the utmost familiarity with it; quotation, illustration, anecdote, seemed ready at his hand for every topic."

And such topics he talked about! Topics like primogeniture in Rome, at what date the tradition was first observed, and about the survival of the law in England. After dinner the famous Talleyrand came in to visit and told Macaulay that he meant very soon to go down to the House of Commons to hear him, "since he had heard all the other great orators."[10]

Perhaps he remembered things too well—this young statesman who spoke so amazingly about every topic, whether it was a topic introduced by himself or by another. Perhaps that memory was becoming a genuine burden to him, a handicap which caused him to settle all questions not by the agency of the reason but by a blind appeal to recollection and precedent, precedent which he seemed always to have, unaccountably, at his tongue's end. Leslie Stephen was one critic who thought so. Macaulay argued a case—any case, Stephen implied—purely by quoting other cases, simply by an appeal to authority: there was no real thinking involved. He accumu-

10. See Greville's *Diary*, II, 151-52 (2 vols. London, 1927).

lated endless facts, but he never, says Stephen, got at the reasons which his facts represented or served to make tangible. Talking with him was like talking with an encyclopaedia! And yet, whether ultimately satisfying or not, the member from Calne was invariably astonishing. Before one had been very long in his presence one began to adopt, naturally, it seems, the rôle of a rapt and bewildered listener.

The diary which Greville kept during the momentous years of the Reform Bill's agitation and passage—years which saw Macaulay's first success in politics—is a work that, after more than a century, still reads as vividly and as convincingly as do those of recent historians. His resentments toward the lower orders, which were those of a gentleman bred to dislike all violence, appear without quibbling in entry after entry. There was Henry Brougham, the Whig orator, whom Greville set down in 1830 as the hero of the rabbleocracy—that is of "the rebels, republicans, associations, and all the disaffected in the country."[11] There was Francis Place, that unbelievably successful organizer of mass protests against the existing order. He was making secret "domicilary visits" to Prime Minister Grey, to the obvious disgust of the diarist. Then there was William Cobbett, the fanatical editor of the *Poor Man's Friend*, and Richard Carlyle, the ramping atheist, both of them either writing or haranguing "to inflame the minds" of a people already violently restless. Distress, Greville thought, "is certainly not the cause of these commotions, for the people have patiently supported far greater privations before." There was a new and sullenly ominous spirit abroad, a spirit which, to this mild-mannered friend of wealth and station, would overturn his England of happy memory, unless a firm hand, like that of Wellington's, were laid upon its usurpations.

Consider the evidence of restlessness that might be picked up anywhere! The Duke of Richmond had gone down to his estate at Sussex and had actually waged a battle with 200 laborers. Of course, his Lordship put these rascals to rout with

11. Leslie Stephen, *Hours in a Library* (3 vols. London, 1879), I, 294-95.

a scant fifty of his own farmers and tenants,[12] but nevertheless, only think of what an outrage like this implied. The laborers were apparently beginning to think that they had rights! And the very next day, moreover, the Duke had captured a man named Evans, a fellow accused of exciting the peasantry, and had found on his person stock receipts amounting to £800 and, "in a secret pocket," a chemical receipt for combustibles. Three days later, the Cabinet sat all morning to consider the violence that now was spreading in all directions through the troubled land. Before it rose, Greville notes, it decided to offer "large rewards for the discovery of offenders, rioters, and burners." A week later, it seemed still, to this observer, that London was like "the capital of a country desolated by cruel war or foreign invasion."[13]

And other reports, all of them distressing, kept filing in from all parts of the island: young lords on horseback having to charge the surly peasants who occupied their property; barns and ricks being everywhere set aflame by a mysterious agent, Captain Swing, who seemed somehow to be in all places at once, a relentless ghostly avatar of the dispossessed. In manufacturing districts like Manchester, too, workmen appeared to be organizing with a fiendish genius and success; and the agriculturists at Wiltshire were doing the same. Greville had talked to Colonel Napier and learned that, in his opinion, "a revolution is inevitable." The diarist recalled what Poet Laureate Southey had said: "If he had money enough he would transport his family to America."[14]

But the crowning indignity took place the following midwinter: "The king went to the play night before last; was well received in the house, but hooted and pelted coming home, and a stone shivered a window of his coach and fell into Prince George of Cumberland's lap."[15] Her Majesty, also present, was terrified almost beyond speech!

12. Greville, *op. cit.*, I, 346 (September 10, 1830).
13. *Ibid.*
14. *Ibid.*, I, 347.
15. *Ibid.*, I, 348 (February 24, 1831).

Back of these eruptions, growing daily more menacing, was a resentment which no one knew how to stop, except by removing the accumulated injustices which caused it. Two hundred families could not hope to control forever the destinies of the richest constitutional monarchy on earth. A few dozen wealthy but short-sighted planters could not hope to impose forever on that people a tariff on wheat which made a loaf of bread so outrageously overpriced that practically a day's wage was required to buy it. Nor could the rising upper middle classes in the industrial towns of the midlands—towns which had sprung up almost with the suddenness of mushrooms—be kept forever from the ballot and a voice in the House of Commons on the argument that, according to a census made three centuries ago and still in force, they deserved no voice, since three centuries ago their thriving towns were wastelands. What did a tradition so obsolete amount to in that constant temporizing with emergency which is politics? Look at those boroughs that once were so prosperous! Many of them were wastelands *today*, unpeopled and poisonous, since across their straggling acres rode injustice in the form of irresponsible lords who controlled them still and sent out puppets in their names to mold the destinies of England. They were rotten boroughs over which flowed no life save the fugitive life of foxes and grouse. These conditions must be changed, wiped out; and other things must be altered too—matters such as the disfranchisement of Catholics and Jews, and the long standing curse of slavery. The patience of the masses was done for.

And young men, like Macaulay, knew it. The Iron Duke himself knew it, the arch Tory statesman who, even at Waterloo, had stood unmoved while the world flamed and crumbled before him. There must be some giving in, some compromise with the forces of disorder, some temperate championing of the cause of those who had gone for so long without any champion at all. Perhaps most things could at length be saved; perhaps the upper middle classes could drift gradually, thanks to ever waxing incomes, into that class which moved in still higher altitudes. Somewhere, in other terms, there was a golden mean, the mean of a reasonable reform that would take the place of both radicalism and revolution. So the Whigs of Macaulay's day thought. And the Ministry which he had dedicated himself without reservation to support set out to frame the bill that would provide it.

VII. Reformer

THAT BILL upon which the apostles of temperate reform set to work was one that, almost from its inception, assumed the mantle of excitement and drama. For though moderate in its ultimate implications, it seemed to those defenders of the established order—the Tory statesmen and Churchmen—not moderate at all, but revolutionary to the point of desperation. Secrecy, therefore, had to be strictly enjoined upon those who were taking part in its framing, lest the proposals they were soon to announce be learned about by the opposition. If this should happen—Lord Grey and his Cabinet well knew—the Tories could solidify their forces and frighten the King and the moderates in the House to such an extent that the measure might never be suffered to come up at all.

Francis Jeffrey, now Lord Advocate (or Secretary) for Scotland, came down in person to London, to draft that part of the bill that applied to his country. A committee of four drew up the general proposals. For secretaries, or amanuenses, the ladies of the Grey household served:[1] no hired assistants could be trusted to withstand Tory bribes.

The Cabinet finally agreed on all details, and Lord Grey went down to Brighton to inform King William of their provisions. His Majesty, holding the preliminary right of veto, had to be consulted beforehand. But after the four Georges—who had become systematically worse as one suc-

1. I am following mainly, in these pages, George Macaulay Trevelyan's *Lord Grey of the Reform Bill* (London, 1929), by long odds the best account of the measure. See especially 275-306.

ceeded the other—William IV proved fairly easy to work with. For one thing, he had come to feel that it was dishonorable in a ruler to listen to advice from members of the party which was not in power. That advice, he knew, would probably be jaundiced. So Grey found his mind receptive, or at least untainted. He saw, what he probably suspected already, that the rather simple minded retired Admiral to whom he talked was dominated by a single fear: the fear that the "radicals" would get control of the government. He would accede to *anything* if it would prevent that catastrophe. Grey's line of argument was, therefore, practically cut out for him. He had merely to persuade the King that a strong reform bill —yet one that kept control in the hands of the propertied classes—was after all the most conservative act that could be passed. Such a measure would destroy the force of the radical revolt: the reformers who were not too extreme would be contented with it and, thus, absorbed into that fast growing sponge which was Whiggery. It was an old trick, one of the oldest in the overthumbed hornbook of political strategy.

The King was soon convinced. He agreed to support "the Bill, the whole Bill, and nothing but the Bill," and though the Tories accused Grey later of imposing upon His Majesty's simplicity, he never shifted his allegiance. To him it was "an aristocratical measure," an opinion which history has confirmed. On March 1, 1831, Lord John Russell, a member of the Cabinet, appeared in the small, stuffy and profoundly uncomfortable House of Commons—too small to seat more than two-thirds of the membership[2]—to read the piece of legislation whose particulars had been so well concealed. "A little fellow not weighing above eight stone," Lord John, with his quiet voice, seemed at first to suggest a law as unpretentious as himself.

But this illusion was soon dispelled, bluntly. Speaking in general terms, he announced that the Reform Bill provided that 60 rotten boroughs of the country were to lose two mem-

2. This was, of course, the old St. Stephen's Chapel, which was burned in 1834.

bers apiece. Forty-seven others, he went on, were to lose one member apiece. So much for England. Having finished with her, he was proceeding calmly to outline the changes that were contemplated for Wales, Ireland, and Scotland, when "an honorable member called on him to name the disfranchised boroughs." Challenged, Russell proceeded to read them out, slowly, a political death sentence for more than 150 members—members who squirmed, hissed, and catcalled bitterly as the lengthening catalogue doomed the lot of them, one by one.

The Grey Ministry became immensely popular, almost overnight. It had got off to a poor start three and a half months before, had been criticized as dilatory and timid; but now those early misgivings were forgotten. Francis Place, a director of radical propaganda, put "the best radical organizations of the country at the service of the Ministers and their measure."[3] William Cobbett, the widely read and respected friend of labor, praised the Bill liberally in his *Two Penny Tracts*. The middle orders, "a term comprising the humblest clerk to the wealthy magnates," naturally favored it; and from the lower classes, anonymous but militant, came a song whose words focused their sentiments in a way which few statesmen could afford to ignore:

> *See, see, we come! No swords we draw,*
> *We kindle not war's battle fires.*
> *By union, justice, reason, law*
> *We'll gain the birthright of our sires*
> *And thus we raise, from sea to sea,*
> *Our sacred watchword, Liberty.*

Reared against these combined forces, the major element that sought to curb them, was the Church. It seemed to those unaware of its recent history ironical in the extreme that an institution dedicated to the ideal of the improvement of man's

3. G. M. Trevelyan, *op. cit.*, 275-306.

spiritual and temporal estate should fight so stubbornly an act almost bound to make the realization of that ideal simpler. But the Church of England had for more than half a century been almost as rotten as the borough of old Sarum itself—that deserted mound which still "returned" two regular members to Parliament. The spirituality of that Church had waned since the age of the Enlightenment began to wax, far back in the previous century. Dissatisfied with its decline, the Wesleys and Whitefield had sought to revive it and, failing, almost lived to see the sects which they had begun formed into a new and vigorous denomination. The Evangelicals had worked, too, in the interest of a spiritual renaissance, had done much to achieve such humanitarian reforms as the limitation of slavery. And now, at Oxford, a new movement, Tractarianism, was slowly getting under way. But the moribund body of the Church itself remained, basically, moribund still, entrenched behind the twin barriers of wealth and privilege. It was in control at Oxford and Cambridge. Its leaders had witnessed, through decade after decade, the steady and relentless exodus of young men from the once prosperous and contented villages of England to the rising dirty industrial towns. They had seen the desperate living quarters in those places, they knew of the incredibly long hours of labor required, they were aware of the lack of any facilities for education or for religious comfort in them.

But they were indifferent to these matters. As for the souls of these ragged masses, the Church left them to the care of the "vulgar" Methodists and Baptists. As for their overtasked bodies and neglected minds, that was something entirely too complex and troublesome to bother with investigating. Ample-bottomed bishops drank their tea and dined in sweet candle-lit security, knowing well that, while the old order held fast, nothing would check the methodical collecting of the taxes levied in the name of the cause they pretended to serve. Yet they were not too dull to realize that a fundamental rearranging of Parliament might bring to an end their otherwise inviolable world. For the masses which the Holy Establishment had bilked but otherwise ignored were now well convinced of at least one thing: that that Establishment took too much from them, and gave too little in return. [4]

Debate on Russell's measure started at once. The particulars of it were, as is generally known, that boroughs of fewer then 2,000 population should lose altogether their representation in the House of Commons, that those of fewer than 4,000 should be permitted to elect only one member. This would eliminate a total of 168. To replace these, fifty-five new representatives were to be permitted from the populous counties of England, seventeen more from Ireland, Scotland, Wales, and London, and thirty-four more from the larger English industrial towns. Suffrage in those towns was to be extended to all male citizens who paid a rate, or property tax, of as much as £10 annually. This limitation, of course, excluded the lower classes entirely from the ballot. [5] Lord John's estimate was that approximately half a million people would be added to the constituency, "all of them responsible." [6]

Macaulay spoke first during the second night. It was his maiden effort in that House before whose membership so many able men, distinguished elsewhere, had failed unaccountably to live up to their promise. Macaulay felt throughout his career that it was the most difficult audience in the world to face.

Several Tories had preceded him. The first had been Sir R. H. Inglis, of the University of Oxford, and Inglis had proved himself as much of an alarmist as ever Macaulay did in his most hysterical moments. "I own," he had warned, "that I approach the discussion of this question with a sensation of awe at the contemplation of the abyss on the brink of which we stand, and into which the motion of the noble

4. *Ibid.*, 290.
5. Hansard, *Parliamentary Debates* (3 series), II, 1082.
6. *Ibid.*, II, 1083.

[111]

Lord [Russell] will, if successful, hurl us."[7] He went on to invoke the authority of the peerless Burke, that venerable defender of venerable institutions. Other speakers, supporting Inglis, had pointed out that some of the boroughs were not rotten and, therefore, should not be abolished. Only those which were admittedly corrupt should be wiped out. Macaulay himself, as he was soon to be reminded, had come into Parliament by way of the system now being threatened. And as for this unthinkable extension of the franchise to every householder who paid £10 yearly in taxes, the proposal, Mr. Horace Twiss had declared, meant nothing less than turning the government over "to men of limited information, of strong prejudices, and of narrow and contracted views, such as shopkeepers and small attourneys."[8] Such men, he exclaimed, are not fitted to vote. And having said this, he turned to the *Book of Ecclesiastes* to prove his point: The potters described in that book are the middle class. It is made up of men who sustain themselves by the work of their hands. They are very useful servants; a city cannot be built without them; "but they should not be sought for in public council nor allowed to sit high in the congregation." The debate was less than a single night old; yet the Church had already taken its stand and summoned to its aid the authority of its Book. This further proof of its decadence must it give, while men still poignantly remembered that it was a clergyman who had read the riot act to the trampled and bleeding masses at Peterloo.

The Whigs had naturally not been silent under these protests. One of them, Mr. H. V. Shelley, had brought a copy of the *Westminster Review* to the House and had quoted lengthy passages from it in support of the following doctrine: "Anarchy is fearful, but it is a passage sharp and short, while misrule under which the nation has suffered every sort of injury, moral, political and financial, is a chronic disease,

7. *Ibid.,* II, 1090.
8. *Ibid.,* II, 1134-35.

a continuous affliction, spoiling the health, the spirits and the temper of a community. Tens of thousands of Englishmen are convinced that a revolution involving temporary anarchy is preferable to the maintenance of an oligarchy of accursed domination. . . . The aristocracy," he concluded, "have had their long and disastrous day; it is now the time of the Demos."[9] Let the Tories, in other words, keep one thing clear: the choice to be made is between reform and revolution. The chair then recognized the honorable gentleman for Calne, Mr. Macaulay.

Things began to look up at once, the discussion to assume a more exalted plane. He was happy, he said, to see that there had up to now been no petty quibbling within the ranks of the reformers, some wanting this little item provided for, others objecting to that little item. Such bickerings would disrupt the party bent on improvement, but they had not been in evidence thus far. The issue, the cleavage, was clearly defined: there were those in the House who wanted reform and there were those who did not want it.

What did the Bill provide for, basically? What was its core, its central provision? Simply this: "To admit the middle class to a large and direct share in the representation, without any violent shock to the institutions of the country."[10] Did worthy gentlemen think that he was convinced of the infallibility of the measure he supported? Did they feel that he regarded it as the perfect solution for the problems of limited monarchies? Mr. Macaulay would not positively say. "I believe that there are some societies in which every man may safely be admitted to vote." The opposition jeered this radical statement, but the speaker was not disturbed. Instead, he proceeded to explain it, in an argument that was eminently sensible. Universal suffrage was a fact in America, and it apparently was successful as practiced there. But there was a marked difference between the condition of the workmen in the old world and those in the new. Across the Atlantic, it appeared,

9. *Ibid.*, II, 1170.
10. *Works*, VIII, 12.

wages were uniformly high, food was relatively cheap, and a large family was "not an encumbrance but a blessing." Men, in short, were independent and therefore free. They trusted their better judgment; they were not the victims of that violence and credulity which befall so often the laborers of the old world when markets decline and poverty threatens.

This latter contingency was the axis around which the whole problem revolved. Men cannot be expected to exercise their better judgment in political affairs until they are relatively secure. Money makes them secure as does nothing else. The conclusion from this fact is obvious. A pecuniary qualification ought to be required in England before a man is extended the ballot.

This point he emphasized over and over. "It is not by numbers but by property and intelligence that the nation ought to be governed." Then he considered the views of those who had criticized the Bill. Gentlemen in the benches opposite had contended that the country was better off now than it had ever been in the past. Macaulay was no "antiquary"; he would not contest their argument. It was irrelevant. But this fact he knew; that in a sense our ancestors were wiser than we, for "they legislated for their own times. They looked at the England which was before them. They did not think it necessary to give twice as many Members to York as they gave to London, because York had been the capital of Britain in the time of Constantius Chlorus; and they would have been amazed indeed if they had foreseen, that a city of a hundred thousand inhabitants would be left without representatives in the nineteenth century, merely because it stood on ground which, in the thirteenth century, had been occupied by a few huts." [11]

And there was Sir Robert Inglis, his honorable friend for the University of Oxford. He had set forth, in alarm, the contention that if the present law were passed "England will soon be a republic." On what did he base his contention, but

11. *Ibid.*, VIII, 16.

on the fear that the middle class which was clamoring for the vote would, within a decade after it had been granted, "depose the King and expel the Lords from their House?" Sir Robert, in saying this, had made a most unfortunate admission: he had acknowledged his belief that "the great body of the middle class look with aversion on monarchy and aristocracy." If this were so, who was to blame? Sir Robert was forgetting the primary end of government, which, Macaulay reminded him (paraphrasing Bentham, without acknowledging it), "is the happiness of the people."[12] Whenever the will of the monarchy and aristocracy conflict with that of "the great body of the middle class"—Macaulay would not admit this to be the case at present—the former group must give way. Those who constitute it will have failed to fulfill their responsibility.

Macaulay proceeded then to answer other objectors. He pointed out to them that action should not be longer postponed. He made plain to them how they had temporized with the emergency the nation now faced, an emergency that was ominous mainly because of their vacillation. The day for further timidity was past. "Reform that you may preserve," the voice of the Age advised. "The danger is terrible. The time is short. If this Bill is rejected, I pray to God that none of those who concur in rejecting it may ever remember their votes with unavailing remorse, amidst the wreck of laws, the confusion of ranks, the spoilation of property, and the dissolution of social order."[13] With that peroration the member for Calne sat down to the ringing applause of both sides of a House; for the gentlemen who heard him, whether in agreement or in disagreement, admired a brilliant performance. And they all knew that in Macaulay's address they had heard one.

But though this applause was general and sustained, it was not universal. There were those present whose resentment

12. *Ibid.*, VIII, 20.
13. *Ibid.*, VIII, 25.

against the Reform Bill was too settled to be relaxed, even in the face of an eloquence almost consummate in its persuasiveness. Lord Mahon was the first to follow Macaulay, and he began his disclaimer with the despairing remark that the Whig Member "had touched on so many phases of the subject that he hardly knew which phase to answer first." The honorable gentleman had charged the Tories with inconsistency. That charge was equally applicable to his own party. Lord Mahon, however, was happy to bear this humble tribute to the eloquence and talent of which the Honorable Member from Calne had addressed the House, finding in him another proof of the utility and advantage of the reviled "close" boroughs. "By what other means could young men of talent [with no fortunes worth noticing] obtain seats in this House?" [14] Macaulay in the course of his speech had used the words "revolution" and "massacre." Pass the Bill, he had argued, and avoid both calamities. What he failed to mention, Lord Mahon argued, was that the Bill itself was identical with revolution. "The Honorable Member from Calne called upon the House to sacrifice the whole constitution in order to preserve it."

Next came "Orator" Hunt, the hero of Peterloo, now a Member of Parliament. Mr. Hunt was still a radical, and the bill, to him, appeared as weak in its provisions as it had appeared overwhelmingly extreme to the Tories. Aspersions had been flung, he reminded his audience, against the intelligence and judgment of the industrial laborers of England. They were unjust aspersions, the fruit of bias and ignorance. Hunt got down to cases. The laborers in cities who attended public meetings, he shouted, are "a great deal more intelligent and better educated than the inhabitants of that most degraded and rottenest of all rotten boroughs, the borough of Calne." [15] Let Mr. Macaulay keep that fact in mind.

Then he turned to the tragedy of Peterloo, for that tragedy

14. Hansard, *op. cit.*, II, 1206.
15. *Ibid.*, II, 1210.

still retained its power to awaken bitterness and remorse in the hearts of those who had been guilty of it. Shouting with a fury too hot and impassioned to be stilled, he went on to proclaim that "a drunken and infuriated yeomenry, with swords newly sharpened, slaughtered fourteen and wounded 685 of as peaceable and well disposed persons as any he saw around him."[16] This, and a great deal more he thundered out, while shouts of "No, No!," "Question," and "Order!" rang hysterically from every part of the House. Orator Hunt was having his revenge; the issue between violent change and violent resistance to any change was throbbing stormily over the heads of the Whig moderators. And Tom Macaulay was in the midst of the conflict, was beginning to take the lead on the side of common sense. He was also, as the price of that leadership, inheriting rather a good deal more than his share of razor-edged vituperations.

Debate over the Bill, which hour by hour had been gaining in popular estimation, went on daily for slightly more than three weeks. Then came the vote on its second reading, the reading that was always critical for a measure. If it passed this reading by a majority vote, some sort of reform was assured; if it did not, many Whigs sincerely believed, a civil war was imminent. One of the best letters Macaulay ever wrote—a letter to a lifelong friend, Thomas F. Ellis—describes possibly as well as any extant account what happened when that vote was counted:

"Such a scene as the division of last Tuesday I never saw, and never expect to see again If I should live fifty years, the impression of it will be as fresh and sharp in my mind as if it had just taken place. It was like seeing Caesar stabbed in the Senate-house, or seeing Oliver taking the mace from the table; a sight to be seen only once, and never to be forgotten. The crowd overflowed the House in every part. When the strangers were cleared out, and the doors locked, we had six hundred

16. For more exact figures on the killed and wounded see G. M. Trevelyan, *British History in the Nineteenth Century*, 189.

and eight members present—more by fifty-five than ever were in a division before. The ayes and noes were like two volleys of cannon from opposite sides of a field of battle. When the opposition went out into the lobby [a regular custom until 1836], an operation which took up twenty minutes or more, we spread ourselves over the benches on both sides of the House; for there were many of us who had not been able to find a seat during the evening. When the doors were shut we began to speculate on our members. Everybody was desponding. 'We have lost it. We have only two hundred and eighty at most. I do not think we are two hundred and fifty. They are three hundred and ninety-nine.' This was the talk on our benches. I wonder that men who have been long in Parliament do not acquire a better *coup d'oeil* for numbers. The House, when only the ayes were in it, looked to me a very fair House—much fuller than it generally is even on debates of considerable interest. I had no hope, however, of three hundred.

"As the tellers passed along our lowest row on the left hand side the interest was insupportable—two hundred and ninety-one, two hundred and ninety-two—we were all standing up and stretching forward, telling with the tellers. At three hundred there was a short cry of joy—at three hundred and two another—suppressed, however, in a moment; for we did not know what the hostile force might be. We knew, however, that we could not be severely beaten. The doors were thrown open, and in they came. Each of them, as he came up, brought some different report of their numbers. It must have been impossible, as you may conceive, in the lobby, crowded as they were, to form any exact estimate. First we heard that they were three hundred and three; then that number rose to three hundred and ten; then went down to three hundred and seven. Alexander Barry told me that he had counted, and that they were three hundred and four. We were all breathless with anxiety when Charles Wood, who stood near the door, jumped up on a bench and cried out, 'They are only three hundred and one.' We set up a shout that you might have heard at Charing Cross, waving our hats, stamping against the floor, and clapping our hands. The tellers scarcely got through the crowd; for the House was thronging up to the table, and all the floor was fluctuating with heads like the pit of a theatre. But you might have heard a pin drop as Duncannon read the numbers. Then again the shouts rang out, and many of us shed tears. I could scarcely refrain. And the jaw of Peel fell; and the face of Twiss was as the face of a damned soul; and Herries looked like Judas taking his neck-tie off for the last operation. We shook hands, and clapped each other on the back, and went out laughing, crying, and huzzaing into the lobby. And no sooner were the outer doors opened than another shout answered that within the House. All the passages and the stairs into the waiting room were thronged by people who had waited till four in the morning to know the issue. We passed through a narrow lane between two thick masses of them; and all the way down they were shouting and waving their hats, till we got into the open air. I called a cabriolet, and the first thing the driver asked was, 'Is the bill carried?' 'Yes, by one.' 'Thank God for it, sir!' And away I rode to Gray's Inn—and so ended a scene which will probably never be equalled till the reformed Parliament wants reforming.

"As for me," Macaulay confessed to his friend, "I am at present a sort of lion. My speech has set me in the front rank, if I can keep there; and it has not been my luck hitherto to lose ground when I have once got it." [17]

2

The subsequent career of the Reform Bill is too familiarly recorded in history to call for much attention here. After passing the second reading by this delicate majority, the measure went into Committee. There it was defeated. A

17. G. O. Trevelyan, *op. cit.*, I, 186-88 (Letter of March 30, 1831).

problem of acute importance was thus brought fairly before King William: He must choose between a new ministry and a much modified Bill, or he must dissolve Parliament and call a general election. [18] Pamphlets, meanwhile, were being circulated in all directions. The newspapers were filled with exciting conjectures or with ill concealed threats. And His Majesty was increasingly alarmed, lest the revolution which the now plaguing edict was expected to avert break forth, in open fury, before the cumbrous mills of legislation could grind it out.

The Whigs, as was natural, wanted dissolution; they knew that the propaganda which they had spread with the help of radical organizations had taken effect. Lord Grey was in conference daily with the King, and, at length, in May, His Majesty gave his consent to what Grey wanted. He would go down to the Lords and explain to them his intentions.

By the time he had made up his Royal mind, it was past noon; and his Royal mind had become convinced that the dissolution could not be postponed a single day longer. But he must reach the Upper Chamber by two o'clock; otherwise his action would have to be delayed. And of course there were the Horse Guards to be called out, the Royal Coach to be made ready, the Royal robes to be donned, and a Royal speech to be prepared, in explanation.

His Majesty was less interested in these forms than were his advisers. The mortal dread in which he stood of the radicals had now brushed aside all other timidities, great and small. He announced that, if necessary, he would ride to Parliament in a hackney coach. But Lord Chancellor Brougham had been busier than his master knew. He had already sent for the Horse Guards; he had already served notice that the Royal Coach was needed, and he had written a draft of His Majesty's speech. Yet who should carry the Sword of State, preceding

18. At this date it was necessary to obtain the Royal permission before Parliament could be dissolved. See G. M. Trevelyan, *British History in the Nineteenth Century*, 236.

the King as he entered the Chamber? Lord Grey assumed this privilege.

And thus it happened that, in a sense, all the due forms were observed. Grey arrived "looking like William's executioner," with William himself, his crown obviously awry, following him as was proper, while crowds shouted and salute guns boomed methodically down the quiet Thames. The King stood forth and read his speech; and in conclusion, to the dismay of the Tories, announced that he had been induced to dissolve the House "for the purpose of ascertaining the sense of my people." It was the sign of a new era in English political history,[19] an era in which the masses, at least indirectly, were beginning to influence the course of legislation.

The election His Majesty called for went as the Whigs knew it would go. It went—in those boroughs not exclusively under the control of wealthy noblemen—almost unanimously in support of the advocates of the Bill. Instead of a majority of one there was now in the House a majority of 136 in its favor.[20]

But before this majority was established, Macaulay had made another speech. He addressed the House the night of July 5, in the middle of that summer through which statesmen labored despite fiendish weather, and in what was, without doubt, a more than normally fetid atmosphere. Members were often sick, often surly; and words that might otherwise have been generous were frequently hot and short. It was no easy task against skilled antagonists to contend for certain abstract rights for more than eight hours of every day, when seats were unavailable, when lobbies were thick with cigar smoke, and when one could not hope to get to his rooms until four o'clock in the morning.

In his speech, Macaulay pointed out, to begin with, that if the argument stressed by certain Tories were allowed— the argument that the franchise was property and that, there-

19. See, on the foregoing, G. T. Garrett, *Lord Brougham* (London, 1935), 263-64.
20. See G. M. Trevelyan, *British History in the Nineteenth Century*, 237.

fore, disfranchisement was robbery—then the whole electoral system must be so classed. For by an "act of Henry VI," an act which fixed the present franchise of English counties, "tens of thousands of electors who had not forty shilling freeholds," were disfranchised. [21] He was using history with decisive effect here, as he had used it in his first address and as he was to use it in almost every other speech he was to make. In a sense it was an appeal to precedent and authority, the type of appeal which he could make with a conviction unexcelled among his contemporaries. It was a dangerous argument, this contention of the despairing opponents of reform. "If in order to save political abuses from the fate with which they are threatened by the public hatred, you claim for them the immunities of property, you must expect that property will be regarded with some portion of the hatred which is excited by political abuses."

And there was the "let well enough alone" argument. Those who advanced it forgot one fact: that revolutions were caused mainly by nations which continued to move onward, while "constitutions stand still." The whole history of the English nation, summarized, was "a history of a succession of timely reforms." There were, he realized, extremists of two sorts in the House—those who wanted a more radical law, and those who wanted no change at all. Macaulay lumped these protestors into two neat and unpleasant categories: "the friends of corruption and the sowers of sedition."

Then there were those who objected to the terms of the Bill. They wanted reform but not the reforms called for in the present measure. The bill has anomalies, these statesmen cry. "But if gentlemen have such a horror of anomalies, it is strange that they should so long have persisted in upholding a system made up of anomalies far greater than any that can be found in this bill." At this point the speaker was forced to pause by reason of the cry of No! No! which rang out from across the House. He was undisturbed. "Yes, far greater," he

21. *Works,* VIII, 27.

insisted. "Answer me, if you can. But do not interrupt me. On this point, indeed, it is much easier to interrupt than to answer. For who can answer plain arithmetical demonstration? Under the present system, Manchester, with 200,000 inhabitants, has no members. Old Sarum, with no inhabitants, has two members." With that bit of fairly devastating extempore evidence, he resumed his original argument.

He did not mean to contend, in any sense, that the present measure would function infallibly for all time. Another generation might find in it the same defects that the Whigs found in the old one. But what he wanted those who demurred to its provisions to keep clearly before them was the fact that change, too long postponed, unalterably leads to evils that prove unmanageable. "It was because the French aristocracy resisted reform in 1783, that they were unable to resist revolution in 1789." The time was ripe, the die cast, and while he wished to spread no unwarranted alarms among his audience, nevertheless he desired his audience to know that the people this time would be denied no longer their already too long withheld prerogatives. This measure he dared label a "Second Bill of Rights—a greater charter of the Liberties of England." Gentlemen murmured loudly at his phrase. But he sat down without changing it. Nor has posterity changed it.

Macaulay was to defend the Ministry's measure once more before it was sent up to the House of Lords. The occasion was the night of September 20, 1831, the second night of the debate on the motion that "the Reform Bill do pass." It was perhaps the least distinguished of the five addresses he delivered while that amply aired piece of legislation was in process of becoming law. Yet, at that, it was a speech that stands out brilliantly from those masses of verbiage in *Hansard* that record the cautious gropings of the British nation toward a reasonably democratic government.

He dealt mainly with two major Tory contentions—the contention that the Bill was dangerous since, if passed, it would bring into the House a body of desperate and illiterate legislators; and the contention that the Bill was futile, since the Upper Chamber, fearing the destruction of the peerage, would certainly throw it out. What did honorable members really mean in contending that this measure was designed to turn over to low, fierce, and desperate men the task of running the government of England—"men who will turn the House into a beer garden, and who will try to turn the monarchy into a republic, mere agitators without honor, without sense, without education, without the feelings or the manners of gentlemen"?[22] Such arguments represented the views of alarmists who were ignorant of history. Having uttered in effect, this plain statement, Macaulay proceeded to establish it by citing instance after instance to support the proposition that during the last half century those members of Parliament who had been actually *elected* to their seats— men like Fox, Sheridan, Tierney, and Sir Samuel Romilly— had been distinguished primarily by their high-minded devotion to statesmanship. There was not a rabble rouser among them. He proceeded to explain to his audience a principle of English government which, three decades later, Walter Bagehot was to make the thesis of his able work on the *English Constitution*. It was the principle of deference. The basis "of all representative government," Macaulay declared, "is that men who do not judge well of public affairs may be quite competent to choose others who will judge better."[23]

And as for the Lords, who have been enjoined by despairing Tories in the House of Commons to crush this savage attack on the country's institutions, let them be lessoned by what has happened across the channel, in France. Have their Lordships never walked by those stately mansions, "now sinking into decay and portioned out as lodging rooms, which line the silent streets of the Faubourg St. Germain? Have they never seen the ruins of these castles whose terraces and gardens overhang the Loire? Have they never heard that from those

22. On this entire speech see *Works*, VIII, 26-38.
23. *Works*, VIII, 41-42.

magnificent hotels, from those ancient castles, an aristocracy as splendid, as brave, as proud, as accomplished as ever Europe saw, was driven forth to exile and beggary, to implore the charity of hostile governments and hostile creeds, to cut wood in the back settlements of America, or to teach French in the schoolrooms of London? And why were those haughty nobles destroyed with an utter destruction? Why were they scattered over the face of the earth, their titles abolished, their escutcheons defaced, their parks wasted, their palaces unmantled, their heritage given to strangers? Because they had no sympathy with the people, no discernment of the signs of their time."[24] He concluded by saying what, in simplified terms, meant this: he believed their Lordships were, though not overburdened with mental discernment, at least not so stupid as to invite upon themselves, through rejecting the Bill, a fate such as he had just described. And when he sat down, amid cheers that rang continuously through the narrow chamber, there were those present, Tories venerable with age, who felt that here was the spirit of Edmund Burke returned again to Parliament, though a Burke seated this time on the sinister side of the House.

The Bill finally passed the Commons, but the Lords proved more stupid than Macaulay had suspected. They threw it out, by a majority of 41 votes. Members of the House, however, were not dismayed. They recognized, what Macaulay had plainly stated already, that though "we are bound to respect the constitutional rights of the Peers. . . . we are bound also not to forget our own." A resolution was accordingly read and debated in the Commons two days after the action of the Lords of October 7, a resolution which pledged continued allegiance to the principles of the measure and to the Ministry.

Macaulay was one of the first to defend this resolution. He argued that theirs was an independent body, a body that should not be intimidated by the action of any Peerage.

24. *Ibid.*, VIII, 43.

Theirs was a body, moreover, fully as competent as the nobility to legislate in the best interests of the nation. The issue now drawn was perfectly clear: the will of the majority was being thwarted by the blind instincts of a small but entrenched group. Did not those men who composed that group know that no law was really valid or enforceable "till public opinion breathes the breath of life into the dead letter?" [25] He called upon history, that servant who so readily obeyed his will, in convincing support of what he argued. The Libel Act of 1819 was passed over popular protest and, as a result, no magistrate dared enforce it. The principle worked both ways. What faced the country now was plain: It must be governed either by public opinion or "by the sword." Those who had spoken in fear of the fatal predicament of mob rule were now being brought face to face with their dread. *The mob shall rule,* if the will of the Peerage wins the deference it is so stubbornly seeking.

He spoke once more on this question the sixteenth of December. The Bill which he defended this time was not identical with the one the Ministry had first submitted, though essentially little had been altered. What changes had been made were designed to meet a few reasonable but minor objections which certain "wavering" Lords had raised to it. The new measure, in other words, gave those waverers an opportunity to save their faces. [26]

Of course, there was little at this stage to be added to what had already been said, either in favor of reform or against it. Macaulay realized this fact perfectly well, and contented himself principally with summarizing his previous arguments, with disposing of the chronic objections of those who sat on the benches opposite, and with paying a glowing tribute to the "middle orders of Britain." Part of that tribute is worth recalling, since the sentiments it contained represented convictions which he never gave up. He had dedicated himself,

25. *Ibid.,* VIII, 50.
26. See G. M. Trevelyan, *British History in the Nineteenth Century,* p. 239.

he said, to the support of that party which had stood from its inception for temperance and sanity in public affairs. "That party is the middle class of England, with the flower of aristocracy at its head, and the flower of the working class bringing up its rear. That great party has taken its immovable stand between the enemies of all order and the enemies of all liberty. It will have reform; it will not have revolution; it will destroy political abuses; it will not suffer the rights of property to be assailed; it will preserve, in spite of themselves, those who are assailing it, from the right and from the left; it will be a daysman between them: it will lay its hands upon them both; it will not suffer them to tear each other in pieces. While that great party continues unbroken, as now it is unbroken, I shall not relinquish the hope that this great contest may be conducted by lawful means, to a happy termination." [27]

That hope was fulfilled, as every one knows: the happy termination did come, as he had predicted. The amended Bill passed the Commons quickly and, in April, 1832, it passed its second reading in the House of Lords by a majority of nine. A last and desperate effort was made by certain Peers to weaken it radically in Committee, but their threat was stopped in May by an equally desperate threat of King William. His Majesty, now actually convinced that civil war was imminent, announced his intention to "pack" the Peerage. He would create a sufficient number of new and liberal lords to assure its success in the Upper House. Their Lordships gave in, and the measure became law.

3

It is probably safe to say that by the time the new law was passed, Macaulay was one of the best known Whigs in Parliament. He had been of distinct service to the Ministry. He had brought to its support a variety of talents, an intellectual genius, which made even his Tory opponents forget that his

27. *Works*, VIII, 72.

family name was undistinguished in English History. True to his own ambitions, he had singled out the remarks of the outstanding members of the opposition in his attacks on what he sincerely regarded as an outworn and decadent political philosophy. J. W. Croker had been called to task for certain utterances, and Sir Robert Peel had been compelled to explain, as best he could, his parliamentary inconsistencies of the past decade. And though both of these men were his superiors in debate—thanks to the experience of many years—neither was his equal in the telling phrase or in the overwhelmingly brilliant general effect.

Macaulay's delivery was in part responsible. As we have seen, it was sustained and loud; it was not very pleasing to hear. There was a lack of variety about it which left, usually, the impression of coldness. One felt, somehow, that the whole speech had been memorized beforehand, was merely being declaimed in one's presence. But what an intellectual stimulant it was to listen to! With what consummate mastery did he range throughout those endless fields of literature and history, plucking the most appropriate evidence to sustain his case! It was like reviewing the whole of one's past education—including those lessons one had never quite learned. And how rapidly it was all set forth! There was scarcely a pause from beginning to end; one could not nod a moment without missing something valuable. Here was a man who had not only, it seemed, taken all knowledge to be his province, but who managed to keep that knowledge at his tongue's end. It was little wonder that, almost from his first speech in the House, something resembling a rush from the smoking rooms to the benches took place whenever it was whispered that Mr. Macaulay was on his legs. Men know that remarks well worth hearing were in store for them.

Thus far—that is, by 1832—the gentleman for Calne had outlined a philosophy of government that was simple enough. His views, condensed, implied the conviction merely that those citizens who had amassed a fair amount of property should be permitted to participate in the business of government. The major responsibility of government, indeed, was the protection of the property rights of such individuals. They were, as their station in the economic world amply testified, thrifty and industrious people, solid and sane and temperate in judgment, in short, the element upon which the security of the nation was built. Their interests, moreover, were so central that they affected the interests of that class above them, the aristocracy, and that other more restless and dangerous element below them. When the middle class merchant was prosperous, that is, the working man would be prosperous too.

Macaulay, to the day of his death, never understood why this last fact was so difficult to grasp, or why, at any rate, the "lower orders" refused to be content with what it implied. For all his talk about the changing nature of society, and of government, he never seems to have allowed for a time when that government would have to admit those "lower orders" to a share in legislation. Unless they possess tangible wealth— the sort government is consecrated to protect—men, he felt, cannot be trusted to legislate. They will unbalance budgets; they will favor their own class and penalize other classes; they will forget the welfare of the whole, the remembering of which is the first rule of statesmanship.

But he could never comprehend that labor itself—the ability to work, one's manual or technical skill—may also be a kind of property; and that being so, a kind for which an economic class is justified in demanding protection. This, and such like considerations, not being immediately pressing, he brushed comfortably aside. They were, he felt, the problems of theorists, of hair-brained philosophers; and Swift, in the third voyage of Gulliver, had disposed of them all for good.

VIII. Hater

N O MAN could reach the literary and political eminence which Macaulay achieved by the time of his thirty-second year without making enemies. To many frailties of human nature he had already proved himself an exception, but not to this. Yet the fact bothered him very little, if at all. One of the best haters of his century, he had already learned to endure the hatred of others with indifference. In all the entries of his copious *Journals*, entries written for no eye to read, not one bears evidence of the least regret that this or the other contemporary had apparently found little if anything to admire in him. He returned indifference or disparagement with contempt. Too often, perhaps, he was contemptuous gratuitously. He was a man, as we shall see, who set up his own standards of rectitude, judging his fellows invariably in terms of whether they found those standards acceptable. It was his Clapham background, flowering out at length into a narrow censoriousness that was blinding him permanently to any generous understanding of the complexities of human nature.

One of these contemporaries, whom he hated with a passion almost more than mortal, was a gentleman twenty-two years his senior, Henry Brougham. Brougham had already distinguished himself as a Whig when Macaulay was still lying before his mother's hearth, engrossed with a slice of buttered bread and a copy of *Paradise Lost*. Educated at Edinburgh, a pupil of Dugald Stewart, he had come down to London in

1805, even then fairly well esteemed as one of the founders of the exciting Whig review. At the age of thirty-one, in 1809, he had entered the House of Commons; and before very long men were beginning to look to him for leadership whenever the questions of mass education or the emancipation of slaves obtruded momentarily amid the more absorbing issue of war.

In truth he was a restless figure, burning inwardly with ambitions too dispersed for any single position of eminence to allay. He must have a hand, and a directing hand, in everything! By the time Macaulay received his Trinity Fellowship, Brougham was probably the most popular person in England, thanks to his brilliant defense of Queen Caroline against the outrageous charges of immorality which had been brought against her by her outrageously immoral husband, George IV. A long gaunt figure with an unforgettable profile, a "formidable" eye, and a trumpet shaped nose that twitched continually, he was the type of person whom his contemporaries never tired of wondering about. The plain clue to his conduct, one English critic remarked, was that he was "the maddest man who has taken part in the public life of this country."[1] There was insanity in his family, it was often recalled, especially when as Lord Chancellor he was found playing hide and seek with the great seal of England, or indulging in a game of leap frog with the children of some noble lord.

Brougham seems to have noticed Macaulay first on the occasion of the anti-slavery meeting in 1824. With Zachary he had for some years been friendly; they thought almost as one on the subject of abolition. Shortly after this meeting, he had offered Zachary advice, we recall, about the course his son should pursue if he desired to prepare himself for the Bar. Several years passed. Macaulay began his career with the *Edinburgh Review*. It was then, by his own story, that Brougham began to see in the younger man a threat to his own authority and popularity as a writer for the magazine—and it was a

1. Lloyd Sanders, *op. cit.*, 278.

threat which his implacable vanity would not suffer him to endure.

The details of this relationship during the next several years have been best recorded by Macaulay's sister Margaret. On November 27, 1831, she took a long walk with her brother, during which time the "conversation turned entirely on one subject,"[2] the subject being Lord Brougham, then so formidable a figure in English politics that the retiring young lady would not "venture to write his name," even in a private journal. "I asked Tom when the present coolness between them began. He said, 'Nothing could exceed my respect and admiration for him in early days. I saw at that time private letters in which he spoke highly of my articles, and of me as the most rising man of the time. After a while, however, I began to remark that he became extremely cold to me, hardly ever spoke to me on circuit [they traveled the northern circuit together], and treated me with marked slight. If I were talking to a man, if he wished to speak to him on politics or anything else that was not in any sense a private matter, he always drew him away from me, instead of addressing us both. When my article on Hallam came out [in the Fall of 1828], he complained to Jeffrey that I took too much of the *Review;* and when my first article on Mill appeared, he foamed with rage and was very angry with Jeffrey for having printed it.'

" 'But,' said I, 'the Mills are friends of his, and he naturally did not like them to be attacked.'

" 'On the contrary,' said Tom, 'he attacked them fiercely himself; but he thought I had made a hit, and was angry accordingly. When a friend of mine defended my articles to him, he said, "I know nothing of the articles. I have not read Macaulay's articles." What can be imagined more absurd than his keeping up an angry correspondence with Jeffrey about articles he has never read? Well, the next thing was that Jeffrey, who was about to give up the editorship, asked

2. See G. O. Trevelyan, *op. cit.*, I, 173-75. The whereabouts of Margaret Macaulay's Journal is unknown, according to her great nephew, G. M. Trevelyan.

if I would take it. I said I would gladly do so, if they would remove the headquarters of the Review to London. Jeffrey wrote to him about it. He disapproved of it so strongly that the plan was given up. The truth was that he felt that his power over the Review diminished as mine increased, and he saw that he would have little indeed, if I were editor.' "

Macaulay then entered Parliament. Brougham had opposed Lord Lansdowne's selection from the first, feeling, perhaps rightly, that Mr. Charles Denman, who as Solicitor General had aided him during the trial of Queen Caroline, deserved the place far more than the young Trinity graduate. " 'I do not complain,' " Macaulay continued to his sister, " 'that he should have preferred Denman's claims to mine. . . . I went to take my seat. As I turned from the table at which I had been taking the oaths, he stood as near to me as you do now, and he cut me dead. We never spoke in the House, excepting once, as I can remember, when a few words passed between us in the lobby. I have sat close to him when many men of whom I knew nothing have introduced themselves to me to shake hands, and congratulated me after making a speech, and he has never said a single word. I know that it is jealousy, because I am not the first man whom he has used in this way. . . .

" 'He is, next to the King, the most popular man in England. There is no other man whose entrance into any town in the kingdom would be so certain to be accompanied with huzzaing and the taking off of horses. At the same time he is in a very ticklish situation, for he has no real friends. Jeffrey, Sydney Smith, Mackintosh, all speak of him as I speak to you. I was talking to Sydney Smith of him the other day, and said that, great as I felt his faults to be, I must allow him a real desire to raise the lower orders, and do good by education, and those methods upon which his heart has always been set. Sydney would not allow this, or any other merit.' "[3]

This portrait of his contemporary Macaulay sketched for his

3. G. O. Trevelyan, *op. cit.*, I, 175.

sister has about it an air of injured virtue that is deceptive. Apparently no more than the simplest record of certain facts, its total impression is grossly misleading. It is notable, like so many of his later portraits, mainly for its suppressions. Read by itself, for example, one could scarcely guess that it was Brougham who, guided by the genius of Bentham, pushed through a stubborn House the earliest legal reforms of the century. One would scarcely guess, again, that before his defense of the Queen had made him popular, he had already jeopardized his political future by defending Leigh and John Hunt against the charge of sedition, a charge brought against the two editors for printing in the *Examiner* an account of a British soldier who was punished with a thousand lashes. The portrait leaves out, too, rather unworthily, the genuine devotion which Brougham felt continuously for Macaulay's father, a devotion which led him to say, at the funeral of Henry Thornton, that the lives of such men as Thornton and Zachary were what made him "realize that there was more in Christianity than the Edinburgh wits had dreamed of." [4]

It leaves out, still further, such a detail as the following, the rumor of which at least must have reached Macaulay in one way or another, before he unburdened his mind to Margaret: In 1827 Brougham had written Lord Lyndhurst, the newly appointed Chancellor: "Let me strongly advise you to give an early token of your favor to young Macaulay. He is the greatest genius now coming into the profession. Make him at once Commissioner of Bankruptcy." [5] And Lyndhurst did just this, at a time when any kind of position was welcome.

There was also the case of Macaulay's brother, Henry. Only as far back as December 4, 1830, Tom had written to MacVey Napier of the *Review* a note confessing that he was "in high good humour" with Brougham. "He has given my brother a living of £300 a year, without the least solicitation, direct or

4. Viscountess Knutsford, *op. cit.*, 481-82.
5. G. T. Garrett, *Lord Brougham* (London, 1935), 216-17.

indirect. It was the first living he had to give, and nothing could have been done more handsomely!"[6]

The plain fact is that, whether deliberately or not, Macaulay failed to be honest with his sister. It was not Brougham's cutting him dead that lay back of his dislike, a dislike that soon became, and remained to his death, an unjust but implacable hatred. The cause was, rather, an incident in itself insignificant enough, though important because it reveals with such emphasis the irresponsibility of the elder man and the inflexible pride of the younger:

The French Revolution of 1830 was an event from which the Whigs felt a good many timely lessons might be drawn. Who, in England, should point those lessons, fraught as they were with so many warnings to governments that delayed too long the enactment of badly needed reforms? Macaulay appears to have thought of the opportunity first. He would go to France, study the causes which led to the overthrow of the monarchy, and write an article which the *Edinburgh Review* would feature. It would enhance his own standing among reformers, and it would strengthen the cause of his party. He informed Napier of his ideas on the subject. Napier was delighted. Macaulay thereupon made a short trip to France and was apparently busy with a lengthy essay when Napier received the following note from Brougham:

"I must beg, and indeed make a point of giving my thoughts on the Revolution [of 1830], and, therefore, pray send off your countermand to Macaulay. The reason is this: all our movements next session turn on that pivot; and I can trust no one but myself with it, either in or out of Parliament. . . . I have already begun my article, and it is of greatest importance that it should stand at the head."[7]

What could the new editor do? The order he received—for it was nothing less—came from one of the founders of the magazine, from a man who had written for it constantly for

6. *Selections from the Correspondence of MacVey Napier* (ed. by his son, MacVey Napier, London, 1879), 99.
7. *Ibid.*, letter of September 8, 1830.

more than a quarter of a century, a man who was soon to be named Lord Chancellor of England, and who had already, for a full decade, enjoyed the reputation of one of the two most popular public men in the country. Napier did as he was told. He apologized to Macaulay at great length, but in the end the article was countermanded.

Macaulay was furious. He let the editor know plainly that he would endure no such relationship with any magazine. He had been put to considerable expense and time to gather his material. He had refused at least one definite offer to write for a rival publication. Mr. Napier should realize that the subject was a timely one; it must be treated now or not at all. Mr. Napier must also make up his mind whether he is to manage the magazine himself, or whether he intends to make it exclusively an organ devoted to publishing the vagaries of the unpredictable Mr. Brougham.[8]

Brougham's was, of course, the article which finally came out. It was entitled "The Late Revolution in France," and as he had requested, it was the opening essay. Also by Mr. Brougham were numbers eight, eleven and thirteen, treating respectively such various topics as "Allen on the Royal Prerogative in England," "Galt's Life of Lord Byron," and "The General Election and the Ministry." For this displacement Macaulay never forgave him. All other affronts hereafter seemed to the younger man but new appendages to that old injustice. And yet, to Brougham's never resting, disordered mind, it was an incident soon buried and forgotten in an infinity of other incidents progressively more important.

2

John Wilson Croker was no personal friend of any member of Macaulay's family. Tom knew, naturally, that he had been for years a regular contributor to the *Quarterly Review*, that Tory publication which had set itself up as a rival to the *Edin-*

8. *Ibid.*, letter of September 16, 1830.

burgh. He knew that under the Tory administration Croker had served as Secretary of the Admiralty. He also knew, or found out very soon, that in the entire House of Commons there was no one except Lord Althorp and Lord John Russell himself who understood the terms of the Reform Bill as thoroughly as this Tory did. The aged Brougham, writing long after both Macaulay and this rival were dead, confessed as much when he called Croker "a most important person in opposition. Nothing could exceed his ability and his thorough knowledge of his subject. He made but one error—committing all his objections to writing and print . . . . and by this we largely profited. Althorp's knowledge of the Reform Bill and Croker's were the two wonders of the day; but Croker debated far better, though with less weight. Althorp muzzled all his party on finding that they, being unacquainted with the details, were perpetually getting him and them in scrapes, Croker watching the sight of the Whig officials unable to explain their own Bill." His talents, Brougham confesses, "were of a very high order, and have not, I think, been sufficiently allowed. He was also a man of great personal kindness to his friends, though a good hater to his enemies, and so much devoted to his opinions that he voluntarily retired from Parliament as soon as the Reform Bill passed, and never returned."[9]

What were those opinions which Croker held so tenaciously —so tenaciously, indeed, that when overwhelmed by other opinions, he chose withdrawal from a debased House to compromise? For one thing, he was fully convinced that the Reform Bill was a step deliberately calculated to place power in the hands of the mob. How else could one reason, he wanted to know, when its provisions catered so obviously to the desires of those people who had led riots in the principal cities, or who had burned ricks throughout the country districts in the name of that savage abstraction, Captain Swing? As for the people in general, this stubborn Tory went on, they were not

9. *Life and Times of Henry, Lord Brougham* (Edinburgh, 1871), III, 498-99.

impatient for reform. Consider the evidence! In 1821, only nineteen petitions were submitted to the House of Commons requesting a basic change in the government. In 1822 there were twelve; in 1823, there were but twenty-nine. And from that date until 1830, a period of seven years, *not one petition had been submitted*. Even in 1830 only fourteen were brought to the attention of Parliament.

Then, Mr. Croker pointed out, a very remarkable thing happened. Parliament was dissolved. And before it could be reconvened, 650 petitions for reform were dumped on the cluttered table of the speaker. Why this sudden and unpredictable shift in popular sentiment? The answer was almost too obvious for comment: the Whigs and their radical friends had been at work, stirring up a contented people to dissatisfaction and to threats of violence. It remained for honorable members to decide whether they would yield to clamors so artificially provoked.[10]

It is true that Croker had been "taken in" about the nature of the Bill, as had, indeed, practically every other Tory. A week before Lord Russell introduced the measure, he reported to a friend that the leading Tories had recently met at the home of Sir Robert Peel and had decided to allow the measure "to make its appearance without serious resistance. Many will concur to turn it out," he added, "who are not ready to shut the door in its face."[11] But this note was written before Croker's friends had any suspicion of the desperate terms of the measure. After it was read the first time, his fears for the future of his country were extreme. "If it is carried," he wrote a friend, "England, no doubt, will still be great and happy; but it will be under a *different* form of constitution and administration from that which has raised her to her present greatness and happiness. No king, no lords, no inequalities in the social system; all will be levelled to the plane of the petty shopkeepers and small farmers. This, perhaps, not with-

10. Speech of March 4, 1831. See L. J. Jennings, *Croker Papers*, II, 95-116.
11. *Ibid.*, II, 108.

out bloodshed, but certainly by confiscations and persecutions. 'Tis inevitable, and this to be perpetrated by a set of men like Lambton and Johnny Russell whom a club in Regent Street would not trust with the management of their concerns."

Shortly after these sentiments were set forth [and while Croker was going about the halls of Parliament greeting his Whig acquaintances as "Citizen Russell" or "Citizen Churchill"], Macaulay made the speech in which occurred his extensive reference to the French Revolution. The Tories, he had said in effect, had been fairly warned by history. Let them give way before the irresistible demands of the people, lest justice, too long delayed, sweep them forever from the citadels of power.

This high sounding bluff was entirely too much for Croker. He proceeded to reply to Macaulay, immediately, in a speech that lasted for more than an hour. It was a smooth reply, and in some respects it was unanswerable. Without doubt it constituted the most thorough lecture on history that Macaulay ever was forced to sit through.

Croker began with a tribute to Macaulay's eloquence. Yet he thought it rather remarkable, he confessed, to see a young man being pushed forward so rapidly and to such dizzy heights by the Whigs. It seemed odd, to him, that the important duty of defending their abortive bill was being left largely "to a gentleman who has never yet appeared in political office and who, notwithstanding his great talents, has hitherto had little opportunity of displaying them, except in the humble station of a practicing barrister." But he would not be misunderstood. Unseasoned as they were, Mr. Macaulay's talents had already put to shame all the talents of His Majesty's Ministry combined.

He turned then to Mr. Macaulay's historical argument, to the elaborate parallel he had drawn between the English Tories and the Aristocrats of eighteenth century France. "Good God, sir," he exclaimed to the chairman, "where has the learned gentleman lived—what works must he have read —with what authorities must he have communed, when he attributes the downfall of the French nobility to an injudicious and obstinate resistance to popular opinion. The direct reverse is the notorious fact—so notorious that it is one of the commonplaces of modern history.[12]

"Allow me, sir, to inform the learned gentleman for Calne. . . ." And on Mr. Croker went, ably, and with infinite patience, lecturing his opponent on a subject upon which Mr. Macaulay had seemed but an hour before so completely the master. The rising young English historian was compelled, in other words, to listen to a good deal more than he had anticipated. It is doubtful whether he ever found out that Croker was himself an authority on the French Revolution, having translated from the French a valuable work on the subject while Macaulay was still an industrious scholar at Cambridge.[13]

Yet Croker's triumph was brief. Macaulay had already condensed his wrath against his imperious enemy in the form of a review of Croker's edition of Boswell's *Life of Johnson*. That review was now in the presses. "See," he had written his sister Hannah, "whether I do not dust that varlet's jacket for him in the next number of the *Blue and Yellow*.[14] I detest him more than cold boiled veal."

That review came out in late September, and it revealed Macaulay at his best, and worst. All of the bitter vituperations and unqualified denunciations which had characterized the outstanding critical essays of the century were apparent in it, in epitome. Jeffrey had set the style more than a quarter of a century before, when first had swum into his ken the innocent ruminations of Wordsworth. Byron, in 1808, had condemned that style, vainly, in *English Bards and Scotch Reviewers*. It had gone on, year by year, gaining strength and

12. See the *Speech of the Rt. Hon. John Wilson Croker on the Question that the Reform Bill Do Pass* (9-22-31), London, John Murray, 1831.
13. G. W. Croker, trans., *Royal Memoirs*, or *The French Revolution* (London, 1823).
14. A frequent name, in Macaulay's correspondence, for the *Edinburgh Review*, a reference, of course, to its cover. See G. O. Trevelyan, *op. cit.*, I, 218.

emphasis, had gone on indeed until it fell upon the early work of Keats with a force so devastating, thought Shelley and Byron, that it had brought that poet to an untimely grave. Croker himself, ironically enough, had written that savage review of *Endymion*. Now its savagery was returning upon him with a fury augmented tenfold.

Although the substance of Macaulay's essays will be treated in another place, this one must be noticed now, since from it stemmed a mutual hatred that colored all their later opinions of each other. Macaulay's introduction was savage: "This work," he began, "has greatly disappointed us. Whatever faults we may have been prepared to find in it, we fully expected that it would be a valuable addition to English Literature; that it would contain many curious facts, and many judicious remarks; that the style of the notes would be neat, clear, and precise; and the typographical execution would be, as in new editions of classical works it ought to be, almost faultless. We are sorry to be obliged to say that the merits of Mr. Croker's performance are on a par with those of a certain leg of mutton on which Dr. Johnson dined, while traveling from London to Oxford, and which he, with characteristic energy, pronounced to be 'as bad as bad could be, ill fed, ill killed, ill kept, and ill dressed.' This edition is ill compiled, ill arranged, ill written, and ill printed."[15]

This was merely the beginning. He went on to speak of Mr. Croker's "ignorance and carelessness" with respect both to facts and dates, to declare that many of his blunders one would be surprised to hear an educated person commit even in conversation: "The notes absolutely swarm with misstatements into which the editor never would have fallen, if he had taken the slightest pains to investigate the truth of his assertions." Then came what looked like a really impressive array of evidence. Date after date and fact after fact were quoted from Croker, held up for ridicule, and then correctly stated by his reviewer. Macaulay's language was never more savage:

15. *Works*, V, 498.

"There is not a forward boy in England who does not know that," or "Can Mr. Croker possibly be ignorant that," or Mr. Croker's statements appear "utterly frivolous," or "Mr. Croker has shown a degree of inaccuracy, or, to speak more properly, a degree of ignorance, hardly credible"—such statements are typical. The learned reviewer appears, by turns, patient, condescending, amazed, disgusted. He concludes his references to the editor by declaring: "We will not multiply instances of this scandalous inaccuracy. It is clear that a writer who, even when warned by the text on which he is commenting, falls into such mistakes as these, is entitled to no confidence whatever." [16] Croker was paying, with usury, the price for leadership in the Tory party.

Yet Macaulay was not allowed to escape unanswered. *Blackwood's* was ready in its next issue with a reply, honestly set forth, with Macaulay's remarks and those of his critic printed in parallel columns. What, it wanted to know, had Mr. Macaulay's imposing list of citations and sacrifices of Truth to Brilliancy amounted to? Lumped together, the evidence meant that Croker had been charged with "gross and scandalous inaccuracy," for having, in three cases, assigned the wrong dates to the deaths of as many minor figures mentioned in the biography. These, the *Blackwood's* author declares, "were errors of the presses." Three other errors, all of them trivial, Mr. Croker had indeed committed: "He attributed to Henry Bate Dudley, the Fighting Parson, the editorship of the old Morning *Herald*, instead of the old Morning *Post;* and he has erroneously said that Burgoyne's surrender at Saratoga took place in March, 1788, instead of October, 1777. He is mistaken, too, in saying that Lord Townsend was not Secretary of State until 1720." He was Secretary in 1714, and was called to office again at the later date. This was the aggregate of the real misstatements in the edition. Yet the perpetration of them "has so incensed the immaculate and infallible reviewer that he has not scrupled to assert that the

16. *Ibid.*, V, 505.

whole of Mr. Croker's part of the work is 'ill compiled, ill arranged, ill expressed, and ill printed.' "[17]

As for the parallel quotations and replies, they do indeed put Macaulay's intellectual integrity in this case under grave doubt. The following specimen will serve to indicate their effect:

MACAULAY.—"In one place we are told that Allan Ramsey, the painter, was born in 1709, and died in 1784; in another, that he died in 1784, in the seventy-first year of his age. If the latter statement be correct, he must have been born in or about 1713."

ANSWER.—"This is but a dishonest trick of his reviewer. The age is indeed stated differently in the two notes; but one note is Mr. Croker's, and one is Mr. Boswell's. Mr. Boswell states colloquially that 'Allan Ramsay died in 1784, in his seventy-first year'; Mr. Croker states, with more precision, that 'he was born in 1709, and died in 1784.' And Mr. Croker is right."[18]

One other example must suffice:

MACAULAY.—"Croker says the Marquess of Montrose was beheaded at Edinburgh. There is not a forward boy in any school in England who does not know that Montrose was hanged."

ANSWER.—"Montrose was both *hanged* and *beheaded;* the beheading incident really is one of the most striking passages in Clarendon. This was Mr. Croker's reason for stressing it."

The most serious inadequacy in Macaulay's review this article failed to touch upon. It was the fact that the young Whig entirely ignored Croker's really unique work in the edition; for Croker had written a number of elderly gentlemen who still had personal recollections of Dr. Johnson, and persuaded them to set down the incidents they remembered or had heard about. Tom Moore, Isaac Disraeli, James Mackintosh, Sir Henry Ellis, the Duke of Wellington, Lord Eldon,

17. See *Answer to Mr. Macaulay's Criticism in the "Edinburgh Review" on Mr. Croker's Edition of Boswell's Life of Johnson* (selected from *Blackwoods*) (London, 1856), 14.
18. *Ibid.*, 3.

Walter Scott—they were all helpful, contributing "hundreds of notes" which, but for Croker's timely interest, would soon have been irrevocably lost. Scott, for example, mentioned one that, if not well known, is none-the-less invaluable. It had to do with the only personal interview which ever took place between Adam Smith, the famous economist, and Johnson. The two men were no sooner introduced than Johnson began to question certain facts in Smith's well-known letter on the death of Hume. Smith proceeded to justify himself. "You lie!" shouted Johnson. "You are a son of a bitch," returned Smith, and walked out. "On such terms," declares Sir Walter, "did these two great moralists meet and part, and such was the classic dialogue between them."[19]

Such editorial details as these the Whig reviewer overlooked. They could not serve his purpose. That purpose—conceived one feels, the moment the book came from the presses—was to damn Croker, to make him appear ridiculous, and by so doing, to fling a final odium upon the waning cause he represented. His brilliant style was being made to serve now, not the imperious goddess of Truth who had blessed him at his birth after all other goddesses had passed him by; it was being brought to serve a purpose much less disinterested and less final.

But Macaulay was content. Every one was reading his article, while the "feeble" reply to it was being hawked about, unnoticed or disdained. And the bitterness of the old Tory was not concealed. He had worked with great patience to bring out his edition, and Macaulay in one stroke had demolished it. "Croker," he wrote his sister in triumph, "looks across the House of Commons at me with a leer of hatred which I repay with a gracious smile of pity."[20]

19. Scott to Croker (January 30, 1829), *Croker Papers*, I, 46.
20. G. O. Trevelyan, *op. cit.*, I, 225.

This hatred of Brougham and Croker was not to be allayed by time, for Macaulay did not grow mellow or charitable with the advancing years. As we shall see, he grew, if anything, even more savagely hostile and contemptuous toward all men whose opinions did not square with his own. Self righteousness settled about him in marble and impenetrable folds. He never admitted to a fault or to a mistake. Rarely, if at all, did he admit even to a doubt. Such confidence in his own unswerving rectitude blinded him increasingly to many of the subtleties of human nature, subtleties which might have given him pause, had not a well nigh infallible memory misled him into thinking that the bare feat of accurate recalling was synonymous with the ability to judge with fairness and honesty. Too many times did the reverse prove true. For Macaulay seldom bothered to recall anything except for the purpose of using it in an argument, or on some similar occasion during which the desire to refute an antagonist displaced all other desires, both high and low.

His subsequent relations with Brougham ran through the above-named unfortunate course. Apparently he shared with his new friends at Holland House the belief that Brougham was too much of an individualist to be trusted within the closest deliberations of his party. One could never tell what he would do, or into what violations of good political strategy his restless appetite for individual acclamation would lead him.[21] Moreover, the great advocate and law reformer was not so well born as he might have been! He seemed not quite acceptable socially![22] At all events, something like a verbal feud went on between the two men for the next quarter of a century. And as might have been expected, the intermediary in this feud, the gentleman to whom each addressed his opinions of the other, was MacVey Napier, of the *Review*.

21. Lord John Russell, *Recollections and Suggestions*, 138-40.
22. J. R. M. Butler, *Passing of the Great Reform Bill* (London, 1914), 261.

The year 1835 focused a good deal of this bitterness, and Macaulay, though then in India, shared in it, at least by indirection. Brougham had been left out of the new Melbourne Ministry, because, said the Prime Minister, of his "omniverous appetite for praise," his "perpetual interference in matters with which he has no direct concern," and, above all, because of his "disregard for truth."[23]

Brougham began from this date a busy correspondence with Napier. The question upon which he wished the editor to think as he did was that of the obligations of the magazine to the Whig Party. Should the *Edinburgh* follow, with blind servility, wherever a misguided Ministry might lead? Was the publication to have no independence at all? Brougham's contention was that it was founded on broad Whig principles, but that it was not obligated to support "any given Ministry *in toto.*" What he in particular wanted was the privilege to attack the government from time to time, if government fell into error. Napier disagreed. This was a time of crisis, he felt: the ministers needed support desperately now, and he meant to render it unreservedly. Brougham was bitter. "Professor Napier"—as he addressed him almost always in contemptuous moments—had sold out to Holland House; and from that point he moved to other points more particular still, to calling over the names of those whom Holland House favored, and to damning them variously, one by one.

In Macaulay's case, he complained of his style. His work is invariably that of a clever young man. But it is far too prolix. Every essay would be helped if it were cut in two. He is too garrulous, can never resist a digression. Napier defended his most brilliant contributor with an unwonted tartness: he is unselfish. "His assistance to the review is invaluable."

"My dear Sir," replied Brougham, who was by this time disgusted with such over praise. "As to Macaulay, I only know that he left his party—which had twice given him seats

23. Russell, *op. cit.*, 140.

in Parliament for nothing—while they were laboring for want of hands in Parliament, and jumped at promotion and gain in India. But what think you of his never having called on me since his return? Yet I made him a Commissioner in Bankrupts in 1827, to the exclusion of my own brother. I gave his father a commissionership, to the exclusion of the Whig supporters, and I gave his brother a place in Africa to the exclusion of a friend of my own. Yet on returning from India he suffers his fears of giving offense at Holland House to prevent him from doing what he never feared to do when I was in office. As he is the second or third greatest bore in society I have ever known, and as I have little time to be bored, I do not at all lament it. But I certainly know that he is by others despised for it, as he is pretty sure one day to hear. That you have done anything very adventurous in encountering the wrath of the Macaulay party, I really do not much apprehend. That he has any better right to monopolize Lord Chatham [Macaulay and Brougham had both written essays on Chatham, and Napier had published Macaulay's] I more than doubt. That he would have done it better than I, I also doubt. For if truth, which he never is in search of, be better in History than turning sentences, and producing an effect of eternal paint and glitter, I am assured that the picture I have done, poor as it is, may stand by any he or his imitator Wm. Empson could have done.

"But that is a trifle. I only mention it to beg of you to pluck up a little courage, and not be alarmed every time any of the little knot of threateners annoys you. *They want to break off all kind of connection between me and the 'Edinburgh Review.'* I have seen it. . . . A *party* and a *personal* engine is all they want to make it."[24]

Napier tempered these strictures considerably and then passed them on to his favorite reviewer. The paradox latent in one section of Macaulay's reply is astonishing to this day. Napier had said nothing to him about Brougham's

24. *Napier Correspondence* (Brougham to Napier, July 4, 1838), 260-61.

estimate of his style. It is therefore remarkable indeed to read Macaulay's appraisal of the style of his antagonist, for nowhere can one find a better summary of his own virtues and defects as a writer. It reads as though, from some vantage point not granted him by time, Macaulay had looked down upon the body of his own work, and passed upon it all, for once, a frigidly impartial judgment. Brougham's late articles, he declared, have when compared with his early ones a merit unusually high. "They are, indeed, models of magazine writing as distinguished from other sorts of writing. They are not, I think, made for duration. Everything about them is exaggerated, incorrect, sketchy. All the characters are either too black or too fair. The passions of the writer do not suffer him even to maintain the decent appearance of impartiality. And the style, though striking and animated, will not bear examination through a single paragraph. But the effect of the first perusal is great: and few people read an article in a review twice. A bold, dashing, scene-painting manner is that which always succeeds best in magazine writing."[25]

Perhaps this estimate, applied to Macaulay's work, is too severe, a shade *too* frigid. After all, he is still read today, at least by students and by specialists in his age. One can never be quite sure. But on this circumstance there seems little doubt: that the first impression produced by his work is one of almost dazzling brilliance; that that impression wanes on second and third reading, since there are few complexities or nuances to sustain it; that Macaulay's characters are, mainly, figures without shadings; and that the polemic nature of his discussions is unmistakable and, at length, rigid and unconvincing. In an age of crumbling standards, in short, one feels that no one is quite justified in maintaining, on all occasions, a tone of infallibility.

He turned next to Brougham's complaint that he had not called on the former Lord Chancellor since returning from India. "As to Brougham's feelings toward myself, I know,

25. G. O. Trevelyan (Macaulay to Napier, July 20, 1838), *op. cit.*, II, 17.

and have known for a long time, that he hates me. If during the last ten years I have gained any reputation either in politics or in letters—if I have had any success in life—it has been without his help or countenance, and often in spite of his utmost exertions to keep me down. It is strange that he should be surprised at my not calling on him since my return. I did not call on him when I went away. When he was Chancellor, and I was in office, I never once attended his levee. It would be strange indeed if now, when he is squandering the remains of his public character in an attempt to ruin the party of which he was a member then, and of which I am a member still, I should begin to pay court to him. For the sake of the long intimacy which subsisted between him and my father, and of the mutual good offices which passed between them, I will not, unless I am compelled, make any public attack on him. But this is really the only tie which restrains me; for I neither love him nor fear him." [26]

The last statement is probably true. For one of the compensations of rectitude, to Macaulay, was that one's own acts could always be justified to the world. And what other fear, among civilized men, could ever arise to haunt a man's heart, except the fear of the world's knowing that within that heart there was something shamefully hidden? His conduct had been almost impeccable from birth. Now even his opinions were model ones. It was all something to be proud of. And Macaulay *was* proud; and also decidedly careful that those relationships upon which that pride was founded were never jeopardized by other relationships of a less exemplary nature. It was the sure way to fortune, and perhaps to a kind of fame.

But in his letters and his *Journal*, on the subject of Brougham, he continued to grumble and to vituperate. An acquaintance had seen Napier in the summer of 1838, and the report he brought back was wretched indeed. Napier was almost distracted, and the reason for his condition was, as usual, Brougham. He was persecuting the poor editor "with the

26. *Ibid.*, II, 18.

utmost malignity. I did not think it possible," Macaulay wrote his friend T. F. Ellis, "for human nature in an educated, civilized man—a man, too, of great intellect—to have become so depraved. He writes to Napier in language of the most savage hatred, and of the most extravagant vaunting. The Ministers, he says, have felt only his little finger. He will now put forth his red right hand. They shall have no rest. As to me, I shall rue my baseness in not calling on him." [27]

Then, suddenly, the air would clear; other prospects would absorb that restless mind, and Macaulay and all his company would fade into a now meaningless past. Five months after the above note was written, Macaulay and his friend Ellis, a barrister, were walking to Lincoln's Inn Fields when they met Brougham. It was an awkward moment. "But he greeted me just as if we had parted yesterday, shook hands, got between us, and walked with us some way." He talked vehemently about issues then pressing in politics, waving his hands, sputtering, and never waiting for a reply. "As we were walking, Allen the Quaker came by. Brougham halloed to him and began to urge him to get up the strongest opposition to Lord John Russell's education plan. I was glad when we parted." [28]

Then, a decade later—long after the two men had ceased to have any relationships in common—the great Jeffrey died, that editor who, in so many ways, had helped them both, to whom both were devoted. It was decided by certain of the famous Whig's friends that a subscription should be taken for the purpose of raising a monument in his honor. The historian Hallam met Macaulay and asked him to attend that meeting, which was to be held at Brougham's house. "I would not go. I will never enter Brougham's house. At Brook's met Dundas. He could not make up his mind to go to Brougham's and abused Richardson for fixing such a place for the meeting. I have little doubt that it is a trick of Brougham's." [29] Macaulay subscribed £20, but he did so by letter.

27. *Ibid.*, II, 21.
28. *Ibid.*, II, 49 (From Macaulay's *Journal*, February 13, 1839).
29. *Journal*, II, 333 (Entry of February 16, 1850).

There was one other entry, brief and dramatic, an entry embodying some of the most concentrated language Macaulay ever used. It was written the year before his death. "Saw Brougham. Strange fellow. His power's gone. His spite immortal. A dead nettle."[30] It was his farewell, as far as we know, to the man whom his father had esteemed as one of the foremost statesmen of the age, a man, moreover, to whom posterity is yet to do full justice.

Twelve years after Macaulay's death, this statesman, still vigorous and busy, published his memoirs under the title *The Life and Times of Henry Brougham, Written by Himself.* They appeared in three stout volumes, so copious in their explanations and allusions that one might almost call them a history of the first two thirds of the century. The book is interesting to us for another reason: in all its crowded pages, the name of T. B. Macaulay does not appear once.

His subsequent relations with Croker were almost identically unpleasant. That solid old Tory, it will be recalled, resigned his seat in Parliament when the Reform Bill was passed, and never afterwards sought to return. The country, he thought, was politically going to the devil. But Macaulay did not forget the lecture he had been forced to listen to on the subject of the French Revolution, nor did Croker forget the Whig's review of his edition of the Life of Johnson.

Nothing happened for eleven years. Macaulay departed for India to make his fortune, and Croker retired to his country seat to meditate upon the disappearance of the old England he loved and had sought to preserve.

Then, in 1843, Macaulay got wind of a bit of gossip about his old enemy. "In a singularly powerful letter," writes G. O. Trevelyan, Macaulay recited "in detail, certain unsavory portions of that gentleman's private life which were not only part of the stock gossip of every bow-window in St. James's Street, but which had been brought into the light of day in

30. Quoted in W. E. Gladstone, *Gleanings of Past Years*, which contains an estimate of Macaulay reprinted in the Everyman Edition of his *Speeches*, xiii.

the course either of Parliamentary or judicial investigations. After illustrating these transactions with evidence which proved that he did not take up an antipathy on hearsay, Macaulay comments on them in such terms as clearly indicate that his animosity to Croker arose from incompatibility of moral sentiments, and not of political opinions. He then proceeds to remark on 'the scandals of Croker's literary life'; 'his ferocious insults to women, to Lady Morgan, Mrs. Austin, and others'; his twitting Harriet Martineau with deafness; his twitting Madame D'Arblay with concealing her age. 'I might add,' he says, 'a hundred other charges.' "[31]

He might indeed. For Macaulay, when his enemies were concerned, had a preternaturally sharp ear for gossip, and a preternatural credulity. Having once concluded that a man was contemptible, he accepted with no trace of discrimination all rumors which tended to support that judgment. His biographer, in this case, seems equally gullible. He tells us that Macaulay's animosity toward Croker arose from an incompatibility of moral sentiments, forgetting that his uncle had hated Croker "worse than cold boiled veal" a dozen years before the alleged scandal became known.

The truth is that there was no real cause for scandal at all. From the years 1821 to 1842 Croker had devoted a great deal of time to looking after the properties of an old friend, Lord Hertford, a gentleman of about £400,000 fortune, but half insane and partly paralyzed. He received no salary for this work, though it was understood that he would be left a sizeable fortune upon his Lordship's death.

Now Lord Hertford was preyed upon during his last years by several parasites. There were the Count and the Countess Zichy, whose mother had been friendly with him. There were the Countess's two sisters. Finally there was Hertford's valet, Nicholas Suesse. The Count and Countess, who practically dominated their erratic patron, finally became unendurably boring to him. He longed for more exciting company, and

31. *Op. cit.*, I, 122-23.

commissioned Suesse to provide it. This was done a number of times. When the Zichys were at his home, Hertford would slip away to a tavern; when they were away, he would entertain new friends in his own house. It was during one of these latter occasions that Croker appeared once on business, and dined with his Lordship and his guest, one Angela Borell. Soon after this, Hertford, returning from a tavern brawl, caught a cold, developed pneumonia, and died.

Croker had been named to administer the estate. In the will he learned with astonishment that the Countess Zichy and her two sisters had been given £100,000 each. £20,000 more had been left to the valet. To Croker went £23,000, though a great deal more had been promised him for his twenty year services as property manager. The family of Hertford, including his immediate relatives, were cut off without a cent. Finally, it developed that an envelope containing 100,000 francs belonging to Hertford was in Suesse's possession. Croker thereupon charged the valet with theft and instituted proceedings. It was at this point that Suesse, in retaliation, began to circulate the story Macaulay had picked up, a story to the effect that Croker and Angela Borell had been guilty of scandalous carryings on with one another.

The sequel to Lord Hertford's history is scarcely important here. Suesse pleaded not guilty, declared that his master had given him the money, and was acquitted, the court decreeing that a gentleman as irrational as Hertford might very well have acted as was claimed. Soon afterwards, the valet married Angela.[32]

The two men crossed once more, in 1849. The first part of Macaulay's *History* had come out, and Croker reviewed it for the *Quarterly*. After 18 years his opportunity had come! Lockhart, the editor, had even given him a lead. "If you could do the book pure justice," he wrote, "nothing more is wanted to give the author sufficient pain. He has written some very brilliant essays—very transparent in artifice, and I suspect

32. See *The Croker Papers* (3 vols. London, 1884, ed. I. J. Jennings), II, 415-20.

[153]

not over honest in scope and management, but he has written *no history;* and he has. . . . committed himself ingeniously in two or three points which, fitly exposed, would confound him a good deal and check his breeze from El Dorado." Lockhart went on, more specifically, to say that Macaulay's savage hatred of the Church of England was obvious, and should be condemned. "I own though," the editor added, "that I read the book with breathless interest." Croker took these hints, and in one of the most bitter and irrational reviews of the age attempted, with no success whatever, to stem the sale of that miraculously selling work. Croker's thesis was simple enough, and fairly true. He contended that Macaulay's book must be regarded chiefly as a historical romance. "It will never be quoted as authority on any question or point regarding the history of England."

But he had written in bad taste, and to no real purpose. On April 25, 1849, Macaulay notes in his *Journal* that a friend had seen the Duke of Devonshire's marks in his copy of the *Quarterly* which contained the article. " 'Spite.' 'Nonsense!' 'Pure Spite!' " and similar phrases had been written in the margin by the Duke on page after futile page.

The same month Macaulay had gone to the British Museum—of which both he and Croker were directors— to look up a quotation the existence of which Croker had denied. He found it, as was to be expected. "His blunders are really incredible," Macaulay wrote that night in his *Journal*. "The article has been received with general contempt. Really, Croker has done me a great service. I apprehend a strong reaction, the natural effect of such a success; and, if hatred had left him free to use his very slender faculties to the best advantage, he might have injured me much. He should have been large in acknowledgment; should have taken a mild and expository tone; and should have looked out for real blemishes, which, as I too well know, he might easily have found. Instead of that he has written with such rancor as to make everybody sick. I could almost pity him. But he is a bad, a very bad, man; a scandal to politics and to letters."

His last notice of Croker occurs the following January. He had attended a meeting of the directors of the Museum, and it was Croker's turn to preside. "I never was in a room with him before, saving the House of Commons. I took no notice of his existence." [33] Thus in his declining years did they pass in review before him, these enemies, and drop, one by one, into the category of the damned. That family—not his own—into which he had been born had drawn from him perhaps all the devotion of which he was capable. For the rest of the world, as shall soon appear, was left, chiefly, contempt or hatred. He was no humanitarian; he could not love everybody. So he elected, in the main, to despise everybody, except that group whose similarity of manners and opinions saved them from the general curse. And this group was limited indeed. Its members could be numbered, almost, upon the fingers of a single hand.

33. *Journal*, II, 219 (January 29, 1850).

IX. Campaigner

"Be you Foxes, be you Pitts
You must write to silly chits.
Be you Tories, be you Whigs
You must write to sad young gigs." [1]

SO VERSIFIED THE JUDICIOUS POET to his
favorite sisters, Hannah and Margaret, traveling in
Wales during July, 1832, to escape the humors of the dog
days. Macaulay remained in London. Already he had received
overtures to stand for Parliament for the thriving industrial
town of Leeds, and a new Parliament was soon to be called
for, one elected according to the provisions of the now epochal
Reform Bill. He was writing reviews for the *Edinburgh*, working himself "to death in the House of Commons," and building
up his political fences. And he was making the rounds
socially.

Would his two silly chits like to know what was going on
in the capital?

"Pitt is preaching, and Croker is lying.
The cholera's raging, the people are dying.
When the House is the coolest, as I am alive,
The thermometer stands at a hundred and five.
We debate in a heat that seems likely to burn us,
Much like the three children who sang in the furnace." [2]

1. G. O. Trevelyan, *op. cit.*, I, 233.
2. *Ibid.*, I, 236.

He continued to write to them, almost every other day, in high spirits now that the glorious political revolution had passed into history without bloodshed. He described the air of the House, that filthiest of all filthy atmospheres, reeking constantly of tobacco and quicklime scattered about to stay the ravages of the cholera. He told them of the endless dinners he attended, dinners arranged by nobleman after nobleman to satisfy the curious heroines who desired to meet him.

When Parliament adjourned, in August, the dining out went on without interruption. After the last business session, he set out for Holland House with Lord Grey, the Chancellor, Lord Palmerston, and Luttrell. He told his sisters about that dinner; for they were always curious to know what occurred behind those almost impassable doors: "Allen," he wrote, "was of course at the head of the table, carving the dinner and sparring with my lady. The dinner was not so good as usual; for the French cook was ill; and her ladyship kept up a continued lamentation during the whole repast. I should never have found out that everything was not as it should be but for her criticisms. The soup was too salt; the cutlets were not exactly *comme il faut;* and the pudding was hardly enough boiled. I was amused to hear from the splendid mistress of such a house the same sort of apologies which ——— made when her cook forgot the joint and sent up too small a dinner to table. I told Luttrell that it was a comfort to me to find that no rank was exempted from these afflictions.

"They talked about ———'s marriage. Lady Holland vehemently defended the match; and, when Allen said that ——— had caught a Tartar, she quite went off into one of her tantrums. 'She a Tartar! Such a charming girl a Tartar! He is a very happy man, and your language is insufferable; insufferable, Mr. Allen.' Lord Grey had all the trouble in the world to appease her. His influence, however, is very great. He prevailed on her to receive Allen again into favor, and to let Lord Holland have a slice of melon, for which he had been petitioning most piteously, but which she had steadily refused on account of his gout. Lord Holland thanked Lord Grey for his intercession. 'Ah, Lord Grey, I wish you were always here. It is a fine thing to be Prime Minister.' " [3]

It is Macaulay at his best, the Macaulay who never forgot his place as real head of his family, and as the one who, because of that place, was charged not only with supporting it but with amusing it. He never allowed the responsibility of his position as public servant to absorb his sense of responsibility to his brothers and sisters. Story after story he would relay to them, about the more comical side of his life as a legislator, carefully selecting those details which his interested, but not too seriously interested readers might enjoy. No adulation of the great—and he received more than his share —was ever able to turn his head. It was the crystallization of his early training as the eldest son of the most conscientious resident of Clapham. Duty had become a word to which instinctively he gave his allegiance.

Meanwhile, he was carrying on another extensive correspondence with his political admirers in Leeds. The leaders of this group wished thoroughly to sound him out before pledging him their support. Well, he wanted them to understand this fact at once: that he had no interest in canvassing for votes. The practice was beneath his dignity as a law maker; it was also an affront to the elector. "To request an honest man to vote according to his conscience is superfluous. To request him to vote against his conscience is an insult." [4] He hoped to see the day when an Englishman would think it as great an offense to be courted and fawned upon in his capacity as elector as in his capacity of juryman. His conduct was before the voters. Let them make up their own minds independently.

Moreover, there was a second point to be plain about. He would make no pledges to any constituency whatsoever. To his opinions all men were welcome, but "I will not bind myself

3. *Ibid.*, I, 240-41.
4. See letter of August 3, 1832, in Frederick Arnold, *Public Life of Lord Macaulay* (London, 1862), 112-19.

to make or support any particular motion." He wanted them to understand his position clearly. He had no wish to appear either haughty or contemptuous. But just as a physician understands medicine better than an ordinary man, and just as a shoe-maker makes shoes better than an ordinary man, so a person whose life is passed in transacting affairs of state becomes a better statesman than an ordinary man." His public had the right to change its representative if dissatisfied with him. But while he was in office—should he be named to office—he would not be tied down. "My opinion is that electors ought at first to choose cautiously; then to confide liberally; and when the term for which they have selected their member has expired, to review his conduct equitably, and to pronounce on the whole taken together." He was taking a stand almost identical with that which Burke had taken fifty years before in his speech to the electors of Bristol, was using, almost identically, Burke's language. But, Burke or no Burke, he was stating his own profoundest convictions.

These convictions met with some protest; Macaulay was asked to modify or to explain his position more patiently. He did neither. Under the old Parliamentary system, he reminded his correspondent, he had never been a flatterer of the great. "Under the new system I will not be the flatterer of the people." This, of all times, was one in which public men should speak the truth as they saw it. "It is not necessary to my happiness that I should sit in Parliament; but it is necessary to my happiness that I should possess, in Parliament or out of Parliament, the consciousness of having done what is right."

His supporters, no little overawed, finally decided upon him as their candidate. There were three men in the race, contesting for two positions. Mr. Marshall was an almost certain choice for one place. The remaining place was sought by Mr. Michael Sadler, a Tory, who had opposed the Reform Bill at every stage, but who had won considerable support through his interest in ameliorating the working conditions of factory children. Two years before, in the *Edinburgh*, Macaulay had attacked Sadler for attempting to formulate a law of population increase. ("We did not expect a good book from Mr. Sadler; and it is well that we did not, for he has given us a very bad one," etc.) [5] There was no love lost between these two, and little between their followers.

It was a lengthy campaign. He went up to Leeds in September, and had a trying stay, but left hopeful. "About half my day was spent in speaking, and hearing other people speak; in squeezing and being squeezed; in shaking hands with people whom I never saw before, and whose faces and names I forget within a minute after being introduced to them. The rest was passed in conversation with my leading friends, who are very honest, substantial manufacturers. They feed me on roast beef and Yorkshire pudding; at night they put me into capital bedrooms; and the only plague which they give me is that they are always begging me to mention some food or wine for which I have a fancy." [6]

His opponents in Leeds kept him busy too. For one thing, he had accepted a position as secretary to the India Board at £1200 a year, and those who opposed his election made much of that fact. Mr. Macaulay was a hireling of the Ministry, a placeman who had been bought by his party. Visiting Leeds in the early fall, he was greeted with these charges the moment he reached the town; they were placarded prominently almost everywhere. He addressed one audience— from certain quarters of which ensued almost continuous interruptions. It was a new sensation for him. At one point, early in the speech, someone shouted a comment upon his private life that he failed to catch. He paused. "I should be extremely obliged if the gentleman who makes any animadversions on my conduct will make them openly; let him state what is the charge he brings against me and I pledge myself to answer it." [7] But the gentleman did not choose to respond.

5. *Works*, V, 419.
6. G. O. Trevelyan, *op. cit.*, I, 245.
7. Arnold, *op. cit.*, 103.

He soon got around to the charge of being a hireling of the Ministry. "I will explain to you gentlemen, fully, under what circumstances I accepted office." And he did explain to them, with great patience, that though his new position had been a sinecure under the Tories, it was capable under the Whigs of becoming an office of much importance. Such he intended to make it, a resolution concerning which the Ministry had already been fully informed. But what does Mr. Macaulay think of the Factory Bill Mr. Sadler plans to submit to the next Parliament? Someone had shouted this question from the floor. Mr. Macaulay could not say, for he had not been privileged to read the bill. Of this, however, his questioner could rest assured: he would assent "to any measure that may seem to me necessary for protecting children from over-working and cruelty."[8]

He met other questions with equal composure, and answered them ably, though the meeting was tumultuous. And he finished his speech with a warning that required a good deal of courage to sound. Let them, he declared, cease to expect a miraculous shower of blessings from the provisions of the Reform Bill. He was certain "that to an assembly so enlightened as this, it must be obvious that the best government cannot act directly and suddenly and violently on the comforts of the people; it cannot rain down provisions into their houses; it cannot give them bread and meat and wine. These things they can obtain only by their own honest industry, and to protect them in that honest industry and secure them in its fruits, is the end of all honest government."[9] But let them not be dismayed. It is true that the national debt is greater today than ever before in the history of Britain. But so is the wealth of the country greater, infinitely greater. It was to the augmentation of that wealth, to the ever increasing domination of world trade by British merchants, that all the policies of the Whigs were dedicated. He foresaw, twenty

8. *Ibid.*, 107.
9. *Ibid.*, 108.

years from this date—if the wisdom of his fellow citizens would but permit these policies to continue—a condition in which the fair city spread about him would have arrived "at a degree of wealth and prosperity such as may now seem visionary to anticipate."

And his prophecy was fulfilled, came true with room to spare. What he failed to foresee was the more nearly final fruit of that policy, which reached its season rather early in the present century. For that philosophy of trade which would make England great and rich would, other statesmen figured, if followed, make their own nations great also. Unfortunate rivalries ensued, and swelled unmanageably, and ten million lives were sacrificed, and other damages still incalculable amassed, before statesmen began even seriously to wonder about the ultimate implications of the words of this candidate for Leeds.

The campaign grew more hectic as it neared its closing weeks. When it was advertised that Mr. Macaulay would address a meeting, his followers would bring a band to the place designated; the band would play lustily while the crowd collected. Sadler's forces also would come, accompanied by a rival set of musicians. The result of so much potential melody concentrated in one place was what might easily be predicted. When Macaulay began speaking, Sadler's artists would break out with a lively march tune. Pleading with them was useless. On several occasions Macaulay, lusty voiced and persistent though he was, was compelled to give up though only half finished. And nearly always at such times he met with interruptions, one after the other, to the effect that "You shan't sit in Parliament," or "Your bloody Reform Bill ain't worth a damn."

On at least one occasion a man who questioned Macaulay at a meeting got a good deal more than he had bargained for. The charge had been spread about that the brilliant young Whig was a Deist or a Socinian; he doubted, it was alleged, the divinity of Christ. Macaulay had been considerably nettled, but had said nothing publicly in answer. Then, at one rally, before either Macaulay or Mr. Marshall had been introduced, a voter who turned out later to be a Methodist preacher shouted to the Chairman that he wished "to know the religious creed of Messrs. Marshall and Macaulay."

Macaulay was on his feet at once. "Who calls for that?"

"I do," a voice answered.

"May I see him stand up."

Pandemonium followed. Macaulay repeated his demand that his questioner mount the platform. His supporters around the embarrassed churchman echoed his demand. Elsewhere confused shouts of "Turn him out," "Shame," and "Hear him" mingled wildly with the Chairman's plea for order. The Reverend finally stood up.

MR. MACAULAY.—"I must say that I have heard with the greatest shame and sorrow the question which has been proposed to me; and with peculiar pain and sorrow do I learn that the question was proposed by a minister of religion. I do most deeply regret that any person should think it necessary to make a meeting like this an arena for theological discussion. I will not be a party to turning this assembly to such a purpose. My answer is short, and in one word—I regret that it should be necessary to utter it. Gentlemen, I am a Christian. (Cheers.) Gentlemen, this is no subject for hearty acclamation. I have done; I will say no more. No man shall have to say of me that I was the person who, when this disgraceful inquisition was entered into an assembly of Englishmen, actually brought forward the most sacred rights to be canvassed here—who brought forward these subjects to be a matter for hissing or for cheering. . . . Gentlemen, I have done. I tell you I will say no more; and if the person who thought fit to ask this question has the feeling of a person worthy of being a teacher of religion, he will not, I think, rejoice that he called me forth." [10]

Other meetings were almost equally tempestuous. Macaulay

10. *Ibid.*, 111.

declared himself for free trade. "I am for a system under which we may sell where we can sell dearest, and buy where we can buy cheapest."[11] He declared himself as favoring remuneration for public services. How else were young men with no great fortunes to rise in the world of politics? The careers of such leaders as Lord Brougham and the immortal Fox would have been impossible had salaries been denied them. And he declared himself, at great length, and to resounding cheers, against the iniquities of the Tory party. Who first debased the currency imprudently, and then restored it imprudently? The Tories. Who compelled us to take paper for gold? The Tories. Who upheld religious disabilities until the country was driven to the point of civil war, and relaxed them only when it was doubtful if we should not lose Ireland as we had lost America? The answer was, again, the Tories. They had ruled England for the last fifty years. "If distress exists then, who is to answer for it?" Once more the answer was patent: "The Tories!"

This did he ride into office, on that wave of protest and accumulated indignation which had placed all the woes of the country upon the now spurned threshold of the conservatives. At the conclusion of the balloting, in December, the count read as follows: Mr. Marshall, 2012; Mr. Macaulay, 1984; Mr. Sadler, 1596. "Slander and hypocrisy," Macaulay wrote his supporters, "threats and caresses, bludgeons and gin have done their worst; and the result is that the cause of Reform has triumphed."[12] He returned to Parliament to do his share toward hurrying on that golden era of progress and always growing prosperity which, now that "the middle orders of Britain" were in control, seemed definitely certain to come.

And yet, inwardly, it was with a heavy heart that he returned. While still campaigning, he had received a letter from Hannah about his other favorite sister Margaret. The

11. *Ibid.*, 124.
12. *Ibid.*, 138-43.

two girls had been visiting in Liverpool at the home of a prominent Quaker, Mr. John Cropper. While there, Margaret and a brother of their host, Mr. Edward Cropper, had fallen hopelessly in love. They were to be married. It required all the common sense and fortitude of Macaulay's nature to adjust him to the thought of "losing" her. The limitations of his way of life were, for the first time, being brought home to him, abruptly.

"The attachment between brothers and sisters" he wrote, "blameless, amiable, and delightful as it is, is so liable to be superseded by other attachments that no wise man ought to suffer it to become indispensable to him. That women shall leave the home of their birth, and contract ties dearer than those of consanguinity, is a law as ancient as the first records of the history of our race, and as unchangeable as the constitution of the human body and mind. To repine against the nature of things, and against the great fundamental law of all society, because, in consequence of my own want of foresight, it happens to bear heavily on me, would be the basest and most absurd selfishness.

"I have still one more stake to lose," he continued in this note to Hannah. "There remains one event for which, when it arrives, I shall, I hope, be prepared. From that moment, with a heart formed, if ever any man's heart was formed, for domestic happiness, I shall have nothing left in this world but ambition. There is no wound, however, which time and necessity will not render endurable: and, after all, what am I more than my fathers—than the millions and tens of millions who have been weak enough to pay double price for some favorite number in the lottery of life, and who have suffered double disappointment when their ticket came up a blank." [13]

His grief had continued, marring even the election day itself. He was sitting in the midst of two hundred friends, he told Hannah in another note, all of them mad with exaltation and thinking him, now that victory was assured, the hap-

13. G. O. Trevelyan, *op. cit.*, I, 258.

piest man in the world. "Yet it is all I can do to hide my tears, and to command my voice, when it is necessary for me to reply to their congratulations. Dearest, dearest sister, you alone are now left to me. Whom have I on earth but thee?" But for her, in the midst of all his success, he would prefer to lie dead beside his friend Hyde Villiers, whom he was replacing on the India Board. "But I cannot go on. I am wanted to write an address to the electors; and I shall lay it on Sadler pretty heavily. By what strange fascination is it that ambition and resentment exercise such power over minds which ought to be superior to them? I despise myself for feeling so bitterly toward this fellow as I do. But the separation from dear Margaret has jarred my whole temper. I am cried up here to the skies as the most affable and kind hearted of men, while I feel a fierceness and restlessness within me quite new and almost inexplicable."

Truly this was a strange case, a fundamentally unhealthy situation. What was his sister to do about it, except to feel miserable over her brother's abnormality? Such a word is severe, but no other word seems quite adequate. He was still fairly young, had barely turned thirty-two. Why was it that a person "formed if ever man's heart was formed, for domestic happiness"—Why was is that the normal expression of the instinct for such happiness should appear unthinkable to him, so unthinkable, in fact, that nowhere, not even once in his copious *Journals*, does a serious reference to it occur? The truth is that he was strangely sexless. For affection he had an almost infinite capacity. There the matter began and stopped. As far as any record shows, he was never once in love.

2

During the year 1833 Macaulay made three important speeches in Parliament. The first was on that vexed subject of Ireland, a subject which had flamed up anew when King

William, aware of the fact that lawlessness was more than normally rampant in the country, petitioned Parliament for a grant of extraordinary powers to enable him to deal with the problem. He wished, he declared, "to preserve and strengthen the union" between the two nations. Mr. O'Connell objected, moving that the House resolve itself into a committee, that the whole problem might be given a full airing. Now this Irish patriot was the real leader of his countrymen; he had been responsible, largely, for organizing them some years before to a point which enabled them to outvote their landlords at the polls. And his success had been so marked that, in 1829, Sir Robert Peel and the Duke of Wellington had put through a law providing for Catholic emancipation. Catholics, in other words, were thenceforth admitted to Parliament, and O'Connell came in with a good many others, determined to keep the problems of his people prominently upon the consciences of the English.

Macaulay touched upon only one point which O'Connell had made in his demurrer: the point that it would be wise to have two separate legislatures, one for England and one for Ireland. The proposal, Macaulay declared, was ridiculous. You cannot have one executive power and two parliaments. He summoned history to support him. If the two houses disagree, to which is the sovereign to conform? But let him be understood. "If on fair trial, it be found that Great Britain and Ireland cannot exist happily together as parts of one empire, in God's name let them separate." He did not wish to see them joined together—"like those wretched twins from Siam who were exhibited here a little while ago—by an unnatural ligament which made each the constant plague of the other, always in each other's way, more helpless than others because they had twice as many hands, slower than others because they had twice as many legs, sympathizing with each other only in evil, not feeling each other's pleasures, not supported by each other's ailment, but tormented by each other's infirmities and certain to perish miserably by each other's dissolution."[14]

No! Emphatically he did not want that. He wanted justice meted out equally to both countries: he wanted every valid cause of complaint removed. But there was something else he wanted, too, and Mr. O'Connell could do a great deal about it. He wanted lawlessness in Ireland stopped. "You try to deter us from putting down robbery, arson, and murder, by telling us that if we resort to coercion we shall raise a civil war. We are past that fear. Recollect that, in one county alone, there have been within a few weeks sixty murders or assaults with intent to murder, and six hundred burglaries. Since we parted last summer, the slaughter in Ireland has exceeded the slaughter of a pitched battle. . . . Civil war, indeed! I would rather live in the midst of any civil war we have had in England during the last two hundred years than in some parts of Ireland at the present moment."

O'Connell had reproached the Whigs for not acting more generously toward his country. "His reproaches are not more stinging than the reproaches which, in times not very remote, we endured unflinchingly in his cause." He was demanding too much of the House; he wanted favors, not justice. "Though a young member of the Whig party, I will venture to speak in the name of the whole body. I tell the honorable and learned gentleman that the same spirit which sustained us in a just contest for him will sustain us in an unjust contest against him. Calumny, abuse, royal displeasure, popular fury, exclusion from office, exclusion from Parliament—we were ready to endure them all, rather than that he should be less than a British subject. We will never suffer him to be more."[15]

O'Connell was on his feet at once. Macaulay, he declared, had totally misapprehended his speech. He had magnified a passing reference in it, a reference to the legislative union, and had passed over the real burden of his complaint, which

14. *Works*, VIII, 86-99.
15. *Ibid.*, VIII, 98.

had to do with the causes of civil unrest in his country. O'Connell was followed by a colleague, Mr. Sheil. What Mr. Sheil objected to was the fact that Macaulay "had with great discursive expatiation," supported a Royal address designed to stop all argument about Ireland. How could any fair-minded law maker do this? Had Macaulay concluded that his arguments were unanswerable, that he had put an end to all the doubts which hedged the problem? If that were his view, Mr. Sheil wished that the learned member "had adverted to the fiscal and moral evils of absenteeism, had explained the causes of the misery and destitution of Ireland, had exhibited the advantages of our provincial dependence, and shown us the benefits of having English members overwhelm, on Irish questions, the majority of Irish members in this House."[16] Mr. Macaulay, in other words, while a brilliant speaker, knew very little about his subject. But on this particular occasion a knowledge of the subject was secondary. The House had done all it could do for Ireland, or at least all that it wanted to do. The motion which Macaulay supported was passed by a majority of 428 to 40.

His second speech was in favor of removing the civil disabilities of the Jews. He felt, along with a vast majority of law makers, that what had been granted the Catholics should in fairness be given the members of this faith. The matter was debated in committee during the month of April, Macaulay rising on the seventeenth to answer a member for Oxford. This Tory gentleman had contended that his party believed in religious liberty: he did not by any means endorse persecution of the Jews; he would not hang them, or flay them, or draw their teeth, or fine and imprison them without cause. But after these magnanimous assertions, he proceeded to point out that they should none-the-less be kept from political office, "for no one has a *right* to political office." It is all a matter of favor, and such a favor, he felt, should be granted only to

16. Hansard, *Parliamentary Proceedings* (3rd Series), XV, 266.

the type of individual who professes the established faith of the country.

The conclusions from such reasoning as this are monstrous to contemplate, Macaulay declared. The Jews *as a race* were being kept from office. "We are about to bring in a bill for the government of India. Suppose that we were to insert in that bill a clause providing that no graduate of the University of Oxford should be a Governor General or Governor of any Presidency, would not my Honorable Friend cry out against such a clause as most unjust to the learned body which he represents? And would he think himself sufficiently answered by being told, in his own words, that the appointment to office is a mere matter of favor, and that to exclude any individual or a class from office is no injury?"[17] It all reduced itself to this, Macaulay went on: there was no logical stopping point to persecutions, once they were begun.

He next proceeded, in support of his views, to cite Scripture at great length, by way of confounding still more deeply the gentlemen on the benches opposite who had been quoting it to their own advantage only a moment before. How can they square their treatment of this race "with that commandment which comprises the law and the prophets"—that we should do unto others as we would have them do unto us? The gentleman had argued, too, that it had been prophesied that the Jews are to be wanderers on the face of the earth, are not to mix on terms of equality with other peoples. Macaulay insisted that the meaning of that sentence was being wilfully misinterpreted, for in the United States the Jews were politically free and settled. This fact therefore proves that the prophecy, *as construed by the Tories*, is false! Again it had been urged that, since the Jews looked forward to the coming of a Great Deliverer who will lead them back to Palestine, "they will always consider England not their country but merely as their place of exile." What gross ignorance of human nature was evident in an argument of this sort! To think that men,

17. *Works*, VIII, 101-10.

dreaming vaguely of some far off divine event, could be led to take no interest in what was tangible and immediate and certain!

The Jews were a great race, a race that in England was exceedingly wealthy. And as Mr. Cobbett had pointed out, "it is impossible to deprive a man of political power if you suffer him to be the proprietor of half a county." Wealth begets such power. Let us therefore grant to the Jew the name and title to that which in reality he already possesses, and uses indirectly day in and day out.

The Tories could only repeat, in the person of Mr. Holcomb, who followed Macaulay, their feckless and by this time thoroughly tiresome arguments. There was a profound feeling in the country, he declared, that church and state must fall together. By tradition a Church of England had been established, and it should not have its existence jeopardized by measures like that now being supported by the Whigs. He proceeded to say once more that there was no abstract right of political power given any group, but that some group had to govern as a matter of practical necessity. He would have his hearers remember that, by venerable usage, adherence to a certain religious creed had been a major qualification for office in England. He was making no charge against the morality of the Jew. He was saying, simply, that a Christian country ought to be governed by Christians.[18] Mr. Holcomb sat down. He had done his duty by the old nobility, but to little purpose. When a vote was called, the Whigs won their measure by a lusty majority. One by one, it seemed to Macaulay, the shackles of intolerance were being courageously struck from all Englishmen of the middle classes.

His last major speech in Parliament for the next six years came in July. The subject was India. During his short period of service as secretary of the India Board, Macaulay had learned a great deal about the history of England's relations with that country. He knew of the first stage—an interval of

18. Hansard, *op. cit.* (3rd Series), XVII, 239.

150 years of quiet trading. He knew of the second stage which culminated with Warren Hasting's impeachment—an interval of fifty years of conquest and plunder. He was himself taking part in the third stage, an interval of organized rule for the mutual benefit of India and England, an interval which had brought in the philosophy of free trade with respect to the province, which had stripped the East India Company of its monopolies and its political authority, and which was designed to unify the territory and to abolish such social barbarisms as Suttee and Thugism.[19] The ultimate implications of this last stage Macaulay was probably as well aware of as anybody. Seen in perspective they appear fairly obvious: India should be westernized, in keeping, doubtless, with that ever widening quest for markets for western goods which was the major economic passion of the nineteenth century.

The specific subject of his address was the Bill proposed by Mr. Charles Grant, President of the India Board, a Bill designed to promote better harmony between the Company and the Board. It called, mainly, for payment to the Company for privileges which it was being made to surrender. The question was, who should settle the amount that was due? It also called for the appointment, subject to the approval of the Directors of the Company, of a supreme council that should manage the land impartially as a benevolent despot.

Of course, there were objectors to the plan. Macaulay spoke long in defense of the fairness of the indemnities offered, admitting, however—which was rare in him—that the sum due the stockholders could not, with absolute certainty, be determined. Then he turned to the idea of the Supreme Council. What other plan for governing the nation had been mentioned? There was the proposal that Parliament should govern it. This was impossible. The job was too complex, and the indifference of members of the House to Indian affairs was proverbial. "A broken head in Cold Bath Fields

19. Compare G. M. Trevelyan, *British History in Nineteenth Century*, 309-14. See also Macaulay ("Government of India" speech), *Works*, VIII, 114-16.

produces a greater sensation among us than three pitched battles in India."[20] What was wanted was a check on the Crown, a ruling body independent of the particular faction in power, "but no more than independent, not a tool of the Treasury, not a tool of the opposition." Mr. Charles Grant's plan was the only one proposed which fulfilled those conditions.

He was sorry, however, that despotism had to be recommended. He knew that the ideal government was a free government. But the people there were not yet ready for freedom. All despotisms are imperfect, but at least he would have the Indian despotism impartial. Consider the collateral proposals of Mr. Grant's measure! One of them called for a plan of civil service in the country: all lesser positions were to be competed for. Now there were gentlemen present who were skeptical about this; they felt that the academically successful would win out, and they objected to such a system on score that there was no relation between success at a university and practical success later.

Gentlemen were misled. Indeed, Sir, this objection will prove far too much for those who use it. "It would prove that there is no use at all in education. Why should we put boys out of their way? Why should we force a lad who would much rather fly a kite or trundle a hoop to learn his Latin Grammar? Why should we keep a young man to his Thucydides or his Laplace, when he would much rather be shooting? Education would be a mere useless torture, if, at two or three and twenty, a man who had neglected his studies were exactly on a par with a man who had applied himself to them, exactly as likely to perform all the offices of public life with credit to himself and with advantage to society. Whether the English system of education be good or bad is not now the question. Perhaps I may think that too much time is given to the ancient languages and to the abstract sciences. But what then? Whatever be the language, whatever be the sciences, which it is in any

20. *Works*, VIII, 121.

age or country the fashion to teach, the persons who become the greatest proficients in those languages and those sciences will generally be the flower of the youth, the most acute, the most industrious, the most ambitious of honourable distinctions. If the Ptolemaic system were taught at Cambridge, instead of the Newtonian, the senior wrangler would nevertheless be in general a superior man to him who was destitute of these accomplishments."[21]

It was Macaulay's high tribute to the life of the mind, and to the value of the discipline it involves in the business of governing a state. He was speaking here his deepest convictions. For unless one distinguishes himself at the University, he always felt, his chances for later distinction have been almost completely thrown away. Years later, in 1859, he learned that the son of a close friend had been rated at his school in the third, or lowest class. He was grieved, and bitter about it, as a note in his *Journal* bears witness: "The Classical Tripos. S—— first. . . . E—— low in the third. Alas, what can he do or be! And for what earthly purpose has he spent the last three years at Cambridge? To waste money and to form bad and disreputable connections, I suppose. For that is all he has done and all that, after his first start, he could reasonably be expected to do. The East India Civil Service is quite out of the question. The best thing that he can do is to join his brother at the Antipodes. I would gladly assist to send him thither."[22]

Mr. Grant's bill was carried without a division, and Macaulay, who had not only spoken so well in defense of it, but who had also aided in framing its provisions, was naturally delighted. "Sir, having heard that speech," said one elderly member, "may console the young people for never having heard Mr. Burke."[23] He was looked upon thenceforth as an authority on Indian affairs, as, next to Mr. James Mill, perhaps the ablest authority in the country. That knowledge,

21. *Ibid.*, VIII, 132.
22. *Journal*, XI, 458.
23. Macaulay to Hannah, July 11, 1833, quoted in G. O. Trevelyan, *op. cit.*, I, 278.

aided no doubt by the peculiar strength of his political ties, had not been acquired for nothing. Macaulay was well aware that, by the provisions of the India Bill, "one of the members of the Supreme Council. . . . is to be chosen from among persons who are not servants of the Company." He added, in this letter to Hannah, a rumor of what proved to be one of the most important circumstances of his life: "It is probable, indeed nearly certain, that the situation will be offered to me."

He went on to explain the terms of the position. The salary was £10,000 a year. One could live in splendor anywhere in the country with half that sum. The remainder of his income, with the accruing interest, he could put by. "I may therefore hope to return to England at only thirty-nine, in the full vigor of life, with a fortune of thirty thousand pounds. A larger fortune I never desired."

Really, he continued, it looked like his only chance. Schisms were developing within the party; soon he was going, in conscience, to be compelled to break with certain of his colleagues. He would sell all his chances of keeping his present office six months longer "for fifty pounds down. . . . In England I see nothing before me, for some time to come, but poverty, unpopularity, and the breaking up of old connections." And of course there was the family to support; at least five members of it were still dependent upon him.

"Yet what shall I feel? And with what emotions, loving as I do my country and my family, can I look forward to such a separation, enjoined, as I think it is, by prudence and by duty? Whether the period of exile shall be one of comfort and, after the first shock, even of happiness, depends on you. If, as I expect, this offer shall be made to me, will you go with me? I know what a sacrifice I ask of you. I know how many dear and precious ties you must, for a time, sunder. I know that the splendor of the Indian Court, and the gayeties of that brilliant society of which you will be one of the leading personages, have no temptations for you. I can bribe you only by telling you that, if you will go with me, I will love you better than I love you now, if I can."[24]

He was asking a great deal of her. It was a six months' voyage, to a land that was looked upon at this date as a barbarous region, fraught with disease and death. It meant a five year separation from the rest of the family, and in the case of two of the members of that family who remained behind, five years proved to be forever. But Hannah consented. They would await the appointment. She would go with him to the ends of the earth.

One untimely political issue threatened that summer to ruin all his chances. The bill which was to emancipate the slaves in the West Indies came up, sponsored by the Ministry under which Macaulay held office. He was bound to support that measure as read. But it contained one clause, a concession to the planter interest, of which none of the abolitionists approved, Zachary Macaulay least of all. The clause set forth that the negroes should become apprenticed laborers, and that as such they should labor for their masters "for a time to be fixed by Parliament." That time, quite freely talked about, was to be a full dozen years.

Here was no freedom at all, declared Zachary; and Mr. Buxton, and the dying Wilberforce, and scores of others agreed with him. Zachary's son agreed likewise. He could not support the measure as it stood. He told the ministers that he would oppose them in committee, and handed in his resignation. He was resigning not only his present place, but his prospect for wealth in India as well. It was probably the most courageous action of his life.

The matter dragged on for more than a month. Macaulay opposed his own Ministry on the floor, as he had warned he would do. At length the Cabinet met to consider his resignation, for, thanks largely to his opposition, the objectionable clause in their bill had been thrown out. But they decided not to accept that resignation. This was, in truth, no more than

24. *Ibid.*, I, 291 (Letter of August 17, 1833).

they should have decided; but their conclusion was unusual and gave their enemies much to gloat over: here was a Ministry, those enemies taunted, which could not keep discipline within the ranks of its own placemen!

Emancipation, then, had come at last! And with justice too, for—unlike America—England had voted her planters £20,000,000 in compensation for the loss of their slaves. Almost everywhere there was rejoicing. Mr. Buxton told the aging Zachary that in his sober and deliberate judgment he had done more toward this consummation than any other man."[25] Wilberforce died just before the measure was in final form, but certain of its early success. Macaulay, writing his sister of that death, has left one of the most revealing paragraphs in all his work.

The great reformer kept his faculties to the very last, he said. "He was cheerful and full of anecdote only last Saturday. He owned that he enjoyed life much, and that he had a great desire to live longer. Strange in a man who had, I should have said, so little to attach him to this world, and so firm a belief in another: in a man with an impaired fortune, a weak spine, and a worn-out stomach! What is this fascination which makes us cling to existence, in spite of present sufferings and of religious hopes? Yesterday evening I called at the house in Cadogan Place, where the body is lying. I was truly fond of him. . . . And how is that? How very little one human being generally cares for another! How very little the world misses anybody! How soon the chasm left by the best and wisest men closes! I thought, as I walked back from Cadogan Place, that our own selfishness when others are taken away ought to teach us how little others will suffer at losing us. I thought that, if I were to die tomorrow, not one of the fine people whom I dine with every week will take a *côtelette aux petits pois* the less on Saturday at the table to which I was invited to meet them, or will smile less gayly at the ladies over the champagne. And I am quite even with them. . . . There

25. *Ibid.*, I, 278.

are not ten people in the world whose deaths would spoil my dinner; but there are one or two whose deaths would break my heart. The more I see of the world, and the more numerous my acquaintance becomes, the narrower and more exclusive my affection grows, and the more I cling to my sisters, and to one or two old tried friends of my quiet days."[26] But he would not go on preaching to her out of Ecclesiastes. He knew her heart—and she knew his, as no one else in the world would ever know it.

The appointment to the Supreme Council was long delayed. Even though rumors that Macaulay would be named were generally spread about, and even though office seekers plagued him unmercifully—while shirt and sock salesmen insisted still more heavily that he order by the dozens those gentlemanly necessities unobtainable in India—he was forced to wait, and wonder, and wait still longer. It was not until December 4 that the directors finally voted him the place. But that vote, when it actually came, proved decisive: nineteen were in favor of him; only three were against him.[27]

One scene, excessively annoying, took place before he left. It was with Lady Holland, whose tyrannies this time went a shade too far for sufferance: He wrote Hannah about it, as usual. "She was quite hysterical about my going; paid me such compliments as I cannot repeat; cried, raved; called me dear, dear Macaulay. 'You are sacrificed to your family. I see it all. You are too good to them. They are always making a tool of you; last session about the slaves; and now sending you to India!' I always do my best to keep my temper with Lady Holland, for three reasons: because she is a woman, because she is very unhappy in her health and in the circumstances of her position; and because she has a real kindness for me. But at last she said something about you. This was too much, and I was beginning to answer her in a voice trembling with anger, when she broke out again: 'I beg your pardon. Pray,

26. Macaulay to Hannah, July 3, 1833. *Ibid.*, I, 285-86.
27. Macaulay to Lansdowne, December 5, 1833. *Ibid.*, I, 306.

[178]

forgive me, dear Macaulay. I was very impertinent. I know you will forgive me. Nobody has such a temper as you. I have said so a hundred times. I said so to Allen only this morning. I am sure you will bear with my weakness. I shall never see you again'; and she cried and I cooled; for it would have been to very little purpose to be angry with her. I hear that it is not to me alone that she runs along in this way. She storms at the Ministers for letting me go. I was told that at one dinner she became so violent that even Lord Holland, whose temper, whatever his wife may say, is much cooler than mine, could not command himself, and broke out: 'Don't talk such nonsense, my lady. What the devil! Can we tell a gentleman who has a claim upon us that he must lose his only chance of getting an independence in order that he may come and talk to you in an evening?' " [28]

He sailed with his sister in February, 1834. He was going to India to make his fortune—true; but not by the old freebooting methods of the previous century. The reforming Whigs had changed all that. He was going out, rather, as a public servant of both nations. He was to act as legal adviser to the Council, was to lead in drawing up a new Penal Code and a new educational system for the country. And in this way—insofar as one mortal *can* manage to effect so overwhelming a task—he was to begin the process of turning those hundreds of millions of slow faces gradually but systematically westward, toward England, toward that country from which flowed, at not too great a price, practically every blessing that flesh is heir to.

28. Macaulay to Hannah, January 1, 1834. *Ibid.*, I, 314.

X. Statesman

A CHEERING GROUP of Falmouth Whigs, led by the mayor, came down to see Macaulay and Hannah set sail on the Indiaman, the *Asia*. He had prepared himself well for the voyage, a half dozen trunks of books having preceded him on board. *John Bull*, too, his father's old nemesis, took equally conspicuous notice of his departure. His new office, this publication had observed, was a mere job, created expressly for him. Last session, in what was to have been one of his greatest speeches, he had palpably broken down. The Ministers were therefore packing him off lest he cause them further embarrassment. Yet the editors, for all that, heartily wished him a pleasant voyage. They wondered also, incidentally, whether there were an export duty on "sweltering venom."[1] If there were, the implication ran, half Mr. Macaulay's first year's salary would have to remain behind with the English customs officers!

An uneventful trip it proved to be—almost four months of outward monotony lifted only for moments by "the catching of a shark, the shooting of an albatross, a sailor tumbling down the hatchway and breaking his head, a cadet getting drunk and swearing at the captain." Hannah proved extremely sociable, dancing with the gentlemen evenings, mornings reading novels or sermons with the ladies. Macaulay added, in this note back home, that he contented himself with being

1. Arnold, *op. cit.*, 184; and G. O. Trevelyan, *op. cit.*, I, 320.

very civil whenever he was with other passengers, but took care to be with them as little as possible.

In truth he was reading, voraciously. "Except at meals, I hardly exchanged a word with any human being." During the whole voyage, he went on to say, he read with keen and increasing enjoyment. "I devoured Greek, Latin, Spanish, Italian, French, and English; folios, quartos, octavos, and duo-decimos." Not since his Cambridge days had he known even an approximation of such leisure, and, in the way which seemed to him eminently valid, he was making the most of it.

It is astonishing to contemplate the list of books he got through: The *Iliad*, the *Odyssey*, all of Virgil, all of Horace, Caesar's Commentaries, Bacon's *Advancement of Learning*, the works of Dante, Petrarch, Ariosto, and Tasso. He also read *Don Quixote*, Gibbon's *Decline and Fall*, seven thick folios of the *Biographia Britannica*, Sismondi's *History of France*, Mill's *History of India*, and, finally, "all the seventy volumes of Voltaire." [2] It is small wonder that, reading with such savage persistence, he had scarcely any time at all to reflect on the pages flowing madly beneath his eyes; small wonder that his criticism of the works should be undernourished or — worse than that—trivial: "I liked the *Iliad* a little less, the *Odyssey*, a great deal more than formerly." Horace charmed him more than ever, Virgil not quite so much as before: Virgil is, often, deficient in portraying character, and his supernatural machinery doesn't convince. He was enraptured with Ariosto; he still thought Dante better than Milton, on a par indeed with Homer, out-topped, indeed, only by Shakespeare. He could do nothing except compare his latest impression with an earlier. What mattered was remembering only. Reading was becoming for him a drug. One took to it to forget or to escape the idle talk of idle persons.

June 10, 1834, the *Asia* anchored off Madras, and Macaulay had his first glimpses of native life in the person of a boatman who rowed out to the ship in a raft. "He came on

2. Letter to T. F. Ellis, July 1, 1834. *Ibid.*, I, 329.

board with nothing on him but a pointed yellow cap, and walked among us with a self possession and civility which, coupled with his nakedness, nearly made me die of laughing." Following him were messengers from the Governor-general, Lord William Bentinck. His Lordship was ill, 400 miles up the country, at Ootacamond. His Council must meet at once, and Macaulay's presence was necessary to make a quorum. There was nothing for the new member to do except to send Hannah on to Calcutta, and to set out for the hill country as his superior requested. He traveled by palanquin, with a train of thirty-eight natives.

Along the way during this eight day trip he met some curious people. One was the Rajah of Mysore, who insisted that his guest examine his wardrobe and picture gallery. Several of his pictures, Macaulay conceded, were not much inferior to those one saw in the sanded parlors of country inns in England. But the jewel of his collection, of which the Rajah was vain beyond measure, was "a head of the Duke of Wellington, which has most certainly been on a sign post in England." Yet the Rajah was a man of both taste and wisdom compared with an Englishman who accosted Macaulay in the same town. "Pray, Sir," he addressed the new councillor, "do you not think that Bonaparte was the Beast?" "No, Sir, I cannot say that I do." "Sir, he was the Beast. I can prove it. I have found the number 666 in his name. Why, Sir, if he was not the Beast, who was?"

It was a tough question, but Macaulay answered it: "Sir, the House of Commons is the Beast. There are 658 members of the House; and these, with their chief officers—the three clerks, the sergeant and his deputy, the chaplain, the door keeper, and the librarian—make 666."

"Well, Sir, that is strange. But I can assure you that, if you write Napoleon Bonaparte in Arabic, leaving out only two letters, it will give 666."

"And pray, Sir, what right have you to leave out two letters? And, as St. John was writing Greek, and to Greeks, is it not likely that he would use the Greek rather than the Arabic notation?"

"But, Sir, everybody knows that the Greek letters were never used to mark numbers."

Macaulay answered the learned divine "with the meekest look and voice possible." "Sir, I do not think that everybody knows that. Indeed, I have reason to believe that a different opinion—erroneous, no doubt—is universally embraced by all the small minority who happen to know any Greek." So ended the controversy. "The man looked at me," Macaulay added, "as if he thought me a very wicked fellow; and, I dare say, has by this time discovered that, if you write my name in Tamul, leaving out T in Thomas, B in Babington, and M in Macaulay, it will give the number of this unfortunate Beast."[3]

Macaulay admired the Governor-general as he admired few men, and his first weeks in the hills he passed pleasantly enough. Yet his stay there coincided with the monsoon. Grey blankets of rain streamed down continuously. During a solid month, he complained, he did not get two hours walking. It was seldom that he could see a hundred yards ahead of him. "He began to be bored," his nephew notes, "for the first and last time in his life." His companions were restless almost to desperation; for the town was new, and one who ventured any distance away ran an imminent risk of being "trodden into the shape of half a crown by a wild elephant, or eaten by the tigers."[4]

But Macaulay saved the situation, at length, and by a method that, if used a hundred years later, would probably have placed it beyond hope of salvation. He brought out a copy of *Clarissa Harlowe*, unabridged of course; and while relentless torrents beat above their heads, the rapt company traced, volume through volume, the methodically darkening fortunes of Richardson's lady. An old Scotch doctor, a Jacobin and a free thinker, cried over the last section until he was too

3. *Ibid.*, I, 328.
4. *Ibid.*, I, 334-35.

ill to come down to dinner. The chief secretary declared that reading the book under the spell of Macaulay's enthusiasm for it was an epoch in his life. The Governor's wife seized one volume, and could scarcely be made to pass it on. The chief justice next gave it up unfinished; his tears had blinded him; he could not continue.

Meanwhile Macaulay was writing home about his prospects in this strange country and about what he hoped to be able to do for the family. Expenses were less than he had anticipated. If he lived, he would get rich fast. The exchange rate in India was greatly in his favor. "After next Christmas," he told his younger sisters, Fanny and Selina, "I expect to lay up on an average about seven thousand pounds a year." Before the present year ended, he planned to send home "a thousand or twelve hundred pounds for my father, and you all." It was most comforting, he felt, to be able to think that within a few years they could all be assured of a good fire, a good joint of meat, and a good glass of wine—all without owing obligations to anybody. "Rely on it, my dear girls, that there is no chance of my going back with my heart cooled toward you. I came hither principally to save my family, and I am not likely while here to forget them." [5]

Yet that family which he had come out to save was soon to face another change, one which was to affect Tom permanently. Hannah had become engaged to Charles Trevelyan, a native of Somerset, who had attended the Charterhouse School, next the East India Company's College in Haileybury, and had set out immediately afterwards for India. He was an intrepid man, one who desired to make the trip southward on horseback, going through Persia and the mountains of Baluchistan. But this rash venture was not permitted. He went by ship, the voyage requiring six dull months. Macaulay, six years his senior, was altogether pleased with his prospective brother-in-law. "I can truly say," he wrote Margaret, "that if I had to search India for a husband

5. See letter of August 10, 1834. *Ibid.*, I, 331-32.

for Hannah, I could have found no man to whom I could with equal confidence have entrusted her happiness."

It was small wonder that he wrote so! Here was a young man who, in his morality, was fully as stubborn and unyielding as Macaulay himself. When only twenty-one and fresh from England, he had charged his popular superior at Delhi with corrupt practices, had produced his evidence, and despite the "perfect storm that was raised against the accuser," had seen that superior sent home in disgrace. The Evangelical fervor which he had inherited from his father, the Reverend George Trevelyan, was not to be bought off. "He has no small talk," Macaulay went on to say. "His mind is full of schemes of moral and political improvement, and his zeal boils over in his talk." Even in courtship the subjects he regaled his betrothed with were "steam navigation, the education of the natives, the equalization of the sugar duties, the substitution of the Roman for the Arabic alphabet in the oriental languages." On all public matters he was, Macaulay added, "rash and uncompromising in his honesty." The aging Zachary was doubtless delighted to know about him.

What faults he had were few, and not incurable. He knew very little English literature "and, which surprises me greatly, he does not know a word of French. But to the little he has read he has brought a mind as active and restless as Lord Brougham's, and much more judicious and honest. . . . His manners are odd, blunt almost to roughness at times, and at other times awkward even to sheepishness."Macaulay explained this shortcoming by the fact that, during his first five years in India, Trevelyan had lived in a remote province where he rarely met with an Englishman. But Hannah, or Nancy as he called her, was improving him already.

"As to his person, nobody can call him handsome, and Nancy, I suppose in order to anticipate the verdict of others, pronounces him ugly. Birth is a thing I care nothing about. But his family is one of the oldest and best in England. Money is a more important matter, and there I think that Nancy

[185]

is fortunate. He has five thousand pounds in England. His salary here at present is about £2000 sterling and will, in all probability, be soon increased. If he lives, there can be no doubt of his rising rapidly to the most lucrative places in the Indian government."

It was a fine letter, the one just quoted, but it had to come to an end. And as he closed it, he thought once more, more personally this time, of what Nancy's marriage meant. When he had parted from Margaret it almost broke his heart, but then he had Nancy, he had his other relations, he had his friends and his country. Now he had nothing left except the resources of his own mind, and the consciousness of having acted not ungenerously. "But I do not repine. Whatever I suffer I have brought on myself. I have neglected the plainest lessons of reason and experience. I have staked my happiness without calculating the chances of the dice. I have hewn out broken cisterns; I have leaned on a reed; I have built on the sand; and I have fared accordingly." It was the tragical dénouement of an absurd plot.

Later, it seemed to him that nothing remained except his intellect and his books, the ability to hold converse with the mighty dead, the power of forgetting with which he had learned to surround himself. Nothing, after all, was really important except books. If at this moment he were given the choice of his life, he would elect to bury himself in one of those immense libraries at the universities they had visited together, and never pass a waking hour without a volume before him.[6] It was all too unfortunate! And to make it even worse, to school him even more deeply in the implacable contingencies of this world, he received a message from England in January, 1835, one which had crossed his own letter on the long voyage north. It informed him that Margaret had died six months before, in July—while Macaulay was lecturing his friends in the hills upon the excellencies of *Clarissa*.

6. This account of Trevelyan is based, mainly, upon a letter of Macaulay's to Margaret of December 7, 1834 (See *ibid.*, I, 339-42); and upon G. M. Trevelyan's *George Otto Trevelyan, a Memoir*, 6-9.

In his rôle as Councillor he was active almost from the time of his arrival in the country. One of the earliest matters which concerned him had to do with the Press. A form of censorship had existed in India for years. Macaulay, in an important minute, pointed out that in reality as much freedom was enjoyed by Indian publishers as by those in England. Why not then extend to them in name a privilege which actually they already possessed? Those who read the English papers were, almost exclusively, either servants of the Company or merchants to whom any threat to the existing order would prove a menace. A colleague had argued that the law restraining the press was a useful emergency measure. Let it be kept on the books, he had urged, in order that when needed it can be enforced. Macaulay pointed out a truth which carried his motion through: the supreme authority in India was vested in the five of them. They could be called together in thirty minutes time. Would it not be better, then, to remove this standing offense to all lovers of liberty, when it was possible, in a single sitting, to enact a law that would stop every press in India? His colleagues agreed. The measure was repealed.

The next problem to which he addressed himself was one for whose sake he endured the most insulting epithets of his life. "Cheat," "Swindler," "Charlatan," and worse were terms used day after day for a time to describe the ardent reformer, in the very papers for whose freedom he had worked. Macaulay was acting as chairman of a commission of four appointed for the purpose of revising the laws of India. In the early stages of their work these gentlemen, realizing that they could profit greatly from the advice of jurists who had enjoyed years of service in the country, issued a circular to all judges and magistrates. The circular explained that the Commission intended frequently to ask the opinion of these officials before drawing up laws in their final form. But an injunction was added, a warning that the jurists to be consulted "will doubtless at once perceive that freedom of correspondence must be materially checked unless the Commissioners are assured that publicity will not be given to any of their letters."[7] The Press, in other words, was to be kept ignorant of the progress of their work. Editors were indignant, and the bulk of their indignation fell upon Macaulay.

What focused that indignation was the announcement, in 1836, of the repeal of a twenty-three year old law which extended exclusively to Englishmen the right to appeal civil cases to the Supreme Court at Calcutta. Such appeals were in future to be heard by the Sudder Courts, which were manned, Macaulay said, "by English gentlemen of liberal education: as free as even the judges of the Supreme Court from any imputation of personal corruption." His complaint with the old law was that, in effect, it implied that there were two types of justice in the country—a coarse type, which was good enough for the natives, and a superior type, meant only for Englishmen.

Agitation was rather slow in starting. A respectful petition of protest was sent in to the Governor-general. His Lordship read it and replied to it negatively. Then the dissension grew, dragging in its wake all other resentments which the commissioners had aroused. Were not these austere Lycurguses bound to make reports from time to time? Where were their reports? Why had they not been published? The Sudder Court law was renamed the Black Act. A public meeting was called on June 18. The papers had declared that they held and did consider "the honorable fourth member of the Council mainly responsible in this enactment." That member was Macaulay.

Eight hundred people attended the meeting. It was held in the Town Hall and presided over by the Sheriff of Calcutta. What was behind all this complaining was a consideration which Macaulay was not slow to point out. There were a number of unscrupulous lawyers who amassed lucrative fees

7. See Arnold, *op. cit.*, 202.

from cases they carried to the Supreme Court. The revised law would stop such practices. One voluble attorney after another addressed the crowd. There was much applauding and shouting. A resolution was drawn up and wildly cheered. Finally one of the orators declared that loyal Englishmen should let the tyrant Macaulay know that

"There yawns the sack, and yonder rolls the sea." [8]

This was going pretty far. It was a plain threat to lynch Macaulay. Then a ludicrous thing happened. A certain Captain Biden arose, and after getting recognition, addressed the assembly as follows: "Gentlemen, I come before you in the character of a British seaman, and on that ground claim your attention for a few moments. Gentlemen, there has been much talk during the evening of laws and regulations and rights and liberties, and all that; but you seem to have forgotten that this, gentlemen, is the anniversary of the Battle of Waterloo." Loud and prolonged cheering and laughter interrupted him. "Gentlemen, I beg to propose, and I call on the statue of Lord Cornwallis and yourselves to join me in three cheers for the Duke of Wellington and the Battle of Waterloo." The Captain sat down, but by this time the laughter and cheering had become uncontrollable. The lawyers shouted their protests. They called the proceedings disgraceful. The chairman clamored for order. But all this was in vain; the meeting was past management. It was decided to adjourn until the following Monday, a day "which at least would not labor under the disadvantage of being the anniversary of the Battle of Waterloo." And though the troublesome Captain attended again, and again disturbed the gathering with his proposals, the strategists present did succeed in getting through a resolution which sent a paid agent to England to advocate their cause. Meanwhile, Macaulay's character continued to be assailed in the papers. He was always talking, it was charged.

8. *Ibid.*, 205.

[189]

He despised public opinion. He disliked society. It was prayed that the government would see the light and recall him.

One section of Macaulay's minute on the Black Act sufficiently explains his attitude. Until its passage, he pointed out, "an Englishman at Agra or Benares who owed a small debt to a native, who had beaten a native, who had come with a body of bludgeon-men and plowed up a native's land, if sued by the injured party for damages, was able to drag that party before the Supreme Court, a court which, in one most important point, the character of the judges, stands as high as any court can stand, but which in every other respect I believe to be the worst in India, the most dilatory, and the most ruinously expensive. Judicial corruption indeed is a most frightful evil, yet it is not the worst of evils. . . . A court may be worse than corrupt—it may be inaccessible."

He proceeded to show that in England many people with a just cause allowed injustice to prevail from lack of money for litigation; "and yet the English are the richest people in the world. The people of India are poor; yet the expense of litigation in the Supreme Court is five times as great as the expense of litigation at Westminster."[9] There was no answering this argument. The gentleman who represented the cause of Macaulay's detractors in London apparently failed to answer it, at any rate; for the resolution proposed on his advice to have the operation of the Act investigated died without a division in the House.[10]

Still more significant of the fact that Macaulay was sincerely interested in making his position no sinecure was his work in drawing up a Penal Code for the whole of India. He was not obligated to undertake this task, though authority to do so had been granted the Supreme Council by Parliament. Yet the criminal procedure of the country fairly cried out for systematizing and for reform. Macaulay, in requesting that

9. *Ibid.*, 232-33.
10. G. O. Trevelyan, *op. cit.*, I, 352. Trevelyan attributes the failure of this resolution to the general indifference of members to Indian affairs.

a commission be named for the purpose, set forth the two principles in the light of which it should proceed—"the principle of suppressing crime with the smallest amount of suffering, and the principle of ascertaining truth at the smallest possible cost of time and money."[11] The ideals of the Utilitarians are nowhere better or more succinctly stated. The request was granted at once, and he was asked to begin the undertaking soon after his arrival.

This Code appeared in 1837. Macaulay had been assisted, in various ways, by the other gentlemen already mentioned; yet it is only fair to say that the entire work bears unmistakably the impression of his genius. His colleagues labored with him only intermittently. They were often ill, or compelled to leave Calcutta, or forced to attend to other matters. Macaulay explained all this to the government, when asked why the efforts of the commission did not proceed more rapidly. He also reminded his questioners "that a code cannot be spoken off extempore, or written like an article in a magazine. I am not ashamed to acknowledge that there are several chapters in the code on which I have been employed for months; of which I have changed the whole plan ten or twelve times; which contain not a single word as it originally stood; and with which I am very far indeed from being satisfied. I certainly shall not hurry on my share of the work to gratify the childish impatience of the ignorant."[12] He then proceeded to dumbfound his critics with an array of comparative figures: The French Criminal Code required seven years to complete. The Criminal Code for Louisiana required four years and a half. A similar leisureness marked the drawing up of the Justinian Code. And in each of these cases, it should be remembered, the jurists who supervised the work had as assistants scores of skilled attorneys. The Indian Penal Code was completed in three years!

It was a most remarkable document. In addition to a

11. *Ibid.*, I, 363.
12. *Ibid.*, I, 364.

prefatory letter to Lord Auckland, the new Governor-general in Council, it contained twenty-six ample chapters, together with explanations, exceptions, and illustrations, and eighteen more fully explanatory notes, each one as long as an essay. The labors of the commission, Macaulay explained in the letter, had been complicated by the fact that the Code could not be based upon a digest of any existing system in the country, since all those systems were foreign to it. They had been imposed, variously, by the Mohammedans and the British upon the earlier regulations of the Hindoos. Furthermore, those extant systems were not uniform throughout the country; the nature of the punishment for crime depended largely upon the region in which it was committed.

Perhaps that feature of the Code which has received most comment has been the part devoted to illustration. Macaulay explained to his Lordship that this device had been resorted to profusely for the simple purpose of facilitating the understanding of the law. The Code was new and the vast majority of those to whom it applied were persons of limited education. But what makes this phase of the work especially interesting in Macaulay's case is that the illustrations serve so remarkably to point out his interest in literature. One was based on the plot of *Macbeth*, another on the plot of *Othello*, another on an incident in the life of Jack the giant-killer. It is probably the one generally readable code in existence.

For example: "A., after wounding a person with a knife, goes into the room where Z. is sleeping, smears Z.'s clothes with blood, and lays the knife under Z.'s pillow, intending not only that suspicion may thereby be turned away from himself, but also that Z. may be convicted of voluntarily causing grievous hurt. A. is liable to punishment as a fabricator of false evidence."[13] It is the very case of Lady Macbeth and the grooms.

Again, in his lengthy notes, Macaulay called upon his

13. See Arnold, *op. cit.*, p. 218 ff. Arnold is much more complete than Trevelyan in his treatment of Macaulay's Indian career.

knowledge of literature and history whenever it was necessary to make plain a legal principle. In amplifying his ideas on the weight which ought to be given the ruling passion in crime, he writes: "Suppose that A. makes a deliberate attempt to commit assassination; in the presence of numbers he aims a knife at the heart of Z., but the knife glances aside and inflicts only a slight wound. This happened in the case of Jean Chatel, of Damien, and of many other assassins of the most desperate character. In such cases there is no doubt whatever as to the intention." And respecting a certain kind of assault he notes that "such an assault produced the Sicilian vespers; such an assault called forth the memorable blow of Wat Tyler."

Illustrations of this sort might be tediously multiplied. It seems more pertinent, however, to inquire about the history of the Code after its publication, to note especially how well it has been esteemed by Macaulay's successors. Mr. Fitzjames Stephen, who once held Macaulay's place on the Council, has praised it without reservation. Pointing out the generally known fact that it was far too daring to gain immediate acceptance (it did not come into operation until 1862), he declares that the practical success of the Code has been complete, that "hardly any questions have arisen upon it which have had to be determined by the courts." Elsewhere we are told that young men in India rode with copies in their saddlebags, while old men carried it in their heads.

These were judgments of the later nineteenth century. More recent commentary has not in any important way discredited them. The most serious critic of the work, during later times, is Sir Hari Singh Gour,[14] whose complaints should at least be briefly noticed. This gentleman remarks, with considerable tartness, that "the enactment known as the Indian Penal Code has come to be associated with the great name of Macaulay. As such, perhaps, it is spoken of as a model of codification and as a perfect piece of legislation. That it is

14. *The Penal Law of British India* (2 vols.), Calcutta, 1925.

neither the one nor the other will be probably frankly conceded by anyone who has made a critical study of the subject. At the same time it is a code which, with all its faults, has stood the test of half a century."

This was written in 1909. Sixteen years later the author was still willing to concede that "as a code, it is by far the most important piece of Indian legislation." He added, however, that it now required a thorough revision "by an expert committee of lawyers."

Specifically, Gour contends that many sections in the work are poorly arranged, that many of its provisions overlap one another, that while some parts of it are pedantically precise, "others are bald and leave much to the ingenuity of construction." Still more specifically considered, Gour's exceptions center around the question of the punishments Macaulay's commission decreed. There were five in number—death, transportation, imprisonment, fine, and forfeiture. Each of these types is treated in detail by this critic:

As for the death penalty, he declares, we are no longer certain that it should be demanded at all. At any rate, it is a complex sociological problem which should be weighed in the light of its complexity. Transportation is now obsolete. Macaulay favored it, doubtless, because he knew in what dread the "black water," or the ocean, was held by natives living far inland. The problem of imprisonment, moreover, as prescribed by the Code, is too loosely treated; a man may be given from one day to ten years, depending on the caprice of the judge in the case. Gour is in sympathy with the fourth type, punishment by fine, seeing in it a means of compensating the offended person and of replenishing the state treasury; yet he regrets that it fails to carry with it the stigma that attends other forms of punishment. The last type, forfeiture, he declares, is no longer practiced in enlightened countries and should therefore be discontinued in India.[15]

Gour's is, probably, the most careful critique of the Code

15. *Ibid.*, "Introduction," clx-clxvi.

which has appeared. Yet to consider his strictures in detail is—one feels justified in saying—to be convinced, at least from the point of view of a layman, that his opening generalizations about Macaulay's work are too severe, are not borne out by the evidence later submitted. Condensed, this gentleman's major complaint is that certain sections of the Code are now obsolete, that certain other sections need rearranging or tightening.[16] What else is to be expected, one wonders, in a world so rapidly shifting almost all its standards, if not discarding them utterly?

One more service he was to render to India before he left, and that service, like his labors with its laws, was to prove of lasting importance. Which way was that constantly growing empire to develop in its intellectual interests? Would it become progressive, westernized, or would the apathy of the Orient continue to shroud it? Macaulay had his convictions about this matter, a thoroughly settled opinion, as might be expected. But for half a year after his arrival he said nothing. Named in July, 1834, as Chairman of the Committee of Public Instruction, he devoted the remainder of the year to a patient study of the attitude of his colleagues. There were ten of them. And he soon discovered that, of that ten, five were convinced past any conversion that the energies and resources of the Committee should be devoted to fostering Oriental learning, and that the other five, with equal tenacity, held out for the learning of Europe.

On February 2, 1835, Macaulay settled this difference for good. "How stands the case?" he asked. "We have to educate people who cannot at present be educated by means of their mother tongue. We must teach them some foreign language. The claims of our own language it is hardly necessary to recapitulate." He went on, however, to itemize these claims at length: the works of imagination written in it are not inferior to those of Greece. Every species of eloquence is to

16. See N. K. R. Iyengar, *The Indian Penal Code*, Madras, 1929. This critic is lavish in his praise of Macaulay's work, complaining only of a slight fault in arrangement. See "Introduction," vii.

be found in it, the best histories, the profoundest metaphysics, the ablest reflections upon morals, jurisprudence, and economics, the most valuable works of science. "Whoever knows that language has ready access to all the vast intellectual wealth which all the wisest nations of the earth have created and hoarded in the course of ninety generations. Nor is this all. English is the language of the ruling classes. . . . It is likely to become the language of commerce throughout the seas of the East. . . . .

"The question now before us is simply whether, when it is in our power to teach this language, we shall teach languages in which, by universal confession, there are no books on any subject which deserve to be compared to our own; whether, when we can teach European science, we shall teach systems which, by universal confession, whenever they differ from those of Europe differ for the worse; and whether, when we can patronize sound philosophy and true history, we shall countenance, at the public expense, medical doctrines which would disgrace an English farrier—astronomy, which would move laughter in the girls at an English boarding school—history, abounding with kings thirty feet high, and reigns thirty thousand years long—and geography, made up of seas of treacle and seas of butter." [17] Thus in a single paragraph did he obliterate all the wisdom and civilization of the Orient, as in a single essay on Bacon the next year he was to obliterate the idealistic philosophy of Greece. The gesture defines, in little, his greatest intellectual limitation.

But his point of view prevailed. Two of the Orientalists resigned from the Committee of Public Instruction and were replaced by others sympathetic with Macaulay's attitude. Some of the minutes he set down in connection with his work as Chairman are highly illuminating:

A master desired to be moved to another town, for what Macaulay believed to be a trivial reason: "We are a little too indulgent to the whims of the people in our employ. We pay

17. Quoted in G. O. Trevelyan, *op. cit.*, I, 354.

a large sum to send a master to a distant station. He dislikes the place. The collector is uncivil; the surgeon quarrels with him, and he must be moved. The expenses of the journey have to be defrayed. Another man is to be transferred from a place where he is comfortable and useful. Our masters run from station to station at our cost, as vaporized ladies at home run about from spa to spa. All situations have their discomforts; and there are times when we all wish that our lot had been cast in some other line of life, or in some other place."

A proposal was made that a coat of arms be provided for Hooghly College. Macaulay declared that he did "not see why the mummeries of European heraldry should be introduced into any part of our Indian system." The propriety of printing certain books of Oriental science was considered. Macaulay felt that the money allotted his committee—only £3000 for all purposes—was far too little to be wasted in any such manner. Later a suggestion was made that stipends be paid adult natives for attending the college and studying English. The notion, he felt, was absurd. "Moghal Jan has been paid to learn something during twelve years. We are told that he is lazy and stupid; but there are hopes that in four years more he will have completed his course of study. We have quite enough of these lazy stupid school boys of thirty." Then came the problem of buying grammar texts for the students. More foolishness! "Grammars of rhetoric and grammars of logic are among the most useless furniture of a shelf. Give a boy *Robinson Crusoe*. That is worth all the grammars of rhetoric and logic in the world."

So it went. Some of the teachers in his system were staging scenes out of Shakespeare. "I can conceive nothing more grotesque than the scene from the *Merchant of Venice* with Portia represented by a little black boy." And the prize books that were being given to brilliant children, books, it seemed, deliberately designed to stultify their taste for English literature! A prize book should be one which afforded the winner of it real pleasure; it shouldn't be the works of Pope, it shouldn't be his friend Moore's *Lalla Rookh*, and it shouldn't, above all, be Dick's *Moral Improvement* or Young's *Intellectual Philosophy*. "I will suggest offhand," he declared, "a better list. Give Bacon's *Essays*, Gibbon's *Rome*, Robertson's *Charles V*, Swift's *Gulliver*, Shakespeare's Works, *Paradise Lost*, *The Vicar of Wakefield*, or Southey's *Life of Nelson*." One of the most pleasant recollections of his life, he added, was the occasion when, at the age of fourteen, his master gave him Boswell's biography of Johnson.[18]

Macaulay's influence survived his departure; the system he inaugurated grew astonishingly, and in the direction he desired. Forty years after he began his work, writes Trevelyan, the budget for public education in India had increased seventyfold, and two hundred thousand boys were profiting by the instruction it made possible. And they were learning, moreover, the ways of the West; they were turning their minds away, finally, from the ageless superstitions and moribund folkways of the Orient. They were becoming, at length, brisk and modern—rationalists drenched in the misty gospel of Progress. And above them all, the brightest star in their new and glittering firmament, shone England, radiant source of blessings. Let these recently discovered dark angels but continue to look homeward for all their needs. Let them but do that, and all other problems would solve themselves.[19]

18. These minutes were collected by H. Woodrow and published in Calcutta (c. 1860). The volume is not now to be found in the British Museum. See *ibid.*, I, 353-61.
19. See, on Macaulay's total achievement in India, Elie Halévy, *A History of the English People, 1830-41* (London, 1927), 234-35.

XI. Scholar

YET IT WAS NOT ALL BUSINESS in India; it was never all business in Macaulay's life. Had it seemed so, he would hardly have felt himself to be living at all. One tended to public matters, as it were, with one's left hand. The main justification for existence, what made it endurable, was reading and writing. And as friends fell away, one by one, or as relatives died, these activities came increasingly to absorb him.

He would write home about his living quarters. The Trevelyans were staying with him—Nancy, Charles, and their daughter, just learning to walk. He arose at five, had an early cup of tea, and sat in his garden, absorbed in a book, until his niece toddled down to greet him. He would give her crusts of toast, and together they would feed the great birds that fluttered about the lawn, birds almost as large as the child herself. It would be getting too hot outside now. He would go in to his bath and his dressing. Then breakfast would be ready—"plenty of eggs, mango-fish, snipe pies, and frequently a hot beefsteak. My cook is renowned through Calcutta for his skill."[1]

The reading he was getting through continued, no doubt, to astonish all who knew of it. He wrote his friend Ellis of Margaret's death. "That I have not utterly sunk under this blow I owe chiefly to literature." It was Greek literature that

1. G. O. Trevelyan, *op. cit.*, I, 368.

mainly consoled him, six lines of old Hesiod especially, lines which he never tired of recalling:

"For if to one whose grief is fresh, as he sits silent with sorrow-stricken heart, a minstrel, the henchman of the Muses, celebrates the men of old and the gods who possess Olympus, straightway he forgets his melancholy, and remembers not at all his grief, beguiled by the blessed gift of the goddesses of song." [2]

But Hesiod was only one among a very great many writers whom he admired. Thucydides he had never been able to appreciate in college. Now, "with a mind accustomed to historical researches and to political affairs," he was astonished at his own former blindness. And what a poet Euripides was— another author he had not cared for in his younger days. "It is all I can do to keep Greek and Latin out of all my letters. Wise sayings of Euripides are even now at my finger's ends." He had just finished a second reading of Sophocles. He was now deep in Plato and intended to go right through his entire works. Had Ellis noted the raillery that all but saturates the Dialogues? That was something else he had failed to appreciate at Trinity. He was just about finished also with a complete edition of Livy; to tell the truth he had never read him fully before. "I admire him greatly and would give a quarter's salary to recover the lost Decades." He talked on about emendations, and emendators. Take that ass Niebuhr, for instance! Read over his conjectural restoration of the inscription "on page 126 of the second volume; and then, on your honor as a scholar and a man of sense, tell me whether in Bentley's edition of Milton there is anything approaching it in audacity." Nothing was so extremely nauseous to him, he went on, as a German professor telling the world, purely on his own authority, "that two of the best Latin poets were ignorant of the quality of a word which they must have used in their exercises at school a hundred times."

2. Quoted in *ibid.*, I, 378. (G. M. Trevelyan has published an interesting monograph, *Marginal Notes of Lord Macaulay*) (London, 1907).

Other famous Romans were engaging his interest too. One of them was Cicero, "whose character, moral and intellectual, interests one prodigiously." He had gone through all of Ovid's poems. "I admire him; but I was tired to death before I got to the end." But Ovid couldn't touch Virgil. Caesar he had read again, and the commentator had risen wonderfully in his regard; Sallust, also reread, had gone down.

By way of being more definite, he cast up his reading account once for Ellis. It extended over a thirteen month period, ending with the year 1835. In all, it included, he wrote: "Aeschylus twice, Sophocles twice, Euripides once; Pindar twice; Callimachus; Apollonius Rhodus; Quintus Calaber; Theocritus twice, Herodotus; Thucydides; almost all Xenophon's works; almost all Plato; Aristotle's *Politics*, and a good deal of his *Organon*, besides dipping elsewhere in him; the whole of Plutarch's *Lives;* about half of Lucian; two or three books of Athanaeus; Plautus twice, Terence twice, Lucretius twice, Catullus, Tibullus, Propertius, Lucan, Statius, Silius Italicus, Livy, Velleius Paterculus, Sallust, Caesar, and lastly, Cicero. I have, indeed, still a little of Cicero left; but I shall finish him in a few days."[3]

More insight into his habits of reading may be found from such pencillings as the following. They appeared in practically all his Greek and Latin books:

"I read Plautus four times at Calcutta.

"The first, in November and December, 1834.

"The second, in January and the beginning of February, 1835.

"The third, on the Sundays from the 24th of May to the 23rd of August, 1835.

"The fourth, on the Sundays beginning from the 1st of January, 1837.

"I have since read him in the Isle of Wight (1850) and in the South of France." (1858)[4]

3. *Ibid.*, I, 389.
4. *Ibid.*, I (Appendix), 409.

Each entry, it should be remembered, implied a complete perusal!

Similar lists might be set down for practically all the classical authors. He knew them almost from memory—as he knew *Paradise Lost*, and *Pilgrim's Progress*, and the Holy Bible from memory. It is a curious case, yet a distressing one; for though an increasing sense of his loneliness in the world doubtless contributed to the habit, it was one fairly well developed long before he left Cambridge. One thinks of the case as distressing when he is forced to contrast the breadth of the knowledge Macaulay had led himself to assimilate with the general shallowness of his own thinking. How sad a circumstance to reflect that a man who had so much of the accumulated wisdom of the western world almost literally at his tongue's end, who could quote that wisdom almost hours without number—how sad to think that it made of him so very little more than a Whig politician, a violently biased reviewer for the *Edinburgh*, a historian blind to the virtues of men who did not share the prejudices of his party! He was, in truth, something beyond this, to be sure. He was a master, the like of which is yet to appear, of certain effects in English prose. But that this gift stemmed in any important way from his reading of the ancients is yet to be proved.

Macaulay wrote two essays for Napier while in India—the review of the works of his friend Sir James Mackintosh, and his lengthy appraisal of Lord Bacon. Before sailing from home, he had made the editor a most generous proposition: Let Napier furnish him with important new works as they came out, or new editions of old works, and he would continue to write for the magazine occasionally without expecting pay. In a letter to Brougham, Napier implied that he would not hear to such a sacrifice on Macaulay's part, but the proposal won his lasting gratitude. Napier, moreover, did keep his most valuable contributor pretty well supplied with books.

But the treatise on Bacon created a problem. The editor checked its length and found that, to print it entire, would demand more than a hundred pages of an issue. Such a thing was unheard of. What made the matter still more perplexing was the fact that Macaulay had informed him that he had never bestowed so much care on anything he had previously written. "There is not a sentence in the latter half of the article which has not been repeatedly recast." Napier turned to Lord Jeffrey for advice, and Jeffrey's reply soon resolved the whole business for good:

"What mortal," he exclaimed, "could ever dream of cutting out the least particle of this precious work, to make it fit better into your Review? It would be worse than paring down the Pitt diamond to fit the old setting of a dowager's ring. Since Bacon himself, I do not know that there has been anything so fine. The first five or six pages are in a lower tone, but still magnificent and not to be deprived of a word."[5]

That settled the matter. Macaulay's "Bacon" occupied 104 pages of the *Edinburgh*. It was accompanied by an editorial in which Napier apologized for its length, but added that he knew the best class of his readers would approve so scholarly and brilliant an exception to his usual practice. Approve a very great many did. And as for those who disapproved, that was not too objectionable either; for they disapproved, in many cases, vociferously, which meant that the essay was publicized. So publicized did it become finally, indeed, that one reviewer, James Spedding, devoted two fat volumes to a vain attempt to answer it and to minimize its still abounding popularity.[6]

Yet Macaulay was homesick, a lonely man despite the fact that he was living in a house in which Nancy was still more than a sister to him, and Charles more than a brother-in-law. "I have no words to tell you how I pine for England, or how intensely bitter exile has been to me, though I hope that I have borne it well. I feel as if I had no other wish than to see my country again, and die." Banishment is no light matter, he

5. Jeffrey to Napier. See *ibid.*, I, 398.
6. See Spedding's *Evenings with a Reviewer* (2 vols.), Privately printed, London, 1848.

continued, whether voluntary or involuntary; it can only be understood through experience. Think what it involves —a complete revolution in all the habits of life; an estrangement from almost every old friend and acquaintance; fifteen thousand miles of ocean between the exile and every thing he cares for. "There is no temptation of wealth or power which would induce me to go through it again."[7]

And so it happened that, with increasing impatience, he watched the revolving seasons as they turned, too slowly, toward January, 1838, at which time he had decided to resign his place. His major public objectives would all be finished by that date; the money he had saved would, if wisely invested, be sufficient to maintain him and the family the rest of their days. About this matter he was now confident, since his uncle, General Macaulay, had died in 1836 and left him a legacy of £10,000. Indeed, by the time he proposed to sail he would be richer than he ever wished to be as a single man, "and every day renders it more unlikely that I should marry."

But what would he do, once he was settled again in London? Two paths, he realized, would be open to him—the paths of politics and literature. Would he take the former one, one which, if taken, would render every friendship he cared about precarious? Would he be willing again, as before, "to sit or stand night after night for ten or twelve hours, inhaling a noisome atmosphere and listening to harangues of which nine-tenths are far below the level of a leading article in a newspaper"? What was he seeking, after all, in those old days, when he labored in Parliament hour after hour, until morning broke over the Thames and he tottered home, with bursting temples, to his bed? Was it fame he had sought? If so, there was a better way. Of that he was convinced. And in its train, the train of a literary reputation, were "health, leisure, peace of mind, the search after truth, and all the enjoyments of friendship and conversation." He would not say positively just yet, because he could not predict his

7. G. O. Trevelyan, *op. cit.*, I, 372.

state of mind once he had returned; but now he felt like abandoning politics altogether and undertaking "some great historical work which may be at once the business and the amusement of my life."[8] It was the first intimation of his desire to write the book upon which his reputation mainly rests.

He sailed in January 1838, as planned, on the *Lord Hunger-ford*, "a huge floating hotel" that ran regularly between London and Calcutta. With him were Nancy, and Charles, and Margaret, or "Baba," their first born. They had left behind a second child; she had died of a fever before reaching the age of two. Years later, surrounded by other children of Nancy, Macaulay remembered that now nameless grave in India, and a tiny thing that had stood beside him, feeding incredulously the glamorous birds. The shining seas of space dissolved; in imagination he was there again with her, holding her hand, and in tears.

8. *Ibid.*, I, 387-88 (To Ellis, December 30, 1835).

XII. Partisan

THE STATELY *Lord Hungerford*, much more a palace than a speedboat, required almost six months to make the voyage home. She was even once given out as lost, and friends of the Macaulay family and anxious Whigs called often at Lloyd's for news of her. Four weeks before the ship landed, Zachary, almost blind, and tragically useless after a strenuous career, died in London. His was the second loved face that his son would not see again upon his return. It was strange the way these things happened. Eight years before, while on a brief trip to Paris, he had learned of the death of a younger sister. Two years after that, while on a visit still briefer, he had read in the *Times* of his mother's death. It was to be that way, in years to come, with a brother and with another sister, Selina. Always, it seemed, on these occasions, it was fated that he should be absent.

His father was buried in Westminster Abbey, a fitting reward for one who while he lived had suffered uncomplainingly far more than his share of abuse. "For forty successive years," read his epitaph, he had worked "to rescue Africa from the woes, and the British Empire from the guilt, of slavery." The toil which that heavy labor had involved he had endured with meekness; the praise he had resigned to others. The condolences the family received were wide and uniformly generous. "His name," wrote one friend, "will ever be dear to those who hate injustice."[1] It is a loss, declared another, "which is not to be replaced."

1. See Arnold, *op. cit.*, 244.

On the heels of this misfortune came another highly disturbing affair. It was an outgrowth of Macaulay's review of a work of his friend Mackintosh. That article, which had appeared in 1835, contained strictures more than normally abusive against Mackintosh's editor, a Mr. Wallace. Now, three years later, these strictures almost forgotten by the author of them, Mr. Wallace had serious business with Macaulay.

In truth, this gentleman, though himself a twaddler, was scarcely to be blamed. He had appended to the work he was editing an account of the life of Mackintosh, and in it had accused his subject of "bad taste and gross negligence" for failing, when young, to appear promptly before a board of medical examiners at Edinburgh. He had also, still twaddling, charged Mackintosh, in an early composition, with misusing the past tense of a Latin verb. This was too much for a man of the world like Macaulay. The latter mistake, he said, was one such as "the greatest scholar might commit when in haste, and the veriest schoolboy detect when at leisure." Mr. Wallace was an arrant pedagogue. He had displayed a contempt toward a great man (a Whig) for whom he was incompetent to serve even as a proof reader. No person, he concluded, who has read Wallace's memoir "will doubt that there are men whose abuse is an honor." [2] Wallace sent him a challenge.

Macaulay wanted no duel. He never in his life learned to fire a pistol; three years before his death, even, he was wondering whether it would not be wise to hire somebody to teach him, since robberies in the city were becoming unusually common. [3] His first impulse, therefore, was to call upon his literary recollections for support. This he did by quoting Junius' remark: "I never will give proof of my spirit at the expense of my understanding."

Moreover, had Mr. Wallace behaved according to the

2. Quoted in G. O. Trevelyan, *op. cit.*, II, 12. Macaulay softened the passage, and all others referring to Wallace, when his collected essays came out. See his note in *Works*, VI, 76.

3. See his *Journal*, XI, 41 (entry for September 28, 1856).

Code? Shouldn't his displeasure be ignored, since he had waited several weeks after Macaulay's arrival in London, before signifying his intention? These were questions that were very pertinent and valid, but they were soon answered in a manner with which Macaulay could find no complaint. The challenge, when it came, was "very properly worded." Wallace's delay in sending it was explained by a second as being due to his feeling of sympathy over Zachary's death: he did not wish to obtrude until the initial effect of that grief was past. Macaulay entrusted his side of the matter to Lord Strafford. It seemed that to avoid a meeting now was impossible.

But the seconds for both men proved remarkably sensible. After an interview, they concluded that Macaulay had been bitter because he felt that Mackintosh had been, in his private character, too violently abused; and that Mr. Wallace was bitter because he felt that, in *his* private character, he had likewise been mistreated. The principals were consulted. Macaulay declared that he had not meant to assail Mr. Wallace, *as a man*. Wallace said the same about Mackintosh. Mutual apologies were extended and accepted. It is an interesting coincidence that, after this settlement, Macaulay, with the single exception of an army chaplain, never again wrote unkindly of English gentlemen who had edited or composed books he happened to be reviewing. And this was the case regardless of whether he approved the ideas the books contained, and regardless of whether the gentlemen were Whigs or Tories. [4]

Mr. Napier wanted him, of course, to do more writing for the *Review*. A fine subject, fairly crying for the proper pen, was Walter Scott. Dead six years now, it was time his own generation pronounced its judgment upon him. Meanwhile, however, Macaulay had been maturing, was beginning to realize rather sharply certain of those personal limitations which maturity brings home to everyone. "I will tell you what

4. Compare, for example, in his early reviews, the strictures upon Croker, Southey, and Robert Montgomery with his later comments on the characters of Leigh Hunt and Gladstone. *Works*, V, VI, and VII, *passim*.

I sincerely think," he wrote the editor, "when I say that I am not successful in analyzing the effects of works of genius." Some of his historical, political, and moral essays he was still not ashamed of; "but I have never written a page of criticism on poetry, or the fine arts, which I would not burn if I had the power." Don't misunderstand, he went on. Works of the imagination he very often profoundly enjoyed. He simply had never taught himself to dissect them. Really great criticism filled him with wonder and despair.

Not that he was without an opinion of Scott! He had a decided opinion, and did not mind communicating it to a friend. He felt that Scott was singularly free from the petty sins which beset men of letters—sins of jealousy and morbid irritability, in particular. Yet as a man of the world, Sir Walter had stood a mighty long way from perfection! He was "in politics, a bitter and unscrupulous partisan" [a Tory!]; he was a wastrel financially, agitated "by the hopes and fears of a gambler." Finally, and worst of all, Scott was "perpetually sacrificing the perfection of his compositions and the durability of his fame, to his eagerness for money." [5] It would naturally be in very bad taste to publish such convictions as these in a Scotch review. Macaulay made no reference in this letter to Scott's novels, or to any of his characters.

Several weeks later he wrote Napier again, announcing an intention which had by this date become fixed. He was going on a tour of the continent, and would remain there until spring. "As soon as I return, I shall seriously commence my History." He went on to say that part one—which would cover the period from the Revolution of 1688 to Sir Robert Walpole's long administration—would require five octavo volumes. He was mapping out, in other words, the work which was mainly to engage his interests for the following ten years.

He left for the tour of Italy in October. Writing to Ellis a little before he set out, he told him, among other things,

5. G. O. Trevelyan, *op. cit.*, II, 15-16 (Letter to Napier of June 26, 1838).

that he had recently been painted by the artist Hayter for his picture of members of the House of Commons. Macaulay could not judge of the merit of the work. He could only say, "as Charles the Second did on a similar occasion, 'Odds fish! if I am like this, I am an ugly fellow.' "[6]

2

The first of the eleven volumes of the highly valuable *Journal* which Macaulay kept, with one nine and a half year lapse, to the closing week of his life begins with this tour made during the fall of 1838.[7] Its major value to the biographer rests in the fact that Macaulay undertook it with no thought of publication. It is hastily written throughout, is for the most part unpolished and direct in style. He seems to have been interested in setting down, purely for the purpose of keeping a record, his impressions of men, books, and places. He often read early parts of it over with considerable pleasure, and confessed as much in later entries. As far as can be determined, his friends and relatives did not know until his death that he kept it. It would have intrigued them no doubt, if they had known; as it would have both intrigued and instructed them could they have read it. For within its pages, without the slightest hesitation, he wrote out judgment after judgment of his contemporaries that, in bitterness, even Carlyle during his most dyspeptic intervals would have despaired to rival.

In France, where he stopped first, he did a good deal of walking in the country. The scenery proved delightful to him. After all, to enjoy nature, one should ramble amidst it. One should not approach it as one goes to see the lions fed at the fair. "The beautiful is not to be stared at, but to be lived with. I have no pleasure from books which equals that of

6. *Ibid.*, II, 22.
7. This *Journal* was given to Trinity College, Cambridge, in 1928 by its owner, G. M. Trevelyan, who has kept a typed copy of the whole except Vol. 7. The lapse is from May 15, 1839, to November 8, 1848, the period of the composition of the first part of the *History*. The *Journal* was kept mostly in unlined notebooks of varying sizes. In length each volume averages approximately 300 pages. The work may be examined with Professor Trevelyan's permission.

reading over for the hundredth time great productions which
I almost know by heart; and it is just the same with scenery."[8]

At Marseilles he paid his respects to the Catholic service
and religion, and incidentally, to certain phases of evangelical
worship which he had noticed at home. The passage is too
illuminating to be condensed:

After walking through the streets for half an hour one
Sunday, without finding a place of worship, he at last heard
bells. "The noise guided me to a church, mean outside and
meaner inside, but crowded as Simeon's church used to be
crowded at Cambridge. . . . I staid a short time, and not
being either edified by the mumbling of the priest or gratified
by the odour of the congregation I went out and was soon
attracted by another peal of bells to another church, nearer
than the former, and if possible fuller. The crowd of the
faithful blocked up the avenues, except one, by which I
squeezed myself in; and found that the mass was nearly over.
The building and its decorations were wretched. There was
a daub of God the Father—a subject which even when treated
by the greatest Italian masters is sufficiently offensive—a
wooden doll without beauty as expressly representing the
Virgin—and so forth. I staid to the end, wondering that so
many reasonable beings could come together to see a man
bow, drink, bow again, wipe a cup, wrap up a napkin, spread
his arms and gesticulate with his hands, and to hear a low
muttering which they could not understand interrupted by
the occasional jangling of a bell. The lowest field preaching
is respectable compared with this mummery.

"However, the Mass seems to have as great attractions for
the people of Marseilles as the oratory of the most celebrated
Evangelical preacher for the pious ladies of London. . . .
They spit indeed in the Church, for the French spit everywhere. I wish they would take a lesson from San Ciapellatto
on that subject. I am certain that either of the two congregations which I saw today at Marseilles contained twice as

8. *Journal*, I (quoted in G. O. Trevelyan, *op. cit.*, II, 23).

many people and ten times as many males as I have before seen engaged in the public worship of the Catholic church on the continent all put together."[9]

He had a good deal more to say about the papal states after staying a while in Rome. "Corruption," he soon decided, "infects all the public offices. Old women above—liars and cheats below—that is the Papal administration. As a specimen of old womaning in the highest place of all—the Pope told some English who waited on him two days ago that he did not like railroads, that he was determined not to tolerate them, for he was sure no man could breathe while travelling twenty miles an hour and he would not suffer the breath of his subjects to be taken away."[10] Such an attitude from a person of importance very naturally would vex any man who has recently invested almost half his fortune in railroad stocks!

Yet there were several redeeming features to this Church, even though old women and liars did control it. Macaulay soon decided that religious ceremonies among its followers served very much the same purpose that levees, coronations, exhibitions, and concerts served at home; they enabled people to kill time pleasantly. "Certainly whatever faults the Catholic system may have, it has the merit of offering an agreeable occupation and diversion."[11] In England, he felt, religion is too often associated with what is dull and serious; one is glad when Sunday is over. But not in Rome. He compared a fine service here to a play in Covent Garden, concluding with the remark that he would prefer the former.

There was another thing to be remembered too. Though he could, for himself, imagine nothing worse than an English gentleman being subject to a pope, or a government in which the only avenue of distinction was through the priesthood, still there was something that appealed to his deepest nature

9. Unpublished *Journal*, I, 27-28 (entry of October 28, 1838). Trevelyan quotes from this entry but deletes its most interesting passages. See *ibid.*, II, 24-25.
10. *Journal*, I, 187 (Entry of November 30, 1838).
11. *Ibid.*, I, 198.

when he reflected upon the "immense antiquity" of the papal tradition. It was one which could "boast of a far longer, clear, known, and uninterrupted succession than any dignity in the world." It linked together the two great ages of human civilization. Compared with the successors of Sylvester and Leo the Great, our modern feudal kings are mere upstarts.

With the possible exception of the paintings, Macaulay liked the churches in Italy more than he liked any other thing he saw. He found what every sensitive traveler to that country finds; that those rich interiors glowing with colors were almost incredible to one familiar only with "cold white naked edifices like St. Paul's." The paintings he studied religiously; it was the beginning of an interest which never afterwards waned. One little painting by Raphael, which he saw in a room of the Palazzo Pitti, almost reconciled him, he confessed, to seeing God the Father on canvas.

But damn the beggars of the country! They were everywhere, unspeakably filthy and brazen. Speculating upon their numbers, and their insolence, he decided that the superstitions of Italy were to blame, superstitions which, among other things, reckon almsgiving as a meritorious act. The beggars were perfectly healthy men, in almost every case! One of them practically halted Macaulay's carriage once and asked for an alms. "Why should I give?" Macaulay inquired. "For the love of God," he was answered. "But I gave him nothing; and indeed I am proud to say that I have given not a single piece of copper coin to a single beggar in Italy." [12]

Another thing he disliked was grand opera. His usual comment was that he looked upon attendance at these performances as "a disagreeable duty." In Naples he met a friend who begged him to take a seat in his box at the San Carlo. This, he was told, was the finest theatre in Italy; and on the night he was asked to go, the Royal family also planned to attend. He went reluctantly, admitting that he would not give a copper "to see every Bourbon, living and dead, of the Span-

12. *Ibid.*, I, 109.

ish branch." He looked around at the interior of the building during the first act. At length, however, he became "bored to death." He fell asleep for at least half an hour. Yet afterwards he went home and read *Gil Blas*. "Charming!" he notes. "I am never tired of it." Books were music enough for him.

And as always, he was reading them—good and bad, ancient and modern, anything he could get his hands on: "Bought *Oliver Twist* and read it. It is certainly clever. But there is no delicacy in the delineation of the characters; there is too monotonous a gloom and squalidity about the whole."[13] Before breakfast, every morning, he was getting through, in the original German, ten or twelve pages of Von Ranke's *History of the Popes*, by way of keeping up his acquaintance with a language he had partly learned on the passage from India. He was also going through Dante and Tasso again. And at intervals he was reading fiction which he knew beforehand to be quite worthless—vile narratives like *Crichton*, or that "execrably stupid novel," *Tylney Hall*. "Why do I read such stuff?" he asked himself. But he left the question unanswered.

Meanwhile, a shaky Ministry wanted his services back home. Lord Melbourne had sent word that he should like to name him Judge Advocate. A seat in Parliament could be obtained for him with little expense. The salary was £2500 a year. But Macaulay was aloof, he was not even tempted, he said. "The money I do not want. I have little, but I have enough. The Right Honorable before my name is a bauble which it would be far, very far indeed, beneath me to care about. The power is nothing." As an independent member of Parliament—as one, that is, not bound to support the government blindly—he would have "infinitely greater power." In fact, as a free writer—his present status—he was a great deal more influential. If he had been asked to be a member of the Cabinet, his attitude would, perhaps, be different. But the present offer would reduce him to slavery. He declined it,

13. *Ibid.*, I, 351.

explaining, politely, that only one consideration could induce him to give up his present liberty and studies, the offer of a place which carried with it the opportunity "to effect great things." For after all, he was now seriously meditating the most important labor of his life, his History, was becoming more and more in love with the subject. "I really think," he had written in his *Journal*, "that posterity will not willingly let my book die."[14] He came back home by easy stages, biding his time, in debt to no man.

3

Almost as soon as he got there—in early February, 1839—he ran across an interesting book by young Gladstone, then a Tory sympathizer. Here was "a capital shrove-tide cock to throw at," almost too good a mark to pass up. He read in it a hundred pages or so and his early impression was confirmed. "The Lord," he declared, "hath delivered him into our hand."[15] He set to work on an article for Napier.

Napier was, as usual, delighted with the review: it was the finest piece of logic ever printed. What Macaulay was proud of, on his part, was that there was not a single line in the whole of it which the staunchest of the old Claphamites could have quarreled with as being at all indecorous.

In the same letter which revealed his satisfaction with this latest literary accomplishment, he informed his sister Hannah that he had been elected unanimously to membership in *the* Club. Lord Lansdowne had just told him the news. It was the old club of Dr. Johnson, Garrick, Goldsmith, Burke, Gibbon, Boswell, and Sir Joshua, still vigorously alive. At present it included, among others, Lord Holland, the Bishop of London, Lord Mahon, Sir Charles Grey, and H. H. Milman. Macaulay attended his first meeting, and was delighted. What delighted him most, perhaps, was a sight of the records, which

14. Quoted in G. O. Trevelyan, *op. cit.*, II, 38.
15. *Ibid.*, II, 48.

were carefully preserved. Turning through them at an odd moment, he "came upon poor Bozzy's signature, evidently affixed when he was too drunk to guide his pen."

But there was no getting around the Whigs' dire need of his help. Internal dissension had weakened them desperately. At the head of the party was Lord Melbourne, but that kindly gentleman sadly lacked the powers that had been granted to Grey and Russell. About him, as Sydney Smith declared, there hung an air of shabby incompetence. He could not inspire trust: "One would suppose from his manner that he was playing at chuck-farthing with human happiness; that he would giggle away the Great Charter, and decide by the method of tee-totum whether my lords and bishops should retain their seats in the House of Lords."[16] The real service he was rendering the country—that of instructing the young Queen Victoria in sound constitutional principles—was not then sufficiently well known to win for his Ministry the support it deserved. But to Macaulay, still fairly fresh from other lands, Melbourne's was the old party still,[17] the glorious band of 1832, now fallen upon evil days. He came to its aid, and —forgetting the high resolves he had made in India—stood for Parliament for Edinburgh[18] and was elected.

And with his candidacy and election came the inevitable abuse from sources friendly to the Tory point of view. The *Times* recalled that he had just recently returned from the Orient, where he had succeeded in making a grand mess of the laws. Confusion reigned in that country now, although before he went out on his holy reform mission, it had been serenely tranquil. The only thing Mr. Macaulay had accomplished there had been to amass a fortune of £30,000 at the expense of the public purse. But Macaulay took no notice of this detraction. After his experience in Calcutta, he probably considered it far too tame to worry over.

16. Quoted in Arnold, *op. cit.*, 251.
17. See his remarks to the Edinburgh electors in *ibid.*, 249-50.
18. His one important speech in support of his candidacy is printed in *Works*, VIII, 143-59.

The Parliament to which he was elected in the early summer of 1839 was in session for only a few months. Macaulay did nothing of importance while it lasted. The opposition to Melbourne's Ministry was indeed so strong that, after a bad division, the Cabinet resigned. Sir Robert Peel was called into the Queen's presence and asked to form a Tory government.

But the taciturn Peel had meanwhile been looking over Her Majesty's Red Book, had been checking upon the political affiliations of the ladies in waiting with whom she was surrounded. They seemed to be, practically all of them, of the Whig persuasion. Peel knew what that meant. It meant that, while he would be advising her in one direction, the attendants of the bed-chamber would be advising her in another. There was no competing with such backstairs influence. Before he could afford to take office, he informed Victoria, she would have to get rid of two of her ladies and replace them with others sympathetic to the Tories.

This was quite too much to be borne! For Her Majesty, though young, had already learned to be obstinate. This ominous Lord, it seemed to her hasty judgment, was trying to get rid of all her attendants! She sent him a curt note to the effect that she could not "consent to adopt a course which she conceives to be contrary to usage and which is repugnant to her feelings."[19] The public sided with her. Melbourne was called back to the palace and asked to suggest another cabinet of Whigs.

One step in his proposed reorganization contemplated the appointment of Macaulay to that Cabinet. He would be made Secretary of War. The offer was tendered him and he accepted it. He was now, in late September, a member of the Privy Council, able to write *Right Hon.* before his name. He must go to Windsor Castle and kiss Her Majesty's hand.

This he did, and while on the visit there occurred what was possibly the most embarrassing incident of his life. On October 1 he wrote his constituents at Edinburgh, explaining in detail

19. Arnold, *op. cit.*, 252.

the reasons which had led him to take the place. He knew it was a difficult one, he knew the Whigs were in straits, he knew that he would be personally much happier out of office. But this was a time when loyalty should be placed before personal interests. The party was being assailed by unscrupulous enemies; he would not be numbered among its faint hearted friends. His letter, which was of course written for publication, was dated from "Windsor Castle."

The Tories could not have hoped for more. So the squat ungainly presence of Mr. Babble-tongue Macaulay was now to be seen at Windsor Castle, frightening the ladies in waiting out of their wits? This man and that wild Irishman Sheil both made privy councillors! "Faugh! Why they are hardly fit to fill up the vacancies that have occurred by the lamented death of Her Majesty's two favourite monkeys." [20] The unspeakable impudence of Babble-tongue, addressing his note "to the canaille of the Edinburgh electors" from the royal residence. We should like to believe that the Scottish papers have been playing us a hoax, that the letter came "not from the Castle but the Castle Tavern, Windsor — ay, and from the most proper part thereof for the purpose, namely the Tap. But no; he has somehow or other been pitch-forked into the Palace; and though, in all probability, he has been admitted as a guest there only for the sake of being made fun of by Lord Melbourne and the ladies, still the 'distinguished honour,' as he calls it, has given his brain another turn. This is evident from the insufferably conceited strain of his epistle to the scum of the Edinburgh electors."

He took office with the new year, 1840, and settled in the same house with the Trevelyans in Great George Street. His brother-in-law had been appointed Assistant Secretary of the Treasury. There was another child in the family now, a boy, George Otto Trevelyan. Macaulay was delighted with this domestic arrangement. The prospect that Hannah and her family might return to India had made the entire autumn of

20. From the *Times*. Quoted in *ibid.*, 254-55.

1839 "most painful" to contemplate. Now that melancholy anticipation seemed over.

Macaulay had not been in office a month when he was called upon to defend the Ministry. A motion that "Her Majesty's government, as at present constituted, does not possess the confidence of the House" was made on January 28. Macaulay himself, as a member of it, had come in for his share of personal abuse. The next night he arose to reply for his colleagues.

His beginning was most unfortunate. The Tory speaker who had just preceded him, Sir James Graham, had once been a good friend. But Sir James on this occasion had seen fit to spice his remarks with colorful allusions to Windsor Castle. Macaulay was nettled. He would give this gentleman a lacing! But he had not spoken five sentences before there occurred a highly exasperating slip of the tongue, a slip caused doubtless by the fact that many of the Tories were catcalling and storming about so lustily as to make it impossible for his words to be understood. "I trust," he shouted (though bellowed would be more accurate), "that the first Cabinet Minister who—when the question is, whether the government be or be not worthy of confidence—offers himself in debate, will find some portion of that generosity and good feeling which once distinguished Englishmen."[21] That was enough! "First Cabinet Minister." "First Cabinet Minister"—the phrase rippled over the insolent benches opposite; whisperings and nudgings gave way to hysterical, contemptuous laughter. It was horribly deflating. It required all his courage to continue at all.

Yet he did continue, changing his tactics to embrace a theme that was all too familiar to members who had heard him during the Reform Bill contentions of the decade before. "If I ever should so far forget myself as to wander from the subject of debate to matters concerning only myself, it will not, I hope, be at a time when the dearest interests of our

21. *Works*, VIII, 160 ff.

country are staked on the result of our deliberations."[22] No! He was pleading for the safety of the Commonwealth, at a time when that safety was being seriously threatened. Having uttered this disclaimer, he proceeded none-the-less to justify himself, in great detail, against charges that had been ignorantly and promiscuously made against him on the basis of one of his campaign speeches at Edinburgh. He had been called a Chartist, because he favored extending the ballot to every ten pound householder, no matter whether that householder lived in the city or the country. This evinced, on his opponent's part, rank ignorance of the term he was using! Is it possible that the gentleman does not know "that the fundamental principle of the plan of government called the People's Charter is that every male of twenty-one should have a vote?" Never, in his wildest imaginings, had Macaulay contemplated such nonsense in England.

Macaulay's party had been accused of agitation. What of it? It was agitation that got through the glorious Reform Bill. It is not a practice which can be condemned without discrimination. "In this country scarcely any great abuse was ever removed till the public feeling had been roused against it. It has been charged that "a government which does not discountenance agitation cannot be trusted to suppress rebellion." Agitation and rebellion, then, have been called the same thing in kind. Absurd! They bear the same relation to each other as the act of the surgeon to the act of the assassin. The right to arouse the public conscience in a good cause has long been looked upon as a settled principle of liberalism.

If the Melbourne Ministry is voted out, he continued, a Ministry with Sir Robert Peel at its head will no doubt become its successor. Look for a moment at the position of Sir Robert, with respect to the supporters amid whom he finds himself. Macaulay meant to utter nothing discourteous,

22. *Works*, VIII, 160. Macaulay slightly revised the phrase when he published his collected speeches.

he said, in making the statement that was to follow: But, Sir, it has been, not Peel's fault, "but his misfortune, to be the leader of a party with which he has no sympathy."

And so, by way of shifting the drift of the criticism then raging away from his own party and toward the party of the clamoring opposition, he proceeded to trace out in detail the career of the Right Honorable Baronet, the member for Tamworth. He demonstrated how Peel, again and again, had sought to inject vitality into the lifeless corpse of Toryism; how, again and again, he had performed the hard task "of translating the gibberish of bigots into language which might not misbecome the mouth of a man of sense." The trouble with Peel was that he was a Whig at heart; he sat on the wrong side of the House.

Then he turned to the Irish Question and to the still untarnished glory of his own party, which was the first to practice justice and mercy in that land bowed low by centuries of oppression. He told the House that he was wholly unable to guess whether his government would stand or fall. "But I know," he told them also, "that there are defeats not less glorious than any victory; and yet I have shared in some glorious victories. Those were proud and happy days," he recalled, "when hundreds waited round our doors till sunrise to hear how we had sped; when the great cities of the north poured forth their population on the highways to meet the mails which brought from the capital the tidings whether the battle of the people had been lost or won." Those days we cannot hope to see again, for two such triumphs would be too much for one life. But a no less honorable task still awaits us, the task of contending against superior numbers, and through years of discomfiture, for those civil and religious liberties which will forever be associated with the noble principles of Milton and of Locke. "We may be exposed to the rage of Laud on one side, and of Praise-God-Barebones on the other. But justice will be done at last."

In spite of its unfortunate beginning, it was a most remarkable speech, though it had strayed far, very far from the point. Gentlemen admired it, but in a few cases wondered mildly what the rage of Laud and Barebones had to do with the competence of the Melbourne Ministry. The House adjourned until the following night, when the chair, as soon as order was called, recognized the Tory, Viscount Powerscourt.

It was a new and most ominous thing, said the Viscount, for a Member of the Cabinet to come down to Parliament and boldly declare himself in favor of agitation. It was a new and highly anomalous thing for a Minister to come down and, instead of facing the serious charges brought against his party, "to fly off and talk about the Reformation—about some nondescript animal, half Roundhead, half Cavalier, about the times of Milton and of Locke, and fifty other things which had no more to do with the matter in hand than if he had talked of the sudden death of King Rufus, or, with his powers of declamation, had entertained the House with a panegyric upon the heroic deeds of King Alfred." [23] Macaulay, in brief, had delivered himself of an interesting essay, but its subject matter had been absurdly irrelevant. The remarks of the Viscount seemed momentarily very effective until one of Macaulay's friends pointed out that the suave Tory appeared to be something of an essayist and declaimer himself, since he had obviously prepared his remarks beforehand in hopes that the Right Honorable Secretary of War would be in his seat. But Mr. Macaulay was unfortunately absent on business. The motion of the Tories against the Ministry was defeated, but by the nervous margin of only ten votes.

His duties in connection with the War Department kept Macaulay busy the first few months of the year. In March he had to submit his budget requests, had to submit, too, to a hectic questioning by members of the opposition eager for an opportunity to prove him—and through him his government —incompetent. But nothing could be established against this

23. Hansard, *Parliamentary Proceedings* (3 series), II, 836.

secretary, no detail could be cited regarding which he did not show an almost staggering amount of information. After two hours of questioning, his opponents gave up altogether. He was granted six million pounds to carry on the responsibilities of his job.

He was to make two other major speeches in Parliament, before the waning confidence in Lord Melbourne's Ministry played out, flatly and finally. The first one, delivered the night of April 7, 1840, was another defense of the government. It had become involved in what looked like a war with China, because, said the resolution condemning its policy, of "a want of foresight and precaution." What had happened was simply that certain English merchants had been imprisoned on suspicion of having been guilty of smuggling opium into the country. Macaulay declared that many of the Englishmen who were maltreated had been altogether innocent of the offense attributed to them. He warned fellow members that they were too remote from China to be able to judge intelligently of the actions of the government in that quarter. He defended the principle of *laissez faire;* let Britishers trade where they please. Strict laws against their doing so will lead inevitably to violations. Moreover, if in trading where they please they become enmeshed in the statutes of other countries, that is their own misfortune. The English government will not interfere.

Yet this was not the case in China. The Chinese authorities had passed legislation which they were not equipped to enforce. Realizing as much, finally, they had resorted to indiscriminate violence against many perfectly guiltless foreigners, including a number of Englishmen. "It became our duty," Macaulay declared then, "to demand satisfaction."

Had gentlemen forgotten with what a glow of pride they read lately the dispatches of Captain Elliot which reported his arrival in a Chinese port with his man-of-war? "As soon as he landed, he was surrounded by his countrymen, all in an agony of distress and despair. The first thing which he did was to order the British flag to be brought from his boat and planted in the balcony. The sight immediately revived the hearts of those who had a minute before given themselves up for lost. It was natural that they should look up with hope and confidence in that victorious flag. For it reminded them that they belonged to a country unaccustomed to defeat, to submission, or to shame; to a country which had exacted such reparation for the wrongs of her children as had made the ears of all who heard of it to tingle; to a country which had made the Dey of Algiers humble himself to the dust before her insulted Consul; to a country which had avenged the victims of the Black Hole on the Field of Plassey; to a country which had not degenerated since the great Protector vowed that he would make the name of Englishmen as much respected as ever had been the name of Roman citizen. They knew that, surrounded as they were by enemies, and separated by great oceans and continents from all help, not a hair of their heads would be harmed with impunity."[24]

Surely the House will not censure a government for bringing such radiant hope to their distant countrymen. "But I rejoice to think," he concluded, "that whether we are censured or not, the national honor will be safe." He sat down. The debate wore on for three tiresome nights before a vote was finally taken. When it was, Macaulay learned that he and his colleagues were safe again, but by that identical, tantalizing ten vote majority.

His next two speeches of importance, though fourteen months apart, were on the same subject, the law of copyright. For this reason, it seems, they should be considered together, even though made in different Parliaments. Incidentally, they form a part of the most friendly debate he ever waged in the House. Mr. Sergeant Talfourd, on January 29, 1841, had introduced a bill to extend the term of copyright to a period of sixty years, reckoned from the death of the writer. On the face of it, the measure seemed eminently fair to all members of that

24. *Ibid.*, VIII, 193.

sadly sweated class. The sentiment of the legislators was heavily on Mr. Talfourd's side, so heavily, indeed, that many members stayed away when the second reading was due: they would let it go through without raising an issue. To those who were present it was not a little startling therefore to find Mr. Macaulay on his legs, protesting against an enactment which, they thought, he should have found peculiarly to his taste.

But the well known Whig had given the question no little study, as the few dutiful members who listened soon learned. Macaulay made plain from the start the fact that he and Mr. Talfourd were interested alike in giving to authors and their immediate heirs as much protection as they needed. The question between them was, then: Is a monopoly of six decades the best answer to the problem?

Macaulay thought not. Take the case of Dr. Johnson, dead now for fifty-six years. "If the law were what my honorable and learned friend wishes to make it, somebody would now have the monopoly of Dr. Johnson's works. Who that somebody would be it is impossible to say, but we may venture to guess. I guess, then, that it would have been some bookseller, who was the assign of another bookseller, who was a grandson of a third bookseller, who had bought the copyright from Black Frank, the Doctor's servant and residuary legatee, in 1785 or 1786. Now, would the knowledge that this copyright would exist in 1841 have been a source of gratification to Johnson? Would it have stimulated his exertions?. . . . Would it have induced him to give us one more allegory, one more life of a poet, one more imitation of Juvenal? I firmly believe not. I firmly believe that, a hundred years ago, when he was writing our debates for the *Gentleman's Magazine*, he would very much rather have had twopence to buy a plate of shin of beef at a cook's shop underground. Considered as a reward to him, the difference between a twenty year's term and a sixty year's term of posthumous copyright would have been nothing, or next to nothing. But is the difference nothing to us? I can buy *Rasselas* for sixpence; I might have had to give five shillings for it. I can buy the *Dictionary*, the entire genuine *Dictionary*, for two guineas, perhaps for less; I might have had to give five or six guineas for it. Do I grudge this to a man like Dr. Johnson? Not at all. . . . . What I do complain of is that my circumstances are to be worse, and Johnson's none the better; that I am to give five pounds for what to him was not worth a farthing."

It was a complex problem, and Mr. Talfourd's measure was, unfortunately, not going to solve it. He had not proposed that copyright descend to the eldest son, or that it be bound up by irrevocable entail. It was to descend as personal property, presumably to all the heirs, was to be divided and divided again and again. These heirs, being human, would doubtless sell out to a publisher and share the proceeds. And how could those proceeds possibly amount to very much? Publishers, or booksellers, have no way of predicting what the unpredictable public will want to read half a century hence; they cannot afford any outrageous gambles. Think for a moment of the reign of Charles the Second. The most popular poet of that era was, perhaps, Cowley. But "overleap sixty years and you are in the generation of which Pope asked, 'Who now reads Cowley?' "

And while copyrights *do* remain in a family, moreover, there is always the menace of squeamish descendants who are bent on suppressing or mutilating parts of a work, their ideas having changed from the ideas of their distinguished ancestors. Richardson's grandson, we know, for example, was a clergyman who thought all novel reading sinful. Had he owned Richardson's copyrights, there is no stating what would have happened to *Pamela* or to *Clarissa*. And there was Boswell's eldest son, who considered his father's entire relationship with Johnson "a blot in the escutcheon of the family."[25] The sad but none-the-less accurate circumstance is that

25. *Ibid.*, VIII, 206.

relatives simply can't be trusted in these matters. Macaulay had finished, regretting again that he had been forced to dissent from the ideas of his learned friend. The House divided. By a vote of 45 to 38, the eloquent reviewer had carried his point.

He carried it again the following year, although his party was no longer in power. Lord Mahon, another friend, sought to amend the existing law by a bill extending the period of copyright to a term of twenty-five years, reckoned from the author's death. Surely this plan would satisfy Mr. Macaulay, lacking, as it seemed, practically every shortcoming he had complained of in the earlier one.

Yet it was actually very far from satisfying. The protection it afforded an author's best work was not long enough; the protection it afforded his earliest and poorest work was too great. Macaulay had a counter proposal. He would give to every work a copyright of forty-two years, reckoned from the date of publication.

Let us compare our two plans, he went on, let us see which will appear the more sensible: "Take Milton. Milton died in 1674. The copyrights of Milton's great works would, according to my noble friend's plan, expire in 1699. Comus appeared in 1634, the Paradise Lost in 1668. To Comus, then, my noble friend would give sixty-five years of copyright, and to Paradise Lost only thirty-one years. Is that reasonable?. . . . My plan would give forty-two years both to Paradise Lost and to Comus." Or, again, consider Shakespeare. "My noble friend gives a longer protection than I should give to Love's Labour [sic] Lost, and Pericles Prince of Tyre;[26] but he gives a shorter protection than I should give to Othello and Macbeth." On he went, citing case after case—from Dryden, Burke, and Jane Austen, from Sophocles, from Cicero, from the French

26. Macaulay's chronology is awry here. The earliest record we have of *Pericles* is in the Stationer's Register, where it was entered May 20, 1608—later than both *Othello* and *Macbeth*. Macaulay's slip with the title of the early comedy is further evidence of the fact that, though he talked a good deal about Shakespeare, he read him very little. The dramatists of the Elizabethan age cannot be classed among his favorites.

classicists, from the Spanish, from the German. And then he uttered one of the most significant literary pronouncements of his life, significant, that is, in revealing a fundamental characteristic of his own taste. Gentlemen, he said, in defending his thesis that the plan he favored gave greater protection to an author's later achievements—Gentlemen, "I know of no work of the imagination of the very highest class that was ever, in any age or country, produced by a man under thirty-five." He would go further, would affirm "that of the good books now extant in the world, more than nineteen-twentieths were published after the writer had attained the age of forty." [27]

Perhaps he was dead right in his view; it may all, again, be a matter of taste. But it appears highly revealing, one feels, to see Macaulay in a single gesture dismissing the collected poems and plays of Shelley, Keats, and Marlowe, all of Byron that is worth reading, to say nothing of the best of Coleridge and Wordsworth, and the finest pastoral elegy in any language. He probably realized fully the implications of what he was saying. Macaulay simply didn't like the romantics, and as far as is known he cared nothing for "Lycidas." At any rate, he had made his point in a speech the theme of which was perfectly to his liking. With minor reservations, the law was framed as he desired it. [28]

But long before it was framed, as has been suggested, back in June of 1841, the Secretary of War and all his vacillating colleagues had been "pinned to an issue out of which they could not wriggle," [29] and swept from office in the worst defeat the Whigs had experienced since 1784. Macaulay had managed to keep his own seat, but by a decidedly uncomfortable margin.

27. *Works*, VIII, 214-15.
28. For replies to Macaulay see Hansard, *op. cit.* (3 series), LXI, 1362.
29. A paraphrase of a remark by Sir James Graham. See G. O. Trevelyan, *op. cit.*, II, 83. The "issue" was the Corn Laws.

XIII. Poet

THE PERIOD 1840-44 represents Macaulay's golden age as a reviewer. All except two or three of his most famous essays fall within this four year interval, an interval at the close of which he gave up his connection with the *Edinburgh* for good. It is the period of the essays on Clive and Hastings, the period of his remarkable study of Frederick the Great, the period of his commentary on the Comic Dramatists of the Restoration, and of other lengthy discussions of Addison, Fanny Burney, Barère, and the Earl of Chatham. A moment's pause will indicate the direction Macaulay's mind was taking: he was beginning to saturate himself,with increasing emphasis, in the literary and social background which he planned to treat in his *History*. But what is more arresting still is that these ample works were being turned out merely during intervals of a very busy life. He was still thoroughly active in Parliament, now as a rather clamorous member of the opposition, was still paying his respects, without restraint, to those reformers there who somehow felt that not all that the average Englishman required for his happiness had been granted to him by the Whigs of 1832.

One body of those reformers went under the name of the Chartists, and although Macaulay had already implied rather strongly what he thought of their program, he had not done so with his customary fullness. Now briefly, of course, the Chartists wanted a democracy. They were asking for universal manhood suffrage and for the removal of all property qualifications connected with the right to vote. They favored equal electoral districts, the payment of salaries for members of the House, and annual elections. [1] All of these endorsements, with the exception of the last, have long since, willingly or not, been granted. But this fact was no concern of Macaulay's when he rose on the night of May 3, 1842. The Chartists on the day before had presented a petition requesting that their doctrines be immediately passed into law. Three million signatures were affixed to that request. [2] After it was placed on the table, a sympathizer urged that the assembly allow either certain of the petitioners, or their counsel, to be heard "at the Bar of the House."

Macaulay, for one, would not think of it! It meant the permitting of an opening wedge, a wedge that might, once it was started, be driven clean through the sacred institution of property. Take the specific requests of this group. There were, in all, six of them. Two of the six were good; regarding two others he might be willing to compromise. But these items were unimportant. The essence of the Charter, Sir, "is universal suffrage. If you withhold that, it matters not very much what else you grant. If you grant that, it matters not at all what else you withhold. If you grant that, the country is lost." [3]

He warmed to his subject. He was convinced, he declared, "beyond dispute," that civilization depended upon the security of property. He was convinced, further, that that security was incompatible with literal majority rule. Was not the majority dispossessed? he asked in effect. Was not the majority of citizens now without property? What prevented them at present from taking the property of others then, even from doing so by violence? Why, the government prevented them. But what if the government should become dominated by these lower orders?

1. G. M. Trevelyan, *British History of the Nineteenth Century*, 252.
2. The figure is Roebuck's. See his reply to Macaulay in Hansard, *op. cit.* (3 series), LXIII, 56.
3. *Works*, VIII, 220.

The result, in such a case, would be perfectly obvious. "Class legislation" would be put through by the new and raging forces in control of the state. The financial wealth and the land which individual Englishmen hold today would be subject to wholesale confiscation. Hungry and unfortunate men, who have been duped by the hysterical promises of agitators, would clamor for a redistribution of the country's resources. And how could the miserable wretches be blamed, fed for so long, as they have been, by propagandists who proclaim to them "that there is enough and more than enough for everybody?" The petitioners are brazenly asking us "to give them power in order that they may not leave a man of a hundred a year in the realm."[4]

The whole philosophy of this movement has been corrupted, he continued, by a major misconception. Its central doctrine is, simply stated, "that it is the business of the government to support the people." The thinking of those who have embraced its creed has been systematically invalidated by this conviction. Once in force, its result will become manifest. "Knowledge will be borne down by ignorance," the public credit will be quickly destroyed, trade will decline, manufactures will languish. After that will follow a harsh but inevitable condition. Out of the confusion a strong military despotism will arise; "the sword, firmly grasped in some rough hand," will give protection of a sort to the miserable wreck of our once prosperous empire.

It was Macaulay at the political crossroads. A certain space would he go, but no further. Society, for all his protests to the contrary in 1831, he really was beginning to think of in terms of something static. It had required once, for its proper and progressive functionings, that the classes of comparative wealth, "the middle orders of Britain," be given a share in the government. That had been done eleven years ago. It had all been settled, he fondly hoped, forever.

Yet unfortunately certain citizens had taken the whole thing

4. *Ibid.*, VIII, 223.

amiss. They had got the notion—from the preceptors of violence, no doubt—that the truly valid goal toward which to work was one in which all men became educated participants in the business of the state. To that end these citizens had encouraged the education movement; they had founded mechanics' institutes, they had organized lecture systems, and they had slowly begun to contend for appropriations that would wipe out—altogether at length, they hoped—the standing curse of illiteracy in the land. For education, they had concluded, is able to work marvelous changes in a man; it is able to make him sane and therefore responsible, regardless of whether he holds a property stake in his government.

Macaulay, as far as we can judge, never thought the problem through, never paused to consider what would inevitably happen to the restrictions hedging his sacred ballot, once a sufficient number of the "lower orders" had become well enough informed to use it with tolerably good sense. Yet, on the other hand, he was never quite just to the inherent craftiness of the property classes. For they formed a group which, through devious machinations, was to prove able at length to extend the ballot and still to retain for the most part its old unchallenged power.

At bottom, it should be further added, Macaulay's views were in the main current of English liberalism. He was following his masters, Locke and Adam Smith, and picking up, incidentally, a few timely hints from Burke. Those masters had taught emphatically that the function of government was to extend the blessing of security to its real owners, was, in the words of a recent critic, "to enable rich men to sleep peacefully in their beds."[5] To Burke's thinking, "the right of property and especially landed property, to an exceptional portion in the state was beyond discussion. The mass of the people had no place in the state."[6] They were the "swinish multitude," to him, as they came to be "a great beast" to

5. See, for an excellent discussion of this topic, Harold J. Laski, *The Rise of Liberalism* (Harpers, 1936).
6. Edmund Burke, *Works* (Bohn ed.), III, 334-35. Quoted in *ibid.*, 225.

Alexander Hamilton. And once this middle or property class achieved power, it sought to forge its chains upon the masses that ranked below it. Its spokesmen declared that "their freedom was the nation's also; they insisted that they could not pursue their own self interest without at the same time achieving that of those who were dependent upon them."[7]

It would be impossible to summarize Macaulay's own views more accurately than in the sentence just quoted. On that doctrine which identified the well-being of his class with the well-being of the nation he took his stand, nor did he ever desert it. The currents that bore a different gospel swept past him unregretted. If they left him at length, stranded, "a man of 1832," he was stranded at least upon solid rock—upon the furthest rock, indeed, he felt, that stood this side an endless precipice.[8]

2

In the fall of 1842 Macaulay published his *Lays of Ancient Rome*. He had labored at the poems in that volume for a long time, had made drafts of the best ones while still in India. One of his reasons for wanting to visit Italy when he returned was that he wished to see the places which he meant to describe in certain of the pieces, or had already attempted to describe as best he could. This desire to verify his topographical allusions was a settled trait with him, whether he was writing history or poetry. Only after he had done this necessary spadework, he said, was he able convincingly to imagine the important events with which he was concerned.

The Preface to Macaulay's volume is one of the most interesting and objective essays he ever wrote. All rhetoric and contentiousness are gone. He is a very learned but very

7. Laski, *op. cit.*, 236-37.

8. Macaulay's speech was ably answered by Roebuck, who took him to task with particular severity for treating contemptuously the wholly lawful petition of 3,000,000 of his countrymen. As for Macaulay's charge that they could not govern themselves sensibly, that was a "a libel," said Roebuck. They were the "heart" of England; and they respected law and order as much as anybody. See Hansard, *op. cit.* (3 series), LXIII, 56.

lucid scholar, talking about his favorite subject, Latin literature. One characteristic of that literature which has always
saddened him, he implies, is the fact that those specimens of
it which have come down to us have all been influenced,
often for the worse, by Greek models. In a sense, this influence
was wholly natural. The Latins, groping slowly toward
refinement, suddenly discovered in the country to the east of
them examples of art, of architecture, and of drama which in
finish and brilliance made their own rude efforts ridiculous.
Their young men of culture and fashion, by way of topping
off their education, flocked regularly to Athens or Rhodes,
and came back with their preferences set almost exclusively
upon foreign models.

This circumstance was in certain ways most unfortunate.
For it meant that the art, and especially the literature, which
had been for several centuries indigenous to the Latin temperament was suffered to fall into neglect. No longer fashionable, it ceased to be thought of as even respectable. It was left
to delight the vulgar, was handed down, in oral tradition only,
while the bright young writers of the country absorbed
themselves in efforts to recapture the ecstasies of legends which
were not their own.

And yet the fact that an extensive early Latin literature
once existed is beyond dispute. It was a literature, moreover,
which "was far more poetical" than anything written at a
later date by Latin authors. Consider for a moment the
legends which survived from that age, survived by the fact
of their inherent vitality alone until some chronicler proceeded
to set them down as history. There are "the love of the Vestal
and the God of War, the cradle laid among the reeds of
the Tiber, the fig-tree, the she-wolf, the shepherd's cabin,"
the rape of the Sabines, the nightly meetings of Numa and
the Nymph by the well in the sacred grove, the fight of the
three Romans and the three Albans, the purchase of the
Sibylline books, the crime of Tullia, the simulated madness
of Brutus, the ambiguous reply of the Delphian oracle to the

Tarquins, the wrongs of Lucretia, the heroic actions of Horatius, the Battle of Regillus won by the aid of Castor and Pollux, the touching story of Coriolanus, the still more touching story of Virginia. These, and many others, Macaulay declared—with an unintended but now highly embarrassing irony—"will at once suggest themselves to every reader."[9]

What he hoped to do then, in his book, was to reverse the process by which these legends have come down to us. Latin historians, like Livy, had written of them unemotionally, after the manner of men of their craft. Macaulay would transform them, on the other hand, "back into the poetry out of which they were made." It was regrettable, in a sense, that this procedure appeared necessary, regrettable, that is, that the original ballads did not themselves still exist. Yet such good fortune would be too much to ask for. When we consider by what happy accidents many of the English ballads, of much later date, were saved for us by the timely industry of Bishop Percy and Sir Walter Scott; "how the snuff of a candle, or a mischievous dog, might in a moment have deprived the world forever of any of those fine compositions"—when we consider these things, it should provoke small wonder that the ancient ballads were lost to posterity.

Four of these Roman stories Macaulay treated at considerable length, prefacing each of them with discussions which treated varying versions of the narratives and other technical problems he had been forced to consider. The most widely known of the poems is, of course, "Horatius." But the remaining three, the "Battle of Lake Regillus," "Virginia," and the "Prophecy of Capys," are all written with the same bounding gusto. They are works, all of them, which one associates unmistakably with Macaulay's nature: sweeping, metallic, obvious, and unadumbrated retellings of once stirring events. There is a minimum of quiet suggestiveness,

9. The Preface may be found in *Works*, VIII, 445-62. His complete poems follow, 463-603.

a maximum of tumultuous action. He was bringing to the attention of his age a quality in verse which it sadly lacked.

"Horatius" is almost too hackneyed for quotation; it has paid the penalty which all poems both good and bad must pay when a race makes them part of its consciousness. It treats, we remember, the kind of hero Macaulay eminently admired: the patriot of almost matchless physical valor. Lars Porsena, we learn in the opening lines, is preparing to march against the Capital City, to avenge the wrongs which have been committed against his illustrious house. Thirty prophets have promised him victory; and as his legions flow relentlessly southward, the terror of his hated name rides down the winds before him to Rome. How shall his invasion be stayed? Wise old men, the voices of prudence, advise that the bridge across the Tiber be cut down. But no! there is not time for that; the enemy's banners are already in sight.

Then it is that Horatius speaks out. All men must die, he says. What death can be more fitting, then, than one incurred against fearful odds? He will defend the bridge until its foundations have been destroyed. Two friends volunteer their help. And soon after their resolve is made known, they are at death grips with three champions of the house of Tarquin.

The Romans are victorious, are victorious again against three other picked men of the enemy. And then, it seems, the tide will be turned, for the great Lord of Luna has marched forth to do single combat with Horatius. He swings the sword, too heavy for another to wield, and the red blood flows in its wake from the hero's thigh. Yet this triumph is brief: Horatius runs him through the head so fiercely that his weapon stands out a hand's breadth behind. The invading forces are daunted now; it seems that another champion cannot be found in their ranks. Yet only for a moment is this true. Sextus emerges, advances thrice against the Roman, but turns back each time in quaking dread.

Meanwhile the bridge is tottering. Come back, cry the citizens to its brave defenders. But only two of them return.

Horatius, bleeding fast, remains in its center, unyielding as before, and addresses the Tiber. At length he leaps into it, and amid cheers from both sides swims at last wearily to the bank. Gifts are showered upon him. His name becomes a household legend, a legend still remembered proudly in the homes of his grateful countrymen.

"The Battle of Lake Regillus," a less interesting narrative mainly for the reason that it depends for its dénouement upon supernatural machinery, was conceived of as "a lay sung at the feast of Castor and Pollux," the real heroes of the story. The subject deals with the war between Rome and the Thirty Cities. Army advances against army, the heroes of each side being catalogued after the fashion of the *Iliad*. The charge of these opposing forces is dwelt on with considerable detail. Great deeds are done on the field, as hero slays hero through the long and bloody day. Finally, the Romans fall back; it seems that the struggle will turn hopelessly against them. Even Herminius, "who kept the bridge so well," meets his death "in a great lake of gore."

But suddenly a new influence pervades the wavering Roman ranks. The heaven-sent twins have come to their aid. The armies of the Thirty Cities flee then in wholesale confusion. The Eternal City has again been saved, to be decked with the spoils of the routed enemy. And in honor of the two great brethren a "stately dome" is built, and a feast day decreed which shall evermore be observed with reverence.

Macaulay approached the subject of Virginia with something akin to his old partisan zest. It was a tale of a monarch, Appius Claudius, who possessed many Tory traits: He was obstinate, a tyrant who had blinded himself to the crying needs of his people. The immediate cause of his dawnfall, the author states, was an attempt Appius made "upon the chastity of a young girl of noble birth." The first part of the poem traces his passion, in bounding but irregular heptameters, from the time the Roman "heard her sweet young voice, and saw her sweet young face, and loved her with the accursed love of his accursed race," to the time Virginia's stolid father slays her to prevent her shame. Afterwards Macaulay portrays the anger of the mob, which finally falls upon Appius and sends him bloody and discredited to his home. It is the end of his reign.

"The Prophecy of Capys" is the shortest of the four pieces, and also the least stirring. Its concern, as its title indicates, is with the prediction of the old seer that the two lads whom the she-wolf nourished shall slay their enemies and found a great city; and that the Greeks, Gauls, and the "ranks of false Tarentum" shall invade their dominion in vain.

What are we to think of these poems? Leigh Hunt, that former friend of Shelley and Keats, now shabby and almost destitute, wrote Macaulay soon after they appeared. He was desperately in need of funds and wished to borrow from his prosperous Whig friend. But he could not stay the promptings of his artistic integrity, even on this delicate occasion. Mr. Macaulay's verse, he declared, lacked "the true poetical aroma which breathes from the *Faery Queene*."[10] They did indeed! And many other valid aromas were also lacking: Macaulay's word sense is singularly dull throughout; his language is even trite in many cases. There is no suggestion in them of evidence that he understood character. He is content to praise the obvious civic virtues in men, their forthright honesty and their courage; or to damn them for their unspeakable villainies.

And yet Mrs. Browning declared of the *Lays* that she "could scarcely read them and keep lying down," and Mrs. Humphrey Ward, in turn, likened the rhythms of the lines to the clear metallic note of a trumpet.[11] And even before these critics had spoken, Professor Wilson, whom we remember in the Ettrick Shepherd dialogues, had discerned the merits of the volume, and forgetting for once the scruples of party, had made known his judgment in the pages of *Blackwoods:*

10. See G. O. Trevelyan, *op. cit.*, II, 112.
11. See D. H. MacGregor, *Lord Macaulay* (London, 1901), 111.

"What! poetry from Macaulay? Ay, and why not. . . . The young poets all want fire; Macaulay is full of fire. The young poets are somewhat weakly; he is strong. The young poets are rather ignorant; his knowledge is great. The young poets mumble books; he devours them. The young poets dally with their subject; he strikes its heart. The young poets are still their own heroes; he sees but the chiefs he celebrates. The young poets weave dreams with shadows transitory as clouds without substance; he builds realities lasting as rocks. The young poets steal from all and sundry and deny their thefts; he robs the face of day. Whom? Homer."[12]

Perhaps the most valid pronouncement which has been made upon these works is that of Macaulay's own grand-nephew, George Macaulay Trevelyan. The style of the poems, this critic declares, Macaulay succeeded in endowing with a cut and thrust narrative, with the rush of battle and of action which are entirely valid devices in ballad poetry. "It is absurd," he adds, to look in the *Lays* "for the highest qualities and subtlest tones of lyrical poetry, and to cry out on him as a Philistine because they are not there. Such an outcry is not criticism. Why look for grapes on a fig tree."[13]

The vigor of this narrative style, Trevelyan states further, is not the only merit of the poems. Macaulay has succeeded in giving an emotional value to many names, places, ancient customs, and forms of life. He made his English audience familiar, that is, with a number of legends of the ancient Roman Republic. Nor was his ability to do this so well the result of chance or of simple facility. He worked hard and long upon nearly all his verses, changing and condensing early versions with the patience of an artist. But artist or not, the *Lays* sold amazingly. By the time of his death, in 1859, more than 35,000 copies had passed into the hands of readers.

Not all the poems Macaulay wrote were included in the

12. G. O. Trevelyan, *op. cit.*, II, 110.
13. See his Introduction to the *Lays* (London, 1928), vi-ix, *passim*.

1842 volume; he had labored at others from his student days at Cambridge. One of the others, the "Lines" written at Edinburgh in 1847, has already been briefly noticed. Another one, a fragment called "The Armada," shows that he was capable of treating English subjects with the same vigorous enthusiasm he had felt for the Romans. There are a few additional battle songs, a few translations, and a few epitaphs on illustrious Englishmen. But the chances are that nowhere did he succeed in combining genuine feeling and an economy of language quite so effectively as in the neglected lines which he wrote in 1845 under the title, "Epitaph on a Jacobite":

> *To my true king I offered free from stain*
> *Courage and faith; vain faith and courage vain.*
> *For him I threw lands, honours, wealth away,*
> *And one dear hope that was more prized than they.*
> *For him I languished in a foreign clime,*
> *Grey haired with sorrow in my manhood's prime;*
> *Heard on Lavernia Scargill's whispering trees,*
> *And pined by Arno for my lovelier Tees;*
> *Beheld each night my home in fevered sleep,*
> *Each morning started from the dream to weep;*
> *Till God, who saw me tried too sorely, gave*
> *The resting place I asked, an early grave.*
> *Oh thou, whom chance leads to this nameless stone,*
> *From that proud country which was once mine own,*
> *By those white cliffs I never more must see,*
> *By that dear language which I spoke like thee,*
> *Forget all feuds, and shed one English tear*
> *O'er English dust. A broken heart lies here.*

One freely forgives the echoes in these lines. The poet, at least once, we feel, had got to the bottom of his mystery.

XIV. Essayist

IN THE SPRING of 1843, while still elated with the unexpected success of his poems, Macaulay published his collected *Essays* in three volumes. "Sensible of their defects," as he was, he had seen those volumes through the press with reluctance. The damned Americans were to blame for the whole business! They were tearing out his writings from the pages of the *Edinburgh*, running off cheap reprints of them, and flooding not only their own but the English market. Macaulay was powerless to stop this piracy, for no international copyright laws existed. Left thus helpless, he decided at length to make available at least one accurate version of what he had written. The Essays were dedicated, as was fitting, to Francis Jeffrey.

Thirty-three of the thirty-six reviews he did for the distinguished Whig Quarterly had been finished by this date; only the studies of Addison, Barère, and Chatham remained unwritten. But of that large number he decided to omit the three papers on the Utilitarians—not, however, be it understood, because he was "disposed to retract a single doctrine which they contain." It was rather that he was unwilling "to offer what might be regarded as an affront" to the memory of James Mill—a man from whose opinions he still dissented, but to whose talents and virtues he had formerly not done justice. Otherwise, the essays were being offered as they first appeared, except that he had taken the liberty to remove a few blemishes "caused by unavoidable haste."[1]

1. See Preface in *Works*, V, xi-xii.

How sorely it went against his taste to reprint the "Milton," filled as it was, by his mature standards, "with gaudy and ungraceful ornament!" But honesty demanded it. There it was, leading the collection, substantially as first written, loaded down with glittering paradoxes. As civilization advances, poetry necessarily declines. Nations, like individuals, first perceive, and then abstract. No person can be a poet, or even enjoy poetry therefore, without a certain unsoundness of mind. He who in an enlightened age aspires to be a great poet, must first become a little child. Milton was great as a literary figure because he overcame the advantages of a classical education![2]

So it went. But though paradoxical to an astonishing degree, it gave new life to Jeffrey's Review, and the editor, when it first appeared, was wondering, in blank amazement, where young Mr. Macaulay could possibly "have picked up that style." We may wonder still, yet with the tentative feeling that for a great deal of its gusto and clarity there was ample precedent in the *Edinburgh* itself. We may also be inclined to regret that the objectivity which for the most part characterized the article came so soon to be buried beneath the heavy prejudices of Whiggery.

His next essay, on Niccolo Machiavelli, was something of a let-down;[3] yet Macaulay did not fall into the vulgar error of classing this statesman, as former generations had classed him, among the world's great villains. The proper way to understand Machiavelli's temperament was through considering the nature of the Italian mind during the century he flourished. To proceed in this manner, the reviewer declared, was to realize very soon that while more northern races were given to admiring honor in men, the Italians of the Renaissance placed their major stress upon "policy," or the art of ingenuity. For example: Iago, in *Othello* has been regarded by Englishmen as a "monster incarnate"; Othello

2. *Works*, V, 7.
3. *Ibid.*, V, 46-82 (March, 1827).

himself, on the other hand, has always been thought well of, for the patent reason that he is a man of essentially lofty motives. Yet the fact is, Macaulay went on, that Iago would have been a perfectly intelligible and normal figure had he appeared in an Italian drama of the sixteenth century, while "Othello would have inspired nothing but detestation and contempt." Machiavelli, in short, has been the victim of anachronistic judgments. When Italy is again free, his memory will receive the homage it deserves.

The essay on Dryden,[4] which appeared in January, 1828, went more deeply than the Milton study into the mysteries of the literary profession. To this writer, Macaulay felt, belonged the very first place "in the second rank of our poets." His misfortune was that, when he appeared, the emphasis of his age was upon science and criticism. The fine arts, as such, had fallen into their dotage. It was an age, therefore, "of critical poetry, or poetry by courtesy, of poetry to which the memory, the judgment, and the wit contribute far more than the imagination." Every age (despite what Thomas Carlyle was beginning to think) molds its leaders into conformity with its preconceptions: Luther would have effected no reformation, had he lived in the tenth century; Bacon would have been a schoolman had he lived in the day of Thomas Aquinas. But Dryden was a poor dramatist, and a poorer critic. As dramatist he was too deferential to French standards; as critic he was too biased, an advocate.

Macaulay's next review purported to discuss a volume by Henry Neele, *The Romance of History.*[5] But the reviewer had so much to say in his own right that Mr. Neele was never mentioned. Instead, he sketched the important ancient historians, turned next to the moderns, and dismissed Hume, Gibbon, and Mitford together with the charge that they were too partial to their favorites. Moreover, they neglected miserably "the art of narration." They neglected, as well, the

4. *Ibid.*, V, 83, 121.
5. *Ibid.*, V, 122-61 (May, 1828).

writers of memoirs, those serviceable folk who so often succeed in flooding with light the manners and morals of an epoch. "The perfect historian," in other words, "is he in whose work the character and spirit of an age is exhibited in miniature. He relates no fact, he attributes no expression to his characters, which is not authenticated by sufficient testimony. But by judicious selection, rejection, and arrangement, he gives to truth those attractions which have been usurped by fiction." It was Macaulay's statement of a creed from which he never wavered.

These ideas were expanded later in the year in his commentary on Hallam's *Constitutional History of England*.[6] In its perfect state, history combines the arts of poetry and philosophy. "To make the past present, to bring the distant near, to place us in the society of a great man or on the eminence which overlooks the field of a mighty battle, to invest with the reality of human flesh and blood beings whom we are too much inclined to consider as personified qualities in an allegory, to call up our ancestors before us with all their peculiarities of language, manners, and garb, to show us over their houses, to seat us at their tables, to rummage their old fashioned wardrobes, to explain the use of their ponderous furniture—these parts of the duty which properly belongs to the historian have been appropriated by the historical novelist." On the other hand, there is a class of writers who are concerned with studying the morality and politics of a period. To put the problem differently, there are Sir Walter Scotts and there are Henry Hallams. The ideal historian should combine their separate talents.

His next three essays dealt with the controversy over Mill's theory of government.[7] They have all been noticed, perhaps sufficiently, in an earlier discussion. We have seen, too, that Macaulay came to regret the spirit in which he had written them. He had been unfair to Mill, had indeed even before

6. *Ibid.*, V, 162-238.
7. *Ibid.*, V, 239-329 (March, June, September, 1829).

setting out for India conferred with him several times about the law reforms he hoped to enact there. Another fact which probably influenced him in deciding against the ultimate validity of these works was that, in spite of his charge that the Utilitarians were theorists grossly ignorant of human nature, he had already lived to see a number of their recommendations enacted into quite practical and sensible laws. The entire quarrel had had its genesis in the flames of a controversy now long expired. And in his essay on Bacon, Macaulay in spirit had already, regardless of his denials, joined the ranks of his former enemies. He could well wish the whole business undone.

With the review of Southey's *Colloquies on Society*[8] Macaulay returned to a favorite theme, the absurdities of the Tories. "It would scarcely be possible for a man of Mr. Southey's talents and acquirements to write two volumes so large as those before us, which should be wholly destitute of information and amusement." This was his opening sentence. The Poet Laureate, he continued, is a capable writer in his field, but it is a pity to find him deserting that field "to lecture the public on sciences of which he has still the very alphabet to learn."

In truth the doctrines of this declining gentleman struck at the foundations of Macaulay's deepest faith. For Southey, through the character Sir Thomas More, whom he brings back to earth, was declaring that the entire industrial civilization which was growing so suddenly and so stridently in England was proving monstrous in its effects on the victims who served it. It was a civilization in whose wake stalked an inexorable tyranny and economic slavery, one "which destroyed the bodies and degraded the minds of those who were engaged in it."[9] Look out, this critic of the New Blessedness continued, upon the hovels that are being thrown up to shelter the multiplying thousands whom it controls. Bare, naked and endlessly identical, they stand screaming against

8. *Ibid.*, V, 330-68 (January, 1830).
9. Compare the lines *ibid.*, V, 339. I have altered only the tense of the passage quoted.

[245]

the once placid and ungutted hills. "Time will not mellow them; nature will neither clothe or conceal them; and they will remain always as offensive to the eye as to the mind."

And consider also our changing philosophy of wealth, another gift of this singular New Blessedness. "All wealth," says Sir Thomas More, "in former times was tangible. It consisted in land, money, or chattels, which were either of real or conventional value. . . . All wealth was real, till the extent of commerce rendered a paper currency necessary; which differed from precious stones and pictures in this important point, that there was no limit to its production. . . . Pursue that notion and you will be in the dark presently. Your provincial bank-notes, which constitute almost wholly the circulating medium of certain districts, pass current today. Tomorrow, tidings may come that the house which issued them had stopt payment, and what do they represent then? You will find them the shadow of a shade."

For the fact was, Southey declared in elaboration, that the demon Plutocracy always intervened when intangible wealth began to increase; the benefits of that wealth were directed into ever narrowing and more exclusive channels. "A people may be too rich, because it is the tendency of the commercial, and more especially of the manufacturing system, to collect wealth rather than to diffuse it. . . . Great capitalists become like pikes in a fish pond, who devour the weaker fish; and it is but too certain that the poverty of one part of the people seems to increase in the same ratio as the riches of another."

All this now almost prophetic wisdom seemed strange jargon to Macaulay, a tangled knot of absurdities and obstinacy. In replying to it he proceeded to show that the poor rate was higher in the country than in the new industrial centers, that the mortality rate was increasing in the agricultural areas and decreasing in the cities. Evidences of progress, moreover, were everywhere! The life span was longer, medical service was better, and whole parishes which formerly dined upon barley now had "wheaten bread" with their meals.

These facts all proclaimed, with matchless eloquence, that the present was "the most enlightened generation of the most enlightened people that ever existed."

The subject "Mr. Robert Montgomery's Poems"[10] proved considerably more to Macaulay's taste. Here was a pious versifier of no merit, but one whose reputation, bloated by unscrupulous "puffers," cried out for a full deflating. That deflating was administered, faithfully. In the two long poems which the reviewer had before him, the most striking fact was that whatever passages were not odious had been lifted. "The poem on the Omnipresence of Deity commences with a description of the creation, in which we can find only one thought which has the least pretension to ingenuity, and that one thought is stolen from Dryden and marred in the stealing." Again, Macaulay pointed out that Byron, "in a passage which everybody knows by heart, has said, addressing the sea:

> "*Time writes no wrinkle on thine azure brow.*"

Mr. Robert Montgomery very casually appropriates the image, and reproduces the stolen goods in the following form:

> "*And thou, vast Ocean, on whose awful face,*
> *Time's iron feet can print no ruin-trace.*"

"So," prays the reviewer, "may such ill got gains ever prosper!"

Montgomery himself never quite got over this castigation. Twenty years afterwards, Macaulay noted in his *Journal* that he had received a letter from the poor creature. He was a churchman, and the review, with each successive reprinting in the collected *Essays*, brought down upon him an increasing embarrassment. Would Mr. Macaulay please be so good as to omit it from subsequent editions, thereby letting his victim

10. *Ibid.*, V, 369-87 (April, 1830).

"out of the pillory?" But Macaulay refused to oblige; to do so would imply that his old asperity had been undeserved.[11]

His next subject was Mr. Sadler,[12] the Tory gentleman he was later to defeat in the Leeds election. For Mr. Sadler's style, as has already been noticed, Macaulay entertained not the slightest sympathy. Of his ideas he was equally contemptuous. Mr. Sadler had set out to refute the pessimistic Malthus by attempting to prove what he termed his law of population. That law he had stated, rather uneuphoniously, as follows: "The prolificness of human beings, otherwise similarly circumstanced, varies inversely as their numbers." Poor, stupid, ludicrously absurd Mr. Sadler! To demolish him is ridiculously simple:

Let us suppose that there is a tract in the back settlements of America, or in New South Wales, "equal in size to London, with only a single couple, a man and his wife, living upon it. The population of London, with its immediate suburbs, is now probably about a million and a half. The average fecundity of a marriage in London is, Mr. Sadler tells us, 2.35. How many children will the woman in the back settlements bear according to Mr. Sadler's theory? The solution of the problem is easy. As the population in this tract in the back settlements is to the population of London, so the number of children born from a marriage in London will be to the number of children born from the marriage of this couple in the back settlements. That is to say—

$$2 : 1,500,000 :: 2.35 : 1,762,500.$$

The lady will have 1,762,500 children, as large an 'efflux of the fountain of life,' to borrow Mr. Sadler's sonorous rhetoric, as the most philoprogenitive parent could possibly desire." That would do for Mr. Sadler!

11. G. O. Trevelyan, *op. cit.*, II, 236-37.
12. *Works*, V, 419-44 (July, 1830). The essay is misplaced in the definitive edition, being made to follow the "Byron." The Byron review appeared in June, 1831, not in June, 1830, as indicated in V, 388.

But the vanquished Tory was not quite satisfied. He rushed through the presses a "Refutation of the *Edinburgh Review* Article," and Macaulay, of course, was called on to dispose of it. [13] Sadler had especially resented the slighting references which had been made to his style. He accordingly ferretted out a number of Macaulay's Cambridge verses, "in the hope of finding," Macaulay commented, "something as bad as his own. And we must in fairness admit that he had succeeded pretty well. We must admit that the gentleman in question [Macaulay] sometimes put into his exercises, at seventeen, almost as great nonsense as Mr. Sadler is in the habit of putting into his books at sixty."

This comment is characteristic of the entire essay; it was written throughout as personal abuse. Sadler's "witticisms, and his table of figures, constitute the only parts of his work which can be perused with perfect gravity. His blunders are diverting, his excuses exquisitely comic. But his anger is the most grotesque exhibition we ever saw." Enough is enough. In the article Macaulay was following, simply, the accepted critical style of the quarterlies of his age, a style with a thirty year sanction behind it. It is only just to remember this fact when one feels inclined to condemn his unmannerliness.

Macaulay had two reasons for speaking well of Tom Moore's *Life of Lord Byron*. [14] Both Moore and his subject, as we have noticed, were highly admired at Holland House. It was an excellently written book, about a great and too-much-maligned English nobleman. One of the most ridiculous spectacles Macaulay knew of was "the British public in one of its periodic fits of morality. In general, elopements, divorces, and family quarrels, pass with little notice. We read the scandal, talk about it for a day, and forget it. But once in six or seven years our virtue becomes outrageous. . . . We must take a stand against vice. . . . Accordingly some unfortunate man, in no respect more depraved than hundreds whose

13. *Works*, V, 470-97 (January, 1831).
14. *Ibid.*, V, 388-418 (June, 1831).

offenses have been treated with lenity, is singled out as an expiatory sacrifice. . . . He is, in truth, a sort of whipping boy, by whose vicarious agonies all the other transgressors of the same class are, it is supposed, sufficiently chastised. . . . At length our anger is satiated. Our victim is ruined and heart-broken. And our virtue goes quietly to sleep for seven years more." This had been the fate of Lord Byron, during the most morally depraved period English society had known since the Restoration!

His next review dealt with John Bunyan,[15] whose *Pilgrim's Progress* he already knew almost literally by heart. He began by comparing the work with Spenser's great allegory. Bunyan's story was given every advantage: "One unpardonable fault, the fault of tediousness, pervades the whole of the Fairy Queen. . . . Of the persons who read the first canto, not one in ten reaches the end of the first book, and not one in a hundred perseveres to the end of the poem. Very few and very weary are those who are in at the death of the Blatant Beast"—and among them, we fear, Macaulay was not to be found, for the Blatant Beast is never slain.[16] Bunyan's allegory, on the other hand, is pervaded throughout with a warm human interest. Each sympathetic reader fancies himself in Christian's place. His work has become a part of the personal recollections of millions of readers. No higher reward can fall to a man of genius.

The article on the "Civil Disabilities of the Jews"[17] contained nothing of importance that was not stated, probably to better advantage, in Macaulay's speech in the House two years afterwards. His contention was the simple and obvious one that it was absurd to exclude this race from politics as long as its members were permitted to amass large fortunes. Wealth invariably implied political influence. The Jews of the country had long been entirely reliable patriots, if for no

15. *Ibid.*, V, 445-57 (December, 1831).
16. See *Faerie Queene*, Book VI, Canto XII, Stanzas 38-41, the last three stanzas preceding the Mutabilitie cantos.
17. *Works*, V, 459-69.

other reason than that their material resources were tied up with the nation's future. The time was fully at hand, he felt, for a Christian people to blot from their statute books the laws intolerance had first written into them.

His next subject was Croker's edition of Boswell.[18] The personal strictures which were heaped upon the editor it is needless to recall. But in appraising the character of Boswell himself Macaulay was almost equally unfortunate. Paradoxes he was rarely able to resist, and this time, it seemed, in the character of the unrivalled biographer, he had hit upon the supreme paradox in literature: "Many of the greatest men that ever lived have written biography. Boswell was one of the smallest men that ever lived, and he had beaten them all. . . . He was the laughing-stock of the whole of that brilliant society which has owed to him the greatest part of its fame. He was always laying himself at the feet of some eminent man, and begging to be spit upon and trampled upon. . . . Servile and impertinent, shallow and pedantic, a bigot and a sot, bloated with family pride, and eternally blustering about the dignity of a born gentleman, yet stooping to be a talebearer and eavesdropper, a common butt in the taverns of London. . . . such was this man, and such he was content and proud to be. Everything which another man would have hidden, everything the publication of which would have made another man hang himself, was matter of gay and clamorous exultation to his weak and diseased mind." Misapprehension, it needs hardly be added, could scarcely go any further.

"John Hampden,"[19] and "Burleigh and his Times,"[20] are two of his most listless works. The subject of the former had no relation to literature nor did he seem of sufficient historical importance to interest Macaulay. As critic, he was left, therefore, with the uninspiring task of tracing the rise of the Puritan party, of paying his scant respects to Archbishop

18. *Ibid.*, V, 498-538.
19. *Ibid.*, V, 539-86.
20. *Ibid.*, V, 587-611 (April, 1832).

Laud, and with setting forth the increasing lust for absolute power that characterized the reign of Charles the First. The Burleigh essay, in a similar manner, turned out to be a study of the statesmanship of Queen Elizabeth. The Queen's greatest mistake lay in her failure to establish perfect freedom of conscience, a failure which colored disastrously the history of England for the following two hundred years. Yet she understood and practiced the basic principles of democracy. "Firm, haughty, sometimes unjust and cruel, in her proceedings towards individuals or towards small parties, she avoided with care or retracted with speed, every measure which seemed likely to alienate the great mass of the people."

The editor of the volume *Souvenirs sur Mirabeau*, M. Etienne Dumont, was one of the Utilitarian Bentham's most successful interpreters. Macaulay, in his review,[21] could not praise sufficiently the abilities of that Englishman "who had found jurisprudence a gibberish and left it a science." Yet this solid philosopher, this twin spirit with Galileo and Locke, had spoken "in an unknown tongue." That his work did not remain in obscurity the world may thank the scholarly French writer who first reduced its confusing elements into a system.

As for Mirabeau, and the revolution with which his name had merged, his career epitomizes the essential difference between the temperaments of the English and French nations. Those privileges which the French finally won at such heavy cost and after so bloody a struggle were no greater than those which the English achieved in 1832 without the loss of a single life. How does one account for "the unparalleled moderation and humanity which the English people have displayed at this great conjuncture? The answer is plain. This moderation, this humanity, are the fruits of a hundred and fifty years of liberty."

Macaulay's review of Lord Mahon's *History of the War of Succession in Spain*[22] contains a number of interesting passages,

21. *Ibid.*, V, 612-37 (July, 1832).
22. *Ibid.*, V, 638-84 (January, 1833).

in particular one of the most entertaining accounts on record of that noted Restoration rake, the Earl of Peterborough. Perhaps an even more pertinent section of the work is the one with which it opens. A noble lord had written an attractive book, had actually distinguished himself in his own right. "Industry and a taste for intellectual pleasures are peculiarly respectable in those who can afford to be idle and who have every temptation to be dissipated." The critic desired to wish every success to a gentleman who had stepped so far aside from the traditions of his class "in search of distinctions which he may justly call his own." It was a rare gesture to emanate from a Tory , so rare as to lead Macaulay to pass over a number of faults he might otherwise expose. This policy, in fact, he followed throughout the essay, devoting its pages to a factual summary of the War itself and leaving the author on surprisingly good terms. Every noble lord, he seems to have felt, should be afforded every encouragement!

"Horace Walpole"[23] gave Macaulay a chance to write again of the times he most loved, the times of Dr. Johnson and Burke. Yet his actual subject was one he could hardly admire. Walpole he looked upon as the most eccentric, artificial, and capricious of men. He was as fond of faction as of amusement. He was grossly ignorant of politics and of history. He greatly preferred the reputation of fine gentlemen to the more "vulgar" distinction that might befall him as a man of letters. Attending to anything so unfashionable as the improvement of his mind was quite too contemptible a matter to bother with. Yet, for all that, one can trace in his character the usual literary vices—the vanity, the jealousy, and the irritability of the third-rate artist. The simple fact is that Walpole was too "Frenchified"; and Macaulay had already learned from his father to distrust any influence, literary or social, that stemmed from so questionable a source.

He turned next to William Pitt, the Earl of Chatham.[24]

23. *Ibid.*, VI, 1-35 (October, 1833).
24. *Ibid.*, VI, 36-75 (January, 1834).

This, too, was for the most part a character study, though cluttered up, like the Walpole essay, with numerous digressions which need not detain us. Pitt, he felt, was undoubtedly a great man, but one whose greatness was not complete and therefore not balanced. He was, for example, extremely affected, an almost solitary instance of a man of real genius "who lacked simplicity of character." Yet in an age of petty as well as wholesale corruption, he stood not as one whom great excitement might cause to ruin his country, but as one "who would never have stooped to pilfer from her." His great service was that, when he became Prime Minister, he infused into the national consciousness a new life and a sadly needed courage.

After the Pitt study came the Mackintosh essay.[25] It was written in India and, as we have seen, came near to embroiling Macaulay in a duel. But Mackintosh's theme, the revolution of 1688, was already beginning to interest his reviewer profoundly. Macaulay liked the book, in general, but found it deficient in narrative, though at that it was without doubt, to him, the best treatment of its subject extant. And what a subject, what an era it was—one from which had grandly stemmed the still unchallenged idea of Progress! "Our Creed is that the science of government is an experimental science, and that, like all other experimental sciences, it is generally in a state of progression. . . . It has always been working itself clearer and clearer, and depositing impurity after impurity"—depositing them, one is forced to conclude now, until only the clean ore of Fascism and Communism remains. "The sound opinion," he goes on, "held for a time by one bold speculator, becomes the opinion of a small minority, of a majority of mankind. Thus the great progress goes on, till schoolboys laugh at the jargon which imposed on Bacon, till country rectors condemn the illiberality and intolerance of Sir Thomas More. . . . We believe that we are wiser than our ancestors."

25. *Ibid.*, VI, 76-134 (July, 1835).

Yet we should be charitable towards past generations; we should not treat them with contempt. Their minds were clouded with the limitations of their epochs. The right question to ask is not, where were they with respect to knowledge accepted today, but, rather, "which way were they going? Did they exert themselves to help onward the great movement of the human race, or to stop it?" Here, Macaulay felt, he had placed his finger upon the secret of Oxford University's decline. For three centuries it had taken the part of bigots and slaves. "The glory of being farther behind the age than any other portion of the British people, is one which that learned body acquired early, and has never lost."

He turned his abounding energies to Lord Bacon,[26] and in the book length essay that was the fruit of this study his doctrine of Progress received its fullest elaboration. Obviously the contents of this work can scarcely be suggested here. Macaulay had little praise for Bacon the man; corrupt though his age was, it was still an age which did not condone bribe-taking, the crime for which the great reformer lost his honors. His punishment was fully deserved.

But if Bacon was behind his age in morality, he was centuries ahead of it as a philosopher. What was the end which he proposed to himself in this field? "It was, to use his own emphatic expression, 'fruit.' It was the multiplying of human enjoyments and the mitigating of human sufferings. It was 'the relief of man's estate.' " Two simple words form the key of the Baconian doctrine—the words "Utility and Progress." To make men perfect was no part of his plan. "His humble aim was to make imperfect men comfortable."

Consider for a moment the intellectual wilderness through which this wise man was forced to struggle, before he could point out the Promised Land whose blessedness we all now share: He was faced with the stern necessity of repudiating two thousand years of solidified superstition. The philosopher whose views epitomized these centuries of mental captivity

26. *Ibid.*, VI, 135-245 (July, 1837).

was Plato—Plato, who had taught that a life protracted by medical skill was really no more than a lingering death; Plato, who believed that the only excuse for astronomy was to lift the mind to a state of pure contemplation; Plato, who would acknowledge no practical value in Arithmetic; Plato, who despised the art of writing because he feared the minds of men would degenerate when they began to trust manuscripts instead of their memories; Plato, who had expounded the absurd doctrine that the end of legislation was to make men virtuous!

"To sum up the whole, we should say that the aim of the Platonic philosophy was to exalt man into a god. The aim of the Baconian philosophy was to provide man with what he requires while he continued to be man. The aim of the Platonic philosophy was to raise us far above vulgar wants. The aim of the Baconian philosophy was to supply our vulgar wants. The former aim was noble; but the latter was attainable. The plain truth is that in those very matters in which alone the ancient philosophers professed to benefit mankind, they did nothing or worse than nothing. They promised what was impracticable; they despised what was practicable; they filled the world with long words and long beards; and they left it as wicked and as ignorant as they found it."

Thus he disposed of Plato for a newer God much more to his liking, for a Deity whose Decalogue had proclaimed, in summary, that "an acre in Middlesex is better than a principality in Utopia." And thus, at the same time, by strong implication, he disposed of Christianity, the gospel of which became generally known only when Plato's thought was allowed to pervade its doctrines. Thus, in brief, he disposed of all the idealisms of the human race: they had filled the world with impracticable promises, and had left it as wicked and as ignorant as they found it.

The study of Sir William Temple[27] returned him to the

27. *Ibid.*, VI, 246-325 (October, 1838).

Restoration. Temple was not a man Macaulay admired. Always decorous, a person of unusual caution, he rendered his country several not trifling services, but he was unwilling to risk anything for her. He possessed neither the warmth or the elevation of sentiment to deserve the name of a virtuous man. His nature was colored by a sort of valetudinarian effeminacy. His virtues were negative; he was a moral coward.

One of the most courteous demurrers Macaulay ever wrote was his review of Gladstone's *The State in its Relations with the Church*.[28] Since he was concerned with treating the views of a leading Tory, however, he proceeded to expand again his own rival theory of politics. But his principal complaint was with Gladstone's thesis that a major end of government should be "the propagation of religious faith." This was carrying paternalism entirely too far, for Gladstone was insisting that conformity to an established church should be made an indispensable qualification for civil office. The young Tory was mistaking the function of government, was asking, in effect, that the old disabilities against Jews and Catholics be reenacted. That issue had been fought out and settled almost a decade ago. To restore its proscriptions would lead inevitably to tyranny.

The study of "Lord Clive"[29] is justly classed among the most readable of Macaulay's shorter works; it is also one of his most detailed biographies. The facts of Clive's life need not be summarized here. What is more important is his critic's discussion of Clive's morality in receiving from an Indian ally a present of "between two and three hundred thousand pounds." It is true that this ally owed his eminence in India to Clive's generalship; it is true that Clive might have received twice that sum had he desired it. It is true, even, that the giving of gifts in the East was a custom which had been sanctioned for centuries. But these reasons did not placate Macaulay. The intrepid leader who had done so much

28. *Ibid.*, VI, 326-80 (April, 1839).
29. *Ibid.*, VI, 381-453 (January, 1840).

for his country was still his country's appointed servant. He should not have accepted even the merest bauble, a cross, or a medal, without gaining beforehand the consent of the authorities at home. By forgetting this principle he made increasingly difficult for the future the task of enforcing honest dealings between the English masters and the native chiefs.

And yet there was something to be remembered in Clive's extenuation. Macaulay realized that in ordinary criminal justice the greatest desert cannot be pleaded even in answer to the slightest transgression: "If a man has sold beer on Sunday morning, it is no defense that he has saved the life of a fellow creature at the risk of his own." Yet Clive was not an ordinary man; he should, therefore, be granted more than ordinary indulgence. If this is done, it will be found, Macaulay felt, that from the first period of the man's service in India dates the renown of English arms in the East, and from his second visit there dates the political ascendency of his countrymen. His name, for this service, should stand high in the lists of those who have done and suffered much for the happiness of mankind.

When Macaulay turned to review Von Ranke's *History of the Popes*,[30] he was treating the work of possibly the greatest historian of the age, and he knew it. There was therefore no dallying with his subject, or with the abilities of Von Ranke's translator. He praised both with ample courtesy and proceeded at once to the central issue the volume had raised— the question of how it happened "that the Church of Rome, having lost a large part of Europe, not only ceased to lose, but actually regained nearly half of what she had lost."

Macaulay skirted the periphery of that question at some length. He noticed that in theology alone his doctrine of progress seemed to have no validity: we know no more today about religious matters than we knew in the days of Thales or Simonides. He traced out the early unsuccessful revolts against the Papal authority. Then came the Reformation,

30. *Ibid.*, VI, 454-89 (October, 1841).

the revolt that proved triumphant. But close behind it, strangely enough, followed another reformation, no whit less vigorous, in the Catholic Church itself. Loyola had appeared, and with him the Order of the Jesuits.

In truth, he went on, the Catholic Church has solved the problem of keeping erring mortals within her fold, solved it with a wisdom of which Protestants have never seemed capable. She knows how to deal with enthusiasts. Instead of excommunicating them, she sends them away on some forlorn hope with her blessings. But with the Protestant enthusiast it is different. He may be a Bunyan, fired with a celestial vision, but otherwise not prone in the least to question the articles or the liturgy of the church to which he belongs. But none-the-less, if he preaches about his vision, on Tower Hill or in Smithfield, he is driven out of his church. He forms a new sect and within a few weeks the Establishment "has lost a hundred families."

But Macaulay could not leave his subject with the implication that the Catholic tradition was the sound one. His firm belief was, he declared, that the northern countries of Europe owe their "great civilization and prosperity chiefly to the moral effect of the Protestant Reformation, and that the decay of the southern countries of Europe is to be mainly ascribed to the great Catholic revival."

The outstanding opinion Macaulay advanced in his essay, "The Comic Dramatists of the Restoration,"[31] is almost too well known to be recalled. The reviewer had not the least idea of recommending that the plays he was discussing be suppressed: no works which have exercised a great influence upon the human mind should be permitted to disappear from the world. And yet it would be difficult to condemn too strongly the dramas of men like Wycherley, Congreve, and VanBrugh. "For in truth this part of our literature is a disgrace to our language and our national character. It is clever, indeed, and very entertaining; but it is, in the most

31. *Ibid.*, VI, 490-532 (January, 1841).

emphatic sense of the words, 'earthly,' 'sensual,' 'devilish.' " Shakespeare and Jonson associated vice in their plays with what was degrading. The dramatists of the Restoration, on the contrary, invariably represent even such crimes as adultery "as the calling of a fine gentleman, as a grace without which his character would be imperfect." It was idle of Charles Lamb to contend that the figures in these works "belong to the regions of pure comedy, where no cold moral reigns." The question is simply this: whether a playwright who attempts systematically to render attractive on the stage the worse sort of rakes and prostitutes does or does not make an ill use of his powers. "We own that we are unable to understand how this question can be answered in any way but one."

The volume, *The Opinions of Lord Holland*, was published in 1841, shortly after that kindly man's death, and Macaulay noticed it briefly in the *Edinburgh*.[32] His old friend, the reviewer declared, was an excellent writer and a sound statesman, one of the ablest Whig liberals of his age. He would not attempt yet to discuss his statesmanship in detail. What was more interesting was to recall the unforgettable society which had distinguished Holland House since the eighteenth century. The site of that dwelling, he reflected, may before long be transformed, to make room for new streets and railway depots, its history forgotten save by a few old men, the last survivors of their generation. Yet they will remember with a strange tenderness, these old men, many objects once familiar to them—the avenue and the terrace, the busts and the paintings, the carvings, and the enigmatic mottoes. They will recall with peculiar fondness the chamber which combined so well the gravity of a college library with the graceful embellishments of a drawing doom, the shelves loaded with varied learning, the portraits which preserved the features of the best and wisest Englishmen of recent times.

32. *Ibid.*, VI, 533-42 (April, 1841). The definitive edition gives this date, erroneously, as July, 1841.

They will remember how the last debate in Parliament was discussed in one corner, and the latest comedy of Scribe in another; while Mackintosh turned over Thomas Aquinas to verify a quotation, and while Talleyrand related his conversations with Barras at the Luxembourg. They will remember, too, the benignant face and cordial voice of him who made them welcome, the temper which years of lameness and confinement seemed only to render sweeter. It was Macaulay's last tribute to probably the only man of his time of whom he invariably spoke with affection.[33]

The study, "Warren Hastings," was another almost book-length essay, Macaulay's longest with the exception of his "Bacon."[34] He wasted little time in getting to the heart of his problem, the story of that great leader's stormy career in India. It should first be remembered, Macaulay pointed out, that Hastings was dealing with no race distinguished for probity. "What the horns are to the buffalo, what the paw is to the tiger, what the sting is to the bee, what beauty, according to the old Greek song, is to woman, deceit is to the Bengalee." His daily weapon is chicanery and falsehood. Hastings soon discovered this; discovered, too, that the traditional English notion that this country was filled with palaces of porphyry heaped with pearls and diamonds was a very far cry from the truth.

Yet it was a truth which the rumpish directors back home would not acknowledge. "Govern leniently," they kept advising their Governor-general, "and send more money." The money was hard to get. A great deal of it was there, to be sure, but honest dealing could not extract it overnight. Still the letters kept coming, insistently. What could he do?

Hastings decided to strike a bargain, one that proved the major crime of his career. Sujah Dowlah was a prince of great wealth. He was also a prince who for personal reasons had set as the supreme ambition of his life the subjugation of

33. I suspect that I have garbled the passage unforgivably in condensing it. See *Works*, VI, 541-42.
34. *Works*, VI, 543-644 (October, 1841).

a rival people, the Rohillas, the most intelligent tribesmen in India. Yet this ambitious ruler knew that his own forces would be powerless without the help of the English. Hastings' bargain was that he agreed to lend a force to Sujah Dowlah in return for £400,000, together with all charges the troops incurred while in the field.

Out of the barbarisms and accusations which followed in the shadow of this bargain swelled the tide of humanitarian protest that culminated only when Burke arraigned Hastings before the House of Lords. It is true that the Governor-general had extorted wealth from other rulers as well; from the hapless Princesses of Oude he had taken a total of £1,200,000. It all proved at length too much for the slowly stirring social conscience of England. "I impeach him," shouted Burke, "of high crimes and misdemeanors. . . . I impeach him in the name of the English nation, whose ancient honor he has sullied." And while smelling bottles were handed around among the females and while Mrs. Sheridan was carried out in a fit, the greatest orator of English history went on to impeach him in the name of the people of India, whose country he had turned into a desert, and in the name of human nature itself. Hastings had become, through the magic of Burke's glowing language, "the common enemy and oppressor of all."

The trial dragged on, for months, for years, was delayed, was resumed, was postponed again, until the whole matter had become thoroughly tiresome. At length, in the spring of 1795, a decision was finally reached and pronounced. Eight years had gone by since Hastings' arraignment, and of the one hundred and sixty nobles who walked in the dazzling court procession on the first day, sixty had been laid in their family vaults. Others present, formerly close friends, had been torn apart by political bitterness. "As Hastings himself said, the arraignment had taken place before one generation, and the judgment was pronounced by another." But, once rendered, it proved a judgment in his favor.

Macaulay, it would seem, wrote his "Frederick the Great"[35] in high zest; for the character of this king had fascinated him for years. Frederick's early home life under his tyrant father proved a particularly absorbing story, one to which the reviewer devoted much more attention than was usual with him. The business of life, this father had decided, was to drill and to be drilled. He hated infidels, papists, metaphysicians, all literature, everything, in short, in which his son appeared to find interest. His rage constantly vented itself in curses and blows. At dinner, for some imagined discourtesy, he had been known to hurl plates at his son's head, had been seen to kick him, to cudgel him, to drag him into closets by the hair. Desperate from this sort of treatment, the Prince once attempted to run away. He was overtaken. His father pointed out that the youth was an officer in the army. His act, therefore, was desertion. A friend who had helped him was tried and executed. It seemed probable that a similar fate would befall the Prince himself, and it is likely, Macaulay said, that only the prompt protest of the States of Holland and the Kings of Poland and Sweden stayed the relentless course of Prussian military justice. Such was the strange soldier's early education.

Once king, he found himself at war, and the account of his desperate campaigns against Austria and other allies fills out the remainder of a very readable work. Interspersed through it are many allusions to Frederick's friendship with Voltaire, another man toward whom Macaulay had an almost endless curiosity. Voltaire had aroused His Majesty's interest in verse making, and that interest seemed to increase in proportion to his military reverses. With enemies all around him, despair in his heart and pills of corrosive sublimate, with which he planned one day to take his life, hidden in a secret pocket, "he poured forth hundreds upon hundreds of lines, hateful to gods and men" alike. It is regrettable that Macaulay was forced to cut short what was in some respects the most

35. *Ibid.*, VI, 645-710.

thorough, even if inaccurate, character study he ever wrote.

"Madame D'Arblay" (Fanny Burney) was the last essay he finished before his collection appeared.[36] Again he was treating the age of Johnson, a period in which he felt as fully at ease as when discussing the Restoration. It was a colorful life he set out to trace, yet a long and anti-climactic one—a life, indeed, so protracted that in its latest stage, the then absurdly affected widow came to hear the judgment of posterity regarding the novels she had finished when young. "She was emphatically," Macaulay declared, "what Johnson called her, a character-monger"; and in painting the whims and passions of characters she had, without doubt, considerable skill. She would not be remembered among the great authors of history—no woman, he believed, had ever earned that rank—but in *Evelina* she had written the first tale by a woman, "purporting to be a picture of life and manners, that lived or deserved to live." There have been a good many less significant contributions to the exacting immortal gallery of enduring prose.

Macaulay's few remaining essays should perhaps be considered along with those already treated. "Addison" appeared in the summer of 1843.[37] The biography he was reviewing had been very carelessly put together by Lucy Aiken, a lady who, Macaulay felt, had very little acquaintance with her subject. How he hated to see his favorites poorly edited, or inaccurately described! He had read some of this work while it was still in manuscript and had mentioned to its publishers a number of errors. But the author had indignantly resented such solicitude. Macaulay was forced to cite those errors in his review; for the motto of the *Edinburgh*, "the judge is condemned when the guilty are absolved," was one which he always took seriously. Except for his strictures in this connection, however, the study is devoted entirely to an account of Addison's important works and of his career in politics. It is

36. *Ibid.*, VII, 1-51 (January, 1843).
37. *Ibid.*, VII, 52-122 (July, 1843).

probably, all things considered, his soundest piece of literary criticism,

"Barère," on the contrary, was one of his most hysterical.[38] The volume he set out to discuss was a defense of the notorious Frenchman's career. Macaulay proceeded to treat his subject from the rival thesis "that Barère approached nearer than any person mentioned in history or fiction, whether man or devil, to the idea of consummate and universal depravity." It was a large order, but to his own satisfaction, at least, he filled it to the limit. His confident charges against his subject now read rather monotonously; one feels that he was too obviously the chief advocate for the prosecution. Yet there is one section in the indictment that has lost none of its vividness after almost a century of reprinting. It is Macaulay's paragraph on the Reign of Terror, a phase of which Zachary had once sampled briefly in distant Africa.

"Then came those days," the passage begins, "when the most barbarous of all codes was administered by the most barbarous of all tribunals; when no man could greet his neighbors, or say his prayers, or dress his hair, without danger of committing a capital crime; when spies lurked in every corner; when the guillotine was long and hard at work every morning; when the jails were filled as close as the hold of a slave ship; when the gutters ran foaming with blood into the Seine; when it was death to be great niece of a Captain of the Royal Guards, or half brother of a Doctor of the Sorbonne, to express a doubt whether assignats would not fall, to hint that the English had been victorious in the action of the first of June, to have a copy of one of Burke's pamphlets locked up in a desk, to laugh at a Jacobin for taking the name of Cassius or Timoleon, or to call the Fifth Sans-cullotide by its old superstitious name of St. Matthew's Day. While the daily waggon loads of victims were carried to their doom through the streets of Paris, the Proconsuls whom the sovereign Committee had sent forth to the departments revelled in an

38. *Ibid.*, VII, 123-203 (April, 1844).

extravagance of cruelty unknown even in the capital. The knife of the deadly machine rose and fell too slowly for their work of slaughter. Long rows of captives were mowed down with grape shot. Holes were made in the bottoms of crowded barges. Lyons was turned into a desert. At Arras even the cruel mercy of a speedy death was denied to the prisoners. All down the Loire, from Saumur to the sea, great flocks of crows and kites feasted on naked corpses, twined together in hideous embraces. No mercy was shown to sex or age. The number of young girls and lads of seventeen who were murdered by that execrable government is to be reckoned by hundreds. Babies torn from the breast were tossed from pike to pike along the Jacobin ranks. One champion of liberty had his pockets well stuffed with ears. Another swaggered about with the finger of a little child in his hat. A few months sufficed to degrade France below the level of New Zealand." And Barère, Macaulay went on to argue, ranked high among those who had sanctioned these crimes.

"The Earl of Chatham"[39] was his last contribution to the *Edinburgh*. In a sense it was a continuation of the essay on Pitt which had been published ten years before. The tone of this study is remarkably judicious; it lacks almost entirely the controversial spirit that he had allowed so often in the past to mar his labors. He began this article, for example, by contrasting the Whig and Tory temperaments in a manner which reflected a much greater degree of toleration than was usual with him. Each party, he said, was a representative of a principle that was indispensable to the welfare of nations. One is, in an especial manner, the guardian of liberty; the other of order. "One is the moving power, the other the steadying power of the state." One is the sail, without which society would make no progress, the other the ballast, without which there would be no safety in a tempest. The tragedy of both these parties—and it was perhaps the first time he ever acknowledged a flaw in Whiggery—was that they lost their

39. *Ibid.*, VII, 204-79 (October, 1844).

distinctive traits for almost half a century following the accession of the House of Hanover; they descended to petty squabblings or to complacency. In time they even reversed their positions: Tories became lovers of freedom; Whigs degenerated into worshippers at the feet of power.

It was mainly as a result of this political confusion that the greatness of England declined during the eighteenth century. Pitt's, almost alone, was the influence which kept the memory of that greatness vital. Ignorant of almost everything except the *Faerie Queene*, in financial matters almost ruinously extravagant, he none-the-less had one desperate passion, the passion of making his country powerful again. This he did, though tried long and sorely by enemies and by blockhead rivals who, among other mistakes, lost the American Colonies to an aroused "peasantry" along the Atlantic seaboard. Yet his personal tragedy remains peculiarly poignant. He died, a broken hearted man, before the nation he had served so unselfishly had attained the ends he gave his life to achieve for it.

2

The essays which have been mentioned in the foregoing pages—perhaps too tediously mentioned—comprise Macaulay's total labors for the *Edinburgh Review*. They comprise, too, every short article he wrote for publication, except the early essays for *Knight's Magazine* and five biographies that were printed in the *Encyclopedia Britannica*.[40] These latter works, the product of the last six years of his life, are, properly, a great deal more restrained than the reviews. Though seldom reprinted, they are also perhaps far more trustworthy, more nearly free of the political or moral prejudices that warped a good deal of his earlier efforts. A possible reason for this circumstance is likely to be found in the fact that in four instances—when he was treating Bunyan, Goldsmith, Dr.

40. *Ibid.*, VII, 283-415.

Johnson, and William Pitt—he was writing about characters toward whom he was predisposed to be generous. And even in the case of Francis Atterbury, he was dealing with a man who had given his life in a lost cause—that of the Stuart pretender—which Macaulay never took very seriously. He belonged with the harmless romanticists of history.

The variety of these thirty-six studies is not nearly so considerable as might at first appear. Only six of them were devoted, mainly, to phases of the history of continental Europe —to phases, incidentally, confined to the last three centuries. The remainder were English in subject. Here, too, an unusual concentration is evident. Of this number, one dealt with Restoration history, another with the subject of history in general. Another one treated the career of an Elizabethan statesman, two more were concerned with statesmen and philosophers of the seventeenth century, another four with public figures of the eighteenth. This brings us to literature, in which his interest was more pronounced. Four of the essays discuss individual authors of the seventeenth century, one the drama of the Restoration, and five others examine individual writers of the eighteenth century. Of the eleven articles left we may say that in every case they treat of problems or personalities that were contemporary when Macaulay wrote them. This list does not allow for his biographies, all five of which fall into the period 1650-1800.

The omissions implied here are startling. Macaulay never seems to have noticed seriously the Middle Ages; to the end of his life they remained for him the dark ages. That he knew the literature of Greece and Rome there can be no question; yet the political, social, and economic history of those countries did not interest him. More startling still is his neglect of the great Elizabethan dramatists—a neglect which all accounts of his reading tend to emphasize sharply. Ben Jonson was the only one of the lot, except Shakespeare, with whom he displayed even an average acquaintance.

The essays, as already implied, were of remarkably unequal merit. The best of them almost without exception deal with seventeenth and eighteenth century England.[41] The early review of Hallam set the cast of his later thinking about the age of the Stuarts. The whole life of Charles I was a lie, he pointed out; the entire Tory version of English history was an absurdity. Laud was a "ridiculous old bigot" who lived with other figures on a canvas of almost wholly unrelieved gloom, until the glorious advent of William the Third. The Walpole study attested the fact that Macaulay knew the eighteenth century as well as he knew the century before it, while "Burleigh" established at an equally early date that his concern with the times of Elizabeth was slight. With Bacon, of course, appeared the most dramatic failure of his life. "The philosopher is exalted beyond all reason, the statesman debased beyond all justice." "Clive" and "Hastings" were his most colorful achievements, the former, if less popular, proving considerably the more accurate of the two. "Though this picture of Hastings is perhaps the most dazzling work of art in the author's gallery, it is one of the most inaccurate of his portraits." Hastings owes his celebrity to Macaulay, but his fame had to wait for vindication at other hands.

One might suggest other factual shortcomings at length. The caricature of the father of Frederick the Great is based on the highly jaundiced memoirs of Wilhelmina, which Macaulay employed without a suspicion of their inaccuracy. The account of Frederick himself is scarcely more valid; his worse traits are selected and magnified. Certain of the author's contemporaries were often bitter about these and similar lapses. The "Ettrick Shepherd," as we have seen, dubbed him an "impertinent puppy" for his surly treatment of Southey.[42] In addition to Spedding's two volume criticism of "Bacon," there were Basil Montague's letters to the author in defense of

41. For opinions regarding the historical accuracy of the essays I am indebted mainly to G. P. Gooch, *History and Historians of the Nineteenth Century* (London, 1913), 295-304, *passim*.
42. Quoted in F. Arnold, *op. cit.*, 59-60.

Bacon's political career,[43] John Mitchell's *Jail Journal*[44] with its cynical references to Macaulay's cocksureness in praise of the gospel of "pudding and profit," and John Harris' arguments denying the uselessness of theology.[45] Macaulay has paid, perhaps with usury, the price for his scorn of the doctrines of idealism.

As for the ideas which reassert themselves in these studies, they are few in number, but driven home with brilliant emphasis. Of course, the central one is his gospel of material progress. One is reluctant to dwell upon either the vulgarities or the menace of that gospel; to do so appears too much to resemble a futile railing against an indestructible dogma. Macaulay, it should be said however, lived his faith in that gospel as truly as he proclaimed it. Money, for example, became a troublesome god to him. He was constantly concerned with his own financial status, was nearly always worrying—long after any real cause for worry existed—about his budget, about his income, about his investments, about trivial purchases, or about requests for charities or loans.

This preoccupation with material things colored his thinking about his contemporaries. Those who were prosperous, unless they were plainly stupid, were tolerably endurable. Those who were in straits he generally despised. It colored his thinking also, as we shall see, about such idealisms as the Oxford Movement, the leaders of which, he soon decided, were both reactionary and fantastic. It biased his judgment hopelessly in the case of spiritual reformers like Carlyle, whom he termed a talker and a writer of gibberish. It blinded him to the best poetry of his time; that poetry was romantic, visionary, and entirely too mystical for serious attention. Macaulay preferred, to state the matter differently, to accept without question the dominant philosophy of the Victorian Age—a philosophy which taught that, once wealth had been

43. *Letter to the Rt. Hon. T. B. Macaulay upon the review of the Life of Lord Bacon* (London, 1841).
44. See edition of 1911 (Dublin), 18-26.
45. *A Review of Macaulay's Teaching on the Relationship of Theology to the Science of Government* (Montreal, 1874).

augmented in England, all other blessings that men can tangibly perceive will follow inevitably in its wake. The world-wide madness which this philosophy engendered went on unchecked, as we have seen, until the fatal summer of 1914. And that check, it is pretty plain now, proved, unfortunately, neither ultimate nor instructive.

A second thesis that recurs rather too frequently is that the Whig Party contained within its ranks practically all the political wisdom of the age. Macaulay's loyalty to this party was commendable. It is unfortunate, however, that in his writing he allowed it to shape for the worse far too great a number of his essays. His treatment of Croker was both ill bred and ill informed. His treatment of Southey was equally in bad taste. The principal offense of these two men, as of Sadler, was that they were Tories long before they became writers, just as it was Mill's principal offense that he was something considerably more radical than a Whig.

The style of these works is a complex subject. Perhaps the saddest realization we come to in thinking of it is that Macaulay's character sense was his greatest defect as an author. He saw men almost always from the outside, in terms of a list of positive or negative traits. What went on behind the surface of their actions rarely if ever concerned him. Their motives he did not inquire about. It is for this reason that so often in his crowded canvasses his figures act without excuse or without intention; it explains the fact that many of them—men like Laud, or Charles I, or James II, or Barère—he was forced to term consummate villains and to dismiss without comprehending. The subtleties of behavior, being attributes of spirit, eluded his clumsy hammer and tong probings. It was infinitely simpler to arraign them all before the cold bar of his own rigid morality and to damn or to pardon them in terms of its laws.

He had other traits almost equally unfortunate. Too often he seems to have failed to distinguish between the demands of a prose essay and the requirements of a speech. He loved

[271]

his adjectives and his rhetoric too well; they led him away into lengthy displays of erudition and into digressions that frequently defaced the unity of his work and brought it to a perfunctory close with the apology that space limitations did not permit him to finish. [46] And of course, there was his love of antithesis and of the paradoxical—the Plato, Bacon contrast; the Cavalier, Puritan contrast; the contrast between Boswell the man and Boswell the writer. Each aspect of the antithesis must be drawn in heavy relief and always with the unhesitating accent of omniscience. It must prove effective at every cost, even at the cost of that truth so dear to the heart of those who practice his craft. The passages must *tell*.

That they did tell, and tell with astounding emphasis, nobody to this good day has doubted. He was the first English writer, declares a recent critic, to make history universally interesting, and it is from him that most of his countrymen still derive their most enduring historical impressions. [47] What was his secret? It seems to have been, simply, that he was in all likelihood the most fascinating story teller who ever wrote in the historical guise. Someone has called him the Rubens of historians, a colorist whose dramatic instinct and whose amazing memory enabled him to enrich his narratives in a way that has proved the despair of all his imitators. This, it would appear, is God's plenty for one man. After all, when emigrants from England set out for India or Australia, as they habitually did, with only three books in their packs— the Bible, a copy of Shakespeare, and the *Essays*—they paid Macaulay perhaps the greatest compliment he ever desired, either from his contemporaries or from posterity.

46. See, in illustration, *Works*, VI, 35, 75, 532.
47. See on this entire paragraph G. P. Gooch, *op. cit.*, 298-99.

XV. Loser

THESE ESSAYS sold amazingly, as did everything else Macaulay wrote. Twelve hundred copies a year were disposed of by his publisher during the first decade after their appearance; 4700 copies became the yearly average for the next decade, and 6000 annually for the next. These figures do not include, of course, various editions of the separate essays or the collected editions which were run off in America and Europe. The market for them in their native country, wrote his nephew in 1875, is so steady and apparently so inexhaustible that it "falls and rises with the general prosperity of the nation; and it is hardly too much to assert that the demand for Macaulay varies with the demand for coal." Such a response attests the gratitude of a people whom he had taught to read literary and social history with enjoyment. He turned his attention to Parliament again.

Matters were not going at all handily there. Sir Robert Peel and his conservatives had been in power since Melbourne's resignation in 1841. They had sent to India as Governor-general their headstrong colleague, Lord Ellenborough; and His Lordship had done a very desperate thing, a thing which, Macaulay felt, might lead to the destruction of many of the best reforms which the Whigs had begun in that country. For an order had come from the Governor's Council that the ruined gates of Somnauth Temple should be restored, and this was a temple sacred to Siva, the destroyer.

What was implied was no less than this, Macaulay contended: Paganism in India was going to be countenanced again. He wanted Ellenborough recalled, and pleaded that the ministry which had sent him out be roundly censured. The religion of the English and of millions of the Queen's Asiatic subjects had been insulted "in order to pay homage to an idol." What was going to follow? The absurd Brahminical mythology would likely soon be revived also, along with the equally ridiculous physics, geography, and astronomy of that caste. Then would be restored their horrible practice of widow burning, and the murderous Thugs would be free again to kill honest men by wholesale. The natives will thus be led to believe that we attach "no importance to the difference between Christianity and heathenism." His audience by this time was murmuring in protest. But let gentlemen look at the express orders which the Home Government committed to the Governor-general! Did not one of them plainly specify that no presents should be made to heathen temples? Did anybody in the House deny that that flat order had been violated? An incompetent man was in authority in Calcutta. Justice and humanity demanded his recall![1]

The Right Honorable Member for Edinburgh was obviously very much exercised again. Mr. Hogg, for Beverley, arose. He termed his opponent's speech eloquent, but entirely too violent. He had wholly mistaken the purpose of Lord Ellenborough's act in restoring the gates of Somnauth. The Governor-general had not in the least intended to flatter one sect there at the expense of another. He had meant to honor the whole people of India. Perhaps the gesture was indiscreet. What then? Mr. Macaulay should remember that a vote of censure or recall is a grave thing. "The thanks of this House are the greatest compliment a public servant can be paid; its censure is the worse rebuke."[2] The truth seems to be that Macaulay had read far too many implications into what was no more than a trivial but generous action. At any rate the

1. See the speech in *Works*, VIII, 228-44 (March 9, 1843).
2. Hansard, *op. cit.* (3 series), LXVII, 628-34.

House thought he had, for the motion of censure to which he gave his support lost by a majority of eighty-five votes.

Once the session was over, he set out for a trip to France. He traveled up and down the Loire River, writing to Fanny long accounts of the places he visited. Long accounts of the miseries of making a journey were added, too: "Groan I" was the railway at Brighton, another "groan" was his passage to Dieppe, still others were the custom house and the inns he was forced to put up with. His major interest while there appears to have been the Gothic cathedrals. He returned in October, to work at his last essays for Napier and to continue the earnest reading sessions which he had already begun in preparation for his *History*.

The report of a certain conversation Macaulay had soon after he reached London implies that he was as great a lover of talking as ever. Fulke Greville is the authority. The diarist had gone to breakfast with George Lewis, to meet the historian Von Ranke. Macaulay was there to meet him also, having reviewed his book, we recall, three years before. "I went," confesses Greville, "prepared to listen to some first rate literary talk between such luminaries as Ranke and Macaulay, but there never was a greater failure. The Professor, a vivacious little man, not distinguished in appearance, could talk no English, and his French, though spoken fluently, was quite unintelligible. On the other hand, Macaulay could not speak German, and he spoke French without any facility and with a very vile accent. It was comical to see the over abundance of his matter struggling with his embarrassment in giving utterance to it, to hear the torrent of knowledge trying to force its way through the impediment of a limited acquaintance with the French language, and the want of habit of conversing in it. But the struggle was of short duration. He began in French, but very soon could bear the restraint no longer, and broke into English, pouring forth his stories to the utterly unconscious and uncomprehending professor." This babble of a breakfast, Greville adds, soon came to an end, and Von Ranke was evidently glad to get away. But after he had gone, long after, Macaulay continued to lecture the others. [3]

In February, 1844, he spoke again in the House. The subject this time was Ireland, which was once more in a desperate state, thanks, he felt, to the determined mismanagement of the Tories. Macaulay realized, he said in beginning his speech, that the woes of that tragic nation could not all be attributed to a single Ministry. Their roots went back for centuries, dated in fact from the first conquest of the country. For it was a conquest of the worst type conceivable: the conquest of a race by a race. Yet they were both white races. This circumstance meant that, while the rival populations intermingled locally, they had never, because of their conqueror-subject status, been morally and politically amalgamated.

Yet even so, the English governments which had honestly sought to reconcile the existing national differences on the island had been Whig governments. The Tories had turned lenient only for reasons of desperate policy. The result was that all the Roman Catholics in Ireland and elsewhere were avowed enemies of the Tory party. Macaulay went on to recite the blunders the Peel Ministry had recently made in its dealings with the natives. Public meetings had been forcibly broken up, O'Connell had been unjustly persecuted; the sympathies of the people were being systematically ignored. That ministry meanwhile had gone on its blind way, enforcing petty and technical edicts, its representatives behaving as attorneys when they should have acted like statesmen. He asked that every member of the House who was sympathetic with the oppressed Catholics in Ireland support him in his vote of censure against these ministers. The division took place. But the enemies of the government failed by ninety-nine votes to carry their point. Members apparently felt, as did one gentleman who replied to Macaulay, [4] that the entire

3. F. Greville, *Diary*, II, 160-61.
4. Hansard, *op. cit.* (3 series), LXVII, 1194.

protest was a party measure, nursed in the rankling hearts of a faction no longer in power.

The other speech Macaulay made during the year was on a question long since dead and forgotten. Certain friends of the Established Church and of the Methodists had put through the Lords a measure designed to deprive dissenting congregations of property they had long enjoyed, on the ground that they did not hold the same religious opinions that had been held by the purchasers from whom they derived their title. The measure was intended, Macaulay felt, against the Unitarians, a sect that had owned much of its land for fully eighty years, but which commanded little political prestige or strength. The Peel Ministry favored a time limit of twenty-five years in these cases, a limit beyond which the law would not apply. Macaulay was solidly behind the government in this case. He looked upon the entire measure as a blow against his sacred institution of property. He had no more interest in protecting the Unitarians, he declared, than he had in looking after the welfare of any other religious body. What he hated to see was a determined attempt by Christian men to nullify the Golden Rule. That attempt had its source in malevolence and downright cowardice. It appears that he was right in his view, and that he helped to persuade a majority of the members to agree with him. For Peel's limitation measure went through by a pronounced majority.

Macaulay's first speech in the Parliament of 1845 gave him a theme which he never tired of amplifying—the evils of slavery. The government was proposing that sugar grown in non-slave holding states be admitted into England at a lower tariff rate than that exacted upon shipments of the product from the West Indies, Brazil, and Louisiana. The latter regions produced their crop by a means which enlightened countries had outlawed, and should, the conservatives felt, be penalized accordingly. The Whigs had objected to the distinction that was being made, charging that the attendant loss in revenue would seriously unbalance the budget.

Macaulay, of course, supported his colleagues in their objections. Why not be consistent? he asked the opposition. Slave grown tobacco is admitted into the kingdom. The growth of it at home is even prohibited. If the government intends to mix moral and fiscal problems, let it go the whole way. The truth is, he went on, that the moral argument so sanctimoniously advanced by the Tories was a smoke-screen. They saw an opportunity, through tobacco imports, to collect a tax of twelve hundred per cent, and the opportunity was too pleasing to be neglected. The Tories had their price. The fact should be honestly admitted.

And yet, he was forced to add, the condition of the slaves in the new world filled him with unspeakable disgust: "If there be on the surface of this earth a country which, before God and man, is more accountable than any other for the misery and degradation of the human race, that country is. . . . the United States." It is idle to stress petty distinctions—to say, for instance, that trade in slaves is forbidden there but allowed to flourish in such countries as Brazil. I affirm that there exists in the United States a slave trade not less but more "odious and demoralizing" than that carried on between Africa and Brazil. He went on to specify his charges: negroes bred in Virginia and North Carolina to be sold like beasts to the planters of the Lower South. Alabama and Mississippi were following suit, doubling and trebling these human animals, that their expanding but exacting markets might be satisfied. The dearest family ties of these unfortunates were broken up by heartless traders. Gangs of negroes, 300 or 400 strong, were herded together, handcuffed, and driven southward to perish in the sugar mills of New Orleans. And always the supply must be renewed, for "very few years of labour in that climate suffice to send the stoutest African to his grave." Moreover, conditions in that country seemed hopeless to the believers in progress. "I think it not improbable that in eighty or a hundred years the black population of Brazil may be free and happy. I see no reasonable prospect of such a change in the United States."[5] So he reasoned, to the accompaniment of much applause. England, thanks to the tireless efforts of the Clapham Sect, had solved her much less complex slavery problem a dozen years before. And Macaulay was enjoying, to the fullest, the complacent sense of superiority which that solution had made possible.

Peel's followers, however, had their way with the sugar duties. The measure he elected to speak on next was one the nature of which left him in a quandary. The Ministry brought in a bill providing support for Maynooth College, in Ireland, the school in which young men were trained for service in the Catholic Church. So the Tories had finally decided to do something for Ireland? After years of intolerance there, they were making gestures of friendship. It appeared to Macaulay that, in happier times, such legislation as this belonged by right to his own party. It seemed almost an usurpation of their once exclusively held liberal principles. But he was determined to favor it, no matter what its source. The education of priests should be encouraged.

His plea that Maynooth be supported was a strong one, based upon the principle of toleration and upon the argument that if a great nation decides to support any program it ought to do so in a dignified and generous way. After defending these assertions he turned to Peel, who was present, a nervous figure harrassed by fears of crumbling authority.

His attack upon Peel was one of the most vicious he ever made. He went back to the year 1827, showing, carefully, how the able Tory had won support from his conservative followers on the plea of favoring their views, only to turn against them when in power by supporting measures indorsed by their enemies. "I am forced to say that the Right Honorable Baronet acts thus habitually and on system." He had talked one way about the Catholic question in 1827, when out of

5. *Works*, VIII, 270-83 (June 6, 1844).

power; he had voted the very opposite way the following year when in power. He had fought the Melbourne Ministry until it was driven from office in 1841. Now he was introducing, to the dismay of his supporters, measures which he had violently condemned four years ago. "It is of the highest importance that the world should not be under the impression that a statesman is a person who, when he is out, will do anything in order to get in, and who, when he is in, will forget all that he professed and promised when he was out."

The gentleman has seen the errors of his ways too late, has delayed too long to side with the liberals. He has arrayed class against class, and the resultant protests are clamorous. Fierce spirits have been let loose in the land; their petitions are whitening our benches like a snow storm. "What did you expect?" he shouted to the Minister. "Did you think, when, to serve your turn, you called the Devil up, that it was as easy to lay him as to raise him? Did you think, when you went on, session after session, thwarting and reviling those whom you knew to be in the right, and flattering all the worst passions of those you knew to be in the wrong, that the day of reckoning would never come? It has come. There you sit, doing penance for the disingenuousness of years. If it be not so, stand up manfully and clear your name before the House and the Country."

Though Macaulay had spoken powerfully, he seems, again, to have misunderstood his opponent's motives. The plain truth is that Peel, who once thought the Reform Bill revolutionary, had finally decided that it had not gone far enough. The man who did most to convert him to liberalism was Cobden. This lucid and eloquent opponent of the Corn Laws had directed to him arguments that finally proved unanswerable. Peel admitted it. He came to see that it was hopeless to attempt "to govern the country through a narrow representation in Parliament without regarding the wishes of those outside." In a sense Macaulay had been right in terming him inconsistent, but at bottom Peel was doing no more than liberals have always done. By the Baconian method of trial and error he had come to decide that the essence of political wisdom is to give the most powerful voting group substantially what it wants.[6]

Nine days later Macaulay spoke again on Maynooth. He was defending a motion that funds that were to go to the college be taken from the revenues of the Established Church in Ireland. He knew that the ministers would not risk their seats by lending support to any measure designed to impair the power of the clergy; nevertheless, he felt compelled to speak his mind, to make known an opinion formed calmly many years ago. That opinion, in substance, was "that of all the institutions now existing in the civilized world, the Established Church of Ireland seems to me the most absurd."

What made it absurd was the simple circumstance that, though established, it was hopelessly the church of the minority. It had long received ample revenues from the government without being able to make any impression whatever "on the great solid mass of the Roman Catholic population." Swift, more than a century ago, "described the prelates of his country as men gorged with wealth and sunk in indolence, whose chief business was to bow and job at the castle." That condition was still true, while half starved thousands were compelled to hear mass under the leaky roofs of miserable hovels. The measure before the House asked no more than that we "make to Ireland a concession, which ought in justice to have been made long ago."[7]

His next speech of the 1845 session caused the ministers no little embarrassment, for the vote which followed it was so close that many looked upon it as a victory for the Whigs. Macaulay was pleading that no religious tests be demanded of professors in the University of Scotland. Such a concession

6. See, on Peel and Maynooth, A. A. W. Ramsay, *Sir Robert Peel* (London, 1928), p. 281; G. M. Trevelyan, *British History in the Nineteenth Century*, p. 269; and *Works*, VIII, 303-15.
7. *Works*, VIII, 316-33 (April 23, 1845).

had recently been granted in the Irish universities, and the cases were similar since in neither country was the Episcopal Church the dominant one. He wanted to know, therefore, why Peel and his followers could not, for once, be consistent.

The most interesting section of his address dealt with his answer to certain Tory gentlemen who had contended "that secular knowledge, unaccompanied by a sound religious faith, and unsanctified by religious feeling, is not only useless, but positively noxious, a curse on the possessor, a curse to society." Really, he declared, such talk appeared almost too ludicrous for grave refutation. Consider what it means when applied to the real concerns of life! It means that it would be much better for the captain of an Indian merchant vessel not to know navigation than for him to be a Socinian. "It is seriously meant that, if a druggist is a Swedenborgian, it would be better for himself and his customers that he should not know the difference between Epsom Salts and Oxalic acid." It is meant that a hundred million of the Queen's Asiatic subjects, who are Mahometans and pagans, should not know how to build a bridge, to sink a well, or to irrigate a field. "If it be true that secular knowledge, unsanctified by true religion, is a positive evil, all these consequences follow."[8]

Macaulay, in short, dealt rather roughly with those churchmen who had too freely displayed their dogmatism. He proceeded to show them that theological tests would make for the ruin of the older universities in Scotland—no Adam Smith or Dugald Stewart could be expected to submit to the impertinence of such measures. Men of their abilities would inevitably be drawn to other schools in which academic freedom was still a reality, instead of a shadow.

Again he traveled on the Continent after Parliament adjourned; the trip was becoming an annual event with him. He came back early in the fall, however, and continued to work as before on the *History*. But the political horizon was growing brighter for his party. It was even possible that the

8. *Ibid.*, VIII, 334-48 (July 9, 1845).

Whigs, discredited for four years now, might again find themselves in power.

What had brought this change about was the vexed question of the Corn Laws. These laws, or tariffs levied to protect English grain growers, had long been a cause of misery and agitation. They kept the price of bread at several times the level that would have been normal had wheat from the United States and other countries been allowed, duty free, to enter English ports. Yet twenty-five years of insistent complaint had served to effect only temporary concessions from the politically entrenched planters, until the activities of Richard Cobden, John Bright, and of their Anti-Corn-Law League began to produce really alarming changes. Cobden had read Adam Smith and had become converted to the philosophy of free trade. And through this league he undertook no less a task than that of teaching the principles of economics to "the lower orders of Britain." In the year 1843 alone the organization circulated 9,000,000 copies of carefully worded tracts, held hundreds of mass meetings, and sent scores of petitions to Parliament.

What made the work of the league so effective was that it gained the support of the underprivileged in both town and country. The agricultural laborer—no longer engaged in raising and selling grain for himself, but usually the propertyless serf of a landlord—saw readily that, the cheaper grain was, the cheaper his loaf would be. The overworked and underpaid factory hand had been aware of this truth for years. Their interests were, therefore, united, and soon augmented by support from many large manufacturers who saw the advantages of lowered food costs for their employees. And then, as if to gain Divine as well as human sanction for the cause, the Irish potato crop failed in 1845 and the English wheat crop was rotted by a two months' rain. Hundreds of thousands in both countries faced a starvation which only cheap foreign wheat could forestall.[9]

9. See, on the preceding two paragraphs, G. M. Trevelyan, *op. cit.*, 267-71.

Which party should take the lead in drafting the legislation that now appeared inevitable? Should the Whigs, whom Macaulay had come to look upon as the traditional defenders of liberal laws? The cry for "total and immediate" repeal was heard everywhere. Everywhere, too, one heard rumors about the Cabinet. "Yesterday morning I learned that the Ministers had gone down to the Isle of Wight for the purpose of resigning." Lord John Russell has been sent for by the Queen and asked to form a Whig government. Will he accept the responsibility? And if he gets through a law abolishing the tariff, will the Lords pass it? Macaulay was as excited as he had been in 1831, but he made up his mind about his own course of action. He would support Peel or anybody else who brought forward a measure designed to repeal the duties. He was on the bandwagon.

He went up to Edinburgh to address his constituents on the subject. "My opinions," he began, "from the day on which I entered public life, have never varied. I have always considered the principle of protection to agriculture as a vicious principle." This he had declared twelve years ago when he stood for Leeds. This he had declared in 1839, when he first presented himself before his present electors. This he had informed Lord Melbourne of, when he was invited to become a member of the Government in 1841. But in the latter year an odd thing had happened. The Ministry decided that all factions could be quieted if the small duty of eight shillings the quarter of a ton were permitted on wheat. Macaulay supported that measure for the sake of party harmony. But the Whigs were defeated. Peel went in with his sliding scale which, unfortunately, stuck at a high level and refused to budge. Since that time, Macaulay declared, he had supported every measure designed to abolish the duties altogether.

He didn't mind telling his audience his reasons. The fact was that no matter what laws are made "we must be dependent on other countries for a large part of our food." This was what made him an advocate of free trade. England is the greatest manufacturing country in the world, he went on, but of what good to the workingman is such a distinction if the foodstuffs which other countries would send us in exchange for our finished products are stopped at our ports and taxed out of all reason? The poorer classes have been too long exploited by the powerful but selfish advocates of the tariff. "By the standard of free trade I pledge myself to stand firmly."[10] He returned to London, and on December 13, Lord John called him in for a conference.

His Lordship, it developed, had not consented to form a Cabinet. He had promised the Queen merely that he would consult his friends and see what could be done. All day these friends talked, held interviews, speculated about foreign politics, and wondered how long, if they assumed power, they might be allowed to keep it. Six days later it seemed that a Cabinet would actually be announced. Macaulay had been asked to take charge of the Pay Office, it being the post that afforded the most leisure. "I shall have two thousand pounds a year," he wrote Hannah, "for the trouble of signing my name." He consented and left, in high spirits. But the next night he learned that the entire plan of a Whig Ministry had been given over. Lord John informed him by note that an irreconcilable difference had developed between Grey, son of the Reform Minister, and Palmerston. Grey especially feared that, if given the Foreign Office he had demanded, the truculent Palmerston would soon embroil the country in war.

This note did not explain the real trouble. It seems now that the Whigs simply lacked the courage to face the crisis; they were no longer the "grand old party of 1832." They feared the opposition in the Lords, and they shrank from alienating the sympathies of the wealthy planters in the Commons. It would be necessary again, they thought, as fifteen years before, to call in, on the one hand, the aid of the Crown with its threat of new peers, and on the other, the help

10. *Works*, VIII, 349-59 (December 2, 1845).

of the masses of the people—even that of the despised Chartists. Macaulay's seemed no longer to be the liberal party; it had made what its critics came to term "the grand refusal."[11] Peel and his conservatives resumed office.

Macaulay made only one speech in the Parliament of this year; he defended a bill making it illegal for young persons and women to be worked more than ten hours a day in factories. The implications of this measure were far reaching, for it meant that in many industries the laboring hours of men would be likewise curtailed, since their part of the job could not be carried on without assistance. Parties divided over the question. Melbourne, Cobden, and Bright opposed it; Russell, Palmerston, and Macaulay supported it. After a stormy and lengthy debate it was defeated by ten votes in 1846, but the following session its advocates carried it through.

Yet before they defeated the bill, in 1846, worthy members had had the opportunity of hearing what was probably the sanest, most logical, and most patient speech of Macaulay's career. Ths specific issues it treated appear almost incredible today; and yet, in principle, they differ scarcely at all from many labor statutes of the twentieth century. For in both cases the problem was the same: that of enacting into enforceable law certain measures which would compel the controllers of industry to think in more human terms about the people who served them. Each concession that has been gained toward this end has been one that came hard, and that was contested bitterly. But out of the conflict have grown the labor unions, unemployment insurance, old age pensions, and other measures, all designed alike to salvage the industrial order from excesses which have threatened—perhaps still threaten— to destroy it. This is not the place to discuss the question of how far these measures have fallen below their ultimate goal, or to what extent violence has marred the relatively imperfect success already achieved. What is important, rather, is to realize that the whole complex issue has been fought out

11. See G. M. Trevelyan, *op. cit.*, 272.

piecemeal, by slow degrees, insistently, with bloodshed, and with many losses in friendships and in other values less tangible but in no sense less real. The problem epitomizes for us, in brief, the method, and the price, of democratic government.

Macaulay's task was the difficult one of explaining the real meaning of the phrase *laissez faire* to opponents who seemed bent upon perverting it for selfish ends. These opponents had taken it far too literally, were saying that to Adam Smith it meant that government should keep entirely out of business, should leave commerce and industry free, that is, to seek its labor always in the cheapest market and to sell its products in the dearest. If men are willing to work sixteen hours a day, if parents are willing to allow their eight year old children to toil for fourteen hours, what concern is that of the state? *Let us alone!* The essence of successful competition is the sanctity of the profit motive.

Macaulay thought otherwise. There are higher laws than those of commerce. When the public interest is involved, the state has always felt justified in interfering. It interferes with our schedule of work, by requiring that one day in every seven be set aside for purposes of worship and recreation. It interferes in the cause of national defense, forcing men, often against their will, to serve in the militia. Back of these and similar cases was a settled and consistent policy. That policy was now being rightfully extended. The government was beginning to interfere "where the health of the community is concerned." It had already long since presumed to interfere in cases involving the public morality. "Rely on it," he warned his hearers, "that intense labour, beginning too early in life, continued too long every day, stunting the growth of the mind, leaving no time for healthful exercise, leaving no time for intellectual culture, must impair all those high qualities which have made our country great." Never, he felt, despite the clamor of economic alarmists, will that

[287]

"which renders a population stronger and wiser succeed ultimately in making it poorer."[12]

During the last week of June, 1846, the long debated Corn Law Bill finally got through the House of Lords. An unwillingness on the part of the Whigs to risk the dangers of assuming the lead in this repeal measure was all that had kept the conservative party together. With its passage, then, Peel's domination was done for. The Cabinet was defeated in the House only a few hours after the Bill was known to have been saved. Lord John Russell was again sent for and ordered to form a Cabinet.

He was willing this time to oblige, and Macaulay received the place he had been tentatively offered the year before, that of Paymaster-general of the army. He went up to Edinburgh to seek reelection, having forfeited his seat by accepting the position. Arriving there, he learned that an opposition had been organized against him. It had been charged that he was too friendly with the Catholics, that his voting for the Maynooth grant had been an outrage to the loyal Protestants of the country. There was something oddly inconsistent about this charge, for the other Edinburgh representative, Mr. Craig, had likewise supported that grant and yet had been returned unanimously. Why, Macaulay wanted to know, was he alone being stigmatized? The question was never answered, nor did it this time prove troublesome. He won by a seventy per cent majority. But the future was not reassuring. Who could tell what strength these irrational opponents might develop within the next twelve months?

All fall and all winter he worked hard at his *History*. The position under government proved entirely to his liking. Its only unpleasant feature, indeed, was the necessity it laid him under of refusing flatly many incompetents who sought favors from him. One of his responsibilities was that of supplying chaplains for army posts. There was one "old hag," as Macaulay termed her, who hounded him regularly in the

12. *Works*, VIII, 360-76 (May 22, 1846).

interest of her three "brats." "She is so moderate as to say that for her son James she will accept, nay, very thankfully accept, even a living of five hundred a year. Another proof of her moderation," he told Hannah, "is that, before she asks for a bishopric, she has the grace to say, 'I am now going to be very bold.' Really the comedy of actual life is beyond all comedy."

During the session of 1847 Macaulay made only one speech of importance before the House. He defended a bill authorizing a fund of £100,000 "for the education of the people"; and if his speech on the Ten Hours Bill was his sanest and his best, as he seemed himself to believe, certainly his arguments on this pressing subject were never more truly in accord with the philosophy of future generations. The Bill had been objected to by the opposition: a committee ought to be named first, it was felt, to inquire into the necessity for so large a grant. Macaulay brushed this contention aside. It was a time-worn device of men unwilling to pay their obligations to a new society they had helped to bring forth.

"The education of the poor," he began, citing Adam Smith in support, "is a matter which deeply concerns the commonwealth. Just as the magistrate ought to interfere for the purpose of preventing the leprosy from spreading among the people, he ought to interfere for the purpose of stopping the progress of moral distempers which are inseparable from ignorance." Let gentlemen who have contended that the doctrine of free trade or *laissez faire* implied no intervention on the part of the state remember this fact! Smith saw, as every sane man can see today, "that the ignorance of the common people makes the property, the limbs, the lives of all classes insecure." Education, in other words, is the safest kind of social insurance. The only alternative to it is brute force, the evils of dictatorship.

One cannot blame mobs, really, for the violence they so often perpetrate. Mobs follow the best light they know. We punish their excesses because we have no choice; yet no one will contend that our summary executions and imprisonments

[289]

represent the ideal solution to the issue they raise. William Penn, George Washington, even Thomas Jefferson—that arch foe of a powerful and centralized state—all realized this fact. That is why, with each of them, the plea to "educate the people" was incessantly made.

Yet consider how far short we have fallen of what they implored us to do! If the statistics are examined, "you will find that about a hundred and thirty thousand couples were married in the year 1844. More than forty thousand of the bridegrooms and more than sixty thousand of the brides did not sign their names, but made their marks. Nearly one third of the men and nearly one half of the women, who are in the prime of life, who are to be the parents of the Englishmen of the next generation, who are to bear a chief part in forming the minds of the Englishmen of the next generation, cannot write their own names."

And is there any wonder! Only think of the conditions under which tens of thousands of our countrymen receive the smattering of education that is all we vouchsafe them. The common day school is usually held in a room crusted with filth, without air, with a heap of fuel in one corner and a brood of chickens in another. The only machinery of instruction is a dog-eared spelling book and a broken slate. And who are the masters at such places? They are the refuse of all other callings —discarded footmen, ruined pedlars, "men who cannot work a sum in the rule of three, men who cannot write a common letter without blunders, men who do not know whether the earth is a sphere or a cube, men who do not know whether Jerusalem is in Asia or America." To such people we have intrusted the minds of the rising generation!

He went on to defend the practical phases of the Bill, to show that jobbery would not defeat its ends, to show that the counties and cities were being called upon to contribute to its general aims. For proof that the measure was no blind or untried experiment, he cited Scotland. The Scotchman of the seventeenth century was spoken of in London as we now

[290]

speak of the Esquimaux. "The Scotchman of the eighteenth century was an object, not of scorn but of envy."[13] The difference was the result of a system of public education that had been established during those intervening years. The Bill was passed by a majority the like of which Peel had never been able to muster for any measure.

Yet this eloquent and reasoned plea for the rights of the common man failed to help Macaulay's case back in Edinburgh. The opposition to him there had been growing; every disaffected element in the town, it seemed, had found in his conduct the cause of its unhappiness. The story of his campaign for reelection in 1847 is a sad one. To the charge that he had sold out to Popery had been added the further charge that he was a placeman, had forfeited his independence by taking an office under government.

In his most important speech to his constituents, Macaulay undertook to answer this charge. His contention was no more than this: that a man does not necessarily betray those citizens who elected him by accepting a position in the Ministry. Indeed, such a man is, if anything, better able to serve his followers in office than otherwise, since his opinion, as a recognized councillor, will be given more weight by his colleagues. But the treatment he received on that occasion was the rudest he ever experienced. He was hissed. Cries of "Question," "Question," interrupted almost every sentence. Wild confusion and fights in the crowd compelled him to break off time after time. Men cried out that he had betrayed them. He was called dishonest, and finally the shout "It's time you were done" became so insistent that he was forced to sit down, though only half finished. He had been dealt with in a thoroughly rotten and disagreeable manner.[14]

Back of all this pronounced underbreeding there seems to have been only two real criticisms. Macaulay, in the first place, had proved altogether unwilling to treat certain

13. *Ibid.*, VIII, 385-405 (April 19, 1847).
14. See the speech in F. Arnold, *op. cit.*, 311-15.

bumptious business men of the town with the deference which they felt was due them. When they would visit him in London, with elaborately prepared lists of grievances they wanted rectified, he had often been known to brush all their arguments aside and to lecture them instead upon their ignorance of the country's first needs. He hadn't the least notion of truckling before them; he would not even treat them with tact. In the second place, he had especially offended the whiskey traders of Edinburgh. They wanted the tax on their commodity reduced, and Macaulay had told them bluntly that he planned to work instead to have it raised. This group, the *Times* reported, controlled almost 500 votes. It is natural to suppose that practically all of them went to his rivals. Macaulay finished third in the poll, 377 votes behind the second winning candidate.

Well, it was over. It was the end, perhaps, of his public life. He would not say so positively, but so he felt the night after the election. Yet he was not depressed. It meant merely that there would be more time for his writing. He went to his room and sat down to a table. And while the friends of those who had beaten him were shouting in triumph beneath his window, he composed the poem we have already noticed, the lines which told of his birthright, and of the one fay who remained with a blessing, after all her glamorous sisters had passed him by. "The world of thought" was still his own, beyond all principle of change.

XVI. Historian

THE EDINBURGH DEFEAT behind him, Macaulay turned with more eagerness than ever to his *History*. Yet the fact that he did so by no means implied that he was without any other political alternative. Almost as soon as he reached London again, letters of condolence began to flood him; for everywhere in the kingdom, it seemed, his dismissal from Parliament had been taken as a public calamity. Would he please consider standing for Ayr? Would he allow his name to be put up at Wigton, at Oxfordshire, at West Riding? With these invitations came messages from Scotland informing him that those who had led the opposition in the recent contest were thoroughly ashamed of their conduct and wished him back. It was all very kind of his friends, and very comforting; but he would not consent to run in another place. "I never can leave public life," he wrote Hannah, "with more dignity and grace than at present."

No! For this new freedom was proving strangely exhilarating; it brought in its train a sense of privacy that had been denied him for far too long. How much more pleasant it was, for example, to assume again that rôle of the Judicious Poet which he had once so ably portrayed—to write Valentine verses to Hannah's daughter "Baba" on sheets that cost a guinea apiece!

> *And canst thou spurn a kneeling bard,*
> *Mine own, mine only Valentine?*

The heart of beauty still is hard,
But ne'er was heart so hard as thine.
Each year a shepherd sings thy praise,
And sings it in no vulgar strain;
Each year a shepherd ends his days,
A victim to thy cold disdain. [1]

The lines flowed on, fluently, convincingly; they proved quite a problem to the young lady of thirteen who received them. Who could the poet possibly be? This time he signed himself "The Broken Hearted Damon." Was it, after all, Uncle Tom, who was always taking her and her brother George Otto sightseeing, who talked so amazingly about all the places they visited, and who wound up the trips, invariably, with elaborate dinners that would have been perfect except for the caviar and raw oysters? He ordered such things, she suspected, just to watch the faces of his guests. One could never be quite sure about him. Vaguely, it seemed, people appeared to consider him a great man, and yet behaved so outrageously whenever he spent an evening at home! He built paper houses and hid underneath them, or jumped from behind dark corners to give one altogether terrifying frights. She would make him confess to the Valentine when next she saw him, though. Who else in the whole world but Uncle Tom would call himself by that name? Certainly never her father.

So he relaxed, at intervals, between the longer intervals of composition and research. At first he had attempted to do both together. When he found it necessary to comment on a place, as it existed in the late seventeenth century, he would seek out the available information, absorb it thoroughly, and then proceed to set down his findings. There was the question of the borough of Leeds, for instance. What was its size in the days of Charles II? He found an old volume by Wardell, in which was listed the number of houses from the records of the

1. G. O. Trevelyan, *op. cit.*, II, 184-85.

tax collectors of the time. They totalled 1400. This fact gave him the clue he was after; for "according to the best statistical writers of the seventeenth century," the average number of persons to a house was 4.3. Leeds at that time, then, "contained about 6000 souls."

He traveled all over the British Isles, went to Holland and France in search of material. "I have done with All Souls [Oxford]," he noted one busy fall evening. "At ten I went to the Bodleian. I got out the Tanner mss. and worked on them two or three hours. Then the Wharton mss. Then the far more remarkable Nairne mss. At three they rang me out. I do think that from ten to three is a very short time to keep so noble a library open." In gathering material for the siege of Londonderry, he went to the town and took a room. He "called upon every inhabitant who was acquainted with any tradition worth the hearing. He drove through the suburbs; he sketched a ground plan of the streets. Alone or in company he walked four times round the walls of the city."[2] And at night, almost regularly, he sat down to read in Thucydides, to him the greatest of all the historians.

Once his information had been thoroughly mastered, the rate at which he wrote it out was astonishing. Almost as rapidly as his pen could move, and that was rapidly indeed, he would sketch through the narrative entire. He had a set of abbreviations of his own: *cle* was made to serve for *castle;* and so it went for practically every word he used, if it ran to more than one syllable. Once this rough draft was finished, he would begin "to fill it in at the rate of six sides of foolscap every morning." This part would be written in so large a hand and marked over with so many revisions, that when copied off for the printer it seldom came to more than two pages. He called this phase of the composition his "task," and unless he completed it daily he never quite seemed comfortable.[3]

2. *Ibid.*, II, 195.
3. See *ibid.*, II, 198-99.

The first part of his *History* was published in November, 1848; and though the second part was not to appear until seven years later, and the last volume not until after his death, the entire work is in one sense a unit and deserves to be so considered, in one place.

He began his first chapter with a characteristic boldness: "I purpose," he said, "to write the history of England from the accession of King James the Second down to a time which is within the memory of men still living." [4] For those who knew his methods of composition, the difficulty with which he got through the much more limited subjects of his essays, this must have seemed a large order indeed. It was one also, we may as well say to start with, which he fell far short of accomplishing. The first chapter of the book sketches the history of his country from Roman times to the Restoration; the second spans the twenty-five years of the reign of Charles the Second. With chapter three, then, or with the year 1685, his detailed picture of the period may properly be said to begin. In the closing chapter of his last volume we find him only sixteen years further along, writing the final paragraphs on the death of his hero, King William. The work is, without much doubt, the most magnificent and ambitious prose fragment in our literature.

It would be hopeless, and probably useless as well, to attempt to summarize the contents of this work in detail. Yet there are passages in almost every chapter which prove fascinating reading. There is the picture of England in the year 1685, for instance, a picture the like of which in thoroughness and interest one despairs of finding in the writings of his contemporaries. He discusses the population of the country, its military system, its revenues, and the state of agriculture. He describes the tyrannical country gentlemen and the state of the clergy. He sets forth the condition under which citizens lived in the principal towns, and tells of the watering places they visited during their holidays. Then liter-

4. *Works*, I, 1.

ature comes in for comment. What did the people read, how fully did French models influence them, how was their mail delivered? It is all there, presented in absorbing language—the coffee houses, the stage coaches, the highwaymen, the general condition of the working class. And pointing it all, giving focus to the whole broad story, are the comparisons Macaulay never tired of drawing between the backwardness of that age and the progressiveness of his own. "The market place which the rustic can now reach with his cart in an hour was, a hundred and sixty years ago, a day's journey with him. The street which now affords to the artisan, during the whole night, a secure, a convenient and a brilliantly lighted walk, was, a hundred and sixty years ago, so dark after sunset that he would not have been able to see his hand, so ill paved that he would have run constant risk of breaking his neck, and so ill watched that he would have been in imminent danger of being knocked down and plundered of his small earnings."[5]

The picture was equally promising when seen from other angles. Bricklayers who fall from their scaffolds today get medical attention the like of which great merchant princes in the days of King James could not have commanded with all their wealth.[6]

Thus it was that, by the simple device of emphasizing a single point—the improved material status of his own age as contrasted with the past—he managed to bring a limitless comfort to the masses who read his book. It would be unfair not to add that with that comfort he helped to usher in also the complacency that proved one of the dominant traits of his era. All past cultures should be judged by its standards, all the figures of history praised or damned by its code. It was the perfect formula for keeping his Philistine countrymen at ease in Zion.

5. *Ibid.*, I, 330.

6. For further illustration of this progress theme in Volume I, see 219-21, 250, 266-67, 272-73, 283, 290, 291-92, 294, 296, 301, 302, 307-8, 324, 326-27, 329, 449, 527. The reader is never allowed to forget it, either in this volume or in the later ones.

Perhaps the most dramatic section of Book One is that which describes the hapless revolt of the bastard son of Charles II, the Duke of Monmouth. Macaulay seems to have felt a strange sympathy for this tender-hearted Protestant weakling, a sympathy that would have been almost complete had he shown more fortitude during the few hours before his execution. At all events, he traces his career carefully—from his early, pleasant years in Holland, through the fateful day at Sedgemoor when, his untrained soldiers wavering before the forces of King James, he took refuge in disgraceful flight and hid in the fields in the ragged disguise of a shepherd. If only he had not deserted those gallant soldiers who had risked everything in his cause! Always popular, he might have died then a hero, his name as cherished as that of anyone in history. But it was not to be. "Vain hopes and the intense love of life prevailed." He was soon captured, speechless with fear, and lodged in the Tower of London.

Letters to his implacable uncle, the King, were sent to no purpose. He was granted an interview with His Highness, but failed to soften his heart. Had he not led a rebellion? Had he not styled himself "King Monmouth"? The prisoner tried one final plea. He was even willing, he hinted, if forgiven, to be reconciled to the Church of Rome. But even this base promise was scorned. He was led back to the Tower and soon afterwards, unable to talk, the blood gone from his face, he learned that within thirty-six hours he was to die.

Those hours were passed in composing pitiful but useless entreaties to James. But they came quickly to an end. And when they did, it seemed that Monmouth at last took on some of the courage that belonged to his race. Bishops were with him, enjoining him to pray for the King. He did so, with difficulty. They then insisted that he address the soldiers and the assembled crowd on the duties of obedience. But there he stopped. "I will make no speeches." And while the churchman asked God to accept his "imperfect repentance," he turned instead to the waiting executioner, John Ketch. "Here are six guineas for you," he said gruffly, "Do not hack me as you did my Lord Russell. I have heard that you struck him three or four times." Monmouth then laid his head upon the block.

"The hangsman addressed himself to his office. But he had been disconcerted by what the Duke had said. The first blow inflicted only a slight wound. The Duke struggled, rose from the block, and looked reproachfully at the executioner. The head sank down once more. The stroke was repeated again and again; but still the neck was not severed, and the body continued to move. Yells of rage and horror rose from the crowd. Ketch flung down the axe with a curse. 'I cannot do it,' he said. 'My heart fails me,' 'Take up the axe, man,' cried the sheriff. 'Fling him over the rails,' roared the mob. At length the axe was taken up. Two more blows extinguished the last remains of life; but a knife was used to separate the head from the shoulders. The crowd was wrought up to such an ecstacy of rage that the executioner was in danger of being torn to pieces, and was conveyed away under a strong guard."[7]

The remainder of this volume is concerned with Lord Chief Justice Jeffreys' tour of the western circuit and with the Bloody Assizes he held in town after town in his relentless search for the followers of Monmouth. He would put the Duke's whole disreputable army to death! Symbolically, he had his courtrooms hung with scarlet, and one by one the prisoners came up to be prosecuted, judged, and sentenced by this fiend. Three hundred and twenty in all were executed during his hurried tour,[8] most of them being drawn and quartered as part of the sentence. Eight hundred and forty-one more were transported.

His methods in court Macaulay often set forth at length. "A prisoner affirmed that the witnesses who appeared against him were not entitled to credit. One of them, he said, was a Papist, and another a prostitute. 'Thou impudent rebel,' ex-

7. *Ibid.*, I, 487-88.
8. See Macaulay's note, *ibid.*, I, 502.

claimed the Judge, 'to reflect on the King's evidence! I see thee, villain, I see thee already with a halter around thy neck.' Another produced testimony that he was a good Protestant. 'Protestant!' said Jeffreys, 'you mean Presbyterian. I'll hold you a wager of it. I can smell a Presbyterian forty miles.' One wretched man moved the pity even of bitter Tories. 'My Lord,' they said, 'this poor creature is on the parish.' 'Do not trouble yourselves,' said the judge, 'I will ease the parish of the burden.' "⁹

This scene proved typical. A favorite maxim of the Lord Chief Justice was "Show me a Presbyterian; and I'll show thee a lying knave." "Impudent rascal," and "What a generation of vipers we do live among" were his characteristic exclamations. The book ended with a savage analysis of the statesmanship of James. This ruler failed, mainly, through his inability to put down national animosities. Instead of turning mediator, he "became the fiercest and most reckless of partisans." In trying to subjugate England by means of Ireland, he relegated the Irish to the status of "hewers of wood and drawers of water" to the English. The calamities which soon overwhelmed him were no more than the logical outcome of his misdeeds.

The character study of William of Orange, with which Macaulay began his second volume, was by long odds the finest of the many portraits with which the *History* abounds. William was a man he intensely admired; he was everything that James was not. "His name at once calls up before us a slender and feeble frame, a lofty and ample forehead, a nose curved like the beak of an eagle, an eye rivalling that of an eagle in brightness and keenness, a thoughtful and somewhat sullen brow, a firm and somewhat peevish mouth, a cheek pale, thin, and deeply furrowed by sickness and by care. That pensive, severe, and solemn aspect could scarcely have belonged to a happy or a goodhumored man." He was a person schooled early in the necessities of statecraft. "Long

9. *Ibid.*, I, 501.

before he reached manhood he knew how to keep secrets, how to baffle curiosity by dry and guarded answers, how to conceal all passions under the same show of grave tranquillity." His knowledge of languages was extraordinary. Dutch of course he knew, and French almost equally well. And though he spoke and wrote English and German inelegantly, he used both with fluency and effect. He also understood Latin, Italian, and Spanish; yet he cared nothing for the polite literatures of these tongues. Cards, chess, and billiards likewise bored him. His interest was, rather, in warfare; and to a battle, even when nigh overwhelmed with illness, he brought a reckless courage and inspired leadership the like of which one rarely finds in the biographies of physically sounder men. This was the figure whose actions were to dominate the *History*, until death closed his career, and the career of the author who idolized him.

There are many fine stretches of narrative in this volume. The account of the efforts of James II to control the two oldest universities of England is told with a quiet thoroughness that makes the injustice of his action all the more obvious and disgusting. The trial of the seven bishops, a result of James's futile effort to discipline the Established Church, is one of the most dramatic episodes in the entire work.[10] Almost equally effective are Macaulay's accounts of the flight of the Queen and the Prince of Wales to France[11] and the long and bitter siege of Londonderry.

The attempt to subjugate this Protestant stronghold in northern Ireland lasted for three and a half months. By the time the final weeks had been reached, Macaulay wrote, "the number of the inhabitants had been thinned more by famine and disease than by the fire of the enemy. Yet that fire was sharper and more constant than ever. One of the gates was beaten in; one of the bastions was laid in ruins; but the breaches made by day were repaired by night with indefati-

10. *Ibid.*, II, 171-79.
11. *Ibid.*, II, 303-6.

gable activity. Every attack was still repelled. But the fighting men of the garrison were so much exhausted that they could scarcely keep their legs. . . . A very small quantity of grain remained, and was doled out by mouthfuls. . . . Dogs, fattened on the blood of the slain who lay unburied round the town, were luxuries which few could afford to purchase. The price of a whelp's paw was five shillings and sixpence. . . . The people perished so fast that it was impossible for the survivors to perform the rites of sepulture. There was scarcely a cellar in which some corpse was not decaying. Such was the extremity of distress that the rats who came to feast in these hideous dens were eagerly hunted and greedily devoured. . . . Leprosies, such as strange and unwholesome diet engenders, made existence a constant torment." [12] These were the afflictions which the loyal troops, their numbers shrunken from eight thousand to fewer than three thousand, endured for the Protestant cause, before the followers of William arrived to relieve them.

The Battle of the Boyne, which put an end to the military pretensions of King James, is one of the several really distinguished passages in the third volume. [13] Even more graphic, however, and more significant in its omissions, is Macaulay's version of the Massacre of Glencoe, the crime which proved perhaps the worst of William's career. The real motive for that massacre, as one of Macaulay's critics soon pointed out, appears to have been the King's determination to show the people of Scotland the extremes of which he was capable when his authority was slighted. He would make of the followers of MacIan, the Macdonalds, an example not to be forgotten. Their reputation for thievery was notorious, and their loyalty to the Crown was doubtful.

William, of course, did not undertake this bloody business himself. Macaulay blames the Master of Stair for it all. It was he who finally sanctioned, and got approved by the King,

12. *Ibid.*, II, 579-80.
13. *Ibid.*, III, 293-302.

the plan of extermination which two earls of the House of Campbell had proposed. His motive, Macaulay weakly adds, was simply misguided public zeal, for he bore the Macdonalds no personal ill will.

The issue can scarcely be argued here. On the first of February, 1692, 120 soldiers commanded by a captain named Campbell marched to Glencoe, the mountain home of the intended victims. To the excited questions of the natives they replied that they came as friends and sought only quarter. "They were kindly received and were lodged under the thatched roofs of the little community." For twelve days they lived there in peace. Five o'clock on the morning of the thirteenth was the time that had been fixed for the deed. Reenforcements were to be sent in at that hour which would cut off every avenue of escape.

Macaulay gives an excellent account of that slaughter— how hardy old Highlanders, who had for almost a fortnight entertained the soldiers with their best beef and wine, were dragged from their beds, bound hand and foot, and murdered in cold blood. A number of children and women were also killed: one lad of twelve was shot dead while clinging to the captain's knees and pleading to be spared. MacIan's wife had a a jewel torn from her fingers by the teeth of one ruffian, and died the next day from other injuries. When dawn came, thirty corpses were to be seen "wallowing in blood on the dunghills before the doors." That any of the clan escaped was due to the fact that the reenforcements failed to arrive in time to block the passes, and that muskets instead of swords were used for the work of slaughter. As soon as the first shots were fired, those natives who were not being forcibly held escaped, to take their chances amid the ice-covered precipices nearby. There, said Macaulay, more died of hunger and cold than were slain, before the survivors dared venture back to the smouldering huts that had before been their homes.[14]

There are numerous other superior passages in the *History*,

14. *Ibid.*, III, 526-30.

passages in which Macaulay, having a good narrative to tell or a glamorous scene to sketch, forgets his prejudices and becomes the true artist, writing objectively as the artist should. His picture of the court of St. Germain, which James kept in France under the sheltering but designing arms of Louis XIV, his account of the last days of this exiled monarch, and his even more moving story of the death of King William—all are told with a mastery that after eighty years still carries conviction.[15] For the irony of Macaulay's case is that to the student of literature his work seems finest when he attempts to do what, essentially, the historical novelist is able to do best. In his most memorable passages he is almost invariably more of the creative author than the historian. To state this fact is scarcely to regret it.

Few philosophical conceptions obtrude in Macaulay's work to complicate it for the average reader he sought to please. One idea, however, which he attributed to the Whig statesman of the Restoration period, shed in his account of it a flood of light on the motives behind the forced abdication of King James. It had become plain to these men, he declared, that the doctrine of the divine right of kings—an obsession with every Stuart—could only be eradicated from the minds of the English through violence. It was equally plain that until that eradication took place, the constitutional rights of the people would remain insecure. "For a really limited monarchy cannot long exist in a society which regards monarchy as something divine, and the limitations as mere human inventions. Royalty, in order that it might exist in perfect harmony with our liberties, must be unable to show any higher or more venerable title than that by which we hold our liberties. The King must be henceforth regarded as a magistrate, a great magistrate, indeed, and highly to be honored, but subject, like all other magistrates, to the law . . . . The best way of effecting this salutary change would be to interrupt the course of descent. . . . On these grounds the

15. See on these passages, *ibid.*, IV, 1-4; 539-44; 554-56.

Whigs were prepared to declare the throne vacant, to fill it by election, and to impose on the prince of their choice such conditions as might secure the country against misgovernment."[16]

At intervals in his work Macaulay was given to interrupting the narrative in order to set forth his ideas upon the particular genius of the English nation. These pauses, or digressions, proved comforting reading always. There was, for example, his analysis of the statesmanship of his country's leaders. The perfect lawgiver, he declared, is a just temper between the mere man of theory, who can see nothing but general principles, and the mere man of business, who can see nothing but particular cases. "Of lawgivers in whom the speculative element has prevailed to the exclusion of the practical, the world has during the last eighty years been singularly fruitful. To their wisdom Europe and America have owed scores of abortive constitutions, scores of constitutions which have lived just long enough to make a miserable noise, and have then gone off in convulsions. But in English legislation the practical element has always predominated, and not seldom unduly predominated, over the speculative. . . . Never to innovate except when some grievance is felt; never to innovate except so far as to get rid of the grievance; never to lay down any proposition of wider extent than the particular case for which it is necessary to provide—these are the rules which have, from the age of John to the age of Victoria, generally guided the deliberations of our two hundred and fifty Parliaments. Our national distaste for whatever is abstract in political science amounts undoubtedly to a fault. Yet it is, perhaps, a fault on the right side. That we have been far too slow to improve our laws must be admitted. But, though in other countries there may have occasionally been more rapid progress, it would not be easy to name any other country in which there has been so little retrogression."[17]

16. *Ibid.*, II, 461.
17. *Ibid.*, II, 464-65.

A second and even more striking illustration of Macaulay's interest in both flattering and instructing his readers may be found in his account of the founding of the first Ministry in Parliament. That account is preceded by an extensive discussion of the duties of Ministers. It reads like an engrossing lecture on a subject which thousands of his contemporaries had heard mentioned but which comparatively few of them really understood.

The Ministry, he began, was what stabilized a legislative group. As everyone knows, a crowd of five or six hundred men, even if they are lawmakers, can easily become a mob, if left without direction and a sense of purpose. It was an awareness of this truth which brought the first Ministry into existence, which created an institution not known of in the days of the Platagenets, the Tudors, or the Stuarts.

The Ministry is, in fact, he explained, a committee of leading members of the two Houses. It is nominated by the Crown; but it consists exclusively of statesmen whose opinions on the pressing questions of the time agree, in the main, with those of the majority of the House of Commons. Each Minister conducts the business of his own office without reference to his colleagues, but all matters of general importance come before the entire group. In Parliament these men act as one on all questions relating to the general government. Should a member object, it is his duty to resign. While the Ministers enjoy the confidence of the majority in Parliament, that majority supports them against opposition and rejects every motion which reflects on them or is likely to embarrass them. If that majority loses its confidence in them, it refuses to pass their measures and thus renders them impotent. The Ministers then resign, and others who are able to command confidence take their places.

These two examples must suffice. Yet it was this sort of writing, repeated over and over—and embellished always with illustrations of the resistless material progress of England—which made Macaulay's *History* read like a fascinating

commentary on the current scene. The comparatively ignorant reader liked it, one suspects, because it was so lucidly
revealing. The comparatively learned, on the other hand,
enjoyed it because it put the obvious in such engaging and
unforgettable language. His volumes became, as he hoped they
would, as popular as the latest popular novel; they were even
perused, the chances are, in the mysterious dressing rooms
of young ladies. What more, one is privileged to wonder,
could an unmarried gentleman-author desire? This had been
his ambition from the beginning.

2

Yet if the ladies enjoyed it, and the lewd and the learned,
critics also managed to give it their close scrutiny; and some
of the judgments they arrived at are still useful. Croker's
opinion we have already noticed. The work was not history,
he decreed heavily; but neither can his review be fairly termed
criticism. It seems much saner to begin with Macaulay's
theory of his calling, to restate his theory of what the historian
should attempt to do. This involves insisting at once that he
regarded history neither as an abstract science, like economics, nor as a pleasing tale, like the novel. It was rather a
harmonious union of these two disparities; and when a writer
divorced them, he implied rather strongly that he lacked the
genius to bring them together. For the truly great historian, he
felt, should reclaim these materials which the writer of fiction
has appropriated. If this were done, we should not then have
to look for the wars and votes of the Puritans in Clarendon
and for their phraseology in the pages of Scott's *Old Mortality*.
A history of England written throughout from this point of
view would become, he was convinced, "the most fascinating
book in the language."

His emphasis was thus on the side of history as a form of
literature. One need hardly wonder that it was. He had read
the great historians of Greece and Rome from boyhood; he

naturally associated its production with the canons of art. It was in the light of this view that he found such contemporaries as Hallam and Palgrave to be wanting. They "miserably neglected the art of narration." He did not mean to condemn them for stressing philosophical principles in their works. It was merely that such an emphasis involved usually far too many valuable sacrifices. In presenting history from the point of view of science, they were unmaking it as literature. Looking at their work from the point of view of Thucydides, it seemed to him that it had become dull and unlovely in the act of becoming profound.[18] He would probably have said the same thing, in confidence, of his friend John Allen and of Lingard.

Consider the losses which the disciples of this new method have suffered! They have formed a notion about the dignity of history. It is, they say, beneath the contempt of men who described the revolutions of nations to dwell, for instance, on such details as those which make biography charming. "They have imposed on themselves a code of conventional decencies." The most characteristic and interesting circumstances are omitted because, we are told, they are too trivial for the majesty of history. Macaulay was thus not ignorant of the moderns; he simply refused to accept them. The perfect writer in this form, he contended, shows us the court, the camp, and the senate, but he also shows us the nation. He considers no anecdote, no peculiarity of manner, no familiar saying as too insignificant for his notice. One such long neglected item may, if properly handled, revive the spirit of an age for us.

But we should notice his critics in more detail. Within a few months after the first part of the work appeared, a pamphlet could be found in most of the London bookstalls condemning Macaulay for his treatment of William Penn.[19] In truth, the

18. Cf. D. H. MacGregor, *Lord Macaulay* (London, 1901), 71-77.

19. W. E. Forster, *William Penn and T. B. Macaulay, Being Brief Observations on the Charges made in Macaulay's History Against the Character of William Penn* (London, 1849). See especially, 15-26.

distinguished Quaker had been handled badly. Macaulay argued that he had hired himself out to Sunderland, who used him for the purpose of extorting heavy fines from certain relatives of the maids of Taunton. These women had been charged with high misdemeanors, and the Queen had decided to give the money, once obtained from them, to her own ladies in waiting. The critic adduced convincing evidence to show that the "Mr. Penne" involved in this unworthy action was really one George Penne, a noted sharper of the time.

Macaulay's next charge against Penn had been that he sought to "bully" the Fellows of Magdalen College, against their wills, to vote for a Catholic as head of the University. Here, it seemed to the author, Penn was blindly following the dictates of King James. Not so, said the critic. With his usual love of harmony, the pious Quaker was merely seeking a compromise that would placate both His Majesty and the college authorities.

For the historian's treatment of the founder of this sect, George Fox, he was likewise taken to task by V. S. Rountree in two indignant lectures.[20] Macaulay had remarked, with obvious contempt, that the writings of Fox were as "unintelligible as corrupt Hebrew." He had gone on to state that Fox's refusal to take off his hat and his well known antipathy to bowing were both dictated "by the most absurd reasons." All this, declared Rountree, was palpably unfair. The famous Whig forgot that Fox was a man of action, not a sentence polisher. He forgot that high and holy considerations—a desire to be like Christ, in fact—had been the real motive behind the Quaker's unwillingness to defer to the ridiculous conventions of society. Finally, Macaulay had passed over without notice the service Fox had rendered the cause of civil and religious liberty, his work in behalf of prison reform, and his success in ameliorating the evils of the penal code. The portrait, in short, was unworthy of its name; it was "a caricature."

20. See his *Two Lectures on Lord Macaulay's Portraiture of George Fox* (York, 1861).

By far the most exacting comtemporary critic of the *History* was the scholarly attorney John Paget, who contributed to *Blackwoods*, in 1859, five essays on as many characters in the work.[21] Paget is especially revealing when he contrasts the author's handling of a man he liked and a man he disliked, when the two were guilty of similar offenses. There was the well known matter of the marital infidelity of both King James and King William. James's interest in Arabella Church-hill and Catherine Sedley the historian termed "highly crim-inal"; moreover, he adds in evident disgust, the one was plain featured, the other "lean and haggard in figure." Yet William, married to a young and faithful wife to whose devotion he owed the crown, maintained during the whole of his marriage an "illicit" connection with Elizabeth Villiers who, Paget reminds us, "squinted abominably." William was more than brazen about this affair, in the bargain. He settled upon his mistress an estate worth £25,000 annually, he named her brother a peer, and made her brother's wife an intimate of the Queen. Yet Macaulay passes all this over as "an instance of the commerce of superior minds."

He failed likewise to understand the character of the Duke of Marlborough, in part because of his uncertainty about passion. The Duke, who in his twenties was favored by the Duchess of Cleveland, is taken heavily to task by Macaulay, for permitting such a relationship to exist. Paget implies that it was no more than a case of a young man's seeking to advance himself as quickly as possible in court circles. Moreover, the historian failed altogether to allow for the fact that, at 28, Marlborough married a beautiful and penniless girl, after an engagement that had been prolonged because of their mutual poverty. And "his faithfulness to her until his death, and hers to him, is proverbial." The truth is that Macaulay was very much like Swift in at least this respect: though they were two of the most vigorous writers of the English language, both of them appear to have been "in total ignorance of all the feelings

21. Reprinted as *The New Examen*, Intro. by Winston Churchill (London, 1934).

which take their rise from the passion of love." Neither, fundamentally, could sympathize with that most powerful of all motives for action.[22]

Paget turned next to a systematic defense of the character of the later Marlborough against the many charges which had been heaped upon it. Macaulay had called him miserly and avaricious. This, said his defender, was a stock charge made first by the libellers and pamphlet writers of the day. The sufficient answer to it is that, when in poverty and disgrace, Marlborough declined to accept the generosity of Princess Anne; he several times refused the governorship of the Netherlands, though the income from that place was £60,000 a year; he was famous for his liberality to his children; and equally famous for the personal aid he repeatedly gave his own officers.

The next charge was that Marlborough had obtained money under false pretenses, and in analyzing it Paget came upon what must in sadness be called Macaulay's worst fault as a historian. For the critic ran down the authority that had been given for this contention. It was the *Dear Bargain*, a Jacobite pamphlet, clandestinely printed, in 1690. No printer's or author's name appears anywhere in the work. Its subject matter is remarkable. King William is accused of contriving the death of English soldiers by sending them over to Holland, where they usually starve. Queen Mary is called, "ungrateful Tullia," a scandal to Christianity. Former King James is referred to as the mistreated King Lear, "our lawful king," a lover of the people, a hater of injustice, and a firm advocate of freedom of conscience. Marlborough, finally, is said to have been guilty of drawing and pocketing for himself the salaries of officers who had been slain months before.

The point is this: Macaulay took this charge against Marlborough as the literal truth. Yet he knew that the charges made elsewhere in the quarto were absurdly false. Why did he place implicit trust in one of the twenty-four

22. *Ibid.*, 8-10.

[311]

pages of the pamphlet and reject altogether the remaining twenty-three? What makes the case even more astonishing is Macaulay's own statement elsewhere in the *History* on the very subject of Jacobite publications. In this instance he was attempting to show that those who blamed King William for the slaughter at Glencoe were the pamphleteering followers of James: "We can hardly suppose he [William] was much in the habit of reading Jacobite pamphlets; and if he did read them he would have found in them such a quantity of absurd and rancorous invective against himself that he would have been very little inclined to credit any imputation which they might throw on his servants."

The dismaying truth is that, when Macaulay needed evidence to support a preconceived opinion, he didn't care where he found it. It was the old technique of the debater coming out again, the technique which he had mastered while still at Cambridge. What mattered, primarily, was to prove one's case. Any evidence, regardless of its source, that would assist one in the fulfillment of that aim was welcome. This explains why Matthew Arnold labelled Macaulay a Whig, or party, historian and regretted the years he had spent in the House of Commons, years in which a search for truth was lost in the artful defense of special measures. It explains why Professor Jebb was able to predict convincingly the way Macaulay would respond to a charge of unfairness in—say—the case of his remarks on the Anglican clergy. He had pictured the clergy of the Restoration in a highly unfavorable light. Had he been challenged regarding the validity of that picture, says Jebb, he would probably "have poured forth a torrent of citations from Restoration literature. He would have quoted Fletcher's *Scornful Lady*, Vanbrugh's *Relapse*, Shadwell's *Lancashire Witches*, Swift's *Directions to Servants*, and a dozen more; then he would conclude that he had proved his point."[23] That either Restoration drama or satire is not an entirely reliable source of information regarding the life of the

23. R. C. Jebb, *Macaulay* (Cambridge, 1900), 28-30.

age is a circumstance that would not have troubled him at all.

Paget offered a number of other defenses of Marlborough which later historians have accepted as valid. His most elaborate discussion, however, dealt with the Glencoe incident. It is needless to treat that discussion in detail. As already suggested, the guilt for that crime, it is pretty well agreed, must rest with Macaulay's hero, King William. If His Majesty was ignorant that it was to be committed, if he had been duped into signing the paper which authorized it, he would certainly have punished the Marquis of Stair, once the affair became generally known. Instead of that, Stair was granted, says Paget, full "pardon and immunity for all his acts." It was clearly a plan of extirpation, conceived against a clan "too weak to offer any effectual resistance but unfortunate enough to serve as a formidable example."

Other demurrers might have been urged by these critics. It might have been suggested, for instance, that the book as a whole has many static intervals, that Macaulay's habit of talking for several hundred pages about the events of a certain year frequently results in a bogging down of his story. The gaps in it are disturbing too. He will discuss King James for two or three chapters, leave him for four hundred pages, and take up his career again at the point where he left it. The effect is jerky and confusing; one wishes that his threads had been kept more nearly together. This confusion is augmented, moreover, by a genuinely distressing lack of dates. One is not made aware of the years following each other, bringing with them their swift and final changes. There is an amorphous quality about the *History*, in short, a lack of unity which we can only deplore.

It might also have been suggested—with somewhat more emphasis, in view of the prominence of the trait—that Macaulay's many attempts at portraying the characters of the Restoration age are almost uniformly unsuccessful. Instead of presenting them, he is generally content to label them with a set of moral adjectives. Illustrations far too plentiful may be cited from any one of the volumes. There was Robert Ferguson—"violent, malignant, regardless of truth, insensible of shame, delighting in tumult, in mischief for its own sake."[24] There was Robert Young who, having narrowly escaped the gallows, "wandered during several years about Ireland and England, begging, stealing, personating, forging."[25] There was Titus Oates, who "had once eked out the small tithes of a miserable vicarage by stealing the pigs and fowls of his parishioners"; who—to relate his story "circumstantially" —had known only "contempt" from those he served, a "vagabond," with a "brazen forehead," an uneven legged coward, "abhorred and shunned" by all men of honor. Late in his career he became "the mortal enemy of the leading Baptists and persecuted them with the same treachery, the same mendacity, the same effrontery, the same black malice which had, many years before, wrought the destruction of more celebrated victims." Those who surrounded him were "hotheaded and foul mouthed agitators." "Savage malignity" was the only emotion he knew.[26]

What makes the portraits unconvincing mainly is that, aside from the moral complacency which informs them, the villains are almost always Tories, and the Whigs are, almost always, the keepers of virtue. This partisanship was rendered even more obvious by the research of Von Ranke during Macaulay's age, for the German scholar proved that the two parties were really not distinct in the 1680's. The Tories, to be specific, urged war with France, arranged the marriage of William and Mary, and were as ready to fetter King James as were the Whig leaders.[27] Macaulay was probably misled here, in part, by his habit of "castle building," a habit to which he was devoted throughout his life. Before he would venture to write of a scene, he would conjure up for himself, he declared, the images of the principal characters who

24. *Works*, I, 414.
25. *Ibid.*, IV, 555.
26. *Ibid.*, IV, 500-3.
27. See Gooch, *op. cit.*, 302-4.

dominated it, would conjure them up, moreover, in details so vivid that they took on in his mind a reality which no later research he might do could question. It was thus, in other words, that the personages of his work became fixed in their traits, often long before he had been able to undertake any considerable reading about them.

What seems to be an uncontrovertable judgment upon the defects and virtues of the *History* has only recently been pronounced. [28] The late Sir Charles Firth studied the volumes with a thoroughness and perspective that will doubtless satisfy completely the needs of the present generation, and the omissions of Macaulay's work he has set down with finality. The great Whig's major oversight, this critic declares, was his failure to discuss England's American and colonial trade. In the next place, he neglected to comment upon the army; we are not told how it was organized and governed, although Macaulay's interest in it is well known. And as for the Continental relations of his country, they, too, are left generally unexplored. There is an insularity about the *History*, in short, that reveals all too plainly the perhaps more engaging insularity of its author. Yet the materials for an investigation of these problems were for the most part available to him.

But the virtues of his book survive, persistently, all efforts that have been made to discredit them. Entirely apart from his triumphant readability, Macaulay rendered one invaluable service to history. History, we should remember, is not only a record but an inquiry, and Macaulay enlarged inquiry into the past far beyond the scope of previous historians. The best evidence of this enlargement is his unique third chapter, "The Condition of England in 1685," a chapter which represents pioneering achievement in the use of materials formerly ignored by writers in this form. He was the first to ransack journalism for his purposes; nothing human, indeed, was in

28. The present MS was completed and in the hands of the publisher before *A Commentary on Macaulay's History of England*, by Charles Firth (London, 1938), was announced. I have therefore been compelled, largely, to rely on the able review of it in the London *Times* for April 9, 1938.

theory foreign to his interest, if he could employ it to enrich his picture of society in late seventeenth century England.

But we return to his style, inevitably—a style which he made perfectly his own, not by any use of strange words, or strained effects, but by means of pure vigor, copious illustration, and an always abiding clarity. One may examine his sentences twice—one often does—for the purpose of understanding what makes them effective, but never out of a necessity to comprehend them.[29] It is this style that lives on, as has been acknowledged, that keeps Macaulay read while many more factually reliable contemporaries have long since fallen away into oblivion. It will probably continue to keep his fame alive in the years that are to come. For that happy faculty of being able to interest almost every type of mind, with as little cheapening of his own nature as one could ask for, was his to a preeminent degree—an art at which he never ceased to work. The critic who approaches him with a consciousness of this fact has learned his first lesson in humility.

29. See, on his style, A. H. Milman, *A Memoir of Lord Macaulay* (London, 1862), 22-23.

XVII. Victorian

WITH THE FIRST PART of his *History* finished, and about to be published, Macaulay took up his *Journal* again, after a lapse of more than nine years. Naturally his earliest entries had to do with the reception of his book. Three thousand copies were sold in ten days. If his abilities did not fail him, he would become a rich man. He hoped he would not also become a coxcomb. He did not feel intoxicated by his good fortune; still "a man may be drunk without knowing it." On the whole, he could remember no success so complete, unless it was the novels of Scott. Even that venerable Tory, the Duke of Wellington, liked it. "A fine old fellow." Four months after its publication, 13,000 copies had been asked for. As early as January his publisher, Longman, was predicting £5000 in royalties for him as a result of the first half year's sale. His agents in the United States wrote him in the spring of 1849 that their countrymen had already bought 60,000 copies, that no book had ever sold like his with the American public, unless it was the Bible. [1]

Of course there were groups of citizens who had not been entirely pleased with certain statements he had made. "I expect," he had noted a week after the first appearance of the work, "furious abuse both from the ultra Evangelicals and the Tractarians, nor shall I be sorry to be so abused." [2] There could be no surer proof that he had been truly impartial. He was not disappointed; the abuse came, and with it more

1. *Journal*, I, 431-517 *passim*.
2. *Ibid.*, I, 434-35.

formal protests. On February 5, 1849, he was waited upon by a delegation of Quakers, five in number, who were calling in the interest of their idol, William Penn. These gentlemen felt that Penn had been brutally treated.

Macaulay, in spite of an outward deference, treated the great Quaker's advocates with equal brutality. He scarcely gave them a chance to speak, but set in to regale them volubly with arguments in the same style that he had formerly used with political delegates from Edinburgh. "Never," he notes, "was there such a riot. They had absolutely nothing to say. Every charge against Penn came out as clear as any case in the Old Bailey. They had nothing to urge but what was true enough: that he looked worse in my 'History' than he would have looked in a general survey of his whole life." That, the author contended, was hardly his fault; he had not attempted a full length biography. "The Quakers were extremely civil. So was I. They complimented me on my courtesy and candor. But I am afraid that they would qualify their compliments if they knew how I laughed at them after their departure."[3]

Two days later came word that the Catholics were upset about certain passages. Ten days after that followed still another and more strange complaint. A friend informed him that "many people had taken offense at what I said of the Old Testament massacres and assassinations. I asked what he would have me say. It seems that he would have had me take the high neological ground and deny the truth of the narrative. A pretty hornet's nest I should have brought about my ears!"[4] Pretty indeed—for had he listened to these critics, he went on, he would have had to question the geology of part of the Bible in order to "explain" it in the light of present knowledge; would have had to question the morality of it, to prevent the record from seeming barbarous. The only criticism he favored with his concern was that which

3. *Ibid.*, I, 492.
4. *Ibid.*, I, 512.

he heard in Hannah's home, the complaint that, in seeking to make himself understood by the masses, he had at times been a little too obvious for the learned. But, alas, how could one hope to please everybody?

He had pleased Queen Victoria, at any rate; invitations to dine at Windsor Palace came rather often. It was quite different there now from the old days—from the time in 1839, for instance, when he had first been asked to dinner with the Royal family. "We all spoke in whispers," he had noted on that occasion, "and when dinner was over almost everybody went to cards or chess. I was presented; knelt down; kissed Her Majesty's hand; had the honor of a conversation with her of about two minutes, and assured her that India was hot, and that I kept my health there." He had been thoroughly bored.

But it was different, now that his fame had been spread abroad. Prince Albert, for one thing, was eager to have him accept a professorship at Cambridge, but on this point Macaulay was unequivocal: the duties of the place would interfere with his writing. Besides, he added in his *Journal*, it would be altogether foolish of him to give up his leisure for a paltry £400 a year, when he might, by reentering Parliament, receive a position in the Cabinet, and an office which paid ten times that sum. But though he refused the Prince, he made himself at ease while there. Occasionally he would stay overnight, reading Jacobite pamphlets by a blazing fire in his own room before dinner time, or strolling down the long corridor to admire the paintings it contained.

"When we went into the drawing room," he notes, of one of these visits, "the Queen came to me with great animation, and insisted on my telling her some of my stories, which she had heard second hand from George Grey. I gave her an account which made her laugh most[5] heartily. She talked for some time, most courteously and pleasantly. . . . Then came

5. This adjective was deemed too unrestrained by G. O. Trevelyan in his life of Macaulay; he accordingly omits it. See *op. cit.*, II, 247. Also see *Journal*, III, 141.

cards, during which I sat and chatted with two maids of honor. The dinner was late and, consequently, the evening short. At eleven precisely the Queen withdrew. I asked Lord Grey who my two maids of honor were. 'The learned one,' said he, 'is Miss Stanley.' Well,' said I, 'and who is the ignorant one?' " Two days later he was on his way to the city again, still talking about whist. Lord Aberdeen had just told him a story of one of the old Scotch judges, one of the few anecdotes of his life Macaulay thought sufficiently well of to record: "The jurist Lord Braxfield, who took the game quite seriously, exclaimed once to the lady with whom he was playing, 'What are ye doing, ye damned auld bitch?' But he recollected himself and, always a gentleman, added immediately, 'Your pardon's begged, madam. I took ye for my ain wife.' "[6]

As a highly successful author, he was being approached often by other members of his craft with plans designed to make them all much better off. "I met Sir Bulwer Lytton, or Lytton Bulwer. He is anxious about some scheme for some association of literary men. I detest all such associations. I hate the notion of gregarious authors. The less we have to do with each other, the better." This was written in 1850. A year and a half later, it seems, the real purpose behind Bulwer Lytton's suggestion came out in a conversation Macaulay had with Longman. The publisher had called to explain "a most absurd plan for corrupting public men in America to make a copyright treaty with us. £2000 wanted. Sir Edward Lytton and Dickens deep in the plot. For my part, I am certain that they are dupes, and are merely throwing good money after bad. It is a vulgar Yankee trick. But if it were otherwise, I would rather that they should commit piracy on me than that I should be detected in bribing them. I will have nothing to do with it— nothing."[7]

He had, he felt, already obligations enough. There were his two sisters, Selina and Fanny to be taken care of. They were

6. *Journal*, III, 143.
7. *Ibid.*, V, 56 (May 29, 1852).

both in their forties now, both unmarried, both therefore entirely dependent upon their eldest brother. He gave them a regular allowance, but Selina, partly an invalid, occasionally exceeded hers, a fact which vexed him sorely. It was not that he was selfish; he was merely an orderly person who liked to be able to live reasonably, to make a financial budget and hold to it. A year after the *History* came out, he noted in his *Journal* that he had just received very disagreeable news. There had been a "fresh call" of one sister "for railway fares, £40." He would pay it, and would do the same for the other, who had not asked it. "But I cannot help being vexed. All the fruits of my book have this year been swallowed up."[8] That these drains upon him were considerable is proved by a statement he made the following October. He had totalled his own personal expenses for the preceding twelve months and had found that they came to £2000 "almost to a shilling." More than twice that sum, then, had been laid out for other purposes.

Naturally, there were charities of all sorts. "Sent £10 to the Literary fund. The third £10 in a week"; "£5 for poor Tom Moore's monument"—such entries fairly crowd the *Journals*. Macaulay, it appears, could rarely refuse indigent authors. He would send them often as much as a hundred pounds, at times without knowing a single fact about their identity. A beggar would come to his door, with an acrostic and a demand for an interview. He would order his servant to give her money and send her away. Or one would write him for thirty shillings "that he might complete his intellectual culture." Another would demand assistance "toward the printing of his poem entitled Letters from Earth to Heaven."[9] And there were poor devils who had known his father vaguely years before, even before Tom Macaulay's birth. Would he, for the sake of that still cherished friendship, assist his correspondent's son to a minor place under government? And

8. G. O. Trevelyan, *op. cit.*, II, 233.
9. *Journal*, IV, 251 (September 30, 1851).

there were remote relatives—one "impertinent vagabond" in particular, who hounded him regularly, month after month. At times it seemed hard to say whether wealth or poverty were the more desirable condition.

And yet on the whole, he was contented; with the passing of each year he attested the fact in his *Journal*. It was St. Crispin's day, 1850, his birthday. "Well," he wrote, "I have had a happy life. I do not know that anybody, whom I have seen close, has had a happier. Some things I regret, but on the whole, who is better off? I have not children of my own, it is true; but I have children whom I love as if they were my own, and who, I believe, love me. I wish that the next ten years may be as happy as the last ten. But I rather wish it than hope it."

He wished it, rather than hoped it because already, it seemed, that solid frame was beginning to weaken, to give out, faintly, its first intimations of decay. It was not that he failed to exercise sufficiently. He had been known to walk twenty-six miles on a stretch. But he was often vaguely in pain, his system was often upset; he was compelled to take "Dr. Bright's pills," which appear to have done him very little good, to apply mustard poultices to his body, to dope himself with paregoric. And there was "a rheumatism" that had haunted him for days. "I can hardly walk," he would write; or again he would complain of being "knocked up," of having to take "ipecac and rhubarb." It seemed that the *Journal* was "becoming that of an invalid." Then there would be a giddiness while reading, an oppression of the chest, a cough if he walked in the east wind. He was restless for spring to come again; winter in London was almost more than he could bear.[10]

These troubles were beginning to affect his disposition, were making him more and more sensitive to trivialities. There was the matter of dogs, to cite an illustration. After breakfast with Ellis, one morning, he went walking with his

10. See especially, *ibid.*, II, 258-65, 274 (February, March, 1850).

host, accompanied by Ellis's two daughters. "The girls are good and intelligent. A couple of ill conditioned curs went with us, whom they were foolish enough to make pets of. So we were regaled by a dog fight and were very near having two or three other fights. My consolation was that the brutes came home well bitten and limping. How odd that people of sense should find any pleasure in being accompanied by a beast who is always spoiling conversation and giving trouble."[11]

But this was far from being his most disgusting experience with canine worshippers. Several years later he took Baba out for an afternoon, and in the course of their stroll they came upon what seemed to him a most singular monument to human folly. The Duchess of York had made a cemetery for her dogs. "There is a gateway like that under which coffins are laid in the church yards of this part of the country. There is a sort of chapel, and there are the gravestones of sixty-four of her Royal Highness's curs, with their names inscribed— Presto, Ginger, Poor Devil, etc., etc. On some of the monuments were inscriptions in verse. I was disgusted by this exceeding folly. Humanity to the inferior animals I feel and practice, I hope, as much as any man, but seriously to make friends with dogs is not to my taste. I can understand, however, that even a sensible man may have a fondness for a dog. But sixty-four dogs! Why it is hardly conceivable that there should be any warm affection in any heart for sixty-four human beings. I had formed a better opinion of the Duchess."[12]

Yes, there were a good many women in the world who struck one as being, for the most part, fools, and there were many elderly men also who fully deserved the same title. The type of female he especially despised was the one who acted too affectionately toward him. The time for such conduct was definitely past. "In the evening to Lady Grey's. The dowager Mrs. L—— seemed inclined to make closer acquaintance with me than I wish for now, whatever I might

11. *Ibid.*, III, 55 (October 21, 1850).
12. *Ibid.*, XI, 24-25 (August 19, 1856).

have desired once, when I was younger and she younger— before I had grey hair and she mustachios. I hope that I am not turning coxcomb in my fiftieth year, imagining such things without reason."[13] Then there was the case of an elderly regency poet. Macaulay learned in the fall of 1850 that he had married. "That old fool," he exclaimed. "I think that I shall be wiser. Yet who knows what dotage may produce. I sincerely hope that I may die before I sink into such a state." What ridiculous people there were in the world!

But if there were many things that disgusted him in life, there was at least one thing which pleased him almost immeasurably. It was the Great Exhibition. There, truly, was something to distend with pride even the most censorious of English hearts! On the day it opened, May 1, 1851, he went out to watch the crowds. The streets were filled with foreigners who had come for the sight, and they were all "respectable and decent"—no Socialists, as had been threatened, no disseminators of violence. He went to Hyde Park and walked along Rotten Row, then over to the promenade by the Serpentine. There must have been three hundred thousand people there at once, he felt. "The sight among the green boughs was delightful. The boats and little frigates darting across the lake; the flags, the music, the guns; everything was exhilarating, and the temper of the multitude the best possible." He fell in with Punch Greville, who was also delighted with the spectacle and the perfect weather. But Greville showed him a letter from a foreigner, Madame de Lieven, who was thought a political oracle in some circles. "She calls this Exhibition a bold rash experiment. She apprehends a horrible explosion. 'You may get through it safe; and, if you do, you will give yourselves more airs than ever.' " More nonsense from another female! "There is just as much chance of a revolution in England as of the falling of the moon."

He made his way into the main building, elbowed con-

13. *Ibid.*, II, 250 (March 6, 1850).

stantly by the crowd but, for once, feeling a part of it, enjoying the elation which everybody seemed to share. "A most gorgeous sight," he pronounced it; "vast; graceful; beyond the dreams of the Arabian romances. I can not think that the Caesars ever exhibited a more splendid spectacle. I was quite dazzled and felt as I did on entering St. Peters."[14]

It was small wonder that he was dazzled and delighted. That great crystal palace covered, literally, acres; mighty elms and beeches stood under its many colored dome, not a single branch cut to make room for the designs of man. The Queen herself had opened the building that morning,[15] a living testimony to her dearest, brilliant Albert, who had conceived the whole thing himself, and had pushed it through to completion despite the objections of many skeptics. The sights that assailed one's eyes there seemed never to end; they were more than could be grasped by one visit, even by the amazing Macaulay.

There was, to begin with, a huge statue of Victoria on horseback, done by Thorneycroft. Rich and glowing silks from Spittalfields were hung everywhere. There was a plaster statue of Apollo, a model of the orchestra at Exeter Hall, a gigantic statue of the old Tory Lord Eldon, whom Macaulay thought privately to be "a liar by habit, a hypocrite, and a thorough specimen of a canting, greedy, pettifogging knave,"[16] but who was certainly impressive done out in shining alabaster. Then there was Dent's clock, the most accurate in all the world, elaborate iron castings from an English manufacturer, specimens of lumber from the Canadian backwoods, Ross's large telescope, railway bridge models, a new and improved light for lighthouses, a forty foot model of the Liverpool docks which Albert had recently dedicated and which would accommodate 1500 small vessels at once.

Elsewhere were sections devoted to the linen and printed

14. From the *Journal*, quoted in G. O. Trevelyan, *op. cit.*, II, 248-49.
15. See Lytton Strachey's superb account of the Exhibition in *Queen Victoria*, Chapter VII.
16. *Journal*, II, 200-1 (January 10, 1850).

fabrics produced in England, and hardware exhibits, and samples of incomparable "metropolitan" furniture. What a variety one could find to interest him in this division—ornamental side walls, elaborate bookcases, oak sofas, and ponderous sideboards! In still other sections mineral showcases could be studied, and sculptured forms, and in one corner, "a whole mediaeval court reflecting the workmanship and skill of our forefathers." [17] All of these things united in chorus to sing a single chant, a mighty melody to the industrial supremacy of England.

For proof of this supremacy one had merely to look at the offerings from other countries that were represented. There was the United States, to cite an example, that country across the Atlantic which good Englishmen could never quite forgive for having sought through violence a destiny of its own. One first noticed, in this section of the Palace, a number of maps of the new nation. Interesting they were, but by no means so good as the French or German specimens. Next came the "much talked of air exhausted metal coffin in which a human body (they say) can be preserved for ages without undergoing the slightest change toward decomposition." The observer was compelled to admit that a bouquet of flowers did remain inside this queer container, as fresh as if newly picked.

This, however, was all that a discriminating visitor could honestly admire from the States. Naturally there were specimen carriages to be seen, elaborately embossed with ornaments and escutcheons, but "for the heraldry of these latter we fear *the College* will not vouch." The walls of this exhibit, it was amusing to remark, "are benefitted by the skill and art of London paperhangers." In still another quarter one found collections of American farming implements, not nearly so impressive as those of the English, "but no doubt effective in their way. . . . Our cousins *come out strong* in the way of raw materials, among which we have some famous chewing

17. See the descriptive pamphlet, *A Visit to the Great Exhibition* (London, 1851), 6-15.

tobacco. Artificial legs, too, and teeth, are shown, the latter no doubt intended to fill up the gaps caused by the chewing tobacco aforesaid."

The same inferiority was traceable in the contributions from other countries. Samples of Russian workmanship were "few and far between." Only a meagre display of "curiosities" was to be seen in the Italian section, while all that could be said of the offerings from Austria, Belgium, and France was that they revealed "the national character." The products of England were so immeasurably superior to those of other lands, in brief, that it was difficult to avoid laughter when one saw them placed side by side.

And what the whole grand spectacle meant was so palpably, so incontestably evident! Moderate liberalism had triumphed. The only economic doctrine of unquestioned validity was that of free trade. Through the once barred doors which this doctrine had flung wide a prosperity was flooding in the like of which few men of past ages had even dreamed of. Let gentlemen but look about them! The renascence of wonder was here indeed, brought to life this time by entirely tangible causes. *Laissez faire* was king.[18] Where that fabulous ruler would lead his subjects in years to come nobody took the trouble to ask. But that he would make them all but grossly rich—if they respected the theories of his favorites, the manufacturers—was a certainty that rested in the cool shades beyond argument.

Thus Macaulay spent his time, during the early fifties, seeing the sights, writing more on his *History*, visiting with noble lords, attending breakfasts and giving them, and talking, talking, almost constantly. Often he was arguing, too, especially about the new rage, phrenology, which was taking in even the staid bishops of the Church. What humbuggery that was, and how ridiculous it made him feel to sit idly by while a fraudulent ignoramus pawed his head! Only

18. See, on the significance of the Exhibition, A. V. Dicey, *Lectures on the Relation Between Law and Public Opinion in England in the Nineteenth Century* (London, 1905), 81.

his friendship for Lord Mahon made him endure it; his Lordship was so eager to have him analyzed. But consider the result of the analysis—the experimenter had pronounced him talented as a landscape artist! Then there were absurd tests of electrical influence, tests designed to show that heavy tables could be moved by the mysterious emanations from one's hands. More quackery! Once the table did move, but the Bishop of Oxford finally confessed that his leg had been the mover, accidentally. [19] What was it that made intelligent people doubt the sufficiency or their five orthodox senses?

But all this while the voters of Edinburgh had been doing penance. Late in the spring of 1852 they held a mass meeting and passed unanimously a resolution in favor of plans to induce Macaulay to run in the coming election. "No man," said one of the speakers who supported him, "has given stronger pledges. . . . that he will defend the rights of the people against the encroachments of despotism and the licentiousness of democracy. If Macaulay has a fault, it is that he is too straightforward, too open; that he uses no ambiguities to disarm opposition." A few weeks later came an inquiry from the Scottish Reformation Society: If nominated again from Edinburgh, would Mr. Macaulay declare himself willing to vote against the grant to the Catholic College of Maynooth?

Mr. Macaulay would promise no such thing! He would promise nothing whatever. He had great respect for his interrogators, but he had nothing to ask of them. He was not a candidate for their suffrages. He had no desire to sit again in Parliament. "If indeed, the electors of such a city as Edinburgh should, without requiring from me any explanation or any guarantee, think fit to confide their interests to my care, I should not feel myself justified in refusing to accept a public trust offered me in a manner so honorable and so peculiar. I have not, I am sensible, the slightest right to expect I shall on such terms be chosen to represent a great constituent

19. See G. O. Trevelyan, *op. cit.*, II, 258-59.

body; but I have a right to say that on no other terms can I be induced to leave the quiet and happy retirement in which I have passed the last four years."[20]

His followers in Scotland were not to be insulted. They put him up for the election, and campaigned for him while he remained complacently in London, definitely curious about the progress of his cause, but definitely too proud to give it active assistance. Five candidates, in all, were entered in the race. When the votes were counted the night of July 8, it was found that Macaulay had led the poll.[21]

He was to go back to Parliament then, was to continue his work in the liberal cause. And how pleasantly it had all come about! Not once had he compromised; not once had he appeared to be interested in the least, except from a sense of duty. People who had never seen him grasped one another's hand on receipt of the news: Macaulay was returned again. Everywhere, in other words, he was being honored—as lawmaker, as author, and as a gentleman who never abandoned his settled principles. Royalties, moreover, continued to swell his income. Only one height of renown remained, he declared, "I am not yet in Madame Tussaud's wax-works." But even this blessing was, at length, to come true. He can be found in that weird mansion today—with a forehead much too narrow, and in robes he never wore, staring blankly, and with evident disapproval, toward his recent Majesty Edward the Eighth.

20. From Letter to Secretary of Scottish Reformation Society. *Ibid.*, II, 263.
21. The count is given in *ibid.*, II, 265.

XVIII. Censor

YET WHEN DO BLESSINGS, unalloyed with evil, ever visit themselves upon men in this world? The same week during which he was reelected, Macaulay came at last to know that his days of abundant health were gone from him forever. He had already, as we have noticed, been often ill, often too out of sorts to continue his writing. Now it was worse than ever. An unaccountable lassitude seemed all too frequently to settle upon him. He would remember other far more vigorous times, times when he worked zestfully for more than twelve hours without show of fatigue. "Why can not I work so now?"

He soon found out. He had planned to go to Edinburgh to thank his constituents for the way they had honored him; yet somehow, as the date drew near, it seemed that he could not possibly summon the strength for the trip. He called in Dr. Bright, and for once was given a thorough examination. Bright found that the action of his patient's heart was "much deranged." He positively forbade him to think of making his intended journey; it was evident that Macaulay could hardly walk. He was ordered, instead, to go to Clifton for a complete rest. When fall came, he seemed to get better, and went with reasonable regularity to Parliament. But winter brought on an attack of bronchitis, and then asthma, and violent fits of coughing. From these last two ailments he never recovered. He became less and less active, gave up his long walks, saving his strength for his book. Thinking over that illness of the past

July, he realized now that it had been a crisis in his life. "I became twenty years older in a week." A mile was a more tedious distance to him now than ten miles had seemed the summer before.[1] When he dined with friends there were "flashes of silence" between parts of what once had been conversation that never paused.

He had more time to be alone, was able to think longer—at intervals during which some degree of physical discomfort was always present—about the ways of the world, and the strange people who were in it. So few of them were really to his liking; so many of them were either quacks or dullards! He filled his *Journal* with his opinions of them, often adding, it is true, little to what he had previously concluded, but generally tending to notice a good many men to whom he had formerly paid no attention. It seems, moreover, that in these estimates the righteous spirit he had inherited from Clapham revived again to color his views. He was not becoming a misanthrope. He was merely, he doubtless felt, a person of standards and settled convictions, from the center of which he reached his unhalting judgments about the passing scene. But he kept them to himself. Macaulay was never a gossip.

His fellow writers came in for ample notice. To begin with, there was Carlyle, whom he had first mentioned in 1850. "At the Atheneum I read Carlyle's trash—Latter Day something or other. Beneath criticism. Yet his evidence before the Commissioners at the British Museum is even more absurd. Truly the world will not be duped forever by such an empty headed bombastic dunce."[2]

Macaulay had obviously made up his mind about Carlyle some years before this note. But he does not seem to have been thrown much with the great Scotchman personally. June 30, 1851, however, Lord Mahon gave a fairly elaborate breakfast. Present were Lord Ashley, the historian Hallam, and a good many others. Among the others was "that ass

1. See quotation from *Journal* in G. O. Trevelyan, *op. cit.*, II, 272-73.
2. *Journal*, II, 280 (April 2, 1850). *Latter Day Pamphlets* is, of course, the book.

Carlyle, who talked more nonsense than I ever heard come from him. I take it that he is accustomed to lay down the law to a set of small persons, and is quite out of his element in general society. Both Van and I encountered him very intrepidly. He instantly lost temper, talked still more absurdly than before, and when he found us resolute and imperturbable, went away in the sulks. His philosophy seems to be made up of such saws as that no bad man can write a good book, that nobody ought ever to look back to the past with pain or pleasure, and other such wisdom." [3] The next night Macaulay met Carlyle at Lord Ashburton's. This time his note was brief. "Carlyle—a humbug—seemed to be sensible of his impertinence of yesterday and to wish to be civil. I was civil. Why not? Nothing is so easy as to be civil where you despise." [4] He was to notice him again. "Got Carlyle's Frederick II. . . . and read it, that is as much as I can read it. I never saw a worse book. Nothing new of the smallest value. The philososphy nonsense and the style gibberish. I have the profoundest contempt for him." [5]

Another gentleman who appears often in the pages of Macaulay's *Journal* is Leigh Hunt, that always financially embarrassed author who had once been intimate with Keats and Shelley. "Leigh Hunt called—Talked all sorts of mawkish nonsense and paid me the £50 which he borrowed three years ago on solemn promise to pay in three months." [6] This note was made in the summer of 1850. A little later in the year he read Hunt's account of Byron. It was such a contemptible performance that Macaulay felt ashamed of himself for having had any dealings with the man. Later he decided that Hunt was improving. But not for long! "Finished Hunt's memoirs," he wrote in November. "A wretched, conceited, ignorant, shallow, vulgar book." [7]

3. *Ibid.*, IV, 151.
4. *Ibid.*, IV, 154.
5. *Ibid.*, XI, 370 (September 30, 1858).
6. *Ibid.*, II, 354 (July 15, 1850).
7. *Ibid.*, III, 85 (November 26, 1850).

What was Hunt's fault? Macaulay gave the matter considerable attention, and finally decided that he had got to the bottom of it. "Read Hunt's book. Amusing, but certainly there never was a happier epithet than that of Cockney. Clever as he is, and observant, there is a shabby genteel air— a frowziness about his style—which produces ridicule and a slight disgust. I was much amused by a passage which I thought very indicative of the laxity of his notions of *meum* and *tuum*, a laxity which he owns and glories in. He speaks of the smallness of Lord Byron's head—Shelley's head too, it seems, was small—so was Keats's. 'They were the only three of my acquaintance whose hats I could never get on.' "[8] Some months later Macaulay added a few more touches to this sketch. "Yesterday," he wrote, "Leigh Hunt borrowed £30 of me. He always borrows in such form—sends long epistles explaining why he wants money just at present. . . . This time it was his daughter. He seems to distrust the post strangely. A queer fellow. He had genius disfigured by a vile vulgar affectation. The genius seems to have taken flight, and only the affectation remains."[9]

Once more this pitiful figure, now seventy, was to annoy the historian and to be roundly damned for it. "Was reading over my strawberries and wine and had put on my clothes for a walk in the garden when Leigh Hunt came and sate, boring me to death. He had brought me some funds which I had lent; but as he told a long story of his disappointments about some expected gains from America I insisted on his keeping the money and would have given as much more to be rid of him. His conversation may formerly have been good. It is now worse than trash. It is positive torture to hear his endless meandering egotism. At last he went. I, in great joy, went out into the garden, but I had not had time to take more than two turns on the lawn when the bell at the gate rang. The dogs began to bark; and soon a visitor appeared, issuing from

8. *Ibid.*, IX, 121 (March 1, 1856).
9. *Ibid.*, XI, 49 (October 19, 1856).

the library window. I could not conceive who it was. T[revelyan], I thought, with some great Indian news. Who should it be but this cursed Leigh Hunt again. God forgive me! He came to say that he was uneasy in mind, that he fancied that I was cold to him, that I must have heard something to his disadvantage, that he implored me to tell him what it was. I hardly knew what to say or how to look. Fortunately it was dark. I was divided between laughing and swearing. However, I protested that he had quite misunderstood my manner—that I had heard nothing about him, etc. Then he began on Dickens's *Bleak House* and the character of Skimpole which, he said, people took for his. Dickens had solemnly affirmed the contrary. But some traits had no doubt been taken from him. And this was most cruel and unfair. Then some protestations of honesty and honour. I was really worried out of all patience. However, I spoke gently and politely and got rid of him. He is intolerable."[10] But Macaulay was not forced to tolerate him further: the tired old gentleman came no more.[9]

Macaulay had despised William Wordsworth since he had first read his verses at Cambridge. After the poet's death, in 1850, the *Prelude* was published. Macaulay managed to get through that work, and he set down his opinion of it briefly in his *Journal*. "It is a poorer *Excursion*," he wrote—"the same sort of faults and beauties; but the faults greater and the beauties fainter, both in themselves and because faults are always made more offensive, and beauties less pleasing, by repetition. The story is the old story. There are the old raptures about mountains and cataracts; the old flimsy philosophy about the effect of scenery on the mind; the old, crazy, mystical metaphysics; the endless wilderness of dull, flat, prosaic twaddle; and here and there fine descriptions and energetic declamations interspersed." The poem seemed to him, to the last degree, Jacobinical, even Socialistic. He un-

10. *Ibid.*, XI, 142-44 (July 9, 1857).

derstood why the conservative Laureate had not brought it out in his lifetime.[11]

He next tried to get through a biography of Wordsworth. "I read, that is as far as I could read, the life of Wordsworth by his nephew. As stupid as the Prelude. More stupid it is impossible to be."[12] Yet to a mild degree Macaulay relented in later years on this subject that had formerly given him occasion to express so much disgust. In 1858 he took up again the life of Wordsworth. "A poor affair," he pronounced it still, adding that it was ridiculous for the writer to call the *Prelude* an autobiography, when Wordsworth had lived fifty years after the time to which it relates. But there were a few items which tended to redeem the poet's reputation. "I like his letters much better than Southey's; and, I think, his taste in literature far better than Southey's. I mean his taste in judging of the works of other people. I was amused and pleased," he confessed finally, "to observe his high and warm commendation of Bentley's Phalaris—the last book that I would have thought him likely to value."[13]

Nor was this his final notice. The last year of his life, in 1859, Macaulay made a tour of the Lake Country. In the course of that trip, he wrote his friend Ellis, he went "to Grasmere Churchyard and saw Wordsworth's tomb. I thought of announcing my intention of going, and issuing guinea tickets to people who wished to see me there; for a Yankee who was here a few years ago, and heard that I was expected, said that he would give the world to see that most sublime of all spectacles, Macaulay standing by the grave of Wordsworth."[14] No man, in the end, was really worth one's anger, especially when one could despise him instead.

One of the few writers of his time whom he seems generally to have admired was Thackeray, and yet the praise he bestowed upon that novelist was guarded, discrete, heavy

11. Quoted in G. O. Trevelyan, *op. cit.*, II, 238-39 (July 28, 1850).
12. *Journal*, IV, 69 (April 26, 1851).
13. *Ibid.*, XI, 360 (August 14, 1858).
14. Quoted in G. O. Trevelyan, *op. cit.*, II, 399.

with characteristic reservations. The two men did not meet until 1849.[15] The next year, Macaulay records, "Thackeray called—talks too much about his Vanity Fair. I suspect that success, coming late, has turned his head. 'L'on voit bien, messieurs, que vous n'etes pas accoutumes a vaincre.' At all events, I am sure that I never, except to a friend of many years' standing, introduced the subject of my own works."[16]

Nevertheless, Macaulay had before this date thought enough of the novelist to propose his name at the Athenaeum Club; he believed him capable of proving a much better member than some of the gentlemen already on the roster. At a breakfast he had attended in January, reference was made to a recent ballot there. "I was interested only in Thackeray. The great majority jealous for him. That wretched creature H.——— threw him out. I never saw a man so little to my taste. . . . Alas, how much I have forgotten my own wrongs in Thackeray's."[17]

The following year, Macaulay attended his friend's series of lectures on the English humorists. Thackeray was treating the eighteenth century, an age about which, as one might suspect, Macaulay's own knowledge was far from slight. "Hannah called," he notes, to take him to the Auditorium. "A large assembly and brilliant. I was glad of it. Thackeray introduced me to his mother and daughter. He lectured, as to manner and voice, much better than the last two times. His style is not to my taste, but there is much cleverness in what he says; and to the majority of his audience his declamation is doubtless more agreeable than it would be if it were in purer taste. He paid me a high compliment, which was cheered."[18] Macaulay attended the later lectures. He heard Thackeray on Fielding, Smollett, and Hogarth, and thought him feeble, superficial, and a little nasty, but felt that he did well enough for the audience. The next occasion proved

15. *Journal*, I, 529 (March 8, 1849).
16. *Ibid.*, II, 27-28 (June 8, 1850).
17. *Ibid.*, II, 219 (January 29, 1850). I am respecting Professor G. M. Trevelyan's wishes, here and elsewhere, in using initials occasionally instead of names.
18. *Ibid.*, IV, 106-7 (May 29, 1851).

equally disappointing, though this time, it appears, the speaker was not wholly to blame. It was a bad, weak lecture on Sterne and Goldsmith. But what made it almost unbearable was the sight of "that hideous woman—if it were not an insult to the sweet sex to call her so—Harriet Martineau, among the hearers." A militant female was always able to spoil an evening for him completely.

There was one more entry which dealt with the greatest satirist of the age, and it, like the others, was qualified in its praise of him. Macaulay had just finished the *Miscellanies* of Thackeray. He felt that the false spelling and the Irish blarney had been overdone in the book. Such cheapness was suitable only for *Punch*, "or in a single character, like the drunken reprobate in *Pendennis*." But Thackeray, he added, is "an excellent writer and shows his abilities even in these papers."[19] His fault, in summary, was the fault of poor Leigh Hunt: he lacked a truly classical, or pure style.

In references less ample Macaulay paid his respects to dozens of his other contemporaries. Taken singly these comments mean little; they read, in isolation, merely like judgments founded on jealousy. But this is scarcely the way to take them. They should be read together. If one is willing to follow this practice, the total effect becomes remarkably significant; it gives one what was, probably, the truth about the Macaulay of the latest stage—a man embittered by prejudices that had long been developing and that had at length, through illness, become crystallized.

There was, to begin with, Walter Savage Landor. John Forster, the friend of Dickens, asked Macaulay to dinner to meet the austere poet. He was a day making up his mind to go. "I do not chuse like Bulwer," he wrote, "to live in a literary coterie. But it does not do to go to the opposite extreme, and to avoid the society of men like F. in a way which looks like the effect of system or of personal antipathy. He wants to introduce me to Landor. I once saw Landor; and

19. *Ibid.*, IX, 121 (March 1, 1856).

then I could not endure him. I like neither the man nor his writings. But I do not chuse to seem to shun him. For many people fear him, and it might be supposed that I have some such feeling." [20] This meeting proved "very civil," he recorded afterwards; yet civilities apparently did not long endure. For Macaulay's next reference was to some "stuff" Landor had written; while the following one expressed the opinion that Landor was a "blustering humbug." [21] One reason for this last opinion seems, without much doubt, to have been a notion of one of Macaulay's friends that the poet was "a greater Latinist than Cicero." Cicero's peer in his native tongue might very possibly be living in Victoria's England, but he had not written any *Imaginary Conversations*. One should look for him among the historians!

Then came a host of others—Tom Campbell, the poet, "a poor creature, who wrote perhaps a hundred good lines and ten thousand middling or bad lines"; D'Israeli, a "coxcomb and charlatan"; William Cobbett, the working man's friend, whose last writings represented a grievous falling off, after "spite had attacked his powers"; Theodore Hook, Zachary's old enemy, who was a blackguard; Harriet Beecher Stowe, from America, a foolish woman who had written a mighty "foolish impertinent book" about England.

And there were others, many, many others. Dickens had published a novel, *Bleak House*, which he tried to read, but at first could not possibly manage. Later he got through it, but was forced to pronounced its pictures of life and manners grossly exaggerated. The biographer Rickman had done a life of that stupid, worthless, drunken, dirty beast Tom Paine, who had nowhere set down any sentiment that any sixth rate radical and infidel might not write, if he would stoop to the job. The sermons of Charles Wesley were available. Macaulay looked through them and pronounced their author an odious fellow.

20. *Ibid.*, IV, 153 (June 30, 1851).
21. *Ibid.*, XI, 248 (January 7, 1858).

His ranging censoriousness drifted abroad, pouncing for a moment on the French stylist Chateaubriand, who half a century before had written a volume, *The Genius of Christianity*, which defended mysticism in the Church much too romantically to suit a rational Englishman. "I was astonished," Macaulay wrote, "at the utter worthlessness of the book, both in matter and manner. The French may be beautiful, as far as mere selection and arrangement of words go. But in the higher graces of style, those graces which affect a foreigner as much as a native, those graces which delight us in Plato, in Demosthenes, and in Pascal, there is a lamentable deficiency. As to the substance, it is beneath criticism. Yet I have heard men of ten times Chateaubriand's powers talk of him as the first of French writers. He was simply a great humbug." An obscure American received a brief line—"Began a queer book called "The Whale,' by Herman Melville—Absurd"; while another American, Horace Greeley, obscure now but then a prominent editor, came in for much more elaborate attention. He had read a biographical study of Greeley, an indescribably absurd and culpable work, the life of a great fool by another great fool. Macaulay remembered Greeley's visit to England in 1851. He had sent letters back to New York, to his paper, in which he talked of the beautiful marble of which most of London was built! Afterwards the vagabond said that Macaulay destroyed his health by opium eating. He was angry for half an hour, "and then came contempt to comfort me."

Mrs. Browning's masterpiece, *Aurora Leigh*, came his way late in life; but that blank verse novel of socialism, slum clearance, and romance failed to please him. It was trash, he decided—unredeemed trash—bad philosophy, bad style, bad versification, gross and sometimes indecent imagery. People would write him often about his own books, occasionally even expressing their opinions in poetry. "By the by," he once noted, "some fool has sent me some doggerel lines on my History. It must be the same poet who formerly mailed me a couplet which he called an impromptu. There cannot be two such asses alive."

Then there was Coleridge. Macaulay once got hold of his "literary remains" and read in them at length. "What stuff!" was his reaction, "what a succession of unintelligible paragraphs! It is quite inconceivable that, if there were any meaning in his philosophy, it should not peep out here and there, through the cloud of gibberish. But I declare that, having read many hundred pages of his writing, I have not the slightest guess at what he means by an idea or by the reason as distinct from the understanding. . . . It is mere hocus-pocus to me." Now and then, though, when Coleridge wrote like a man of the world, Macaulay confessed that he read him with pleasure.[22]

The books kept coming; there seemed no end to them, and Macaulay kept looking inside them and setting down his opinions. A Yankee had sent him an ill written angry book in which he defended the doctrine of the eternity of the torments of hell. Macaulay turned over some pages, but was so disgusted by the writer's asperity, conceit, shallowness, and ignorance that he laid the volume down. Another fool had sent him some equally absurd, thoughtless, ill natured nonsense—not a Yankee fool, but an Irish fool.

One could continue these citations at length, could vary them to include his disgust for people like the one he met on a trip to Italy—"an eccentric, rambling fellow, a Radical and yet a High Churchman, full of Puseyism and Ruskinism and Voluntaryism, and half a dozen other isms mixed in the queerest manner."[23] His contempt—the word comes easily—for Newman and the other leaders of the Oxford movement was ill concealed but amply expressed. He could detect their influence even in architecture. Visiting Oxford, in 1858, he paused to examine the chapel of Balliol College. It was "a tawdry thing— half cockney, half Puseyite." He could imagine

22. *Ibid.*, XI, 564 (September 16, 1859).
23. *Ibid.*, X, 186-87 (September 8, 1858).

nothing worse than those two influences yoked together, unless it was Pre-Raphaelitism joined with them. But this last fashion simply *could* not endure for long. He went to the Royal Academy to an exhibit, and the walls of the place were all but cluttered with the work of members of the school. Pre-Raphaelitism was definitely spreading. "I am glad to see it so," he wrote tersely, "glad because it is by spreading that such affectations perish."

His condemnations ranged through the proud peerage of England in a way that, if published even now, might still prove somewhat embarrassing to see. So many twaddlers, "princes of twaddlers," "idle dolts," "fools," "idiots," and "conceited asses" were to be found in that peerage; so many "stupid parties" they gave; so many "babbling bluestockings" were numbered among the ladies of rank! And there was the Prince of Wales, later Edward VII, who could perhaps be a capable lad if brought up normally. "Gibbs came," Macaulay writes in 1856, "and insisted on introducing me to the P. of W. I had to go to H.R.H.'s room—to stand before a boy of fourteen—sirring him and bowing to him. Wretched work! How much happier he would be with a more manly education. I feel, too, for that nice girl the Princess Royal—To be betrothed to a foreigner whom she cannot care a rush for. And all from a senseless family pride unknown to the great old sovereigns of England. Why cannot she marry as the daughters of the Plantagenets married?"[24]

Macaulay hated to dine out in the fifties; it was trying to his health and often trying on his nerves. When he went, almost invariably he was displeased if he found a great crowd present. "Glad to get home" was his usual comment at such times. But occasionally even large affairs had to be attended, and, occasionally, too, they proved, if generally, at least not altogether bad. The banker, Baron Rothschild, gave such an entertainment once, and in writing about it Macaulay went into some detail. "Decent, fine house," he notes, to begin

24. *Ibid.*, IX, 53-55 (January 29, 1856).

[341]

with, "bad pictures—and the most stupid of stupid parties. Half a dozen Jews of family—some Jewesses. A diplomat or two—that foolish prig Lord John Manners, who was always my aversion, the silliest speaker in England except his brother and the worst poet except his sister—with a solemn coxcombry that turns my stomach. He always seems to be trying to resemble one of Jane Porter's insufferable heroes. There was Lord Duro and his wife—Alas! Alas! that everything beautiful must fade. How beautiful once. There was Wharburton, the brother of the writer—agreeable enough, and Lady Mary Wood, a very superior woman, but both far from me. I was wedged between a Jew from Naples and the envoy from Copenhagen, both talking broken English. Yet I learned something both about Italy and about Denmark. I myself said very little. The dinner good and the wine, as the dinners and wines of Israelites generally are. . . . I stole away as soon as I could."[25]

Yet there were other dinners at which not even a once beautiful woman could be found, to prompt one's mind to meditations upon eternal things. A celebrated duke gave such a one, while people were still talking with freshness about the *History*. An "odious party," it proved. N.S.——— was there, "whom I abominate as a detestable writer, and who abominates me as a successful one. And the Duchess must not only present us to each other ostentatiously, but must insist on my giving her my arm, though it is not *heraldically* the proper thing, and on my talking to her at dinner. I never in my life was more disagreeably seated. I was between Miss S.——— and Lady D.——— I hate the genus bluestocking, and in the whole genus I hate no two women like these two. The stuff that they talked was incredible. I could have died with laughing except for vexation at my own place in so absurd a group. Then there was an absurd Lord C.——— haranguing on twenty subjects in a strange flighty way. I did my best to be polite. Talkative it was not necessary to be."

25. *Ibid.*, II, 40-41 (June 27, 1850).

Yet he was still able, at times, to refuse these nobles who insisted upon lionizing him, now that the world had acclaimed him a great writer. He once set down his notions on this practice rather plainly. The Duke of Bedford had asked him to come for a week-end. But Macaulay wrote "a short courteous excuse." He preferred his own fireside, or Hannah's, to "any duke's palace" in the world. He added that he did not wish to imitate "the airs of Diogenes. But I have really nothing to ask of the great but that they stand out of my light and let me enjoy my own tub." [26] The Duke would have to look elsewhere for entertainment.

The foregoing comments should perhaps be sufficient to indicate a good deal about the character of Macaulay. They make plain that he disliked dullards, and that he had little respect for financial failures who turned suppliants and plagued him with tales of their calamities. Women he had a hearty contempt for, when they became conscious of their learning, or when they failed to remember that respectable gentlemen of fifty odd could not be lured by wiles proper to girls in their 'teens. As for members of the nobility, no matter what their sex, he cared nothing for them unless they proved themselves interesting intellectual companions. Their five hundred year old names were meaningless, by themselves. And of course there were the mystics, toward whom his disgust was settled and complete, whether they were widely admired poets like Wordsworth, or equally widely marveled at poet-philosophers like Coleridge. Such men should keep their opinions upon the solid rock of rationality and correctness, just as they should keep their styles untawdry, dignified, and uncolloquial. To say that Macaulay was a poor critic of his fellow authors is needless; posterity, it is plain, has reversed the judgments of the *Journal*, in the case of practically every writer to whom he referred. It is probably better to say that he was no critic at all when he read exclusively for his own pleasure. Every author was judged in the light of his

26. *Ibid.*, II, 185 (December 24, 1849).

social and moral, in short of his personal, status; and no one ever entirely escaped censure, because no one ever turned out, unfortunately, to be a perfect likeness of Macaulay himself!

And yet he was not always bitter, was not always damning people as he damned the Glenmore Highlanders, who burned him in effigy for declaring that "their ancestors had had the itch." There was a place in his heart, at least one place, that never hardened; there were recollections that centuries, were he to know them, could never render less poignant or dissolve. "Home," he wrote in 1856, "and passed the day arranging papers. Some things that met my eyes overcame me for a time—Margaret, alas, alas. And yet she might have changed to me. But no, that could not have been. To think that she has been twenty-two years dead; and I am crying for her as if it were yesterday." [27]

27. *Ibid.*, IX, 204 (April 19, 1856).

XIX. Sage

ONLY TWO MORE SPEECHES of any importance were yet to be made by the member for Edinburgh—one to his constituents for reelecting him, and one, in great triumph, before the House itself. In November, 1852, still weak from his illness, he managed to get up to Scotland, to fill the engagement he had had to postpone the summer before. It had been five years since he last stood before them, he said, years filled with many losses which time would never restore. There was Sir James Craig, whose labors for freedom had begun before Macaulay's birth. There was the incomparable Jeffrey, gone too, forever, from among the well remembered faces. There was still another man, poor Charles Buller, who had carried to the grave so much eloquence and wit, so many fair hopes and engaging qualities. And there was Sir Robert Peel.

It was difficult to imagine the House of Commons without him. Twenty-two years ago, when Macaulay had first appeared before it, Sir Robert held the highest position among the Ministers of the Crown. During all the subsequent years of his service, he scarcely remembered one important discussion in which Peel had not borne a conspicuous part. "His figure is now before me: all the tones of his voice are in my ears; and the pain with which I think I shall never hear them again would be embittered by the recollections of some sharp encounters that took place between us, were it not that at last there was an entire and cordial reconciliation, and that, only a very few days before his death, I had the pleasure of receiving from him marks of kindness and esteem of which I shall always cherish the recollection." And all this was but to name a few of the many who were gone. It seemed almost strange for him to be speaking. Those whom he most admired had fallen away to dust.

Yet he went on, as was fitting, to live up to the occasion, to survey the world from the vantage point of wisdom and age, to suggest what menaced it, and to point out those blessings which men might rightfully anticipate from the future. Wild passions and wilder theories had recently been abroad in Europe, fermenting savagely under what seemed to be calm surfaces. From the borders of Russia to the Atlantic Ocean these forces had at last broken loose, and civil blood had flowed in their wake in the greatest capitals of Europe. "The house of Orleans fled from France; the Pope fled from Rome; the Emperor of Austria was not safe in Vienna." And the same confusion had reigned in Florence, in Naples, and in Germany. It was perhaps, Macaulay felt, all basically the result of the stubborn postponement of long overdue reforms. But a circumstance so widespread in its scope had brought home to him a saddening truth: Adam Smith and Gibbon had been wrong in predicting that the dark ages were gone forever, merely because the enlightened part of the world had grown powerful and cunning while the savage part remained weak. They had asked, these men, with glowing confidence, where the Huns and Vandals that would destroy civilization were to come from; and the question ten years ago had seemed quite unanswerable. But now it was different. It had not occurred to the two learned gentlemen "that civilization itself might engender the barbarians who who should destroy it." That they had not destroyed England already was a debt which all owed "to a wise and noble constitution, the work of many generations of brave men."[1]

But let the audience not be misled. Extending the franchise

1. See his speech in *Works*, VIII, 414-28 (November 2, 1852).

had not been the act which saved England. There was the current plan of Mr. Walpole, for instance, a man who felt otherwise, who believed that everybody who had served two years in the army should be allowed to vote. What did this bold plan really call for? It called, first, for young men. It called, in the next place, for ignorant men. Finally, it called for men who were five feet, two inches or more in height! No. The secret of progress among nations was not that those which had most advanced had been most liberal with the ballot. Economic conditions were reassuring in countries like the United States, rather, because there was "a boundless extent of fertile land" in the new world. Yet he would not have his hearers discouraged. "Under the benignant system of free trade," Britain will be drawn closer to these more prosperous nations, will share in all the good fortune they enjoy. Having said this, he could say no more. He was exhausted.

Parliament convened, and he went to its sessions dutifully. But he took care of himself during the winter. When dull speakers were on their legs, he remained in the lobby, reading or resting, or he walked out into the bracing air. He was independent now; no place with the government could interest him. To many of his younger colleagues he seemed a venerable survivor of an age that had departed, one of the old defenders of liberalism, one of the immortals around whom clung a reputation almost mythical in its proportions. It was known that his health was failing, but, still, one afternoon or evening, men hoped, the cause would come that would arouse him as of old; the Burke of the age would be heard again.

That day was a long time arriving. For more than half a year Macaulay remained practically silent in the House. Winter gave way to spring; spring was ready to give way to summer. It was Wednesday, the first of June; and Wednesday was always the dullest day of the week in Parliament. Sent there by the *Times* to report the routine matters that took place, you found yourself, wrote a reporter, loitering in the halls outside the committee lobby, wondering what room you should enter next. Suddenly a stout gentleman emerged from nowhere, bumped against you, apologized, and hurried on, running and plainly out of breath. You wondered what strange business was able to propel like mad those gouty limbs toward the assembly hall. And while you wondered, staring after him, two more members trotted past you, followed by five more, actually dashing for the entrances. Then more doors open; more members rush out; men are tearing past you now, from all points, but headed in the same direction. "Then wigs and gowns appear. Their owners tell you, with happy faces, that their committees have adjourned; and then come a third class, the gentlemen of the Press, hilarious. Why, what's the matter? Matter? Macaulay is up! It was an announcement that one had not heard for years, and the passing of the word had emptied the committee-rooms as, of old, it emptied clubs.

"You join the runners in a moment, and are in the gallery in time to see the senators, who had start of you, perspiring into their places. It was true. He was up, and in for a long speech. He was in a new place; standing in the second row above the Treasury Bench; and looking and sounding all the better for the elevation, and the clearer atmosphere for an orator. The old voice, the old manner, and the old style— glorious speaking! Well prepared, carefully elaborated, confessedly essayish; but spoken with perfect art and consummate management; the grand conversation of a man of the world, confiding his learning, his recollections, and his logic to a party of gentlemen, and just raising his voice enough to be heard through the room. Such it was while he was opening his subject, and waiting for his audience; but as the House filled, which it did with marvelous celerity, he got prouder and more oratorical; and then he poured out his speech, with rapidity increasing after every sentence, till it became a torrent of the richest words, carrying his hearers with him into enthusiasm, and yet not leaving them time to cheer.

A torrent of words—that is the only description of Macaulay's style, when he has warmed into speed. And such words! Why, it wasn't four in the afternoon; lunch hardly digested; and the quiet reserved English were as wild with delight as an opera house, after Grisi, at ten. You doubt it? See the division; and yet, before Mr. Macaulay had spoken, you might have safely bet fifty to one that Lord Hotham would have carried his bill. After that speech the bill was not thrown out, but pitched out. One began to have a higher opinion of the House of Commons, seeing, as one did, that, if the Macaulay class of minds would bid for leadership, they would get it. But it was not all congratulation. Mr. Macaulay had rushed through his oration of forty minutes with masterly vigor; but the doubts about his health, when you meet him the street—when you take advantage of the sphinx-like reverie,

Staring right on with calm, eternal eyes,

to study the sickly face—would be confirmed by a close inspection on Wednesday. The great orator was trembling when he sat down; the excitement of a triumph overcame him; and he had scarcely the self-possession to acknowledge the eager praises which were offered by the ministers and others in the neighborhood."[2]

What was he saying to his excited audience, an audience so rapt and entranced by his words that it obeyed his will blindly, ignoring the fact that the measure he had asked them to throw out had been passed twice by its previous vote? It was really an issue of no great significance, nor did Macaulay make the least claim that it was. Lord Hotham had proposed, simply, that the Master of the Rolls be declared incapable of sitting in the House. And Macaulay had contended, with equal simplicity, that if this were done, an able man would be lost to the Commons and relegated to the Upper Chamber.

2. See London *Times*, June 2, 1853. Quoted in G. O. Trevelyan, *op. cit.*, II, 28-82.

Why, he wanted to know, should a six century old practice which had produced no evil effects be changed?

For the bill against which he was contending contained one remarkably grave flaw. It had been argued that the Master of the Rolls, being a judge, should not be a politician also. Yet as drawn up, the new measure did nothing to deprive him of this latter status. As it at present read, he was still left free to act as the soul of a great party, as the favorite tribune of a stormy democracy, or the chief spokesman of a haughty aristocracy. He was merely forbidden to act in this fashion in the House of Commons. "He must go a hundred and fifty yards hence. He must sit on a red bench instead of a green one. He must say 'My Lords,' and not 'Mr. Speaker.' He must say 'Content,' and not 'Aye.' " But for all these nice distinctions, he may still be the most stirring politician in the country. Law reforms were needed desperately in England, and the advice of legally trained minds was needed to frame them. It was not a question, this time, of doing either the liberal or the conservative act. "For myself, Sir, I hope that I am at once a Liberal and a Conservative politician; and, in both characters, I shall give a clear and conscientious vote in favor of the amendment moved by my noble friend." The amendment he referred to was one designed to kill the measure. It passed by a majority of one hundred and one votes. [3]

It proved his last triumph in that Chamber; for his going out of it lacked the glamor of his entrance sadly. In truth he should have retired before now; but the question of the India Civil Service was up again, and about that question he had long been certain in his ideas. When his determination to speak again was made known, certain friends attempted to arrange that he should be heard at a time least taxing to his strength, about two hours after lunch or dinner. The pain in his chest was too great before then; and if he waited much longer he became too faint to stand. But their plans went awry. A political opponent had the floor by right, and refused to

3. See the speech in *Works*, VIII, 429-42 (June 1, 1853).

yield it. "I know as much about India as Macaulay does," he had said, "and my health is as bad as his."

Yet finally, toward eight o'clock on the night of June 24, Macaulay's chance came. He delivered himself of what was perhaps as masterful a defense of the principle of competitive appointments as was heard in the House during his age. Most of his arguments, true enough, he had stated twenty years before in his remarks on the India Bill; but this time they seemed more impressive, based as they were upon the observations of almost a lifetime. He saw nothing but calamities in store for his country, if the objectives for which he had pled vainly in 1833 were allowed, again, to be thrown out by the enemies of efficient government. "My firm opinion is," he declared, "that the day on which the Civil Service of India ceases to be a close service will be the beginning of an age of jobbing—the most monstrous, the most extensive, and the most perilous system of abuse in the distribution of patronage we have ever witnessed. Every governor-general will take out with him, or would soon be followed by, a crowd of nephews, first and second cousins, friends, sons of friends, and political hangers on; while every steamer arriving from the Red Sea would carry to India some adventurer bearing with him testimonials from people of influence in England."

But this was not all. He warmed to his subject, elaborating it in his old and always engrossing manner. "The Governor-general would have it in his power to distribute residences, seats at the Council board, seats at the Revenue board, places of from four to six thousand pounds a year, upon men without the least acquaintance with the character or habits of the natives and with only such knowledge of the language as would enable them to call for another bottle of pale ale, or desire their attendant to pull the punka faster. In what way could you put a check on such proceedings? Would you, the House of Commons, control them? Have you been so successful in extirpating nepotism at your own door, and in excluding all abuses from Whitehall and Somerset House, that you should fancy that you could establish purity in countries the situation of which you do not know, and the names of which you cannot pronounce? I believe most fully that, instead of purity resulting from that arrangement to India, England itself would soon be tainted; and that before long, when a son or brother of some active member of this House went out to Calcutta, carrying with him a letter of recommendation from the Prime Minister to the Governor-general, the letter would be really a bill of exchange drawn on the revenues of India for value received in Parliamentary support in this House."[4]

He returned next to one of his favorite arguments—that excellence at one's studies in school was a pretty certain indication of future excellence in life. "Take down, in any library, the Cambridge calendar. There you have the list of honors for a hundred years. Look at the list of wranglers and junior optimes; and I will venture to say that, for one man who has in after life distinguished himself among the junior optimes, you will find twenty among the wranglers." Compare the great men of the country who were Oxford bred. Those who finished in the third class there will be far outnumbered by those who won firsts. The same point could be made by references to graduates of the other leading schools of England. He talked on at length, but with increasing physical difficulty, driving his points home with careful elaboration. But at last he became too faint to continue. There was much more that he wished to add, he declared, but he did not believe he could mention it at this time. He was exhausted.

Before he became silent forever in the House he was to make one talk more—for speech he never regarded it—on a subject of peculiar interest to the people who had elected him. It dealt with the grim question of taxes levied in support of the Established Church of Scotland, was a defense of a compromise measure designed to distribute those taxes more justly. Edinburgh complained, he declared, that the burden

4. Macaulay did not reprint this speech, since he was unable to finish it in the House. Excerpts may be found in G. O. Trevelyan, *op. cit.*, II, 287-93.

of the Establishment was enormously great in view of the population of Scotland; that the people best able to pay the tax were exempt; and that the Crown lands which should mainly have borne the charge had been taken away by the State. He proceeded, in proof of these charges, to uncover a good deal of official rottenness in Scotland. He pointed out, that is, that members of the College of Justice—the judges, advocates, and officers of the courts—had managed to get complete exemption from the levy. These men represented the real aristocracy of the county, now that Court was no longer held in their capital; yet they were shunning the duties which their positions entailed. They had passed on this burden to the already overburdened poor.

A member raised a question at this point regarding Mr. Macaulay's consistency. Why was it that, years ago, he had favored the complete abolition of the Establishment in Ireland, and yet was unwilling to propose the same measure for Scotland? The cases were similar : in neither country was the Episcopal form of worship the dominant one. But the worthy member got a ready retort. Macaulay explained that he was asking for as much as he knew there was any chance of his getting. Had he felt that a possibility existed of persuading the House to do away with the Establishment, he would plead strongly that such action be taken. As it was, however, he was asking merely that certain abuses in the system be eliminated. It was all a matter of practical politics. He was supporting a compromise measure. "It proposes to diminish the charge and to diminish the number of the clergy; but it does not propose—and I trust I shall never live to see the day when an English Parliament will ever countenance such a proposal, under any circumstances whatever—to interfere with any of the vested rights of property."[5] It was his last effort before them, ending, happily, with a frank confession of two principles which had proved central in all his thinking about

5. See his remarks in Hansard, *Parliamentary Proceedings* (3 series), CXXIX, 451-59 (July 19, 1853).

politics. One of these was that the rights of property are sacred. The other implied that the only safe way for a government to remedy existing abuses is through the piecemeal correction of the worst of them, one by one.

2

A sick man he was when Parliament adjourned the summer of 1853, thoroughly in need of a long rest. He went to Tunbridge Wells, taking with him a pile of books. He would read, he hoped, and work at his *History*, and take long walks again, if his health mended. The moment he got there his spirits seemed to improve. He began to write Ellis about the beauties of Plato, whom he was going through again thoroughly. "The more I read, the more I admire his style, and the less I admire his reasonings." Next he would be talking about "the childish quibbling of Socrates." It seemed odd that such trumpery fallacies as were said to have puzzled Protagoras should have imposed on so powerful a mind. Yes, Plato was full of absurdities. One should look in him for poetry and for fine Greek, but for little more. But these delicious excursions into the classics were abruptly and rudely terminated. After only a few weeks at the resort, he received a notice which declared that, "*by special license,*" one Mr. Vizetelly was about to publish the "collected speeches of Macaulay." He was raging mad. Longman heard of the intended work and advised his friend to bring out his own edition. In no other way could the imposter be punished. Macaulay consented; there was nothing else to be done.

He appended a Preface to the work which proved that, when aroused, he was still able to write with as implacable a bitterness as ever. The Preface began with an apology: as works of literature, he did not think the speeches really worth a reprinting. Again, he was interested in writing something which was much more important, and was reluctant to spare the time necessary to edit them. Moreover, he hated to revive the animosities of two decades ago, a period during which, to cite a particular case, he had spoken of Sir Robert Peel with an acrimony which by no means did justice to the virtues of that great man. Of Peel he wished to say in this place that the two had become reconciled in late years, and that Macaulay lamented his untimely death as both a private and a public calamity.

But all these objections to seeing his speeches in a volume he had had to brush aside. "A bookseller, named Vizetelly, who seems to aspire to that sort of distinction which Curll enjoyed a hundred and twenty years ago, thought fit, without asking my consent, without even giving me any notice, to announce an edition of my Speeches, and was not ashamed to tell the world in his advertisement that he published them by special license. When the book appeared, I found that it contained fifty-six speeches, said to have been delivered by me in the House of Commons. Of these speeches a few were reprinted from reports which I had corrected for the Mirror of Parliament or the Parliamentary Debates, and were therefore, with the exception of some errors of the pen and the press, correctly given. The rest bear scarcely the faintest resemblance to the speeches which I really made. The substance of what I said is perpetually misrepresented. The connection of the arguments is altogether lost. Extravagant blunders are put into my mouth in almost every page. An editor who was not grossly ignorant would have perceived that no person to whom the House of Commons would listen could possibly have been guilty of such blunders. An editor who had the smallest regard for truth, or for the fame of the person whose speeches he had undertaken to publish, would have had recourse to the various sources of information which were readily accessible, and, by collating them, would have produced a book which would at least have contained no absolute nonsense. But I have unfortunately had an editor whose only object was to make a few pounds, and who was willing to sacrifice to that object my reputation and his own.

He took the very worst report extant, compared it with no other report, removed no blemish however obvious or however ludicrous, gave to the world some hundreds of pages utterly contemptible both in matter and manner, and prefixed my name to them."[6]

Macaulay proceeded to illustrate his charges against Vizetelly with a thoroughness which left little doubt that his indignation was justified. He then added a final note in explanation of the diction of his works. He could not always give the actual language he had spoken in the House. Not even the best reports of Parliamentary proceedings were of much help to him on this point, and for an obvious reason: His delivery had been too rapid. "Very able shorthand writers have sometimes complained that they could not follow me, and have contented themselves with setting down the substance of what I said." But he had been as accurate as he was able to be.

Various tasks and diversions interested him in turns, once the disagreeable business of the speeches was disposed of; but above them all hovered the problem of his *History*. He had not yet quite despaired of finishing it, though the chances of doing so grew each day more remote. He served as chairman of a committee to draw up plans for the Indian Civil Service. His impetuous brother-in-law Trevelyan, who held a relatively minor place in government, was eager about these plans, so eager, in fact, that he made determined enemies in high places through his hot endorsement of them. Macaulay feared for a time that the man would lose his position, in his blind zeal against "jobbery and corruption."

In 1854 the Trevelyans moved to the village of Esher, in Surrey, and Macaulay took a house in the same community. He read and walked, as usual, for relaxation. But mostly he wrote and wrote, overtaxing his strength, finally realizing that if more of his great work was to see the light, a much

6. Preface to Speeches in *Works*, VIII, 6-7.

[356]

greater degree of concentration would have to be given to it than in the past. He had almost stopped attending Parliament. At times he would go in for a visit, to listen, and to greet old friends. Almost invariably, on these infrequent occasions, a crowd would gather about him, and every encouragement would be thrown out to start him talking. And once he was started, the regular business of the House seemed practically to come to an end.

Again he would drop in at much less impressive places, places where no one knew him except as a rather stern looking stranger with gray hair and tired eyes. "As I walked back from Esher a shower came on. Afraid for my chest, which at best is in no very good state, I turned into a small ale house, and called for a glass of ginger-beer. I found there a party of hop-pickers come back from the neighborhood of Farnham. They had had but a bad season and were returning, nearly walked off their legs. I liked their looks, and thought their English remarkably good for their rank of life. . . . The poor people had a foaming pot before them; but as soon as they heard the price, they rose, and were going to leave it untasted. They could not, they said, afford so much. It was but four pence-half-penny. I laid the money down; and their delight and gratitude quite affected me. Two more of the party soon arrived. I ordered another pot, and when the rain was over left them, followed by more blessings, I believe, than were ever purchased for ninepence."[7] Yet even delightful little incidents like this he soon was compelled to leave unnoticed in his *Journal*. During the last eight months before the second part of the *History* was finished, he did not take time to write in it once.[8]

That great labor was finally announced for the last week of December, 1855. "Thank God," he wrote, it is over at last. He had now but to wait for the result. He was more anxious about this second part than about the first: there were so

7. From *Journal*. See G. O. Trevelyan, *op. cit.*, II, 320.
8. See *Journal*, VIII, 141-42 (November 6, 1855).

many highly raised expectations to satisfy. But in his favor there was one helpful circumstance which gave him an unwonted confidence. It was the "general sterility, the miserably enervated state" of the literature of his time. That confidence proved well founded, as Longman soon made plain to him. For the full first edition of 25,000 copies had been asked for six weeks before the book came out.[9]

9. *Ibid.*, VIII, 173 (November 26, 1855).

XX. Lord

ONORS CAME THICK upon Macaulay, and from all directions, once the *History* began to be read. He was made a member of the Academies of Utrecht, Munich and Turin. He was made a Knight of the Order of Merit by special decree of the King of Prussia. He was voted a member of the Institute of France. He was named a trustee of the British Museum. Finally, he was awarded the degree of Doctor of Civil Law by Oxford, the university which he had described in his book as having been backward and inferior for the last three hundred years. This last gesture seems to have been more than normally kind, since almost everyone knew how thoroughly he had disparaged the school. When he entered the hall in which the ceremonies were being held, somebody, he notes, "called out 'History of England'! Then came a great tumult of applause and hissing; but the applause greatly predominated."[1] Yet such conduct was not in the least disconcerting to a gentleman who had harangued the turbulent Leeds bagmen, and been shouted down by the Calvinists of Edinburgh.

These Calvinists, henceforth, would have to manage without him. During the early weeks of 1856 he wrote his friends there a sincere and melancholy letter. The experience of the last two years, he said, had convinced him that he could never again expect to be "capable of performing, even in an imperfect manner, those duties which the public has a right

1. *Journal*. Quoted in G. O. Trevelyan, *op. cit.*, II, 329.

to expect from every member of the House of Commons." He was grateful to them, deeply grateful. They had borne with his infirmities in a manner more than just. Not from a single citizen, he added, had he received one line of reproach or complaint. The electors of the city, in turn, deplored his resigning, by unanimous vote. Their reply touched him deeply. It was sad beyond measure thus to give way to the stern exactions of an illness that would not be stayed.

For fifteen years, while he had remained in London, Macaulay had lived near Picadilly Circus at the New Albany, in a suite of rooms on the second floor. The steps to those rooms were now growing too nearly interminable to mount. Hannah and several of his friends had for months been urging him to move. Yet he hated to think of it. One comes to regard his home, he said, as one regards the people he loves. At last, however, in May 1856, an ideal place was found for him. It was Holly Lodge, a villa near Holland House, in a quiet neighborhood rarely disturbed by traffic. The change distressed him, for all partings were distressing, but he went through with it. Once more he mounted the endless steps. He had been happy in these rooms. "Everything that I do is colored by the thought that it is for the last time. One day there will come a last in good earnest." [2]

His trips to the continent went on as usual, Ellis almost invariably going with him. In 1856 they set out early and were in France before the end of August. For the most part, Macaulay spent his time looking at the churches, admiring scenery, and judging pictures. He paid scarcely any attention to political conditions in the country. He rarely bothered with calling on distinguished foreigners, was usually annoyed when one, distinguished or lowly, met him and made demands upon his time.

His comments during this particular visit had a pungency about them that could come only from the seasoned traveler, from one who had seen a great deal and who was not to be

2. *Ibid.*, II, 333 (May 1, 1856).

easily impressed. In the Duomo, in Novara—they had gone on to Italy—"I early found out the famous St. Bartholomew which I had not noticed before. I might as well not have noticed it now: for I saw nothing to praise in it. It may perhaps be a good imitation; but a good imitation of what ought not to be imitated is a bad thing." [3] And the food was no better than the painting. "We dined indifferently, as usual, and were glad to get to bed." The next morning, he added, "We dined, very ill, and set out for the station."

As he went about the older cities, his imagination, almost by instinct, would recreate them as they had been in ancient times. Especially was this the case of Rome. "Everything carries back the mind to a remote age; to a time when Cicero and Virgil were hardly known in Italy." Or on the highway between stops he would pass a scene which had inspired some much more recent poet. "Saw the Euganean Hills at a distance at the south of our road and remembered a very bad poem on them by Shelley, which I read in Jesus Lane when I was a freshman and which still runs in my head." [4] That amazing memory could at times prove a positive curse.

Religious paintings always interested him, though that interest never became idolatry. "I suppose it is speaking within compass," he wrote after one practically full day with such works, "to say that almost every great Venetian painter must have painted a hundred virgins with babes— fifty *Ecce Homos*—twenty crucifixions—twenty annunciations, and twenty assumptions. Art, however exquisite, employed on these subjects, moves me more and more faintly every day." [5]

The trip lasted six weeks. Yet it might have been protracted indefinitely, as far as the mere expense of it mattered, for he was now a "rich man" in earnest. The *History* was selling so well that Longman and his partners thought best

3. *Journal*, X, 36-38 (September 2, 1856).
4. *Ibid.*, X, 51 (September 5, 1856).
5. *Ibid.*, X, 93-95 (September 10, 1856).

to advance their author some of the royalties he would be due the following December. Macaulay, on his part, was entirely willing that they should. A check was accordingly made out to him for twenty thousand pounds. In all the chronicles of the book trade, he said, no single sum equal to that amount had ever been paid to an English author.[6]

He was living comfortably now, was spending close to three thousand pounds yearly, exclusive of travel expenses.[7] Some of the details of these expenses—if they were kept up at the rate itemized several years before[8]—are sufficiently interesting to record. He spent close to £200 annually for spirits, which was a remarkably liberal allowance when one considers their price before the day of heavy taxation in England. He was spending approximately £300 yearly for clothes. For "pocket money" he allowed himself another £700. A scant £50 was required for taxes.

He had invested his fortune most carefully, in conservative and diversified securities. The safest holdings in the United States, Denmark, English steamship and railway companies were in his possession; a reliable three and a half percent paper afforded him much more comfort than a "passive" six. (Passive bonds he defined as those which "profess to pay interest neither now or at any future time.") His personal business philosophy, declares his nephew, was supremely simple. He treated all official and literary gains as capital, and he paid all bills within twenty-four hours. "I think," he once said, "that prompt payment is a moral duty, knowing, as I do, how painful it is to have such things deferred."

But though he appeared eminently sane in his notions about business, his charitable gestures proved increasingly to trouble his friends and relatives. He was so absurdly soft hearted, allowed himself to be outrageously put upon by so many rank imposters! His gifts a few years before seemed meager compared to those he was making now. "I have been forced

6. See G. O. Trevelyan, *op. cit.*, II, 345-46.
7. See *Journal*, IX, 89 (February, 1856).
8. See figures in *Journal*, II, 164-65 (December 2, 1849).

to refuse any further assistance to a Mrs. Y——— who has had thirty-five pounds from me in the course of a few months, and whose demands came thicker and thicker. I suppose that she will resent my refusal bitterly. That is all that I ever got by conferring benefits on any but my own dearest relations and friends." Later he wrote to one of his sisters. "I suppose," he said, "that you told Mrs. Z——— that I was not angry with her; for today I have a letter from her, begging for money most vehemently, and saying that, if I am obdurate, her husband must go to prison. I have sent her twenty pounds, making up what she has had from me within a few months to a hundred and thirty pounds." And of course there were, as always, the poor scholars and authors—forty pounds to one writer, thirty to another, a hundred more to a seedy gentleman who represented himself as an unlucky philologist. He could scarcely refuse such persons, unless they mingled scurrilities with their requests. One he did refuse abruptly, however. He had written to say that he had recently learned that Macaulay had made thirty thousand pounds by his "malignant abuse of good men." Did he not feel like passing on to another a portion of those ill obtained profits? He became at last convinced that charities to authors followed an unvarying and therefore predictable course. One gave money, one gave it again, one gave still again, but at length one stopped giving. Then, in return, one found himself outrageously abused in some magazine or newspaper.[9] It was the way of the world.

Yet there were compensations for such impertinent notes as this. August 28, 1857, was a day the most of which Macaulay spent in very low spirits. The Sepoy Mutiny was raging in India. He did not doubt that the English would prove able to control it, but the thought of so much bloodshed was infinitely saddening. He went to dinner profoundly depressed. But he had hardly begun to dine, he notes in his

9. *Ibid.*, XI, 229 (December 17, 1857). See, for further evidence of Macaulay's troubles with importunate beggars, *Letters of George Gissing* (coll. and arranged by Algernon and Ellen Gissing, London, 1927), p. 139.

Journal, when a messenger came with a letter from Palmerston, now Prime Minister. An offer of a peerage, it was; "the Queen's pleasure already taken. I was very much surprised. Perhaps no such offer was ever made without the slightest solicitation, direct or indirect, to a man of humble origin and moderate fortune, who had long quitted public life. I had no hesitation about accepting with many respectful and grateful expressions; but God knows that the poor women of Delhi and Cawnpore are more in my thoughts than my coronet. It was necessary for me to choose a title off hand. I determined to be Baron Macaulay of Rothley. I was born there: I have lived much there; I am named for the family which long had the manor; my uncle was rector there. Nobody can complain of my taking a designation from a village which is nobody's property now." He was right; nobody did complain, either about the name he chose or about his receiving the honor itself. Few titles have been more honestly earned.

2

Never in his entire career did Macaulay write a more stimulating series of letters than when, in reply to the entreaties of the American biographer, H. S. Randall, he set forth his opinions on the subject of the Constitution of the United States and the fate that would probably befall this country, once its frontier lands had all been claimed and settled. One might add that he never appeared more courteous than when he made these comments, more considerate of an opposite point of view, or more fully the scholar-gentleman who felt that good breeding should prevail, no matter how fundamentally gentlemen disagreed about principles. Randall had sent Macaulay, in January, 1857, an autograph of Washington. He had remarked, in sending it, that the first president had been exalted by most of his countrymen into a god, while Jefferson, the great democrat, was regarded merely as Washington's foil. This was news to Macaulay. But he felt bound to trust it, because Randall was at work upon a life of Jefferson and therefore should know. Yet what made the statement hard to believe was the fact that nineteenth century America was becoming increasingly democratic, seemed more and more to be falling in line with the ideals which Jefferson had cherished for it. Macaulay confessed his astonishment at this fact, and added that, personally, he had never cared for Mr. Jefferson's views. It was this last remark that brought on the two really valuable letters which followed. Randall asked him for his frank opinion of the American form of government. And he got it.

"You are surprised to learn that I have not a high opinion of Mr. Jefferson," Macaulay wrote, "and I am surprised at your surprise. I am certain that I never wrote a line, and that I never, in Parliament, in conversation, or even on the hustings—a place where it is the fashion to court the populace—uttered a word indicating an opinion that the supreme authority in a state ought to be intrusted to the majority of citizens told by the head; in other words, to the poorest and most ignorant part of society. I have long been convinced that institutions purely democratic must, sooner or later, destroy liberty or civilization, or both. In Europe, where the population is dense, the effect of such institutions would be almost instantaneous. What happened lately in France is an example. In 1848 a pure democracy was established there. During a short time there was reason to expect a general spoliation, a national bankruptcy, a new partition of the soil, a maximum of prices, a ruinous load of taxation laid on the rich for the purpose of supporting the poor in idleness. Such a system would, in twenty years, have made France as poor and barbarous as the France of the Carlovingians. Happily the danger was averted; and now there is a despotism, a silent tribune, an enslaved press. Liberty is gone, but civilization has been saved.

[365]

"I have not the smallest doubt that if we had a purely democratic government here the effect would be the same. Either the poor would plunder the rich, and civilization would perish; or order and prosperity would be saved by a strong military government, and liberty would perish. You may think that your country enjoys an exemption from these evils. I will frankly own to you that I am of a very different opinion. Your fate I believe to be certain, though it is deferred by a physical cause. As long as you have a boundless extent of fertile and unoccupied land, your laboring population will be far more at ease than the laboring population of the Old World, and, while this is the case, the Jefferson politics may continue to exist without causing any fatal calamity. But the time will come when New England will be as thickly peopled as old England. Wages will be as low, and will fluctuate as much with you as with us. You will have your Manchesters and Birminghams, and in those Manchesters and Birminghams hundreds of thousands of artisans will assuredly be sometimes out of work. Then your institutions will be fairly brought to the test. Distress everywhere makes the laborer mutinous and discontented, and inclines him to listen with eagerness to agitators who tell him that it is a monstrous iniquity that one man should have a million, while another cannot get a full meal. In bad years there is plenty of grumbling here; and sometimes a little rioting. But it matters little. For here the sufferers are not the rulers. The supreme power is in the hands of a class, numerous indeed, but select; of an educated class; of a class which is, and knows itself to be, deeply interested in the security of property and the maintenance of order. Accordingly, the malcontents are firmly yet gently restrained. The bad time is got over without robbing the wealthy to relieve the indigent. The springs of national prosperity soon begin to flow again: work is plentiful, wages rise, and all is tranquillity and cheerfulness. I have seen England pass three or four times through such critical seasons as I have described.

Through such seasons the United States will have to pass in the course of the next century, if not this.

"How will you pass through them? I heartily wish you a good deliverance. But my reason and my wishes are at war, and I can not help foreboding the worst. It is quite plain that your Government will never be able to restrain a distressed and discontented majority. For with you the majority is the Government, and has the rich, who are always a minority, absolutely at its mercy. The day will come when in the State of New York a multitude of people, none of whom has had more than half a breakfast, or expects to have more than half a dinner, will choose a Legislature. Is it possible to doubt what sort of a Legislature will be chosen? On one side is a statesman preaching patience, respect for vested rights, strict observance of public faith. On the other is a demagogue ranting about the tyranny of capitalists and usurers, and asking why any body should be permitted to drink champagne and to ride in a carriage, while thousands of honest folks are in want of necessaries. Which of the two candidates is likely to be preferred by a working-man who hears his children cry for more bread? I seriously apprehend that you will, in some such season of adversity as I have described, do things which will prevent prosperity from returning; that you will act like people who should in a year of scarcity devour all the seed-corn, and thus make the next a year not of scarcity, but of absolute famine. There will be, I fear, spoliation. The spoliation will increase the distress. The distress will produce fresh spoliation. There is nothing to stop you. Your Constitution is all sail and no anchor.

"As I said before, when a society has entered on this downward progress, either civilization or liberty must perish. Either some Caesar or Napoleon will seize the reins of government with a strong hand, or your republic will be as fearfully plundered and laid waste by barbarians in the twentieth century as the Roman Empire was in the fifth; with this difference, that the Huns and Vandals who ravaged the

[367]

Roman Empire came from without and that your Huns and Vandals will have been engendered within your own country by your own institutions.

"Thinking thus, of course I can not reckon Jefferson among the benefactors of mankind. I readily admit that his intentions were good, and his abilities considerable. Odious stories have been circulated about his private life; but I do not know on what evidence those stories rest, and I think it probable that they are false, or monstrously exaggerated. I have no doubt that I shall derive both pleasure and information from your account of him."[10]

The famous Whig's strictures and predictions proved by no means comforting to Mr. Randall. In October, 1858, Macaulay received from him a copy of his biography of Jefferson, accompanied by a letter which contained several objections to them. Macaulay replied with uncommon patience. He had noted, he said, Mr. Randall's dissent "from some opinions which I have long held firmly but which I should never have obtruded on you except at your own earnest request, and which I have no wish to defend against your objections. If you can derive any comfort as to the future destinies of your country from your conviction that a benevolent Creator will never suffer more human beings to be born than can live in plenty, it is a comfort of which I should be sorry to deprive you. By the same process of reasoning one may arrive at many very agreeable conclusions, such as that there is no cholera, no malaria, no yellow fever, no negro slavery in the world. Unfortunately for me, perhaps, I learned from Lord Bacon a method of investigating truth diametrically opposite to that which you appear to follow. I am perfectly aware of the immense progress which your country has made, and is making, in population and wealth. I know that the laborer with you has large wages, abundant food, and the means of giving some education to his children. But I see no reason for

10. These letters were published as a pamphlet, *Macaulay on American Institutions*, in 1925, by the New York Public Library. They may also be found in G. O. Trevelyan, *op. cit.*, II, 407-12 (Appendix).

attributing these things to the policy of Jefferson. I see no reason to believe that your progress would have been less rapid, that your laboring people would have been worse fed, or clothed, or taught, if your government had been conducted on the principles of Washington and Hamilton. Nay, you will, I am sure, acknowledge that the progress which you have been making ever since the middle of the seventeenth century, and that the blessings which you now enjoy, were enjoyed by your forefathers, who were loyal subjects of the kings of England. The contrast between the laborer of New York and the laborer of Europe is not stronger now than it was when New York was governed by noblemen and gentlemen commissioned under the English great seal. And there are at this moment dependencies of the English crown in which all the phenomena which you attribute to purely democratical institutions may be seen in the highest perfection. The colony of Victoria, in Australia, was planted only twenty years ago. The population is now, I suppose, near a million. The revenue is enormous, near five millions sterling, and raised without any murmuring. The wages of labor are higher than they are even with you. Immense sums are expended on education. And this is a province governed by the delegate of an hereditary sovereign.

"It therefore seems to me quite clear that the facts which you cite to prove the excellence of purely democratic institutions ought to be ascribed not to those institutions, but to causes which operated in America long before your Declaration of Independence, and which are still operating in many parts of the British Empire. You will perceive, therefore, that I do not propose, as you thought, to sacrifice the interests of the present generation to those of remote generations. It would, indeed, be absurd in a nation to part with institutions to which it is indebted for immense present prosperity from an apprehension that, after the lapse of a century, those institutions may be found to produce mischief. But I do not admit that the prosperity which your country enjoys arises from those parts of your polity which may be called, in an especial manner, Jeffersonian. Those parts of your polity have already produced bad effects, and will, unless I am greatly mistaken, produce fatal effects if they shall last till North America has two hundred inhabitants to the square mile."

These citations comprise the substance of Macaulay's remarks. Randall attempted to draw him out further, but to no purpose. He had said his say, and that was the end of it. Perhaps it is still too early to attempt to estimate the truth of his gloomy forebodings about America; for the possibility of two hundred inhabitants to the square mile here is, fortunately, still remote. Yet this much is at least apparent: Macaulay to the last thought of society in terms of static and distinct classes. There was the lower class, then the middle class of property and respectability, and there was, finally, the aristocracy at the top. This last group, the nobility, could never quite be trusted, he felt, since its position depended upon inheritance instead of natural merit. But the peculiar genius of the English people sprang from the fact that it was possible for members of the middle class to rise to positions of authority. This was eminently sensible, he believed. It was also safe—safe because from birth this class had been taught to respect the rights of property. Those who composed it were at heart conservative.

Actually, of course, his idea of the middle class was an abstraction as intangible as any he had ever despised in Plato. There was no line which divided these respectable burghers from the great chaotic group beneath them. Englishmen might make all the distinctions they could think of: they might partition off their ale houses into two or three neat sections forever. They might stretch their ropes between the twelfth and thirteenth rows of seats at their theaters until Doomsday. Or they could demand that one pay a ten pound property tax to the State before he should be allowed the ballot. It did not matter; it was not by these means that one could distinguish with blind certainty the men of prudence

[370]

and judgment from the fomentors of revolution. For all such discriminations followed purely economic lines; and with the rise of a system of generally accessible public education, they were already, in Macaulay's day, becoming meaningless. It was fortunately conceivable, in other words, that even from the lowest classes a statesman might arise—like Alexander Hamilton or Herbert Hoover, for instance—who would be in his ways of thought as conservative as Lord Eldon, certainly as conservative as Lord Grey or Lord Macaulay.

Again, he seems to have grievously underestimated the resourcefulness of which the American type of capitalist is capable. Men of the Jay Gould, Jay Cooke, or John D. Rockefeller the Elder type had not yet appeared in this country, nor had the Fourteenth Amendment, which sanctified their corporations by rendering them practically immune to restraint, appeared either. In short, Macaulay had no prevision of the America we know—an America in which the plutocratic, or capitalist class—through its instruments of propaganda, the press and the radio, and through its threat of unemployment—is able to control with reasonable effectiveness those "lower orders" from which he feared so much mischief.

He failed likewise, it seems, to reckon with Jefferson's well known observation that if the majority of citizens should ever come to be deprived of real property—of land—the democracy in which he believed would probably cease to work. And as for the revolution which, Macaulay predicted, would occur when economic conditions became unsupportable in America—such upheavals, as he himself was well aware, have a way of coming regardless of whether "the people" are already in power. One had occurred in France a few years before his birth, while that country was ruled by a despot. The test, on this point, will perhaps always be whether the governing authority is sufficiently considerate of what is demanded by those who are governed.

It is probably inadvisable to consider more closely the

[371]

relation of Macaulay's views to the present political scene in this country. He could not know that scene—would scarcely, one feels, have wished to know it any too well! And yet it might be added that out of our own conflict between the Conservatives, the New Deal, and the more extreme Labor reformers of the United States (all of them alike in having had parallels in Macaulay's day) may come within the next decade the fulfillment or the refutation of his prophecy. The issue, moreover, will likely be decided upon fundamentally moral grounds. It will be the issue of whether the almost endless opportunity for the amassing of fortunes which this country offered resourceful men during the past century prove finally, through the greed which it engendered, a barrier against all reasonable compromise between warring factions. Certainly it is true that no greater temptation to acquire material wealth has ever been presented a nation equipped with modern industrial instruments. If failure attends the efforts of those who would adjust the ambitions of these hostile interests, Macaulay's prediction will in spirit have come true. A great adventure in government will have been tried, and, at length, superseded.

XXI. Victim

THE YEAR 1859 began as cheerfully as the aging writer could ask. Five weeks before, "Baba" had married Henry Holland, the son of Macaulay's old friend, Sir Henry Holland, the physician. He heartily approved the match and gave his niece £500 as a present. They would remain in London; he would see her as often as before.

Yet this event was soon followed by another the thought of which may almost be said to have haunted him to his grave. His brother-in-law, Charles Trevelyan, was offered in January the governorship of Madras. It had been a position which he had longed for since young manhood. It would enable him to send back possibly six thousand pounds a year to invest.[1] Still Macaulay was bitter about his going. Trevelyan had many admirable qualities, he confessed, but he was rash and extravagant. "That a man who has such a home and who values it and loves it should banish himself from it, for a mere delusion, a mere fancy. He cannot get India out of his head. To be governor there was his earliest day dream and he must indulge his fancy at whatever cost."[2] For one who had enjoyed his fill of honors it seemed now that nothing could replace the quiet joys of a home in a civilized country and of a life free from the uncertainties of authority. Hannah and her son George Otto, and the youngest child, Alice, would follow him later in the year. Of all whom he loved, only Baba would be left, and she engrossed in her husband and her

1. See Macaulay's figures in *Journal*, XI, 418 (January 9, 1859).
2. *Ibid.*, XI, 434 (February 10, 1859).

new home. The dearest ties were falling apart, when one needed them most to bind together the remnants of one's crumbling world.

Before Trevelyan set sail, in February, he called to see Macaulay. "You have always been a most kind brother to me," he said. Macaulay had tried to be so. Would they ever meet again? He did not expect it. "My health is better; but another sharp winter will probably finish me." All this was in his *Journal*, for he would not reveal his heart to another man. But he knew that the imperious demands of their natures were parting them forever from each other.

Occasionally, he would go to the House of Lords. There were his eminent rivals and allies of other years—Lord Brougham, Lord Ellenborough, Lord Darby, and many others. But his mind was fixed chiefly upon Parliaments long dissolved; he was saving his strength for the last years of King William's reign. Once he had planned to speak from the plush benches, but he refrained. He was tired, and, besides, the opponent whom he had thought to answer was satisfactorily replied to by a more vigorous Whig colleague. Macaulay kept silent. Yet that he was in no sense overawed by the distinguished company about him is amply indicated by such comments as the following: "Debate in committee on the words 'Faith of a Christian.' The Chancellor very poor. L—— weak physically, but in full intellectual vigour. Lord L—— mad and drunk. The Bishop of C—— absurd beyond the absurdity of either madness or drunkenness." Parliament had lost its interest for him.

It was better to remain in his rooms, to work when he could upon the endless *History*, to keep up with nephew George's activities at Cambridge, and to read—to read mornings, afternoons, and evenings, in a never quite successful effort to forget the coming departure of those he loved. He looked through the files of the *Quarterly Review* for 1830-1832, reexamining the articles which Southey, Croker, and other Tories had written. Some books of Southey—the *Life of*

Wesley for one—he could still appreciate. But not those tedious political articles. They were mostly "mere trash—absurd perversions of history, parallels which show no ingenuity, and from which no instruction can be derived." They were all forgotten now, all gone to the dogs. And Croker was below Southey. The latter at least had a good style, but "Croker had nothing but italics and capitals as substitutes for eloquence and reason."

There would be other mental exercises much more aimless than the reading he was keeping up. He would suddenly discover that his knowledge of German was escaping him, would take down a volume of Schiller, and run through a hundred pages of it during a morning. Or he would pass an evening in comparing the average duration of the lives of archbishops, prime ministers, and lord chancellors in England; still other evenings in working out evidence to support his view that the senior wrangler at the university, as a rule, far outstripped his less brilliant contemporaries in the race for honors later in life.[3] Tests almost innumerable he would propose to himself, all of them designed alike to prove that no "mental decay" had set in, regardless of how nearly complete was becoming the disintegration of his body. In truth, the possible decline of his intellectual powers was the one event most intolerable to contemplate. Over and over did he pray that "the curtain might drop" before that calamity took place. To be pitied was one of the few truly unendurable conditions.

Occasionally Americans would come to visit him or would write him. Those whom he admired were identified more or less closely with the Boston Brahmin group—men like J. T. Fields, the publisher, or Edward Everett, or the historians Prescott and Motley. Fields called once and impressed him as a proud aristocrat, who "abominated the whole system of government" in America. Of Prescott he spoke often with marked kindness, especially in April of 1859, on the occasion

3. See G. O. Trevelyan, *op. cit.*, II, 379.

of a visit to the Palace. He had just learned of the historian's death. "After dinner," he notes, "came the circle, the short conversations tete-a-tete with Her Majesty, and everything else that makes the Palace the dullest house in London. She asked my opinion of Carlyle's *Frederick II*. I could not praise and did not like to blame; so I got away as fast as I could to poor Prescott, whom I could praise heartily."[4] Two months later Everett wrote him that he was sailing for England with his son, whom he planned to enroll at Trinity. Macaulay was pleased to think that he would see his old friend again, but was worried about the boy. He had heard that he was "an odd, priggish, very Yankeyish youth, certain, therefore, to be unhappy at Cambridge."[5] But these apprehensions proved groundless; he met the young man and liked him. He had obviously been brought up respectably. This was the trait which Macaulay admired about the Brahmins in general. They seemed well bred, urbane, aristocratic. And if they were remarkably complacent too, it was a fact that he failed to notice. He was inclined that way himself, rather heavily.

But the departure of his sister's family grew, with each day, a more melancholy anticipation. In May he went up to Cambridge, to visit his nephew George. "A pleasant party," he notes. "I talked with spirit but my heart was very sad. I find that Hannah means to go to Madras in the autumn of next year with Alice. George will probably follow them a few months later. He wants me to go too, and to return at the close of the cool weather. But I think that this would only make the pain, which must be borne, more severe. I can hardly look at little Alice without tears. I may live till the others return. But when I part with her it will be forever. Yet what weakness to be crying, in May, 1859, for what will not happen till November 1860. How many events may, long before November, 1860, confound all our calculations."[6]

This mood persisted. "A letter from Hannah," he wrote

4. *Ibid.*, XI, 471 (April 13, 1859).
5. *Ibid.*, XI, 514 (June 15, 1859).
6. *Ibid.*, XI, 485 (May 1, 1859).

again in July. "Very sad and affectionate," I answered her. There is a pleasure even in this exceeding sorrow; for it brings out the expression of love with a tenderness which is wanting in ordinary circumstances. But the sorrow is very, very bitter. The Duke of Argyle called, and left me the sheets of a forthcoming poem of Tennyson. I like it extremely—notwithstanding some faults. The parting of Lancelot and Guinevere, her penitence, and Arthur's farewell, are all very affecting. I cried over some passages; but I am now 'with the tears near the eyes,' as Medea says." [7]

Later in the month he visited the Trevelyans at Lake Windermere, following a short stay there with a two weeks' tour through the Western Highlands. Hannah and Alice accompanied him. This trip assumed almost the nature of a triumphal march. Practically everywhere, on steamers and at railway stations, people would recognize him and join in to make him comfortable, or to cheer. At hotels he would not be allowed to pay for the dinners he ordered. It was often highly embarrassing; but of course it pleased him too, to see such honest evidence of the world's esteem.

Thus summer passed, yielded to fall, to the heavy days that grew always darker and more brief. The Trevelyans had changed their plans; they would have to leave within a few months. "A sad day," he declared October 16. "Many tears." He had just written to Hannah. "I tried to work on Chapter XXIV but could do nothing. I read, however, and found, as I have always found, that an interesting book acted as an anodyne, even in times of the greatest trial. After all is it not better that she should go soon than there should be a long parting—a parting protracted through a twelvemonth? And yet, Alice is going too. George will follow. Baba will be left, a great comfort indeed. But even if I should live to see them all again, what can compensate for so many happy years taken from a life which must be drawing to its close."

7. G. O. Trevelyan, *op. cit.*, II, 398. The phrase from Euripides Macaulay wrote in Greek.

And in a pitiful hand that trailed off into gradual illegibility, he added these words: "I wish I were dead. I hardly know what I write—"[8] the words of a once proud spirit, crushed now, completely, by disease and by a hopeless grief.

He could rally at intervals, however, could work for a brief space at his book, or write to his nephew at Trinity upon topics which should never cease to appear important to gentlemen who were also scholars. "Dear George," he began one such note of late October, "I take the liberty to point out to you a false spelling of which you are guilty, a false spelling, too, particularly censurable in a scholar—'to *pander* to the insatiable love of rhetoric.' Now you are surely aware that the word *pandar* is simply the proper name of the warrior whom Homer calls Pandarus, and who is prompted by Minerva to break the treaty between the Greeks and Trojans. The poets and romancers of the middle ages, knowing generally that he had been represented by Homer as a faithless and dishonorable man, made him connive, and more than connive, at the gallantries of his niece Cressida. Thence the name Pandarus or Pandar was given to pimps. When Falstaff wishes Pistol to carry a love letter to a married woman, Pistol exclaims. 'Shall I Sir Pandarus of Troy become?' It is therefore most incorrect to spell the word *pander*. In fact this spelling, like *Syren*, like *Sybil*, like *pigmy*, and some other spellings which might be mentioned, raises a strong presumption that the person who is guilty of it does not know Greek."[9]

What did he think about the subject of religion during these last dense months? Unfortunately, he did not leave a record; the matter seems to have troubled him as little then as at other times. G. M. Trevelyan, the modern historian, suggests that he failed to set down his views on the problem largely because he never formulated them to himself. Perhaps, he adds, "the term 'agnostic,' in the stricter sense of that misused word,"

8. *Journal*, XI, 578 (October 16, 1859). Chapter XXIV was the next to last of the *History*.
9. G. M. Trevelyan, *George Otto Trevelyan, A Memoir*, 43-44.

might have fitted him appropriately.[10] For evidence, one must depend upon such accidental comment as is to be found in Macaulay's marginal notes. In the last sentence of one of the controversial pieces of Middleton occur these words: "But if *to live strictly and think freely; to practice what is moral and to believe what is rational*, be consistent with the sincere profession of Christianity, then I shall acquit myself like one of its truest professors." Macaulay underlined the italicized words in this statement. And beside them he wrote another statement of his own: "Haec est absoluta et perfecta philosophi vita." Whether the absolute and perfect life of philosophy or not, one feels confident in saying that the quotation represents the doctrine in the light of which, from the beginning, he had consciously tried to live.

December had come round, and his decline had remained steady. Nothing, it seemed, could cheer him for long now, not even the most glowing reports from his publisher. On the third, one such report did arrive, and he sat down to calculate his total fortune. He was rich, he said. "Indeed, I cannot reckon my whole property—copy rights included—at less than eighty thousand pounds. Twenty-five years ago I was worth exactly and literally nothing." Moreover, he had acquired it all himself, except for the one legacy from Uncle Colin. "And yet I am unhappy—more unhappy than I have been these many years. I am sick of life. I could wish to lie down and sleep, never to wake."[11]

It would be useless and unfair to trace out in more detail the entries of the few weeks that remained to him. Almost each successive one is briefer and more grief-laden than the last. It would be very cold. He would have no strength for work. He would be dull, torpid, and languid. He would often drop off to sleep. "I feel as if I were twenty years older since last Thursday, as if I were dying of old age." The doctors called and pronounced his trouble "a simple heart com-

10. See *ibid.*, 15. See also on this topic, Leslie Stephen, *Hours in a Library* (3 series, London, 1879), 301-2.
11. *Journal*, XI, 606 (December 3, 1859).

plaint." It was perhaps less simple than they thought, or could ever know.

On the twenty-eighth of the month he summoned enough strength to dictate a letter addressed to a poor curate. In it he inclosed a sum of money—twenty-five pounds. Later in the evening George Otto called, but found him too exhausted to speak, except in monosyllables. Before him, unheeded, lay the first number of Thackeray's *Cornhill Magazine*, open at the beginning of that writer's new novel, *Lovel the Widower*. George went away to summon his mother. But before the two could reach his steps, the maids of the house ran out crying to them in the darkness. They went inside and found him in his library, dressed as usual, the magazine still open. It seemed for a moment that he was merely sleeping. But no, it was otherwise; the tired heart had stopped. The last farewells he had dreaded so deeply would not have to be taken.

Bibliographical Note

The primary sources of information about Macaulay are his own Works (I have used the "Edinburgh Edition," in eight volumes, edited by his sister, Lady Trevelyan); his *Life and Letters*, by his nephew G. O. Trevelyan; and his *Journals*, in eleven volumes, which are now to be found in the library of Trinity College, Cambridge. These *Journals* were published only in part in the definitive life. Almost equally valuable are the *Parliamentary Proceedings* of Hansard, which report his speeches in the House, along with those of the men who preceded and followed him in his various debates.

There have been eight biographies, or biographical studies, in addition to the truly invaluable one which Trevelyan brought out in 1876. It may be useful to mention these chronologically here, since they have not all been previously listed:

R. D. Urlin, *On the Late Lord Macaulay, his Life and Writings* (London, 1860).

H. G. J. Clements, *Lord Macaulay, his Life and Writings* (London, 1862).

H. H. Milman, *A Memoir of Lord Macaulay* (London, 1862).

Frederick Arnold, *The Public Life of Lord Macaulay* (London, 1862).

J. G. Kinkel, *Macaulay, Sein Leben und sein Geschichstwerke* (Basel, 1879).

J. C. Morison, *Macaulay* (E.M.L.S.) (London, 1882).

G. Buelow, *Thomas Babington Macaulay, Sein Leben und Sein Werke. Ein Gedenkblatt zur Hundertyahrigen Wiederkehr seines Geburtstages* (Schweidnitz, 1901).

Arthur Bryant, *Macaulay* (London, 1932).

I have consulted all these works. Of the lot, decidedly the most valuable—exclusive of that of Trevelyan, which no student of Macaulay can ignore—is Arnold's. It contains a number of Macaulay's hustings speeches that are not elsewhere available. It is also much more detailed than Trevelyan's on the subject of his career in India. Morison's is useful as criticism, but is entirely too severe. Bryant, who was permitted to examine the complete *Journals*, has written a very readable book, but it is extremely slight and in no real sense critical. Milman knew Macaulay well, and his account, which ran to four editions, derives a certain value from that fact. The other studies are little more than essays, based almost entirely upon second hand material.

The *Journals* were given to Trinity College, Cambridge, in 1928 by Macaulay's grand nephew, the historian George Macaulay Trevelyan. They may be used with Professor Trevelyan's consent. Macaulay began Volume One on November 20, 1838. Volume Eleven breaks off December 23, 1859, five days before his death. These *Journals* were kept up with unusual consistency, except for one gap of nine and a half years—May 15, 1839, to November 18, 1848—which occurs in Volume One. I have naturally, in preparing my own book, consulted a good many works other than the ones here cited. But most of them it has seemed to me sufficient to refer to in the notes. I see little reason, in other words, for troubling the student with a suggestion of my general reading; one can never be quite sure where true helpfulness shades off into ostentation.

Index

Index

[385]

Lansdowne, Lord, 47, 85-86
Luttrell, Henry, 98

Macaulay, Aulay, grandfather of Zachary, 21
Macaulay, Aulay, brother of Zachary, 22
Macaulay, Charles, brother of T. B. M., 42
Macaulay, Colin, brother of Zachary, 22, 23, 204
Macaulay, Frances, sister of T. B. M., 32
Macaulay, Hannah, sister of T. B. M. (Lady Trevelyan), 40, 73-74, 84, 156, 165-66, 175, 178, 180, 184, 186, 199, 205, 218, 285, 293, 318, 343, 373, 376, 377, 380, 381
Macaulay, Jane, sister of T. B. M., 32
Macaulay, John, father of Zachary, 22
Macaulay, John, brother of T. B. M., 32
Macaulay, Margaret, sister of T. B. M., 40, 73-74, 132-34, 156, 165-66, 184, 186, 344
Macaulay, Selina Mills, mother of T. B. M., 12, 14, 15, 17
Macaulay, Selina, sister of T. B. M., 32, 184, 321
Macaulay, Thomas Babington:
  as essayist, thirty-six studies for *Edinburgh Review* and five for *Encyclopaedia Britannica* cited chronologically and criticized, 242-72.
  as fellow, and contributor to *Knight's*, 57-59
  as poet, *Lays of Ancient Rome*, etc., 233-40
  as student during adolescence, 37-45
  at Trinity College, Cambridge, as student, 45-52
  begins writing for *Edinburgh Review*, 63
  birth, 20
  called to bar, 62-63
  candidate for Leeds, 158-64
  chairman of India Civil Service Board, 356
  challenge to duel by Wallace, 207-8
  childhood, 31-36
  chronic illness, 322, 330
  contents and criticism of *History*, 296-316
  controversy with Utilitarians, 81-85
  criticism of American Democracy, 364-72
  criticism of his contemporaries, 331-44
  defeat in Edinburgh election (1847), 291-92
  elected to The Club, 215-16
  first public address, against slavery, 59-62
  his reading on voyage to India, 181; after his arrival, 199-202
  honors received in later years, 359-63
  investments and expenses, 362-63
  invited to stand for Parliament for Calne, 85-86
  last illness, 379-80

made Paymaster general of the Army, 288
made Secretary of War in Melbourne ministry, 217
named Commissioner of Bankruptcy, 80
named to Supreme Council of India, 178
publication of *History*, 296
Reform Bill speeches, 113-15, 121-27
reforms accomplished in India: the press, 187; the courts, 187-90; the Penal Code, 190-95; public education, 195-98
refuses position of Judge Advocate in Melbourne ministry, 214-15
research for the *History*, 294-95
resigns seat in House, 359-60
sale of *History*, 357-58, 361-62
speech in defense of Melbourne ministry, 219-22
speech on Chartism, 230-32
speech on Church taxes in Scotland, 352-54
speech on Dissenters, 277
speech on Education Bill, 289-91
speech on Factory Bill, 286-87
speech on India Bill, 172-74
speech on Ireland (1844), 276
speech on Irish Question, 166-69
speech on Jewish Disabilities, 169-71
speech on Master of the Rolls, 347-50
speech on Maynooth, 281-82
speech on Somnauth Temple, 273-74
speech on Sugar Duties, 277-79
speech on war with China, 223-24
speech to Edinburgh electors, 346-47
Speeches, publication of, 354-56
speeches on Copyright Law, 224-28
stands for Edinburgh, and is elected, 328-29
tour of the continent and comments on society there (1838), 210-14
unfinished speech on Indian Civil Service, 351-52
Macaulay, William, brother of T. B. M., 32
Macaulay, Zachary, father of T. B. M., 3-20, 21-22, 28, 30, 35-36, 41, 44-45, 49-52, 54-56, 61, 64, 72, 87-88, 131, 176, 206, 208
Mahon, Lord, 116
Manners, Lord John, 342
Martineau, Harriet, 337
Melbourne, Lord, 214-15, 216, 217, 218, 284, 286
Melville, Herman, 339
Mill, James, 72, 81, 83-84, 174, 241
Milner, Isaac, 23, 25, 27, 37
Moore, Tom, 98, 321
More, Hannah, 12, 13, 30, 31, 34, 35-36
More, Jacob, 12, 13
More, Patty, 12, 34
Motley, G. L., 375

Napier, Macvey, 85, 136, 146-49, 202, 208
Newman, John Henry, 340
Newton, Isaac, 45
Newton, John, 13

O'Connell, Irish patriot, 167-68

Paget, John, 310-11
Palmerston, Lord, 65, 285, 364
Peel, Sir Robert, 128, 167, 217, 220, 273, 279-81, 345, 355
Penn, William, 318
Peterloo, 49-50, 116
Pitt, William, 9, 28
Place, Francis, 103
Powerscourt, Viscount, 222
Preston, Rev., schoolmaster of T. B. M., 37-39, 41-42
Pre-Raphaelitism, 341
Prescott, W. H., 375-76

Randall, H. S., 364, 368, 370
Ranke, German historian, 275-76
Religious Tract Society, 19
Rogers, Samuel, 98
Rothschild, Baron, 341-42
Ruskin, John, 340
Russell, Lord John, 108, 111, 137, 139, 284-85, 286, 288

Sadler, Michael, 159, 162, 165
Scott, Sir Walter, 208-9, 317
Shelley, H. V., 112-13
Shore, John, Baron Teignmouth, 24
Sierra Leone Company, 3-11, 18, 28, 55

Simeon, Charles, 27, 37
Smith, Adam, 65, 232, 283, 287, 289
Smith, Sydney, 65, 76-78, 98
Southey, Robert, 104, 245-47
Stephen, Leslie, 102-03
Stewart, Dugald, 64-65, 130

Talford, Sergeant, 224-25
Talleyrand, 102
Thackeray, W. M., 335-37, 380
Thornton, Henry, 23-24, 30
Trevelyan, Alice, 373, 376, 377
Trevelyan, Chas., brother-in-law of T. B. M., 184-86, 199, 205, 218, 356, 375
Trevelyan, G. M., 239, 294, 378-79, 381, and *passim* in notes.
Trevelyan, G. O., nephew of T. B. M., 21, 218, 373, 376, 377, 378, 380, 381
Trevelyan, Margaret ("Baba"), 199, 205, 293-94, 323, 373

Venn, John, 19, 27
Victoria, Queen, 319-20, 325, 376

Washington, George, 364, 365, 369
Wellington, Duke of, 22, 80, 105, 167, 317
Westminster Review, 81, 82, 112
Wilberforce, William, 22-23, 24, 30, 60, 62, 85-86, 176, 178
William IV, 107-8, 120-21, 127, 374
Wilson, John ("Christopher North"), 86-89, 238-39
Wordsworth, 46, 334-35, 343
Wren, Christopher, 45